LOEB CLASSICAL LIBRARY

FOUNDED BY JAMES LOEB 1911

EDITED BY

JEFFREY HENDERSON

PLAUTUS

II

LCL 61

PLAUTUS

CASINA · THE CASKET COMEDY · CURCULIO · EPIDICUS · THE TWO MENAECHMUSES

EDITED AND TRANSLATED BY

WOLFGANG DE MELO

HARVARD UNIVERSITY PRESS

CAMBRIDGE, MASSACHUSETTS

LONDON, ENGLAND

2011

50 YBP 6/11 24.00

First published 2011

LOEB CLASSICAL LIBRARY® is a registered trademark
of the President and Fellows of Harvard College

Library of Congress Control Number 2010924480
CIP data available from the Library of Congress

ISBN 978-0-674-99678-6

*Composed in ZephGreek and ZephText by
Technologies 'N Typography, Merrimac, Massachusetts.
Printed on acid-free paper and bound by
The Maple-Vail Book Manufacturing Group*

CONTENTS

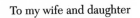

To my wife and daughter

PREFACE

Miser Catulle, desinas ineptire,
et quod uides perisse, perditum ducas.

Poor Catullus, stop behaving like a fool; what you can see has
been lost you should consider as lost.

In my school days, the opening lines from the eighth poem
by Catullus were a favorite with lovesick teenage boys;
now, many years later, I cannot look at them without think-
ing of generations of scholars who tried to reconstruct
the lost Greek originals of our Latin plays. Much has in-
deed been lost, but reconstruction is not as futile a busi-
ness as it might seem. Where it can contribute something
to our understanding of Plautus, I have not hesitated to
mention it in the introductions to individual plays. In the
Curculio, for instance, signs of compression are clearly vis-
ible and the Greek original must have been longer and in
places more explicit in its plot structure. I also thought it
worth mentioning that the Greek original of the *Epidicus*
is unlikely to have ended with a half-sibling wedding, even
though claims to that effect can occasionally still be heard.
In the *Cistellaria* it is some of the Latin plot that needs to
be reconstructed, due to the deplorable state of the manu-
script transmission. But on the whole I have tried to focus

on the Latin texts we have and not on what is no longer available.

My work would not have been possible without support from many sides. Settimio Lanciotti and Walter Stockert sent me their excellent texts of the *Curculio* and the *Cistellaria*; I received the latter even before it appeared in print. Without these critical texts my work would have been much delayed. J. N. Adams answered many questions on grammatical problems. Colleagues in Urbino and Oxford gave me offprints of many relevant articles. But the greatest help came again from John Trappes-Lomax, who read the entire text and commented on every aspect of my work in detail. The book would not be what it is without his generous support.

While I was writing this book, my life underwent several drastic changes. I left the peace and tranquillity of All Souls College in Oxford and moved to Ghent, where I had to adapt to a different way of life and learn a new language well enough to survive my teaching duties and faculty meetings. Without the generous help provided by many new colleagues in Ghent this would not have been possible. Much support also came from my parents, my brother, and old friends. But as always the most important help was provided by my wife, to whom this book is dedicated. Our daughter also did her part: despite not yet being a year old, she was always well behaved and often keen to listen to a bit of Plautus in the original, if only in order to fall asleep more easily.

CASINA

INTRODUCTORY NOTE

The *Casina* is undoubtedly one of Plautus' most farci-
cal creations. It remains unclear to what extent its bawdy
character goes back to the lost but named Greek original,
the *Kleroumenoi* ("Men Casting Lots") by Diphilus (ll. 31–
32). Adaptations were certainly made, the more obvious of
which I shall point out in what follows. Already in antiquity
the play was named for its pivotal figure, Casina, a slave girl
who does not actually come onstage at all. But it is possible
that the Latin play was called *Sortientes* by Plautus, a di-
rect translation of Greek *Kleroumenoi*; this all depends on
how we interpret ll. 31–32: *Sortientes* could be the name of
the Latin play, or it could be a translation of *Kleroumenoi*
for the benefit of those in the audience who were not fa-
miliar with Greek.

As in other comedies, a father and his son are in love
with the same woman, in this case the slave girl Casina.
The father, called Lysidamus in the Ambrosian palimpsest
and this edition, remains nameless in the Palatine manu-
scripts, which may reflect the original situation; scene
headings containing the names of characters were added
relatively late. Lysidamus sent off his son Euthynicus on a
business trip in order to get rid of his rival. However, be-
fore he left, Euthynicus told his slave Chalinus to ask for
the girl in marriage so that he, the young master, could en-

3

joy her. Lysidamus also has a proxy: his slave Olympio, who is a somewhat crude overseer on the family's country estate.

As Cleostrata, the wife of Lysidamus, has her suspicions, she supports her son and Chalinus. Since she raised Casina, whom a slave brought home when he saw her being abandoned as a baby, she has a certain right to give her in marriage to whomever she wants. But Lysidamus as head of the household can overrule her. Naturally, he does not want his wife to be suspicious of his true motives, so he first tries to persuade her to give Casina to Olympio by discrediting Chalinus. When Cleostrata remains intransigent, Lysidamus promises Chalinus his freedom should he give up; Cleostrata does the same with Olympio. However, both slaves resist the temptation to give in. In the end Lysidamus, who does not dare to overrule his wife directly, decides to resort to casting lots as to who is going to marry Casina. This scene (ll. 353–423), during which Lysidamus makes several Freudian slips by saying that he wants to marry the girl, must go back to Diphilus, who named his play for it; but it is clear that Plautus has introduced changes. For instance, in New Comedy there are at most three speaking actors onstage, but in this scene there are four: Lysidamus, the two slaves, and Cleostrata. Since the three men are necessary in the scene, it is likely that Cleostrata is the person that Plautus added. At the end of the scene, Olympio and Lysidamus win and Cleostrata has to prepare the wedding.

Things take a turn for the better when Chalinus overhears a conversation between Lysidamus and Olympio. Lysidamus plans to tell his wife that he will accompany the couple to their country estate. In reality they intend to go next door; Lysidamus has persuaded his neighbor Alcesimus to send over his wife Myrrhina, a close friend of Cleostrata, so that she can help with the wedding preparations. Alcesimus wants to send everyone off so that Lysidamus can sleep with Casina in his house before they all go to the countryside. Chalinus immediately tells his mistress everything, and she can now counteract her husband's plans.

Cleostrata begins to stir up trouble for her husband by telling him that Alcesimus refused to send his wife over, while telling Alcesimus, who is actually keen to help Lysidamus, that his wife is not needed. The ensuing argument between Lysidamus and Alcesimus does not last long, though, and Myrrhina goes next door. Next Pardalisca, a slave girl working for Cleostrata, comes out, seemingly in panic. She tells Lysidamus that Casina has a sword and intends to kill her future husband. Again Lysidamus, fearing for his life, makes Freudian slips. Then the wedding preparations are drawn out for so long that Lysidamus decides to leave with the couple without having a wedding dinner. The women bring out a very special bride—Chalinus wearing a concealing veil.

It has sometimes been argued that the wedding involving a male bride is a Plautine insertion. It is true that a number of ritual elements have a distinctly Roman character, and these must be Plautine. For instance, the bride is admonished to cross the threshold carefully in order to avoid stumbling, a bad omen (ll. 815–17); and more generally, Greek brides were not given advice for their married life on the big day, while Chalinus/Casina gets much advice, albeit unrealistically anti-male. On the other hand, there are Greek elements in the ceremony that must go

5

back to the original, for Plautus would not have introduced unfamiliar customs himself. Thus it was common in Rome for the husband to wait in his own home for the bride, who was accompanied by three boys and the guests. In the *Casina*, Greek customs are followed: the bride and groom go to their new home, accompanied only by a close friend, here Lysidamus.

When the women have left, Lysidamus and Olympio take Chalinus to their neighbor's house. We hear about what happened inside when Olympio comes out; unfortunately the text is damaged from l. 870 onward. Olympio's speech (from l. 875 onward) is witnessed and commented on by Cleostrata, Myrrhina, and Pardalisca, who come out again to watch the "wedding games" (cf. ll. 759–62). Thus we again have more speakers onstage than the Greek original would have allowed. Olympio tells us that, not wanting Lysidamus to have sex with his bride before him, he went into a room and tried to sleep with her, but fled after getting a beating.

In l. 937 Lysidamus enters, followed by Chalinus, which means that there are now six speaking actors onstage, a state of affairs impossible in a Greek play. Lysidamus tells of his experience, which closely resembles that of his companion: he was beaten with the walking stick that old men in Roman comedy habitually carry. In the end he is pardoned by his wife.

Schoell was probably right in giving the epilogue to Pardalisca. She foretells the future: Casina will be discovered to be the neighbor's daughter and therefore freeborn, and she will marry Euthynicus. From ll. 64–66 we can draw the conclusion that this was still a vital part of the Greek original. Plautus probably cut out these scenes in order to expand on the farcical elements, but it remains difficult to say how much is Plautine expansion and how much is Diphilean original.

The date of the Plautine play is relatively certain because of the mention of Bacchanalian revels; admittedly such references occur in several plays and are generally not very important, but in the *Casina* it is said that these days no such revels take place (l. 980). This seems to be a reference to the *Senatus consultum de Bacchanalibus* of 186, which severely curtailed such ceremonies. If the play was written after 186, it was one of Plautus' last plays, perhaps the very last, since he died in 184. The frequent use of song supports such a view, as it is well known that Plautus expanded the sung passages later in his career.

The prologue was written on the occasion of a later production. Since it is said that the older spectators got to know the play in Plautus' lifetime while the younger ones do not know it (ll. 11–14), we can assume that the prologue was written around 165–150. It would help us to date the prologue with greater precision if we knew what is meant by the worthless "new coinage" mentioned in l. 10. Perhaps the writer of the prologue did not intend to refer to any type of coin in particular, but only to the frequent devaluations in general. But a very attractive alternative hypothesis has been advanced. Silver coins were no longer minted after 170; instead, bronze was used. Silver coins were then reintroduced in 157. If the writer of the prologue was conservative and critical of the new type of coins, he could in our passage be referring to their reintroduction, in which case the prologue would date to 157 or shortly thereafter.

SELECT BIBLIOGRAPHY

Editions and Commentaries

MacCary, W. T., and M. M. Willcock (1976), *Plautus: Casina* (Cambridge).

Questa, C. (2001), *Titus Maccius Plautus: Casina* (Urbino).

Criticism

Cody, J. M. (1976), "The *senex amator* in Plautus' Casina," in *Hermes* 104: 453–76.

González Vázquez, C. (2007), "*Casina* de Plauto, la comedia de los sentidos," in *Latomus* 68: 900–17.

MacCary, W. T. (1973), "The Comic Tradition and Comic Structure in Diphilos' Kleroumenoi," in *Hermes* 101: 194–208.

O'Bryhim, S. (1989), "The Originality of Plautus' *Casina*," in *American Journal of Philology* 110: 81–103.

Raffaelli, R., and Tontini, A. (eds.) (2003), *Lecturae Plautinae Sarsinates VI: Casina (Sarsina, 28 settembre 2002)* (Urbino).

Tontini, A. (1991), "Plaut. *Cas.* 987 (un verso ritrovato)," in *Maia* N.S. 43: 9–13.

——— (1992), "Sull'interpretazione di *Cas.* 344: *vorsis gladiis depugnarier*," in I. Mazzini (ed.), *Civiltà, materiale e letteratura nel mondo antico: Atti del seminario di studio (Macerata, 28–29 giugno 1991)* (Macerata).

Williams, G. (1958), "Some Aspects of Roman Marriage Ceremonies and Ideals," in *Journal of Roman Studies* 48: 16–29.

Zehnacker, H. (1976), "Les 'nummi novi' de la 'Casina,'" in *Mélanges offerts à Jacques Heurgon*, vol. 2: *L'Italie préromaine et la Rome républicaine* (Rome), 1035–46.

CASINA

ARGVMENTVM

Conseruam uxorem duo conserui expetunt.
Alium senex allegat, alium filius.
Senem adiuuat sors, uerum decipitur dolis.
Ita ei subicitur pro puella seruolus
Nequam, qui dominum mulcat atque uilicum.
Adulescens ducit ciuem Casinam cognitam.

CASINA

PLOT SUMMARY

Two fellow slaves are keen to marry a fellow slave girl. Their old master commissions one, his son the other. The lot favors the old man, but he is deceived by tricks. A wicked slave is palmed off on him instead of the girl. He beats up his master and the overseer. The young master marries Casina after she is recognized as a citizen.

PLAUTUS

PERSONAE

OLYMPIO seruos
CHALINVS seruos
CLEOSTRATA matrona
PARDALISCA ancilla
MYRRHINA matrona
LYSIDAMVS senex
ALCESIMVS senex
CHYTRIO coquos

SCAENA

Athenis

CHARACTERS

OLYMPIO a slave; overseer on Lysidamus' country estate
CHALINUS a slave; more faithful to Lysidamus' son than to Lysidamus himself
CLEOSTRATA a married woman; wife of Lysidamus
PARDALISCA a slave girl; works for Cleostrata
MYRRHINA a married woman; wife of Alcesimus
LYSIDAMUS an old man; in love with Casina
ALCESIMUS an old man; neighbor of Lysidamus
CHYTRIO a cook; hired to prepare the wedding banquet

STAGING

The stage represents a street in Athens. To the left it leads to the countryside, to the right to the city center. On the street are the houses of Alcesimus, to the left, and of Lysidamus, to the right.

PROLOGVS

PRO saluere iubeo spectatores optumos,
        Fidem qui facitis maxumi—et uos Fides.
        si uerum dixi, signum clarum date mihi,
        ut uos mi esse aequos iam inde a principio sciam.
5   qui utuntur uino uetere sapientis puto
        et qui lubenter ueteres spectant fabulas;
        antiqua opera et uerba quom uobis placent,
        aequom est placere ante ⟨alias⟩ ueteres fabulas:
        nam nunc nouae quae prodeunt comoediae
10   multo sunt nequiores quam nummi noui.
        nos postquam populi rumore intelleximus
        studiose expetere uos Plautinas fabulas,
        antiquam eius edimus comoediam,
        quam uos probastis qui estis in senioribus;
15   nam iuniorum qui sunt non norunt, scio;
        uerum ut cognoscant dabimus operam sedulo.
        haec quom primum acta est, uicit omnis fabulas.
        ea tempestate flos poetarum fuit,
        qui nunc abierunt hinc in communem locum.
20   sed tamen apsentes prosunt ⟨pro⟩ praesentibus.
        uos omnis opere magno esse oratos uolo
        benigne ut operam detis ad nostrum gregem.
        eicite ex animo curam atque alienum aes ⟨foras⟩,
        ne quis formidet flagitatorem suom:

7 antiqua *P*, anticua *Camerarius*   8 alias *add. Ritschl*

PROLOGUE

Enter the SPEAKER OF THE PROLOGUE.

SPEA I give you my greetings, best of spectators, you who hold
Good Faith in highest esteem—and vice versa. If I've
spoken the truth, give me a clear sign, so that I may know
right from the start that you are well-disposed to me. I   5
think people who drink old wine are wise, and so are
those who enjoy watching old plays. Since you like old
works and words, it's only right that you like old plays
above others. Why, the new comedies coming on stage
now are worth even less than the new coinage. Since we   10
learned from what everybody says that you're very keen
on Plautine plays, we're staging an old comedy of his
which found the approval of those of you who are among
the older generation. For those of the younger genera-   15
tion don't know it, I'm sure. But we'll do our best to get
them to know it. When it was first staged, it surpassed all
other plays. In that era the cream of poets lived, who've
now gone away to the place to which all men go. But even   20
so they benefit us in their absence as if they were present.
I want to appeal earnestly to you all to pay benevolent at-
tention to our troupe. Throw worries about your debts
out of your mind, let no one be afraid of his creditor. The   25

---

13 antiquam *P*, anticuam *Camerarius*
20 pro *add. Seyffert*   23 foras *add. Foster*

25   ludi sunt, ludus datus est argentariis;
             tranquillum est, Alcedonia sunt circum forum:
             ratione utuntur, ludis poscunt neminem,
             secundum ludos reddunt autem nemini.
             aures uociuae si sunt, animum aduortite:
30   comoediai nomen dare uobis uolo.
             "Κληρούμενοι" uocatur haec comoedia
             graece, latine "Sortientes"; Diphilus
             hanc graece scripsit, postid rursum denuo
             latine Plautus cum latranti nomine.
35   senex hic maritus habitat; ei est filius,
             is una cum patre in illisce habitat aedibus.
             est ei quidam seruos qui in morbo cubat,
             immo hercle uero in lecto, ne quid mentiar;
             is seruos—sed abhinc annos factum est sedecim
40   quom conspicatust primulo crepusculo
             puellam exponi. adit extemplo ad mulierem
             quae illam exponebat, orat ut eam det sibi:
             exorat, aufert; detulit recta domum,
             dat erae suae, orat ut eam curet, educet.
45   era fecit, educauit magna industria,
             quasi si esset ex se nata, non multo secus.
             postquam ea adoleuit ad eam aetatem ut uiris
             placere posset, eam puellam hic senex
             amat efflictim, et item contra filius.
50   nunc sibi uterque contra legiones parat,
             paterque filiusque, clam alter alterum:

27 neminem poscunt *P, transp. Camerarius*
50 nunc sibi Ω, *transp. Camerarius*

games are on, and we have played a game with the bankers. It's calm, it's the halcyon days[1] throughout the forum. They're being reasonable: during the games they don't demand anything from anyone, but after the games they don't return anything to anyone. If your ears are empty, pay attention: I want to give you the name of the comedy. 30 This comedy is called *Kleroumenoi* in Greek, in Latin "Men Casting Lots." Diphilus wrote it in Greek, and after that Plautus with the barking name[2] wrote it again in Latin. (*pointing to the house of Lysidamus*) A married 35 old man lives here. He has a son, and that son lives together with his father in that house. He has a certain slave who lies in illness, or rather, to tell you the truth, in bed. This slave—but it was sixteen years ago when he saw 40 a girl being abandoned at the start of twilight. He went right up to the woman abandoning her and asked her to give the girl to him. He persuaded her and took the baby away. He brought her home directly, gave her to his mistress, and asked her to look after her and raise her. His 45 mistress did so and brought her up with great care, as if she were her own daughter, not much differently. After she reached such an age that she could attract men's attention, this old man fell madly in love with her, and, in opposition to him, his son did so too. Now each of them, 50 father and son, is preparing his legions against the other

---

[1] The time when kingfishers were believed to hatch their eggs in nests floating on the calm sea (14–28 December, one week before and one after the winter solstice). This period is mentioned because it was proverbially calm and quiet, not because the play was actually staged during it. [2] *Plautus* is also the name of a type of basset hound with soft, broad ears.

pater allegauit uilicum qui posceret
sibi istanc uxorem: is sperat, si ei sit data,
sibi fore paratas clam uxorem excubias foris;
55   filius is autem armigerum allegauit suom
qui sibi eam uxorem poscat: scit, si id impetret,
futurum quod amat intra praesepis suas.
senis uxor sensit uirum amori operam dare,
propterea una consentit cum filio.
60   ille autem postquam filium sensit suom
eandem illam amare et esse impedimento sibi,
hinc adulescentem peregre ablegauit pater;
sciens ei mater dat operam apsenti tamen.
is, ne exspectetis, hodie in hac comoedia
65   in urbem non redibit: Plautus noluit,
pontem interrupit, qui erat ei in itinere.
sunt hic inter se quos nunc credo dicere:
"quaeso hercle, quid istuc est? seruiles nuptiae?
seruin uxorem ducent aut poscent sibi?
70   nouom attulerunt, quod fit nusquam gentium."
at ego aio id fieri in Graecia et Carthagini,
et hic in nostra terra in ⟨terra⟩ Apulia;
maioreque opere ibi seruiles nuptiae
quam liberales etiam curari solent;
75   id ni fit, mecum pignus si quis uolt dato
in urnam mulsi, Poenus dum iudex siet
uel Graecus adeo, uel mea causa Apulus.
quid nunc? nil agitis? sentio, nemo sitit.
reuortar ad illam puellam expositiciam:
80   quam serui summa ui sibi uxorem expetunt,

72 terra in Apulia Ω, terra, ⟨terra⟩ in Apula *Seyffert*, terra in ⟨terra⟩
Apulia *Lindsay*   79 illam puellam Ω, *transp. Pylades*

behind the other's back. The father has commissioned his
overseer to ask for her in marriage. He hopes that if she's
given to him, he'll have night watches ready for himself
outside, behind his wife's back. The son, on the other   55
hand, has commissioned his orderly to ask for her in mar-
riage. He knows that if he succeeds he'll have the object
of his love within his stable. The old man's wife has real-
ized that her husband is bent on a love affair and for this
reason she supports her son. But after the father realized   60
that his son was in love with that same girl and was a hin-
drance to himself, he sent off his lad abroad. Even so, his
mother knowingly supports him in his absence. In case
you're waiting for him, he isn't returning to the city in this   65
comedy today. Plautus didn't want him to, he demolished
a bridge on his way. There are people here who I be-
lieve are now saying to each other: "Please, what's that? A
slave wedding? Are slaves going to marry or ask for a
wife? They've brought us something new, something that   70
doesn't happen anywhere in the world." But I insist that
it does happen in Greece and Carthage, and here in our
land in the land of Apulia. There, an even greater effort is
made for slave weddings than for those of free men. If   75
anyone wishes to, let him bet a pitcher of honey-wine
against me that this isn't the case, provided that the ref-
eree is a Carthaginian or a Greek, or an Apulian for all I
care. Well then? No takers? I see, nobody is thirsty. I'll
return to that abandoned girl. The girl whom the slaves   80
seek as their wife with all their effort will turn out to be

ea inuenietur et pudica et libera,
ingenua Atheniensis, nec quicquam stupri
faciet profecto in hac quidem comoedia.
mox hercle uero, post transactam fabulam,
85   argentum si quis dederit, ut ego suspicor,
ultro ibit nuptum, non manebit auspices.
tantum est. ualete, bene rem gerite, [et] uincite
uirtute uera, quod fecistis antidhac.

ACTVS I

I. i: OLYMPIO. CHALINVS

OL   non mihi licere meam rem me solum, ut uolo,
90   loqui atque cogitare sine ted arbitro?
    quid tu, malum, me sequere?
CHAL   quia certum est mihi,
    quasi umbra, quoquo tu ibis, te semper sequi;
    quin edepol etiam si in crucem uis pergere,
95   sequi decretum est. dehinc conicito ceterum,
    possisne necne clam me sutelis tuis
    praeripere Casinam uxorem, proinde ut postulas.
OL   quid tibi negoti est mecum?
CHAL   quid ais, impudens?
    quid in urbe reptas, uilice hau magni preti?
OL   lubet.
CHAL   quin ruri es, in praefectura tua?
100   quin potius quod legatum est tibi negotium,
    id curas atque urbanis rebus te apstines?
    huc mihi uenisti sponsam praereptum meam:
    abi rus, abi dierectus tuam in prouinciam.

87 et uincite *P*, uincite *A*

both chaste and free, a freeborn Athenian, and indeed
she won't commit anything in the way of fornication, at
least not in this comedy. But soon, when the play has
reached its end, I suspect if anyone gives her money 85
she'll marry him willingly and won't wait for the augurs.
That's all. Farewell, be successful, and be victorious
through true bravery, as you've done so far.

Exit the SPEAKER OF THE PROLOGUE.

ACT ONE

Enter OLYMPIO from the left, followed by CHALINUS.

OL   Aren't I allowed to talk and think about my business 90
      alone, as I like it, without you as my witness? What the
      hell are you following me for?

CHAL Because I'm resolved to follow you like a shadow wher-
      ever you go. Yes, even if you want to go on to the cross,
      I'm determined to follow you. So figure out the rest, 95
      whether or not you can snatch Casina away as your wife
      with your machinations behind my back, as you count on
      doing.

OL   What business have you with me?

CHAL What do you say, you shameless creature? What are you
      crawling around for in the city, you worthless overseer?

OL   I feel like it.

CHAL Why aren't you in the country, in your own territory? 100
      Why don't you rather look after the business that was as-
      signed to you and stay away from city matters? You've
      come here to steal my betrothed from me. Go to the
      country, go to your own province and be hanged!

OL   Chaline, non sum oblitus officium meum:
105   praefeci ruri recte qui curet tamen.
    ego huc quod ueni in urbem si impetrauero,
    uxorem ut istanc ducam quam tu deperis,
    bellam et tenellam Casinam, conseruam tuam,
    quando ego eam mecum rus uxorem abduxero,
110   ruri incubabo usque in praefectura mea.
CHAL tun illam ducas? hercle me suspendio
    quam tu eius potior fias satiust mortuom.
OL   mea praeda est illa: proin tu te in laqueum induas.
CHAL ex sterculino effosse, tua illaec praeda sit?
115 OL   scies hoc ita esse.
CHAL   uae tibi!
OL   quot te modis,
    si uiuo, habebo in nuptiis miserum meis!
CHAL quid tu mi facies?
OL   egone quid faciam tibi?
    primum omnium huic lucebis nouae nuptae facem;
    [postilla ut semper improbus nihilique sis,]
120   postid locorum quando ad uillam ueneris,
    dabitur tibi amphora una et una semita,
    fons unus, unum ahenum et octo dolia:
    quae nisi erunt semper plena, ego te implebo flagris.
    ita te aggerunda curuom aqua faciam probe
125   ut postilena possit ex te fieri.
    post autem ruri nisi tu aceruom ⟨erui⟩ ederis
    aut quasi lumbricus terram, quod te postules
    gustare quicquam, numquam edepol ieiunium
    ieiunum est aeque atque ego te ruri reddibo.

107 istanc *BJ*, istant *VE*, istam *A*   119 *uersum secl. Guyet*
126 erui *add. Leo*

22

OL Chalinus, I haven't forgotten my duty. I've put someone 105
  in charge on our country estate who'll look after it prop-
  erly despite my absence. If I achieve what I've come here
  for, to the city, that is, to marry the woman you are in love
  with, the pretty and tender Casina, your fellow slave,
  when I've taken her to the country with me as my wife, 110
  then I'll permanently sleep in the country, in my own ter-
  ritory.

CHAL *You* should marry her? I'd rather die by hanging than let
  you get hold of her.

OL She's my booty, so you might as well put your neck in a
  noose.

CHAL You creature dug out from a dung heap, she should be
  your booty?

OL You'll know that this is so. 115

CHAL Curse you!

OL In how many ways I'll torment you at my wedding, as
  truly as I live!

CHAL What will you do to me?

OL What will I do to you? First of all you'll carry the torch for
  this new bride. [Then, in order that you're worthless and
  useless for good,] Then, when you come to the country 120
  estate, you'll be given one jug and one path, one spring,
  one copper pail, and eight vats. Unless they're constantly
  full, I'll fill you with lashes. I'll make you so properly
  stooped from carrying water that you could be turned 125
  into a crupper. But afterward, at the farm, when you'd
  like to taste some food, Hunger itself is never as hungry
  as I'll make you at the farm, unless you eat a heap of

130   postid, quom lassus fueris et famelicus,
     noctu ut condigne te cubes curabitur.
  CHAL quid facies?
  OL   concludere in fenstram firmiter,
     unde auscultare possis quom ego illam ausculer:
     quom mi illa dicet, "mi animule, mi Olympio,
135   mea uita, mea mellilla, mea festiuitas,
     sine tuos ocellos deosculer, uoluptas mea,
     sine amabo ted amari, meus festus dies,
     meus pullus passer, mea columba, mi lepus,"
     quom mi haec dicentur dicta, tum tu, furcifer,
140   quasi mus, in medio pariete uorsabere.
     nunc ne tu te mi respondere postules,
     abeo intro. taedet tui sermonis.
  CHAL   te sequor.
     hic quidem pol certo nil ages sine med arbitro.

ACTVS II

II. i: CLEOSTRATA. PARDALISCA

  CLEO opsignate cellas, referte anulum ad me:
145   ego huc transeo in proxumum ad meam uicinam.
     uir si quid uolet me, facite hinc accersatis.
  PAR prandium iusserat senex sibi parari.

   137 te amari *P*, amari te *A*
   140 pariete Ω, parieti *Guyet*

24

vetch, or earth like a worm. Then, when you're tired and 130
starving, an effort will be made that at night you sleep the
way you deserve.

CHAL What will you do?

OL You'll be fastened firmly in the window frame, so that you
can hear it from there when I kiss her. When she says
to me, "my sweetheart, my dear Olympio, my life, my 135
honey, my joy, let me kiss your eyes, my pleasure, let me
please love you, my day of delight, my little sparrow, my
dove, my hare," when these words are said to me, then
you, you criminal, will wriggle in the middle of the wall 140
like a mouse. Now so that you won't presume to give me a
reply, I'm off inside. I'm fed up with your talk.

Exit OLYMPIO into the house of Lysidamus.

CHAL I'm following you. You definitely won't do anything here
without me as witness.

Exit CHALINUS into the house of Lysidamus.

ACT TWO

Enter CLEOSTRATA from her house.

CLEO (*into the house*) Seal the pantries and return the ring to
me. I'm going next door here to my neighbor. If my hus- 145
band wants anything from me, do fetch me from here.

*Enter PARDALISCA from the house of Lysidamus, handing
over the signet ring.*

PAR The old master had ordered that lunch should be pre-
pared for him.

CLEO st!

149–50   tace atque abi; nec paro neque hodie coquetur,
    quando is mi et filio aduorsatur suo

152–54   animi amorisque causa sui,

155   flagitium illud hominis! ego illum fame, ego illum siti,
    maledictis, malefactis amatorem ulciscar,
    ego pol illum probe incommodis dictis angam,
    faciam uti proinde ut est dignus uitam colat,
    Accheruntis pabulum,

160   flagiti persequentem,
    stabulum nequitiae.
    nunc huc meas fortunas eo questum ad uicinam.
    sed foris concrepuit, atque eapse eccam egreditur!
    non pol per tempus iter huc mi incepi.

II. ii: MYRRHINA. CLEOSTRATA

165–66 MYR sequimini, comites, in proxumum me huc. heus uos,
    ecquis haec quae loquor audit?
    ego hic ero, uir si aut quispiam quaeret.

168–69   nam ubi domi sola sum, sopor manus caluitur.
170–71   iussin colum ferri mihi?

CLEO   Myrrhina, salue.

172–73 MYR salue mecastor. sed quid tu es tristis, amabo?

174–75 CLEO ita solent omnes quae sunt male nuptae:
176–77   domi et foris aegre quod siet satis semper est.
    nam ego ibam ad te.

MYR   et pol ego istuc ad te.
    sed quid est quod tuo nunc animo aegre est?

180–81   nam quod tibi est aegre, idem mi est diuidiae.

---

163 ipsa *A*, ea ipse *P*, eapse *Bothe*
176–77 sit Ω, siet *Schoell*

CLEO Hush! Be quiet and be off. 150

Exit PARDALISCA into Cleostrata's house.

CLEO I'm not preparing any and it won't be cooked today since he's opposing me and his son for the sake of his pleasure and love, that disgrace of a man! I'll take revenge on that 155 lover with hunger, with thirst, with harsh words, and with harsh treatment, I'll torture him thoroughly with uncomfortable words, I'll make sure he leads the life he deserves, this fodder for the Underworld, seeker of dis- 160 grace, heap of infamy. Now I'm going here to my neighbor to complain about my lot. (*stops to listen*) But the door has creaked, and look, she's coming out herself! I haven't come here at a suitable time.

Enter MYRRHINA from her house.

MYR (*into the house*) Follow me, girls, next door here. Hey 165 there, you, can anyone hear what I'm saying? (*as two maids appear in her door*) I'll be here (*points to Cleostrata's house*) if my husband or anyone else is looking for me: when I'm at home alone, sleep deceives my hands. 170 Didn't I tell you to bring me my distaff? (*the maids go back in*)

CLEO (*in a sad voice*) Hello, Myrrhina.

MYR Hello. But what are you upset about, please?

CLEO This is what all women are like who are unhappily mar- 175 ried. At home and outside there's always enough that's distressing. In fact, I was coming to you.

MYR And I to you. But what is it that distresses you now? What 180 distresses you disturbs me.

	CLEO	credo, ecastor, nam uicinam neminem amo merito magis
		quam te
183		nec qua in plura sunt
183ᵃ		mi quae ego uelim.
	MYR	amo te, atque istuc expeto scire quid sit.
185–86	CLEO	pessumis me modis despicatur domi.
	MYR	hem, quid est? dice idem—nam pol hau satis meo
		corde accepi querellas tuas—opsecro.
	CLEO	uir me habet pessumis despicatam modis,
190		nec mihi ius meum optinendi optio est.
	MYR	mira sunt, uera si praedicas, nam uiri
		ius suom ad mulieres optinere hau queunt.
	CLEO	quin mihi ancillulam ingratiis postulat,
		quae mea est, quae meo educta sumptu siet,
195		uilico suo se dare,
195ᵃ		sed ipsus eam amat.
	MYR	opsecro,
		tace.
	CLEO	nam hic nunc licet dicere:
197–98		nos sumus.
	MYR	ita est. unde ea tibi est?
		nam peculi probam nil habere addecet
200		clam uirum, sed quae habet, partum ei hau commode
		est,
		quin uiro aut suptrahat aut stupro inuenerit.
		hoc uiri censeo esse omne quicquid tuom est.
	CLEO	tu quidem aduorsum tuam amicam omnia loqueris.
204–5	MYR	tace sis, stulta, et mi ausculta. noli sis tu illi aduorsari,
206–7		sine amet, sine quod lubet id faciat, quando tibi nil domi
		delicuom est.

CLEO I do believe you; I'm quite right not to be fonder of any
neighbor than of you, and there is none who has more
qualities in her that I'd wish for for myself.

MYR I'm fond of you and I'm keen to know what is the matter.

CLEO He despises me terribly at home.   185

MYR Oh, what's that? Say it again, please—I haven't fully got
your complaints in my head.

CLEO My husband holds me in terrible contempt, and I have no   190
opportunity to obtain my right.

MYR That's strange, if you're telling the truth: it's husbands
who can't obtain their right from their wives.

CLEO No, he demands to give my slave girl, who is mine, who
was brought up at my expense, to his overseer, against my
will; but he himself is in love with her.

MYR Please, be quiet.   196

CLEO But surely now I can speak here: we're alone.

MYR That's true. Where do you have her from? A decent
woman ought not to have any property of her own behind   200
her husband's back, but a woman who does hasn't ac-
quired it in an acceptable way, but is stealing it from her
husband or got hold of it through sexual liaisons. I be-
lieve that everything that's yours is your husband's.

CLEO You're speaking against your friend with every word you
utter.

MYR Do be quiet, silly, and listen to me. Just don't oppose him, 205
let him love, let him do what he likes, since you don't lack
anything at home.

196–98 *partes sic distribuit Acidalius* (tace . . . sumus *et* unde ea tibi
est *dat Myrrhinae P, reliquom Cleostratae*)
200 et *P*, set *Seyffert*

208–9   CLEO satin sana es? nam tuquidem aduorsus tuam istaec rem
             loquere.

      MYR   insipiens,

210–12   semper tu huic uerbo uitato aps tuo uiro—

      CLEO   quoi uerbo?

      MYR   "i foras, mulier."

213   CLEO st! tace.

      MYR   quid est?

      CLEO   em!

      MYR   quis est, quem uides?

      CLEO   uir
             eccum it. intro abi, appropera, age amabo.

      MYR   impetras, abeo.

215   CLEO mox magis quom otium ⟨et⟩ mihi et tibi erit,
             igitur tecum loquar. nunc uale.

      MYR   ualeas.

II. iii: LYSIDAMVS. CLEOSTRATA

     LYS   omnibus rebus credo ego amorem et nitoribus nitidis
              anteuenire
              nec potis quicquam commemorari quod plus salis plus-
              que leporis [hodie]
              habeat; coquos equidem nimis demiror, qui utuntur
              condimentis,

220   eos eo condimento uno non utier, omnibus quod praes-
              tat.
              nam⟨que⟩ ubi amor condimentum inerit, quoiuis placi-
              turam ⟨escam⟩ credo;

208–9 ista *B*, istam *VJE*, istaec *Bothe*
213 est *P*, st *Gruterus*   hem *P*, em *Müller*
215 mihi et tibi erit *BVE*, et michi erit et tibi *J*
217 ego amorem credo *P, transp. Hermann*

CLEO Are you in your right mind? You're speaking against your
      own cause.

MYR   Stupid, always avoid this word from your husband— 210

CLEO (*interrupting*) Which word?

MYR   "Go away, woman."[3]

CLEO (*looking around*) Hush! Be quiet.

MYR   What is it?

CLEO There!

MYR   Who is it, who can you see?

CLEO Look, my husband's coming. Go inside, be quick, come
      on, please.

MYR   Yes, yes, I'm going.

CLEO Soon when both you and I have more time I'll speak to 215
      you. Goodbye for now.

MYR   Goodbye.

Exit MYRRHINA into her house.
Enter LYSIDAMUS from the right.

LYS   (*to the audience*) I believe that love surpasses all things
      and neat neatnesses and that nothing can be mentioned
      which has more wit and charm. I'm highly surprised that
      cooks, who use spices, don't use this one spice which sur- 220
      passes all others. Yes, I believe that everybody will like a
      dish which contains love as a spice. Nothing without love

---

[3] The regular divorce formula.

---

218 hodie *del. Guyet*
221 que *add. Camerarius* inierit *BVJE[1]*, inerit *E[3]M* escam *add. R.
Klotz*

nec salsum nec suaue esse potest quicquam, ubi amor
  non ammiscetur:
fel quod amarum est, id mel faciet, hominem ex tristi le-
  pidum et lenem.
hanc ego de me coniecturam domi facio magis quam ex
  auditis;
225 qui quom amo Casinam, magis niteo, munditiis Mundi-
  tiam antideo:
myropolas omnis sollicito, ubiquomque est lepidum un-
  guentum, unguor,
ut illi placeam; et placeo, ut uideor. sed uxor me excruciat
  quia uiuit.
tristem astare aspicio. blande haec mi mala res appellan-
  da est.
229 uxor mea meaque amoenitas,
229ᵃ quid tu agis?
  CLEO abi atque apstine manum.
230 LYS heia, mea Iuno, non decet
230ᵃ ess' te tam tristem tuo Ioui.
231 quo nunc abis?
  CLEO mitte me.
  LYS mane.
231ᵃ CLEO non maneo.
  LYS at pol ego te sequar.
232 CLEO opsecro, sanun es?
  LYS sanus quom ted amo.
  CLEO nolo ames.
  LYS non potes impetrare.
  CLEO enicas.
  LYS uera dicas uelim.
  CLEO credo ego istuc tibi.

32

mixed in can be well-seasoned or sweet. It turns bitter gall into honey, a grumpy man into a charming and mild one. I draw this conclusion from myself, from my own case, rather than from hearsay. Now that I'm in love with 225 Casina, I'm better groomed, I surpass Neatness herself in neatness. I keep all perfumers busy; wherever there's a pleasant ointment, I use it in order to please her. And I do seem to please her. But my wife's torturing me by being alive. I can see her standing here, grumpy. I must address this bad bit of stuff coaxingly. (*turning to Cleostrata, trying to caress her*) My wife and my pleasure, how are you?

CLEO Go away and keep your hand off me.

LYS Goodness, my Juno,[4] you shouldn't be so unfriendly to 230 your Jupiter. Where are you off to now?

CLEO Let go of me.

LYS Wait.

CLEO I won't wait. (*turns to go*)

LYS But I'll follow you.

CLEO Please, are you in your right mind?

LYS I am, since I love you.

CLEO I don't want you to love me.

LYS You can't succeed.

CLEO You're killing me.

LYS (*aside*) I wish you were telling the truth.

CLEO (*overhearing him*) I believe you in that.

---

[4] Wife of Jupiter, the king of gods (who is notoriously unfaithful).

---

225 quam *P*, quom *Reiz* inicio *BJ*, initio *V*, innitio *E*, niteo *Gulielmus* mundicianti deo *BJ*, muntianti deo *E¹*, munditianti deo *VE²*, munditiam antideo *Camerarius*

232 quam *P*, quom *codices Langiani*

235	LYS	respice, o mi lepos.
	CLEO	nempe ita ut tu mihi es.
236		unde hic, amabo, unguenta olent?
236ᵃ	LYS	oh perii! manufesto miser
237		teneor. cesso caput pallio detergere?

              ut te bonus Mercurius perdat, myropola, quia haec mi
                dedisti.

CLEO eho tu nihili, cana culex, uix teneor quin quae decent te
                dicam,

240   senectan aetate unguentatus per uias, ignaue, incedis?

LYS   pol ego ⟨eam⟩ amico dedi quoidam operam, dum emit
                unguenta.

CLEO   ut cito commentust!
       ecquid te pudet?

LYS   omnia quae tu uis.

CLEO   ubi in lustra iacuisti?

LYS   egone in lustra?

CLEO   scio plus quam tu me arbitrare.

LYS   quid id est? quid [tu] scis?

CLEO te sene omnium se⟨num homi⟩nem neminem esse
                ignauiorem.

245   unde is, nihili? ubi fuisti? ubi lustratu's? ubi bibisti?
       mades mecastor: uide palliolum ut rugat!

LYS   di me et te infelicent,
       si ego in os meum hodie uini guttam indidi.

CLEO immo age ut lubet bibe, es, disperde rem.

240 senecta *P*, senectan *Schoell*
241 eam *add. Leo* commendatus est *BVJ¹E¹*, commentatus est *J²Eᶜ*,
commentust *Pylades*   243 tu *del. Geppert*
244 omnium senem *P*, omnium se⟨num homi⟩nem *Spengel*
246 adest *P*, mades *Schoell*

34

LYS   Look back at me, my delight.   235

CLEO (*turning round, with sarcasm*) Yes, just as you're mine.
Please, where does the smell of perfumes come from?

LYS   (*aside*) Oh, I'm dead! Poor me, I'm caught in the act.
Why am I slow to wipe my head with my cloak? May good
Mercury[5] ruin you for giving me this stuff, perfumer.

CLEO Hey there, you worthless creature, you gray-haired gnat,
I can barely keep from calling you what you deserve. Are 240
you promenading the streets in your old age perfumed,
you good-for-nothing?

LYS   Well, I was assisting a certain friend while he was buying
ointments.

CLEO (*aside*) How fast he's come up with it! (*to Lysidamus*)
Don't you feel shame for anything?

LYS   For everything you wish.

CLEO What dens of vice did you throw yourself into?

LYS   I in dens of vice?

CLEO I know more than you think I do.

LYS   What's that? What do you know?

CLEO That there isn't any more worthless old man than you
among all old men. Where are you coming from, you 245
worthless creature? Where have you been? Where did
you whore? Where did you drink? You really are tipsy.
Look how your cloak is all crumpled.

LYS   May the gods curse me and you, if I've put a drop of wine
into my mouth today.

CLEO Go on, drink as you like, eat, throw away your money.

[5] The god of trade.

249–
50   LYS   ohe, iam satis, uxor, est; comprime te; nimium tinnis,
            relinque aliquantum orationis, cras quod mecum litiges.
            sed quid ais? iam domuisti animum, potius ut quod uir
                uelit
            fieri id facias [potius] quam aduorsere contra?

  CLEO   qua de re?
  LYS   rogas?
            super ancilla Casina, ut detur nuptum nostro uilico,
255   seruo frugi atque ubi illi bene sit ligno, aqua calida, cibo,
            uestimentis, ubique educat pueros quos pariat ⟨probe⟩,
            [potius] quam illi seruo nequam des, armigero nili atque
                improbo,
            quoi homini hodie peculi nummus non est plumbeus.

  CLEO   mirum ecastor te senecta aetate officium tuom
260   non meminisse.

  LYS   quid iam?
  CLEO   quia, si facias recte aut commode,
            me sinas curare ancillas, quae mea est curatio.

  LYS   qui, malum, homini scutigerulo dare lubet?
  CLEO   quia enim filio
            nos oportet opitulari unico.

  LYS   at quamquam unicust,
            nihilo magis ille unicust mi filius quam ego illi pater:
265   illum mi aequiust quam me illi quae uolo concedere.
  CLEO   tu ecastor tibi, homo, malam rem quaeris.

  LYS   subolet, sentio.
            egone?

  CLEO   tu. nam quid friguttis? quid istuc tam cupide cupis?

      253 potius *del. Pylades*   256 probe *add. Geppert*
      257 potius *del. Ussing*
      264 unicus est ille *P*, ille unicust *Geppert*

LYS Hey there, my wife, it's enough now. Control yourself. 250
You're making too much noise. Save some speech for
something to argue about with me tomorrow. But what
do you say? Have you tamed your passion now, so as to do
what your husband wants done rather than oppose him?

CLEO What about?

LYS You ask? About the slave girl Casina, so that she can be
given in marriage to our overseer, a useful slave and one 255
where she'll be well supplied with wood, hot water, food,
and clothes, and where she can properly raise the chil-
dren she bears, rather than that you give her to that use-
less slave, the worthless and troublesome soldier's ser-
vant, who doesn't have so much as a lead coin in his
private funds today.

CLEO It's strange that you don't remember your duty in your 260
old age.

LYS How so?

CLEO Because, if you were doing the right and proper thing,
you'd let me look after the female slaves, which is *my* job.

LYS Why the hell do you want to give her to the shield-
bearer?

CLEO Because in fact we ought to help our only son.

LYS But even though he's our only one, he's no more my only
son than I am his only father. It's more appropriate for 265
him to make a concession to my wishes than for me to
make one to his.

CLEO You're looking for trouble, my good man.

LYS (*aside*) She's got wind of it, I can feel it. (*to Cleostrata,
nervously*) I?

CLEO Yes, you. Why are you stuttering? Why do you desire that
match so eagerly?

37

LYS	ut enim frugi seruo detur potius quam seruo improbo.
CLEO	quid si ego impetro atque exoro a uilico causa mea

270   ut eam illi permittat?

LYS   quid si ego autem ab armigero impetro
          ⟨ut⟩ eam illi permittat? atque hoc credo impetrasse.

CLEO iam conuenit. uis tuis Chalinum huc euocem uerbis foras?
          tu eum orato, ego autem orabo uilicum.

LYS   sane uolo.

CLEO iam hic erit. nunc experiemur nostrum uter sit blandior.

275 LYS Hercules dique istam perdant, quod nunc liceat dicere.
          ego discrucior miser amore, illa autem quasi ob indus-
             triam
          mi aduorsatur. subolet hoc iam uxori quod ego machinor:
          propter eam rem magis armigero dat operam de indus-
             tria.

II. iv: CHALINVS. LYSIDAMVS

LYS   qui illum di omnes deaeque perdant!

CHAL   te uxor aiebat tua . . .

280   me uocare.

LYS   ego enim uocari iussi.

CHAL   eloquere quid uelis.

LYS   primum ego te porrectiore fronte uolo mecum loqui;
          stultitia est ei te esse tristem quoius potestas plus potest.
          probum et frugi hominem iam pridem te esse arbitror.

271 ut *add. Guyet*
283 te esse *J*, esse *BVE*

38

LYS So she's given to a worthy slave rather than a worthless one.

CLEO What if I persuade the overseer and talk him into giving her up to that man for my sake? 270

LYS But what if I talk the orderly into giving her up to the other? And I believe I shall succeed.

CLEO Agreed. Do you want me to call Chalinus out here on your instructions? You ask him, and I shall ask the overseer.

LYS Yes, I'd like that.

CLEO He'll be here in a minute. Now we'll test which of us is more persuasive.

Exit CLEOSTRATA into her house.

LYS May Hercules and the gods destroy her, which I can say 275
now. I'm being tortured by love, poor me, and she opposes me as if she did it on purpose. My wife's already got wind of what I'm scheming. Because of that she's deliberately giving greater support to the orderly.

Enter CHALINUS from the house of Lysidamus.

LYS (*half aside, as he sees him*) May all the gods and goddesses ruin him!

CHAL No, you . . . were calling me, your wife said. 280

LYS Yes, I had you called.

CHAL Tell me what you want.

LYS First I want you to speak to me in a more respectful way. It's stupidity to be sulky with someone who has greater authority. (*pauses*) I've considered you a decent and useful person for a long time now.

39

CHAL   intellego.

284–
85   quin, si ita arbitrare, emittis me manu?

LYS   quin id uolo.
      sed nihil est me cupere factum, nisi tu factis adiuuas.

CHAL quid uelis modo id uelim me scire.

LYS   ausculta, ego ‹e›loquar.
      Casinam ego uxorem promisi uilico nostro dare.

CHAL at tua uxor filiusque promiserunt mi.

LYS   scio.

290   sed utrum nunc tu caelibem te esse mauis liberum
      an maritum seruom aetatem degere et gnatos tuos?
      optio haec tua est: utram harum uis condicionem accipe.

CHAL liber si sim, meo periclo uiuam; nunc uiuo tuo.
      de Casina certum est concedere homini nato nemini.

295 LYS intro abi atque actutum uxorem huc euoca ante aedis
          cito,
      et sitellam huc tecum efferto cum aqua et sortis.

CHAL   satis placet.

LYS   ego pol istam iam aliquouorsum tragulam decidero.
      nam si sic nihil impetrare potero, saltem sortiar.
      ibi ego te et suffragatores tuos ulciscar.

CHAL   attamen

300   mi optinget sors.

LYS   ut quidem pol pereas cruciatu malo.

CHAL mi illa nubet, machinare quidlubet quouis modo.

LYS   abin hinc ab oculis?

CHAL   inuitus me uides, uiuam tamen.

LYS   sumne ego miser homo? satin omnes res sunt aduorsae
          mihi?

287 loquar *P*, eloquar *Müller*

40

CHAL *(with irony)* I see. Why don't you free me if you consider 285
me to be like this?

LYS Indeed, I want to. But there's no point in me wishing it
done if you don't support me with your actions.

CHAL I'd like to know what you'd like.

LYS Listen, I'll tell you. I promised our overseer to give him
Casina in marriage.

CHAL But your wife and son promised her to me.

LYS I know. But do you prefer to be an unmarried freeman 290
now or to spend your life as a married slave, you and your
children? This is your choice. Pick which of these options
you like.

CHAL If I were free, I'd live at my own expense; now I'm living
at yours. About Casina I'm resolved not to give in to any-
one.

LYS *(angrily)* Go inside and immediately call out my wife 295
here in front of the house fast, and bring an urn out here
with you, with water and lots.

CHAL Suits me well enough.

LYS I'll parry that spear of yours one way or another now: if I
can't prevail upon you like this, at least I'll draw lots.
There I'll take revenge on you and your supporters.

CHAL But the lot will fall to me. 300

LYS Yes, it'll be your lot to die through terrible torture.

CHAL She'll marry me, devise any plot you like in any way you
like.

LYS Won't you go out of my sight?

CHAL You see me against your will, but I'll live nevertheless.

Exit CHALINUS into the house of Lysidamus.

LYS Aren't I a wretch? Isn't everything against me? I'm afraid

41

iam metuo ne Olympionem mea uxor exorauerit

305 ne Casinam ducat: si id factum est, ecce me nullum se-
    nem!

si non impetrauit, etiam specula in sorti est mihi.

si sors autem decolassit, gladium faciam culcitam

eumque incumbam. sed progreditur optume eccum
    Olympio.

II. v: OLYMPIO. LYSIDAMVS

OL   una edepol opera in furnum calidum condito

310 atque ibi torreto me pro pane rubido,

    era, qua istuc opera a me impetres, quod postulas.

LYS saluos sum, salua spes est, ut uerba audio.

OL   quid tu me ‹tua›, era, libertate territas?

    quin si tu nolis filiusque etiam tuos,

315 uobis inuitis atque amborum ingratiis

    una libella liber possum fieri.

LYS quid istuc est? quicum litigas, Olympio?

OL   cum eadem qua tu semper.

LYS   cum uxoren mea?

OL   quam tu mi uxorem? quasi uenator tu quidem es:

320 dies ac noctes cum cane aetatem exigis.

LYS quid agit, quid loquitur tecum?

OL   orat, opsecrat

    ne Casinam uxorem ducam.

LYS   quid tu postea?

OL   negaui enim ipsi me concessurum Ioui,

    si is mecum oraret.

306 in sortita sunt *P*, in sorti est *Guyet*, in sortitust *Acidalius*
311 quam istam opera *BV*, quam istam operam *JE*, qua istuc opera
Brix   313 tua *add. Leo*   314 quid *P*, quin *Acidalius*
318 uxore *P*, uxoren *Bentley*, uxori *Lindsay*

now that my wife might have persuaded Olympio not to   305
marry Casina. If that's happened, then I'm a dead old
man! If she hasn't succeeded, I still have a little hope in
the lot. But if the lot trickles away, I'll make a pillow of my
sword and throw myself on it. But look, perfect, Olympio
is coming out.

Enter OLYMPIO from the house of Lysidamus.

OL   (*into the house*) You could as soon put me in a hot oven   310
    and bake me as dark bread, my mistress, as obtain from
    me what you ask.

LYS   (*aside*) I'm safe, my hope is safe, that's how I hear his
    words.

OL   (*still into the house*) Why are you threatening me with
    your talk about my freedom, mistress? Even if you and
    also your son don't want it, I can become free for a far-   315
    thing[6] against your wishes and against the will of both of
    you.

LYS   What's that? Who are you arguing with, Olympio?

OL   With the same woman you are always arguing with.

LYS   With my wife?

OL   What wife are you talking about? You're like a hunter: 320
    day and night you spend your life with a bitch.

LYS   What's she doing, what's she talking about with you?

OL   She begs and entreats me not to marry Casina.

LYS   What did you say then?

OL   Well, I told her I wouldn't give in to Jupiter himself, if he
    were to plead with me.

[6] The *libella* was worth only one-tenth of a *denarius*.

	LYS	di te seruassint mihi!

LYS   di te seruassint mihi!

325   OL   nunc in fermento tota est, ita turget mihi.

        LYS   ego edepol illam mediam dirruptam uelim.

        OL   credo edepol esse, siquidem tu frugi bonae es.

               uerum edepol tua mihi odiosa est amatio:

               inimica est tua uxor mihi, inimicus filius,

330   inimici familiares.

        LYS   quid id refert tua?

               unus tibi hic dum propitius sit Iuppiter,

               tu istos minutos caue deos flocci feceris.

        OL   nugae sunt istae magnae. quasi tu nescias

               repente ut emoriantur humani Ioues.

335   sed tandem si tu Iuppiter sis mortuos,

               quom ad deos minores redierit regnum tuom,

               quis mihi subueniet tergo aut capiti aut cruribus?

        LYS   opinione melius res tibi habet tua,

               si hoc impetramus, ut ego cum Casina cubem.

340   OL   non hercle opinor posse, ita uxor acriter

               tua instat ne mi detur.

        LYS   at ego sic agam:

               coniciam sortis in sitellam et sortiar

               tibi et Chalino. ita rem natam intellego:

               necessum est uorsis gladiis depugnarier.

345   OL   quid si sors aliter quam uoles euenerit?

        LYS   benedice. dis sum fretus, deos sperabimus.

326 ego edepol *J*, edepol ego *BVE*

LYS   May the gods preserve you for me!

OL   Now she's all in a seething rage, to judge from the way   325
she's swelling with anger at me.

LYS   I wish she'd burst right down the middle.

OL   I believe she has, at least if you are good for anything.[7]
But your love affair is annoying me. Your wife is my en-
emy, your son is my enemy, the other members of the   330
household are my enemies.

LYS   What does this matter to you? So long as this Jupiter
alone (*points to himself*) is favorable to you, you needn't
care a straw about those minor deities.

OL   That's a load of rubbish. As if you didn't know how sud-
denly human Jupiters die. But to come to the point, if   335
you, my Jupiter, die, when your kingship devolves upon
the minor deities, who will come to my protection, for my
back or head or shins?

LYS   Your situation's better than you think if we enable me to
sleep with Casina.

OL   I don't think you can, seeing how strongly your wife op-   340
poses her being given to me.

LYS   But I'll act like this: I'll put lots into an urn and draw them
for you and Chalinus. I see that the situation's come to
this: it's necessary to change swords and fight in earnest.[8]

OL   What if the lot settles it differently from how you want it?   345

LYS   Speak good omens. I trust in the gods, we'll put our hope
in them.

---

[7] Olympio interprets "burst right down the middle" in a sexual
sense.

[8] The phrase *uorsis gladiis* (partly explained by Caper GLK 7. 104.
12–13) refers to the change from blunt to dangerous weapons; before
the real fight, gladiators put on a harmless show (Cic. *de orat*. 2. 325).

	OL	non ego istuc uerbum empsim tittibilicio;
		nam omnes mortales dis sunt freti, sed tamen
		uidi ego dis fretos saepe multos decipi.
350	LYS	st! tace parumper.
	OL	quid uis?
	LYS	eccum exit foras

Chalinus intus cum sitella et sortibus.
nunc nos collatis signis depugnabimus.

II. vi: CLEOSTRATA. CHALINVS. LYSIDAMVS. OLYMPIO

	CLEO	face, Chaline, certiorem me quid meus uir me uelit.
	CHAL	ille edepol uidere ardentem te extra portam mortuam.
355	CLEO	credo ecastor uelle.
	CHAL	at pol ego hau credo, sed certo scio.
	LYS	plus artificum est mihi quam rebar: hariolum hunc habeo
		domi.
		quid si propius attollamus signa eamusque obuiam?
		sequere. quid uos agitis?
	CHAL	assunt quae imperauisti omnia:
		uxor, sortes, situla atque egomet.
	OL	te uno adest plus quam ego uolo.
360	CHAL	tibi quidem edepol ita uidetur; stimulus ego nunc sum
		tibi,
		fodico corculum; assudascis iam ex metu, mastigia.
	LYS	tace, Chaline.
	CHAL	comprime istum.

354 metuam *P*, mortuam *Ritschl*

OL   I wouldn't buy that kind of talk for total tripe:[9] all mortals trust in the gods, but even so I've often seen those who trust in the gods being fooled.

LYS   Hush! Be quiet for a bit.   350

OL   What do you want?

LYS   Look, Chalinus is coming out with the urn and the lots. Now we'll engage in a pitched battle.

Enter CLEOSTRATA and CHALINUS, the latter with an urn and lots, from the house of Lysidamus, without noticing anyone.

CLEO   Chalinus, tell me what my husband wants from me.

CHAL   He wants to see you dead, burning outside the gate.[10]

CLEO   I do believe that that is what he wants.   355

CHAL   But I don't just believe it, I know it for sure.

LYS   (*to Olympio*) I have more experts than I thought: I have this man as a soothsayer at home. What if we bring our standards closer and go toward them? Follow me. (*to his wife and Chalinus*) What are you two doing?

CHAL   Everything you ordered is present: your wife, the lots, the urn, and myself.

OL   With you there is one more person present than I want.

CHAL   To you it seems like that. I'm your cattle prod now, I'm 360 stabbing your little heart. You're already sweating for fear, whip fodder.

LYS   Be quiet, Chalinus.

CHAL   Subdue that chap.

[9] According to Fulgentius (*serm. ant.* 117. 13–16 Helm), *tittibilicium* refers to dirty threads in weaving. Paul the Deacon (p. 504 Lindsay) thinks that the word has no meaning.

[10] Burials always took place outside the city.

OL   immo istum qui didicit dare.

LYS   appone hic sitellam, sortis cedo mihi. animum aduortite.
       atqui ego censui aps te posse hoc me impetrare, uxor
         mea,

365   Casina ut uxor mihi daretur; et nunc etiam censeo.

CLEO tibi daretur illa?

LYS   mihi enim—ah, non id uolui dicere:
       dum "mihi" uolui, "huic" dixi, atque adeo mihi dum cu-
         pio—perperam
       iam dudum hercle fabulor.

CLEO   pol tu quidem, atque etiam facis.

LYS   huic—immo hercle mihi—uah! tandem redii uix ueram
       in uiam.

370 CLEO per pol saepe peccas.

LYS   ita fit, ubi quid tanto opere expetas.
       sed te uterque tuo pro iure, ego atque hic, oramus.

CLEO   quid est?

LYS   dicam enim, mea mulsa: de istac Casina huic nostro uili-
       co
       gratiam facias.

CLEO   at pol ego nec facio nec censeo.

LYS   tum igitur ego sortis utrimque iam ‹diribeam›.

CLEO   quis uotat?

375 LYS   optumum atque aequissumum istuc esse iure iudico.
       postremo, ‹si› illuc quod uolumus eueniet, gaudebimus;

362 comprime istunc *P*, comprime istum *Pylades* immo istunc *P*,
immo istum *scripsi concinnitatis causa*
  364 atque *P*, atqui *Pius* mecum *P*, me *Lambinus*
  371 atque ego *P, transp. Camerarius*
  374 diribeam *add. Schoell*
  376 si *add. Camerarius*

OL   (*also to Lysidamus*) No, subdue that one: he has learned how to submit.[11]

LYS   (*to Chalinus*) Put the urn here and give me the lots. (*to all*) Pay attention. (*to Cleostrata*) And yet I thought I could persuade you, my dear wife, that Casina should be   365 given in marriage to me. And even now I think so.

CLEO She should be given to *you*?

LYS   Yes, to me—oh, I didn't mean to say that; when I meant "to me," I said "to him," and when I desired that to me— I've been making mistakes in speech for a while already now.

CLEO Yes, you have, and in action too.

LYS   To him—no, to me—bah! at last I've just about managed to return to the right path.

CLEO You're making a lot of mistakes.   370

LYS   That's what happens when you want something so much. But, recognizing your right, we both, I and he, appeal to you.

CLEO What do you mean?

LYS   I'll tell you, my honey: do our overseer here a favor about that Casina of yours.

CLEO No, I'm not doing him any favor, and I'm against it.

LYS   In that case I'll distribute the lots on both sides now.

CLEO Who forbids it?

LYS   I rightly judge that this is best and most fair. Then, if what   375 we want happens, we'll be happy. If it turns out other-

---

[11] Chalinus means "keep in check" when he says *comprimere* "subdue"; but the verb also means "force to have sex," which is Olympio's interpretation, who also speaks of *dare*, "offering oneself for anal intercourse."

sin secus, patiemur animis aequis. tene sortem tibi.
uide quid scriptum est.

OL   "unum."

CHAL   iniquom est, quia isti prius quam mi ‹data› est.

LYS   accipe hanc sis.

CHAL   cedo. mane, unum uenit in mentem modo:

380   uide ne quae illic insit alia sortis sub aqua.

LYS   uerbero,
men te censes esse?

CLEO   nulla est. habe quietum animum modo.

CHAL quod bonum atque fortunatum [tuum] sit mihi—

OL   magnum malum
tibi quidem edepol credo eueniet; noui pietatem tuam.
sed manedum: num ista aut populna sors aut abiegna est
     tua?

385 CHAL quid tu id curas?

OL   quia enim metuo ne in aqua summa natet.

LYS   eugae! caue. conicite sortis nunciam ambo huc. eccere!
uxor, aequa.

OL   noli uxori credere.

LYS   habe animum bonum.

OL   credo hercle, hodie deuotabit sortis si attigerit.

LYS   tace.

OL   taceo. deos quaeso—

CHAL   —ut quidem tu hodie canem et furcam feras.

390 OL   —mi ut sortito eueniat—

CHAL   —ut quidem hercle pedibus pendeas.

378 data *add. Geppert*
382 quid *P*, quod *Camerarius* tuum *del. Guyet*
386 auge *B¹VE¹*, aeuge *B³*, age *JE³*, euge *Camerarius*

wise, we'll bear it with patience. (*handing a lot to Olympio*) Take your lot. Look what's written on it.

OL "One."

CHAL It's unfair that he was given his earlier than me.

LYS (*to Chalinus*) Take this one, will you?

CHAL Give it to me. Wait, one thing's just occurred to me. (*to* 380
Cleostrata*) Check that there isn't another lot there under the water.

LYS (*to Chalinus*) You criminal, do you think I'm you?

CLEO (*also to Chalinus*) There's none. Just have a calm mind.

CHAL May this turn out well and luckily for me—

OL (*interrupting*) You'll get a thorough trashing, I believe; I know your piety. But wait: is that lot of yours made of poplar or fir?

CHAL Why are you interested in that? 385

OL Because I'm afraid it might swim on the surface of the water.[12]

LYS Well said! (*anxiously*) Watch out. Now throw the lots in here, both of you. (*to Cleostrata, as they obey*) Here we go! My wife, shake them up fairly.

OL Don't trust your wife.

LYS Take heart.

OL I believe she'll bewitch the lots if she touches them.

LYS Be quiet.

OL Yes, I'm quiet. I pray to the gods—

CHAL (*interrupting*)—that you carry a chain and a yoke today.

OL —that it falls to me through the lot— 390

CHAL —(*interrupting again*) that you hang from your feet.

---

[12] Poplar and fir are light woods and swim on the water, allowing for manipulation; the usual lots were of hard wood or fire-baked clay and would sink to the bottom.

OL   —at tu ut oculos emungare ex capite per nasum tuos.

CHAL quid times? paratum oportet esse iam laqueum tibi.

OL   periisti.

LYS   animum aduortite ambo.

OL   taceo.

LYS   nunc tu, Cleostrata,
ne a me memores malitiose de hac re factum aut suspi-
ces,

395   tibi permitto: tute sorti.

OL   perdis me.

CHAL   lucrum facit.

CLEO bene facis.

CHAL   deos quaeso . . . ut tua sors ex sitella effugerit.

OL   ain tu? quia tute es fugitiuos, omnis te imitari cupis?

CHAL utinam tua quidem ⟨ista⟩, sicut Herculei praedicant
quondam prognatis, [ista] in sortiendo sors deliquerit.

400 OL   tu ut liquescas ipse, actutum uirgis calefactabere.

LYS   hoc age sis, Olympio.

OL   si hic litteratus me sinat.

LYS   quod bonum atque fortunatum mihi sit!

OL   ita uero, et mihi.

CHAL non.

---

394 suspi *B1*, suspicere *B3E3*, suscipere *VJ*, suspices *Pylades*

395 ⟨tum⟩ lucrum *Luchs* (*clausula fortasse ferendum est si* lucrum
facit *quasi una pars orationis est*)

398–99 ista *transp. Guyet*

400 *uersum Olympioni dat Ussing*

402 est *P*, sit *Pylades*

---

13 Actually Hercules' great-great-grandsons Cresphontes and Aris-
todemus. Cresphontes and the children of Aristodemus wanted Mes-

OL —but that *you* blow your eyes out of your head through your nose.

CHAL What are you afraid of? You already ought to have a noose ready for yourself.

OL You're dead.

LYS Pay attention, both of you.

OL I'm quiet.

LYS Now, Cleostrata, so that you don't say or suspect that I've cheated in this matter, I leave it to you: you make the draw yourself.   395

OL You're killing me.

CHAL Then he's making a profit.

CLEO (*to Lysidamus*) Thank you.

CHAL (*to Olympio*) I pray to the gods . . . that your lot has fled from the urn.

OL Do you say so? Because you are a runaway, you wish that everybody imitates you?

CHAL May that lot of yours dissolve in the drawing, as they say happened to Hercules' children long ago.[13]

OL You'll be so warmed up with rods in a minute that you yourself will dissolve.   400

LYS Olympio, pay attention please.

OL If only this man of letters[14] were to let me.

LYS May this turn out well and luckily for me!

OL Yes, and for me.

CHAL No.

senia; Temenus, the arbitrator, gave Cresphontes a fire-baked clay lot and the children of Aristodemus a sun-baked one. The latter dissolved in the water.

[14] A title given to Chalinus because of his mythological allusion, but also because a thief is often called "man of three letters" (*fur*).

OL	immo hercle.
CHAL	immo mihi hercle.
CLEO	hic uincet, tu uiues miser.
LYS	percide os tu illi odio. age, ecquid fit? caue obiexis manum.
405 OL	compressan palma an porrecta ferio?
LYS	age ut uis.
OL	em tibi!
CLEO	quid tibi istunc tactio est?
OL	quia Iuppiter iussit meus.
CLEO	feri malam, ut ille, rursum.
OL	perii! pugnis caedor, Iuppiter.
LYS	quid tibi tactio hunc fuit?
CHAL	quia iussit haec Iuno mea.
LYS	patiundum est, siquidem me uiuo mea uxor imperium exhibet.
410 CLEO	tam huic loqui [qui] licere oportet quam isti.
OL	quor omen mihi uituperat?
LYS	malo, Chaline, tibi cauendum censeo.
CHAL	temperi, postquam oppugnatum est os.
LYS	age, uxor [mea], nunciam sorti. uos aduortite animum. prae metu ubi sim nescio. perii! cor lienosum, opinor, habeo, iam [iam] dudum salit,
415	de labore pectus tundit.
CLEO	teneo sortem.
LYS	effer foras.

410 loqui qui *BVE1*, loqui cui *J*, loqui *Ec*
412 mea *del. Bentley* iam nunc *P*, nunciam *Camerarius*
413 praebe tu *P*, prae metu *Ussing*   414 iam *del. Pylades*

CASINA

OL   Yes.

CHAL Yes, for me.

CLEO *(to Olympio)* He *(points to Chalinus)* will win and you will live as a wretch.

LYS *(to Olympio)* Hit the face of this tedious creature. Go on, are you doing anything? *(to Chalinus)* Don't raise your hand.

OL   Should I hit him with my fist or with the flat of my hand? 405

LYS Do as you wish.

OL   *(punching Chalinus)* Take that!

CLEO What did you touch him for?

OL   My Jupiter told me to.

CLEO *(to Chalinus)* Hit his cheek in return, like him. *(he obeys)*

OL   I'm dead! I'm being hit with fists, Jupiter.

LYS *(to Chalinus)* What did you touch him for?

CHAL My Juno told me to.

LYS I have to bear it if my wife is in command while I'm alive.

CLEO This man of mine should be allowed to speak just like 410
     that one of yours.

OL   Why is he spoiling my omen?

LYS Chalinus, I think you should be careful not to get a beating.

CHAL A timely warning, after my face has already been battered.

LYS Go on, my wife, draw now. *(to the slaves)* You two pay attention. *(aside)* I don't know where I am for fear. I'm dead! I have a splenetic heart, I believe, it's been jumping for a long time already, it's thumping my chest from dis- 415
     tress.

CLEO I've got hold of a lot.

LYS Pull it out.

CHAL iamne mortuo's?

OL   ostende. mea ⟨haec⟩ est.

CHAL   mala crux ea est quidem.

CLEO uictus es, Chaline.

LYS   quom nos di iuuere, Olympio,
       gaudeo.

OL   pietate factum est mea atque maiorum meum.

LYS intro abi, uxor, atque adorna nuptias.

CLEO   faciam ut iubes.

420 LYS scin tu rus hinc esse ad uillam longe quo ducat?

CLEO   scio.

LYS intro abi et, quamquam hoc tibi aegre est, tamen fac ac-
       cures.

CLEO   licet.

LYS eamus nos quoque intro, hortemur ut properent.

OL   numquid moror?

LYS nam praesente hoc plura uerba ⟨fieri⟩ non desidero.

II. vii: CHALINVS

CHAL si nunc me suspendam, meam operam luserim
425   et praeter operam restim sumpti fecerim
       et meis inimicis uoluptatem creauerim.
       quid opus est, qui sic mortuos equidem tamen?
       sorti sum uictus, Casina nubet uilico.
       atque id non tam aegre est iam, uicisse uilicum,
430   quam id expetiuisse opere tam magno senem,
       ne ea mi daretur atque ut illi nuberet.

416 haec *add. Geppert* crucias *P*, crux ea est *Camerarius*
418 meorum *P*, meum *Pylades*
420 ruri *P*, rus hinc *Langen*
423 fieri *add. Camerarius*

CHAL *(to Olympio)* Are you dead already?

OL *(to Cleostrata)* Show me. *(as she holds it up)* It's mine.

CHAL Then it's evil torture.

CLEO You've lost, Chalinus.

LYS I'm happy the gods have helped us, Olympio.

OL It's happened because of my piety and that of my forefathers.

LYS Go inside, my wife, and prepare the wedding.

CLEO I'll do as you tell me.

LYS Do you know that it's far from here to our farmhouse in 420
the country, where he's taking her?

CLEO Yes, I do.

LYS Go inside and make sure you prepare it, even though it
upsets you.

CLEO Yes.

Exit CLEOSTRATA into her house.

LYS *(to Olympio)* Let's go inside ourselves, too, and let's urge
them to hurry up.

OL Am I delaying?

LYS Because I don't desire any more words to be said in the
presence of this chap *(points to Chalinus)*.

Exeunt LYSIDAMUS and OLYMPIO into their house.

CHAL If I were to hang myself now, I'd have wasted my effort, 425
and besides the effort I'd have spent money on a rope,
and I'd have made my enemies happy. What's the point?
I'm dead as it is. I was beaten by the lot, Casina will marry
the overseer. And I'm not so upset about the overseer
having won as I am about the old man having been so 430
keen that she shouldn't be given to me and should marry

ut ill' trepidabat, ut festinabat miser!
ut sussultabat, postquam uicit uilicus!
attat! concedam huc, audio aperiri fores,
435   mi beneuolentes atque amici prodeunt.
hinc ex insidiis hisce ego insidias dabo.

II. viii: OLYMPIO. LYSIDAMVS. CHALINVS

OL   sine modo rus ueniat: ego remittam ad te uirum
      cum furca in urbem tamquam carbonarium.

LYS   ita fieri oportet.

OL   factum et curatum dabo.

440 LYS uolui Chalinum, si domi esset, mittere
      tecum opsonatum, ut etiam in maerore insuper
      inimico nostro miseriam hanc adiungerem.

CHAL recessim cedam ad parietem, imitabor nepam;
      captandust horum clanculum sermo mihi.
445   nam illorum me alter cruciat, alter macerat.
      at candidatus cedit hic mastigia,
      stimulorum loculi. protollo mortem mihi;
      certum est, hunc Accheruntem praemittam prius.

OL   ut tibi ego inuentus sum opsequens! quod maxume
450   cupiebas, eius copiam feci tibi.
      erit hodie tecum quod amas clam uxorem.

LYS   tace.
      ita me di bene ament ut ego uix reprimo labra
      ob istanc rem quin te deosculer, uoluptas mea.

435 mihi *P*, mei *Müller*
443 cedam *P Nonius*, dabo me *Paul. Fest*.

him. How nervous he was, how he was making a fuss, the
wretch! How he was jumping up and down after the over-
seer won! (*surprised*) Oh! I'll walk over here, I can hear
the door opening. My well-wishers and friends are com- 435
ing out. From this ambush I'll ambush them.

*Enter OLYMPIO, dressed in white, and LYSIDAMUS, carrying
a wallet, from their house without noticing anyone.*

OL   Just let him come to the farm. I'll send him back to you to
the city under the yoke just like a charcoal seller.[15]

LYS   That ought to be done.

OL   I'll sort it out and see it through.

LYS   If he were at home, I'd have liked to send Chalinus shop- 440
ping with you so as to give our enemy yet another misery
in his grief.

CHAL   I'll retreat to the wall and imitate a scorpion. I need to
eavesdrop on their talk secretly: one of them's torturing 445
me, the other's agonizing me. But this whipping post is
strutting about all in white,[16] the treasure chest of cattle
prods. I'll postpone my suicide. I'm resolved to send him
to the Underworld first.

OL   How submissive I've shown myself to you! I gave you
possession of what you desired most. Today you'll have 450
the object of your love behind your wife's back.

LYS   (*looking around*) Be quiet. As truly as the gods may love
me well, I can barely hold my lips in check because of this
and not kiss you, my darling.

---

[15] The charcoal-seller would carry his wares slung from a forked
stick over his shoulder; but the fork is also an instrument of torture for
slaves.   [16] The regular color for bridegrooms.

CHAL quid, deosculere? quae res? quae uoluptas tua?
455   credo hercle effodere hic uolt uesicam uilico.
OL   ecquid amas nunc me?
LYS   immo edepol me quam te minus.
         licetne amplecti te?
CHAL   quid, "amplecti"?
OL   licet.
LYS   ut, quia te tango, mel mi uideor lingere!
OL   ultro te, amator, apage te a dorso meo!
460 CHAL illuc est, illuc, quod hic hunc fecit uilicum:
         et idem me pridem, quom ei aduorsum ueneram,
         facere atriensem uoluerat sub ianua.
OL   ut tibi morigerus hodie, ut uoluptati fui!
LYS   ut tibi, dum uiuam, bene uelim plus quam mihi.
465 CHAL hodie hercle, opinor, hi conturbabunt pedes:
         solet hic barbatos sane sectari senex.
LYS   ut ego hodie Casinam deosculabor, ut mihi
         bona multa faciam <clam> meam uxorem!
CHAL   attatae!
         nunc pol ego demum in rectam redii semitam.
470   hic ipsus Casinam deperit. habeo uiros.
LYS   iam hercle amplexari, iam osculari gestio.
OL   sine prius deduci. quid, malum, properas?
LYS   amo.
OL   at non opinor fieri hoc posse hodie.

455 effodere hercle hic uolt credo P, *transp. Bothe*
468 clam *add. Pius*

---

[17] Through anal intercourse.
[18] *Ianua* "door" is a common euphemism for the anus.
[19] Metaphor for sexual intercourse.

CHAL What, you'd kiss him? What on earth? What, "your dar- 455
    ling"? I do believe he wants to dig out the overseer's blad-
    der.[17]

OL Do you love me at all now?

LYS Yes, I love myself less than you. Can I hug you?

CHAL What? "Hug" him?

OL You can.

LYS (*embracing him from behind and kissing him*) How I
    seem to be licking honey now that I'm touching you!

OL Away with you, lover, get off my back!

CHAL That's it, that's why he made him overseer. And some 460
    time ago, when I'd come to meet him, he also wanted to
    make me the doorkeeper down by the back entrance.[18]

OL How submissive I've been to you today, how much plea-
    sure I've given you!

LYS So much so that I should be more of a friend to you than
    to myself as long as I live.

CHAL Today they'll conjoin their feet,[19] I think. This old man 465
    really has a habit of chasing after bearded men.

LYS How I'll kiss Casina today, how I'll do myself a lot of good
    turns behind my wife's back!

CHAL Goodness! Now at last I'm back on the right track. He 470
    himself is in love with Casina. I've got them where I want
    them.

LYS I'm keen to embrace her right now, to kiss her right now.

OL Let her be taken home first. Why on earth are you in a
    rush?

LYS I'm in love.

OL But I don't think it can happen today.

LYS   potest,
      siquidem cras censes te posse emitti manu.
475 CHAL enim uero huc aures magis sunt adhibendae mihi:
      iam ego uno in saltu lepide apros capiam duos.
LYS   apud hunc sodalem meum atque uicinum mihi
      locus est paratus: ei ego amorem omnem meum
      concredui; is mi se locum dixit dare.
480 OL   quid eius uxor? ubi erit?
LYS   lepide repperi.
      mea uxor uocabit huc eam ad se in nuptias,
      ut hic sit secum, se adiuuet, secum cubet;
      ego iussi, et dixit se facturam uxor mea.
      illa hic cubabit, uir ab[i]erit faxo domo;
485   tu rus uxorem duces: id rus hoc erit
      tantisper dum ego cum Casina faciam nuptias.
      hinc tu ante lucem rus cras duces postea.
      satin astu?
OL   docte.
CHAL   age modo, fabricamini,
      malo hercle uostro tam uorsuti uiuitis.
490 LYS scin quid nunc facias?
OL   loquere.
LYS   tene marsuppium,
      abi atque opsona, propera, sed lepide uolo,
      molliculas escas, ut ipsa mollicula est.
OL   licet.

474 manumitti *B*, mitti manu *VJE*, emitti manu *Camerarius*
478 omnem amorem *P, transp. Pylades*
484 abierit *P*, aberit *Camerarius*
488 at tute *B*, at tutae *V*, arture *E¹*, astute *JE²*, astu *Bothe* docte *B²*,
omittunt ceteri Palatini

62

LYS   It can, if you believe you can be freed tomorrow.

CHAL   I have to stick my ears further into this: now I'll kill two   475
        birds with one stone.[20]

LYS   In the house of this friend and neighbor of mine a place
        has been prepared for me (*points to the house of Al-*
        cesimus). I confessed all my love to him. He said he'd
        give me a place.

OL   What about his wife? Where will she be?   480

LYS   I've found a lovely solution. My wife will invite her over
        to the wedding so that she's here with her, helps her, and
        spends the night with her. I told her to do so, and my wife
        said she would. She'll sleep here. I'll make sure that her
        husband's away from home. You will take your wife to the   485
        farm; that farm will be this one here (*points to the house*
        of Alcesimus) for as long as I'm consummating the mar-
        riage with Casina. From here you'll take her to the farm
        afterward, tomorrow before light. Isn't that smart?

OL   Clever.

CHAL Just go on, you two, make your plots, you'll pay a high
        price for being such tricksters.

LYS   Do you know what you should do now?   490

OL   Tell me.

LYS   Take my wallet, go and buy food, hurry, but I want it in
        a lovely way, tender bites, just as she's tender herself.
        (*hands over his wallet*)

OL   Yes.

---

[20] Lit. "catch two boars in one brake."

LYS emito sepiolas, lepadas, lolligunculas,
hordeias—

CHAL immo triticeias, si sapis.

495 LYS —soleas.

CHAL qui quaeso potius quam sculponeas,
quibus battuatur tibi os, senex nequissume?

OL uin lingulacas?

LYS quid opust, quando uxor domi est?
ea lingulaca est nobis, nam numquam tacet.

OL in re praesenti ex copia piscaria

500 consulere quid emam potero.

LYS aequom oras, abi.
argento parci nolo, opsonato ampliter.
nam mihi uicino hoc etiam conuento est opus,
ut quod mandaui curet.

OL iamne abeo?

LYS uolo.

CHAL tribus non conduci possum libertatibus

505 quin ego illis hodie comparem magnum malum
quinque hanc omnem rem meae erae iam faciam palam.
manufesto teneo in noxia inimicos meos.
sed si nunc facere uolt era officium suom,
nostra omnis lis est. pulchre praeuortar uiros.

510 nostro omine it dies; iam uicti uicimus.
ibo intro, ut id quod alius condiuit coquos,
ego nunc uicissim ut alio pacto condiam,

493 lepidas *BVE*, lepadas *Camerarius*
500 abis *P*, abi *Camerarius*

64

LYS Buy cuttlefish, limpets, squid, barley fish,[21]—

CHAL No, wheat fish, if you're smart.

LYS —soles.   495

CHAL Why only those, please, rather than entire clogs to smash
     your face with, you worthless old man?

OL   Do you want tongue?

LYS What's that necessary for, since I have a wife at home?
     She's our tongue: she never shuts up.

OL   When I'm there I'll be able to decide what to buy from 500
     the fish market.

LYS Fair enough; off you go. I don't want to save money, buy
     plenty. I still need to meet this neighbor of mine so that
     he takes care of what I've told him.

OL   Shall I go now?

LYS Yes, do.

*Exit OLYMPIO to the left. Exit LYSIDAMUS into the house of
Alcesimus.*

CHAL I couldn't be hired for my freedom three times over not 505
     to create big trouble for them today and not to reveal the
     entire business to my mistress right now. I've caught my
     enemies in the act, red-handed. But if my mistress now
     wants to do her duty, the case is all ours. I'll get the better
     of them beautifully. The day is proceeding with an omen 510
     favorable to us. We, the losers, are the winners! I'll go
     inside to season in a different way in my turn now what
     another cook has seasoned, so that the meal won't be pre-

---

[21] The *hordeia* is an unknown fish whose name sounds similar to
hordeum "barley." Hence the pun with the non-existent "wheat fish."

quo id quoi paratum est ut paratum ne siet
sitque ei paratum quod paratum non erat.

ACTVS III

III. i: LYSIDAMVS. ALCESIMVS

515 LYS nunc amici, anne inimici sis imago, Alcesime,
mihi sciam, nunc specimen specitur, nunc certamen cer-
   nitur.
quor amem me castigare, id ponito ad compendium,
"cano capite," "aetate aliena" eo addito ad compendium,
"quoi sit uxor," id quoque illuc ponito ad compendium.
520 ALC miseriorem ego ex amore quam te uidi neminem.
LYS fac uacent aedes.
ALC   quin edepol seruos, ancillas domo
certum est omnis mittere ad te.
LYS   oh, nimium scite scitus es.
sed facito dum merula per uorsus quod cantat ‹tu› colas:
"cum cibo cum quiqui" facito ut ueniant "quasi eant Su-
   trium."
525 ALC meminero.
LYS   em, nunc enim te demum nullum scitum scitiust.
cura, ego ad forum modo ibo: iam hic ero.
ALC   bene ambula.

513 quod *P*, quoi *Müller*
523 tu *add. Lindsay*
525 tu demum nullo scito scitus es *P*, te d. nullum scitum scitiust
Dousa

---

22 Proverbial expression (Festus p. 406 / 408 Lindsay). Soldiers

pared for the man it was originally prepared for, and so that a meal that wasn't prepared for him will be prepared for him.

Exit CHALINUS into the house of Lysidamus.

ACT THREE

Enter LYSIDAMUS and ALCESIMUS from the latter's house.

LYS   Now I'll know whether you are the likeness of a friend or 515
of a foe, Alcesimus, now the evidence is evidenced, now
the contest is contested. As for reproaching me with the
question why I'm in love, stow it away; "with your gray
head," "at an unsuitable age," stow that away, too; "you
who have a wife," stow that away as well.

ALC   I've never seen anyone more lovesick than you. 520

LYS   Make sure your house is empty.

ALC   Yes, yes; I've decided to send all slaves and slave girls
away from my home over to yours.

LYS   Oh, you're incredibly smart. But make sure you comply
with what the blackbird sings in its song; make sure they
come "with food, with everything, as if they were going to
Sutrium."[22]

ALC   I'll remember. 525

LYS   There you go, now at last no writ has more wit than you.
Take care of things, I'll just go to the forum; I'll be back
soon enough.

ALC   Have a good walk.

were normally asked to bring their own food. Sutrium (modern Sutri) was captured by M. Furius Camillus in 389 and then again in 386.

LYS fac habeant linguam tuae aedes.

ALC   quid ita?

LYS   quom ueniam, uocent.

ALC attatae! caedundus tu homo es: nimias delicias facis.

LYS quid me amare refert, nisi sim doctus ⟨ac⟩ dicaculus?

530   sed tu caue in quaesitione mihi sis.

ALC   usque adero domi.

III. ii: CLEOSTRATA. ALCESIMVS

CLEO hoc erat ecastor [id] quod me uir tanto opere orabat
          meus,
          ut properarem arcessere hanc ⟨huc⟩ ad me uicinam
          meam,
          liberae aedes ut sibi essent Casinam quo deducerent.
          nunc adeo nequaquam arcessam, ⟨ne illis⟩ ignauissumis
535   liberi loci potestas sit, uetulis ueruecibus.
          sed eccum egreditur, senati columen, praesidium popli,
          meus uicinus, meo uiro qui liberum praehibet locum.
          non ecastor uilis emptu est modio qui uenit salis.

ALC miror huc iam non arcessi in proxumum uxorem meam,
540   quae iam dudum, si arcessatur, ornata exspectat domi.
          sed eccam, opino, arcessit. salue, Cleostrata.

CLEO   et tu, Alcesime.
          ubi tua uxor?

---

529 ac *add. Kiessling*   531 id *del. Camerarius*
532 huc *add. Bach*   534 ne *add. Saracenus* illis *add. Koch*
538 modius Ω, modio *Dousa*   541 opinor Ω, opino *Bothe*

---

[23] Pun on *uocare* "invite" and *uacare* "be empty." I have rendered
the preceding *fac habeant linguam tuae aedes* ("make sure your house
has a tongue") as "make sure your house is hungry" in order to get some
pun.   [24] Salt was proverbially cheap.

LYS   Make sure your house is hungry.

ALC   How so?

LYS   When I come it should be empty.[23]

ALC   Goodness! You ought to be cut down to size: you're getting above yourself.

LYS   What's the point of me being in love unless I'm clever and witty? But make sure I don't have to look for you.   530

ALC   I'll be at home throughout.

Exit LYSIDAMUS to the right; exit ALCESIMUS into his house.
Enter CLEOSTRATA from her house.

CLEO   So that was why my husband was so keen that I should hurry up to bring this neighbor of mine over here! It was so that they'd have an empty house to take Casina to. Now I won't bring her over here at all so that those vile creatures don't have any chance of an empty place, the   535 old wethers.

Enter ALCESIMUS from his house.

CLEO   But look, he's coming out, that pillar of the senate, that guardian of the people, my neighbor, who is providing my husband with an empty place. This creature wouldn't be cheap at the price of a peck of salt.[24]

ALC   (*to the audience*) I'm surprised that my wife is not yet being sent for to go next door. She's all dressed up and has   540 been waiting at home for a long time already in case she's sent for. But look, I think she's come to fetch her. (*turning to Cleostrata*) My greetings to you, Cleostrata.

CLEO   And mine to you, Alcesimus. Where's your wife?

ALC   intus illa te, si se arcessas, manet;
       nam tuos uir me orauit ut eam isto ad te adiutum mitte-
           rem.
       uin uocem?
CLEO   sine eam: te nolo, si occupata est.
ALC   otium est.
545 CLEO nil moror, molesta ei esse nolo; post conuenero.
ALC   non ornatis isti apud uos nuptias?
CLEO   orno et paro.
ALC   non ergo opus est adiutrice?
CLEO   satis domi est. ubi nuptiae
       fuerint, tum istam conuenibo. nunc uale, atque istanc
           iube.
ALC   quid ego nunc faciam? flagitium maxumum feci miser
550   propter operam illius hirqui improbi, edentuli,
       qui hoc mihi contraxit; operam uxoris polliceor foras,
       quasi catillatum. flagitium hominis, qui dixit mihi
       suam uxorem hanc arcessituram [esse]; ea se eam negat
           morarier.
       atque edepol mirum ni subolet iam hoc huic uicinae
           meae.
555   uerum autem altrouorsum quom eam mecum rationem
           puto,
       si quid eius esset, esset mecum postulatio.
       ibo intro, ut subducam nauim rursum in puluinaria.

543 istuc Ω, isto *Spengel*
544 eam it A, *om. P*, eam te *Goetz*, maneat *Leo*
553 esse *del. Acidalius*

ALC She's waiting inside for you to send for her: your husband asked me to send her over to your place to help. Do you want me to call her?

CLEO No, let her be. I don't want to bother you if she's busy.

ALC She's free.

CLEO Never mind, I don't want to be a nuisance to her. I'll meet 545
     her later.

ALC Aren't you getting ready for a wedding there at your place?

CLEO Yes, I'm getting ready for it and preparing it.

ALC Don't you need a helper then?

CLEO I have plenty at home. When the wedding's over, then I'll meet her. Goodbye now, and give her my regards. (*walks toward her door*)

ALC What should I do now? Poor me, I've committed a great disgrace thanks to that worthless, toothless goat that 550
     drew me into it. I'm promising my wife's services to others as if she were to go and lick the plates. What a disgraceful creature he is! He told me his wife would send for her. But she says she doesn't need her. (*pauses*) It would be odd if this neighbor of mine hasn't got wind of this already. But on the other hand I get the impression 555
     that if it were like that, she'd be having an argument with me. I'll go inside to haul the ship back onto her berth again.

CLEO   iam hic est lepide ludificatus. miseri ut festinant senes!
        nunc ego illum nihili, decrepitum meum uirum ueniat
          uelim,

560   ut eum ludificem uicissim, postquam hunc delusi alte-
          rum.
        nam ego aliquid contrahere cupio litigi inter eos duos.
        sed eccum incedit. at quom aspicias tristem, frugi cen-
          seas.

III. iii: LYSIDAMVS. CLEOSTRATA

LYS   stultitia magna est, mea quidem sententia,
        hominem amatorem ullum ad forum procedere,
565   in eum diem quoi quod amet in mundo siet;
        sicut ego feci stultus: contriui diem,
        dum asto aduocatus quoidam cognato meo;
        quem hercle ego litem adeo perdidisse gaudeo,
        ne me nequiquam sibi hodie aduocauerit.
570   nam meo quidem animo qui aduocatos aduocet
        rogitare oportet prius et ⟨per⟩contarier
        assitne ei animus necne ⟨ei⟩ assit quem aduocet:
        si neget adesse, exanimatum amittat domum.
575   sed uxorem ante aedis eccam. ei misero mihi!
        metuo ne non sit surda atque haec audiuerit.
CLEO audiui ecastor cum malo magno tuo.
LYS   accedam propius. quid agis, mea festiuitas?
CLEO te ecastor praestolabar.
LYS   iamne ornata rest?
        iamne hanc traduxti huc ad nos uicinam tuam
580   quae te adiutaret?

571 contarier *P*, percontarier *Pylades*
572 ei[2] *add. Seyffert*   578 res est Ω, rest *Pareus*, res *Bothe*

72

Exit ALCESIMUS into his house.

CLEO (*turning round*) Now I've made fun of him in a lovely way. How the old wretches are running around! I wish that useless, decrepit husband of mine would turn up now, so that I could make fun of him in turn, after I've 560 had my fun with this other one: I'm keen to create some argument between the two. (*looking around*) But look, here he comes. When you see him look so solemn, though, you'd think that he's a decent human being.

Enter LYSIDAMUS from the right.

LYS It's great stupidity, in my opinion at least, for any lover 565 who has something to love available for that day, to go to the forum. That's what I did, idiot that I am. I wasted the day while I was standing there as an advocate for a certain relation of mine. I'm happy he lost the case, so that he didn't ask me to be his advocate without any effect today: 570 in my opinion a man who calls advocates ought to ask first and find out if the man he's calling has a mind to help him or not. If he says no, he should send him home mindless. (*pauses*) But look, my wife's in front of the house. Poor me! I'm afraid that she isn't deaf and has heard all this. 575

CLEO (*aside*) I have heard it and it'll cost you dearly.

LYS (*aside*) I'll come closer. (*loudly*) How are you, my joy?

CLEO I was waiting for you.

LYS Is everything arranged already? Have you already brought this neighbor of yours over to our place to help 580 you?

73

CLEO   arcessiui, ut iusseras.
       uerum hic sodalis tuos, amicus optumus,
       nescioquid se sufflauit uxori suae:
       negauit posse, quoniam arcesso, mittere.
LYS   uitium tibi istuc maxumum est: blanda es parum.
585 CLEO non matronarum officium est, sed meretricium,
       uiris alienis, mi uir, subblandirier.
       i tu, [atque] arcesse illam: ego intus quod facto est opus
       uolo accurare, mi uir.
LYS   propera ergo.
CLEO   licet.
       iam pol ego huic aliquem in pectus iniciam metum;
590   miserrumum hodie ego hunc habebo amasium.

III. iv: ALCESIMVS. LYSIDAMVS

ALC   uiso huc, amator si a foro rediit domum,
       qui me atque uxorem ludificatust, larua.
       sed eccum ante aedis. ad te hercle ibam commodum.
LYS   et hercle ego ad te. quid ais, uir minimi preti?
595   quid tibi mandaui? quid tecum oraui?
ALC   quid est?
LYS   ut bene uociuas aedis fecisti mihi,
       ut traduxisti huc ad nos uxorem tuam:
       satin propter te pereo ego atque occasio?
ALC   quin tu suspendis te? nemp' tute dixeras
600   tuam arcessituram esse uxorem uxorem meam.
LYS   ergo arcessiuisse ait sese, et dixisse te
       eam non missurum.
ALC   quin eapse ultro mihi
       negauit eius operam se morarier.

587 atque *deleui*   602 eapsaltro *A*, eam ipsa ultro *BVE1*, ea
ipsa ultro *JEᶜ*, eapse ultro *Bothe*

CLEO I invited her, as you'd told me. But this mate of yours, your wonderful friend, somehow got annoyed with his wife. When I invited her, he said he couldn't send her.

LYS This is your greatest shortcoming: you aren't charming enough.

CLEO My dear husband, it's not the job of wives, but of prosti- 585
tutes, to charm other men. You go and fetch her yourself.
I want to prepare indoors whatever's needful, my dear
husband.

LYS Then hurry up.

CLEO Yes. (*aside*) Now I'll inject some fear into his heart. I'll 590
give this lover-boy a very hard time.

Exit CLEOSTRATA into her house.
Enter ALCESIMUS from his house.

ALC I'm popping by here to see if our lover has come back
from the market, who has made fools of me and my wife,
the devil. But look, he's in front of the house. (*turning to
Lysidamus*) I was coming to you this very moment.

LYS And I to you. What do you say, you good-for-nothing? 595
What did I entrust you with? What did I ask you for?

ALC What's that?

LYS How well you've emptied your house for me, how you
took your wife over here to us! Aren't I and my opportu-
nity sufficiently ruined because of you?

ALC Why don't you hang yourself? You'd said your wife would 600
send for my wife.

LYS Well then, she says that she sent for her and that you said
you wouldn't let her go.

ALC But she herself told me of her own accord that she didn't
need her assistance.

LYS quin eapse me allegauit qui istam arcesserem.
605 ALC quin nihili facio.
LYS   quin me perdis.
ALC   quin bene est,
   quin etiam diu morabor, quin cupio tibi—
LYS quin—
ALC   —aliquid aegre facere.
LYS   quin faciam lubens.
   numquam tibi hodie "quin" erit plus quam mihi.
ALC quin hercle di te perdant postremo quidem!
610 LYS quid nunc? missurusne es ad me uxorem tuam?
ALC ducas, easque in maxumam malam crucem
   cum hac cum istac, cumque amica etiam tua.
   abi et aliud cura, ego iam per hortum iussero
   meam istuc transire uxorem ad uxorem tuam.
615 LYS nunc tu mi amicus es in germanum modum.
   qua ego hunc amorem mi esse aui dicam datum
   aut quot ego umquam erga Venerem inique fecerim,
   quoi sic tot amanti mi obuiam eueniant morae?
   attat!
620   quid illuc clamoris, opsecro, in nostra est domo?

III. V: PARDALISCA. LYSIDAMVS

PAR nulla sum, nulla sum, tota, tota occidi,
   cor metu mortuom est, membra miserae tremunt,
   nescio unde auxili, praesidi, perfugi
   mi aut opum copiam comparem aut expetam:
625   tanta factu modo mira miris modis

617 quod Ω, quot *Lindsay*
625 factis Ω, factu *Schoppius*

LYS But she herself commissioned me to send for her.

ALC But I don't care. 605

LYS But you're the ruin of me.

ALC But that's good. But I'll even delay her for a long time. But I wish—

LYS (*interrupting*) But—

ALC (*continuing*)—to do you some harm.

LYS But I'll do the same to you, and with pleasure. You won't have more buts than me today!

ALC But, once and for all, may the gods destroy you!

LYS What now? Are you going to send your wife over to me? 610

ALC Take her and go and be hanged with my wife, with your own wife, and also with your girlfriend! (*calming down*) Go and worry about something else, I'll now tell my wife to go over to your place to your wife through the garden.

LYS Now you are my friend in true brotherly fashion. 615

Exit ALCESIMUS into his house.

LYS Under which omen should I say that this love was imposed on me, or what have I ever done to offend Venus? I'm lovesick and yet I have to face so many delays like this! (*hearing noise from his house*) Goodness! What's 620 that shouting in our house, please?

Enter PARDALISCA from the house of Lysidamus, seemingly in panic.

PAR I'm dead, I'm dead, I've perished utterly, utterly, my heart has died from fear, my limbs are trembling, poor me. I don't know from where I should get or seek the opportunity for help, protection, refuge, support: I've seen 625 such strange goings-on in strange ways inside just now, a

77

		intus uidi, nouam atque integram audaciam.
		caue tibi, Cleostrata, apscede ab ista, opsecro,
		ne quid in te mali faxit ira percita.
629		eripite isti gladium,
629ᵃ		quae sui est impos animi.
630	LYS	nam quid est quod haec huc timida at-
630ᵃ		que exanimata exsiluit [foras]?
631		Pardalisca!
	PAR	perii! unde meae usurpant aures sonitum?
	LYS	respice modo ad me.
	PAR	o ere mi.
	LYS	quid tibi est? quid timida es?
	PAR	perii.
	LYS	quid, periisti?
	PAR	perii, et tu periisti.
	LYS	a, perii? quid ita?
634	PAR	uae tibi!
	LYS	immo uae tibi sit.
634ᵃ	PAR	ne cadam, amabo, tene me.
635–36	LYS	quicquid est, eloquere mi cito.
	PAR	contine pectus,
		face uentum, amabo, pallio.
	LYS	timeo hoc negoti quid siet,
		nisi haec meraclo se uspiam
640		percussit flore Liberi.
	PAR	optine auris, amabo.
	LYS	i in malam a me crucem!
		pectus, auris, caput teque di perduint!
		nam nisi ex te scio, quicquid hoc est, cito, hoc

630ᵃ exsiliuit *A*, exiluit foras *BVE*, exilunt foras *J*, exsiluit *Merula*
634 immo uae *A*, immo istuc *P*

78

new, unheard-of audacity. (*into the house*) Be on your guard, Cleostrata, go away from her, please, so that she doesn't do you any harm in her rage. Take the sword away from that girl! She has no control over her mind.

LYS   (*aside*) What on earth is the reason why she's rushed out 630 here, all fearful and anxious? (*loudly*) Pardalisca!

PAR   I'm dead! Whence do my ears catch that sound?

LYS   Just look back at me.

PAR   (*turning to him*) Oh my dear master.

LYS   What's wrong with you? What are you scared of?

PAR   I'm dead.

LYS   What, you're dead?

PAR   I'm dead, and you are dead, too.

LYS   Eh? I'm dead? How so?

PAR   Curse you!

LYS   No, curse *you*!

PAR   Please hold me so that I don't fall.

LYS   (*grabbing her*) Whatever it is, tell me quickly.   635

PAR   Hold my breast, fan me with your cloak, please.

LYS   (*aside*) I'm anxious about what this may mean, unless she's confused herself with the undiluted bouquet of 640 Liber.[25]

PAR   Hold my ears, please.[26]

LYS   Get away from me and get hanged! May the gods destroy you, breast, ears, and head! Unless you tell me quickly what this is all about, I'll smash your brains to pieces with

[25] Bacchus, the god of wine.

[26] This can be interpreted as a request to kiss her.

		iam tibi istuc cerebrum dispercutiam, excetra tu,
645		ludibrio pessuma adhuc quae me habuisti.
	PAR	ere mi . . .
	LYS	quid uis mea me ancilla?
	PAR	nimium saeuis.
	LYS	numero dicis.

sed hoc quicquid est eloquere, in pauca confer:
quid intus tumulti fuit?

PAR   scibis, audi.

650   malum pessumumque hic modo intus apud nos
tua ancilla hoc pacto exordiri coepit,
quod haud Atticam condecet disciplinam.

LYS   quid est id?

PAR   timor praepedit dicta linguae.

654 LYS   possum scire ego istuc ex te quid

654ᵃ   negoti est?

PAR   dicam.

655   tua ancilla, quam tu tuo uilico uis
dare uxorem, ea intus—

LYS   quid intus? quid est?

PAR   imitatur malarum malam disciplinam,
uiro quae suo interminetur: uitam—

659 LYS   quid ergo?

PAR   ah!

LYS   quid est?

PAR   interemere

659ᵃ   ait uelle uitam,

660   gladium—

LYS   hem!

PAR   gladium—

LYS   quid eum gladium?

PAR   habet.

this here (*holds up his walking stick*) this instant, you serpent. You've been making a fool of me all this while, you wicked woman. 645

PAR My dear master . . .

LYS (*still angry*) What do you want from me, my dear maid?

PAR You're too harsh.

LYS You're saying that too soon. But tell me about it, whatever it is, sum it up briefly: what was that uproar inside?

PAR You'll soon know; listen. At our place your slave girl has just begun to undertake something bad and terrible in this way, something which is inappropriate to Attic manners. 650

LYS What's that?

PAR Fear keeps tripping my tongue up.

LYS Can I know from you what's the matter?

PAR I'll tell you. Your slave girl, the one you want to give in marriage to your overseer, inside she— 655

LYS (*interrupting*) What's she doing inside? What is it?

PAR She's imitating the bad behavior of bad women, since she's threatening her husband: his life—

LYS (*interrupting*) So what is it?

PAR Ah!

LYS What is it?

PAR She says she wants to take his life. A sword— 660

LYS (*interrupting*) What?

PAR A sword—

LYS (*interrupting*) What about this sword?

PAR She has it.

---

658 interminetur *A*, interminatur *P*

	LYS	ei misero mihi! quor eum habet?
	PAR	insectatur omnis domi per aedis
		nec quemquam prope ad se sinit adire:
		ita omnes sub arcis, sub lectis latentes
665		metu mussitant.
	LYS	occidi atque interii!
		quid illi obiectum est mali tam repente?
	PAR	insanit.
	LYS	scelestissumum me esse credo.
	PAR	immo si scias dicta quae dixit hodie . . .
	LYS	istuc expeto scire. quid dixit?
	PAR	audi.
670		per omnis deos et deas deierauit,
		occisurum eum hac nocte quicum cubaret.
	LYS	men occidet?
	PAR	an quippiam ad te attinet?
	LYS	uah!
	PAR	quid cum ea negoti tibi est?
	LYS	peccaui:
		illuc [dicere], "uilicum," uolebam.
675	PAR	sciens de uia in semitam degredere.
	LYS	numquid mi minatur?
	PAR	tibi infesta soli est
677		plus quam quoiquam.
	LYS	quam ob rem?
	PAR	quia se
677ᵃ		des uxorem Olympioni,
678		nec se tuam nec se suam nec
		uiri uitam ⟨asseuerat⟩ sinere in
680		crastinum protolli: id huc
		missa sum tibi ut dicerem,
682–83		ab ea uti caueas tibi.

82

LYS	Poor me! Why does she have it?
PAR	She's chasing everybody at home throughout the house and doesn't let anyone come near her: everybody's hiding under chests and couches and keeping quiet out of fear. 665
LYS	I'm dead and done for! What harm has so suddenly come her way?
PAR	She's mad.
LYS	I think I'm the most wretched man ever.
PAR	If only you knew what words she uttered today . . .
LYS	I'm keen to know that. What did she say?
PAR	Listen. She swore by all the gods and goddesses that 670 she'd kill the man who she sleeps with this night.
LYS	She'll kill me?
PAR	Why? Does that have anything to do with you?
LYS	Bah!
PAR	What business do you have with her?
LYS	I made a mistake. I meant to say, "the overseer."
PAR	You're deliberately leaving the straight road for a wind- 675 ing path.
LYS	She isn't threatening me, is she?
PAR	With you alone she's angry, more than with anyone.
LYS	What for?
PAR	Because you're giving her in marriage to Olympio. She's adamant that she won't let your life, her own life, or her husband's life continue till tomorrow. I've been sent here 680 to tell you about this, so that you may be on your guard against her.

---

674 dicere *del. Fleckeisen*
678 neque se suam *P,* neque suam *A*
679 asseuerat *add. Leo*
682–83 ut Ω, uti *Leo* dig⟨nus es⟩ *add. Leo*

LYS   perii hercle ego miser!

PAR   dig⟨nus es⟩.

LYS neque est nec fuit me senex quisquam amator

685 adaeque miser.

PAR   ludo ego hunc facete;

nam quae facta dixi omnia huic falsa dixi:

era atque haec dolum ex proxumo hunc protulerunt,

ego hunc missa sum ludere.

LYS   heus Pardalisca!

PAR quid est?

LYS   est . . .

PAR   quid?

LYS   est quod uolo exquirere ex te.

690 PAR moram offers mihi.

LYS   at tu mihi offers maerorem.

sed etiamne habet nunc Casina gladium?

PAR habet, sed duos.

LYS   quid, duos?

PAR   altero te

occisurum ait, altero uilicum hodie.

LYS occisissumus sum omnium qui uiuont.

695 loricam induam mi optumum esse opinor.

quid uxor mea? non adiit atque ademit?

PAR nemo audet prope accedere.

LYS   exoret.

PAR   orat.

negat ponere alio modo ullo profecto,

nisi se sciat uilico non datum iri.

700 LYS atqui ingratiis, quia non uolt, nubet hodie.

nam quor non ego id perpetrem quod coepi,

ut nubat mihi? illud quidem uolebam,

"nostro uilico."

LYS   Poor me, I'm dead!

PAR   (*aside*) Serves you right.

LYS   (*aside*) There isn't and there hasn't been an old lover as   685
wretched as me.

PAR   (*aside*) I'm fooling him wittily: what I told him has happened was a lie from first to last. My mistress and this
woman from next door have hatched this trick, and I've
been sent to fool him.

LYS   Hey there, Pardalisca!

PAR   What is it?

LYS   (*hesitating*) There is . . .

PAR   What?

LYS   There is something I want to ask you.

PAR   You're delaying me.   690

LYS   And you are saddening me. But does Casina still have a
sword?

PAR   She does; two, actually.

LYS   What, two?

PAR   She says she's going to kill you with one and the overseer
with the other today.

LYS   I'm the most killed man of all who live. I think it's best for   695
me to put on a breastplate. What about my wife? Hasn't
she approached her and taken them away?

PAR   No one dares come near her.

LYS   Let her persuade her.

PAR   She's asking her. She says she'll only put them down if she
knows she won't be given to the overseer.

LYS   (*angrily*) But since she won't marry willingly, she'll marry   700
against her will today. Why shouldn't I see through what
I've begun, that she should marry me? I meant, "our
overseer."

	PAR	saepicule peccas.
	LYS	timor praepedit uerba. uerum, opsecro te,
705		dic me uxorem orare ut exoret illam
		gladium ut ponat et redire me intro ut liceat.
	PAR	nuntiabo.
	LYS	et tu orato.
	PAR	et ego orabo.
	LYS	at blande orato, ut soles. sed audin?
		si effexis hoc,
		soleas tibi
710		dabo et anulum in
		digito aureum et
		bona pluruma.
	PAR	operam dabo.
	LYS	face ut impetres.
715	PAR	eo nunciam,
		nisi quippiam
		remorare me.
	LYS	abi et cura.
		redit eccum tandem opsonatu meus adiutor, pompam ducit.

III. vi: OLYMPIO. CHYTRIO. LYSIDAMVS

720	OL	uide, fur, ut sentis sub signis
720ᵃ		ducas!
	CHYT	qui uero hi sunt sentes?
721	OL	quia quod tetigere, ilico rapiunt,
721ᵃ		si eas ereptum, ilico scindunt:
722		ita quoquo adueniunt, ubiubi sunt,
722ᵃ		duplici damno dominos multant.
723	CHYT	heia!
	OL	attat! cesso magnufice

PAR You make mistakes a little often.

LYS Fear keeps tripping up my words. But, I entreat you, say 705
     that I'm asking my wife to persuade her to put down the
     sword and to let me return inside.

PAR I'll tell her.

LYS And you, ask her.

PAR And I shall ask her.

LYS But ask her coaxingly, in your usual way. (*as she turns to
     move away*) But are you listening? If you succeed, I'll
     give you sandals and a golden ring for your finger and lots 710
     of good things.

PAR I'll try my best.

LYS Make sure you succeed.

PAR I'm going now, unless you delay me in some way. 715

LYS Go and take care of it.

Exit PARDALISCA into the house of Lysidamus.

LYS Look, finally my helper's returning from shopping, he's
     leading a procession.

*Enter OLYMPIO with CHYTRIO and his assistants from the
right.*

OL   See to it, you thief, that you keep these briars in line! 720

CHYT In what way are these men briars?

OL   Because they immediately cling to whatever they touch.
     If you pull them away, they immediately tear it to pieces:
     wherever they go, wherever they are, they punish their
     employers with double damage.

CHYT Come off it!

OL   (*spotting Lysidamus*) Oho! Should I not clothe myself in

723ᵃ		patricieque amicirier atque ita ero
723ᵇ		meo ire aduorsum?
724	LYS	bone uir, salue.
	OL	fateor.
	LYS	quid fit?
725	OL	tu amas: ego esurio et sitio.
	LYS	lepide excuratus [in]cessisti.
	OL	aha, hodie ***.
	LYS	mane uero, quamquam fastidis.
	OL	fy fy! foetet tuos mi sermo.
	LYS	quae res?
	OL	haec res.
	LYS	etiamne astas?
	OL	enim uero πράγματά μοι παρέχεις.
729	LYS	dabo tibi
729ᵃ		μέγα κακόν,
730		ut ego opinor, nisi resistis.
	OL	ὦ Ζεῦ,
		potin a med abeas,
		nisi me uis
		uomere hodie?
	LYS	mane.
	OL	quid est? quis hic est homo?
735	LYS	erus sum.
	OL	quis erus?
	LYS	quoius tu seruo's.
	OL	seruos ego?
	LYS	atque meus.
	OL	non sum ego liber?
		memento, memento.
	LYS	mane atque asta.
	OL	omitte.

88

	grand, aristocratic style and approach my master like this	
	as quickly as possible?	
LYS	Greetings, my good man.	
OL	I admit it.	
LYS	What's up?	
OL	You are in love; I am hungry and thirsty.	725
LYS	You've strutted around elegantly turned out.	
OL	Ah, today ***. (*walks on*)	
LYS	But wait, even though you're giving yourself airs.	
OL	Faugh, faugh! It stinks when you speak.	
LYS	What's the matter?	
OL	This is the matter.	
LYS	Won't you stand still?	
OL	You really are giving me a hard time.	
LYS	I'll give you a hard beating, I think, unless you stand still.	730
OL	O Zeus! Can't you leave me, unless you want me to vomit today?	
LYS	Wait.	
OL	What is it? Who is this?	
LYS	I'm master.	735
OL	What master?	
LYS	The one whose slave you are.	
OL	I'm a slave?	
LYS	Yes, mine in fact.	
OL	Aren't I free? Remember, remember.	
LYS	Wait and stand still. (*grabs him*)	
OL	Let go.	

---

726 incessisti Ω, cessisti *Müller*

727 (ede)pol *A*, ey ey *P*, fy fy *Spengel*

728 *spatium ante* etiamne *BV*, *Lysidamo dant JE*[3] (*nullum spatium E*[1])

	LYS	seruos sum tuos.
	OL	optume est.
	LYS	opsecro te,
		Olympisce mi, mi pater, mi patrone.
	OL	em,
740		sapis sane.
	LYS	tuos sum equidem.
	OL	quid mi opust seruo tam nequam?
	LYS	quid nunc? quam mox recreas me?
	OL	cena modo si sit cocta.
745	LYS	hisce ergo abeant.
	OL	propere cito intro ite et cito deproperate.
		ego iam intus ero, facito cenam mihi ut ebria sit.
747		sed lepide nitideque uolo,
747ª		nil moror barbarico bliteo.
748		stasne etiam? i sis, ego hic habeo.
748ª		numquid est ceterum quod morae siet?
749	LYS	gladium Casinam intus habere ait, qui me ac te interimat.
750	OL	scio. sic sine habere;
		nugas agunt: noui
		ego illas malas merces.
		quin tu i modo mecum
		domum.
	LYS	at pol malum metuo.
755		i tu modo, perspicito prius quid intus agatur.
	OL	tam mi mea uita
		tua quam tibi cara est.
		uerum i modo.
	LYS	si tu iubes, em ibitur tecum.

746 facite Ω, facito *Geppert*
757 tua quam *A*, quam tua *P*

LYS	(*sweetly*) I'm your slave.
OL	That's perfect.
LYS	I entreat you, my dear little Olympio, my father, my patron.
OL	There you go, you really show sense. 740
LYS	I'm yours.
OL	What do I need such a useless slave for?
LYS	What now? How soon are you restoring me to life?
OL	If only the dinner were cooked!
LYS	Let these people go in then. 745
OL	(*to Chytrio and servants*) Go inside fast and quickly and hurry quickly. I'll be inside in a moment, make sure that my dinner is sumptuous. But I want it neat and lovely, I don't care for barbarian trash. Are you still standing there? Do go, I live here.

Exit CHYTRIO into the house of Lysidamus, followed by his assistants.

OL	Is there anything else to cause delay?
LYS	She says Casina has a sword inside, to kill me and you with.
OL	(*skeptically*) I know. Let her have it like that. They're 750 talking rubbish. I know those bad pieces. Just go home with me.
LYS	But I'm afraid of trouble. Just go yourself and have a look 755 first what's going on inside.
OL	(*timidly*) My life is as dear to me as yours is to you. (*giving him a push*) All the same, come along.
LYS	If you tell me, well, I'll go with you.

Exeunt OLYMPIO and LYSIDAMUS into their house.

91

ACTVS IV

IV. i: PARDALISCA

PAR nec pol ego Nemeae credo neque ego Olympiae
760 neque usquam ludos tam festiuos fieri
quam hic intus fiunt ludi ludificabiles
seni nostro et nostro Olympioni uilico.
omnes festinant intus totis aedibus,
senex in culina clamat, hortatur coquos:
765 "quin agitis hodie? quin datis si quid datis?
properate, cenam iam esse coctam oportuit."
uilicus is autem cum corona, candide
uestitus, lautus exornatusque ambulat.
illae autem armigerum ilico exornant duae
770 quem dent pro Casina nuptum nostro uilico.
sed nimium lepide dissimulant, quasi nil sciant
fore huius quod futurum est; digne autem coqui
nimis lepide ei rei dant operam, ne cenet senex,
aulas peruortunt, ignem restinguont aqua:
775 illarum oratu faciunt; illae autem senem
cupiunt extrudere incenatum ex aedibus,
ut ipsae solae uentris distendant suos.
noui ego illas ambestrices: corbitam cibi
comesse possunt. sed aperitur ostium.

IV. ii: LYSIDAMVS. PARDALISCA

780 LYS si sapitis, uxor, uos tamen cenabitis,
cena ubi erit cocta; ego ruri cenauero.
nam nouom maritum et nouam nuptam uolo

---

[27] Two places where athletic competitions took place.

ACT FOUR

Enter PARDALISCA from the house of Lysidamus.

PAR   I don't believe that at Nemea or Olympia[27] or anywhere   760
else such jolly games take place as the game-making tak-
ing place inside here at the expense of our old master and
our overseer Olympio. Everybody's rushing around in-
side through the entire house. The old man's shouting in
the kitchen and urging on the cooks: "Why won't you get   765
on with it today? Why aren't you giving us anything if you
are giving us something? Hurry up, dinner ought to be
cooked already." And that overseer is walking around
with a garland, dressed in white, bathed and adorned.
The two women, on the other hand, are adorning the or-
derly there so that they can give him in marriage to our   770
overseer in place of Casina. But they're pretending ever
so charmingly that they don't know that anything will
happen of what will happen. And the cooks for their
part take care ever so charmingly that the old man won't
get his dinner; they knock over the pots and extinguish
the fire with water. They're doing so at the women's re-   775
quest. And the women want to throw the old man out
of the house without dinner, so that they themselves are
the only ones to stuff their bellies. I know those glut-
tons: they can gobble up a shipload full of food. (*looking
around*) But the door is opening.

Enter LYSIDAMUS from his house.

LYS   (*into the house*) If you're wise, my wife, you'll dine never-   780
theless when dinner is cooked. I'll dine on our country
estate: I want to accompany the new groom and the new

rus prosequi—noui hominum mores maleficos—
ne quis eam abripiat. facite uostro animo uolup.
785   sed properate istum atque istam actutum emittere,
tandem ut ueniamus luci; ego cras hic ero.
cras habuero, uxor, ego tamen conuiuium.

PAR   fit quod futurum dixi: incenatum senem
foras extrudunt mulieres.

LYS   quid tu hic agis?

790 PAR   ego eo quo me ipsa misit.

LYS   ueron?

PAR   serio.

LYS   quid hic speculare?

PAR   nil equidem speculor.

LYS   abi.
tu hic cunctas, intus alii festinant.

PAR   eo.

LYS   abi hinc sis ergo, pessumarum pessuma.
iamne abiit illaec? dicere hic quiduis licet.
795   qui amat, tamen hercle, si esurit, nullum esurit.
sed eccum progreditur cum corona et lampade
meus socius, compar, commaritus uilicus.

IV. iii: OLYMPIO. LYSIDAMVS

OL   age tibicen, dum illam educunt huc nouam nuptam foras,
suaui cantu concelebra omnem hanc plateam hymenaeo
      meo.

799 miω A, meio P

bride to our estate—I know the wicked ways of the peo- 785
ple—so that no one abducts her. Enjoy yourselves, but be
quick to send her and him out at once, so that we can get
there while it's light. I'll be back tomorrow. I'll have my
banquet tomorrow despite everything, my wife.

PAR   (*aside*) What I said would happen is happening: the
women are throwing the old man out of the house with-
out dinner.

LYS   (*spotting Pardalisca*) What are you doing here?

PAR   I'm going where my mistress has sent me. 790

LYS   Really?

PAR   Yes, seriously.

LYS   Why are you spying here?

PAR   I'm not spying at all.

LYS   Go away. You are dawdling here, the others are rushing
around inside.

PAR   I'm going.

LYS   Then go away, will you, you worst of all women.

Exit PARDALISCA into the house of Lysidamus.

OL   Is she gone now? I can say anything here. A lovesick man 795
doesn't feel hunger at all, even if he does feel hunger. But
look, the overseer's coming out with a garland and torch,
my comrade, partner, and co-husband.

*Enter OLYMPIO from the house of Lysidamus, with a flower
garland on and a wedding torch in his hand.*

OL   Go on, flute player, while they're bringing that new bride
out here, make this entire street ring with a sweet wed-
ding song for me.

800 LYS + OL Hymen Hymenaee, o Hymen!

    LYS   quid agis, mea Salus?

    OL   esurio hercle, atque adeo hau salubriter.

    LYS   at ego amo.

    OL   at ego hercle nihili facio. tibi amor pro cibo est,
         mihi iaiunitate iam dudum intestina murmurant.

    LYS   nam quid illaec nunc tam diu intus remorantur remeligi-
         nes?

805   quasi ob industriam, quanto ego plus propero, procedit
         minus.

    OL   quid si etiam suffundam hymenaeum, si qui citius pro-
         deant?

    LYS   censeo, et ego te adiutabo in nuptiis communibus.

    LYS + OL Hymen Hymenaee, o Hymen!

    LYS   perii hercle ego miser! dirrumpi cantando hymenaeum
         licet:

810   illo morbo quo dirrumpi cupio, non est copiae.

    OL   edepol ne tu, si equos esses, esses indomabilis.

    LYS   quo argumento?

    OL   nimis tenax es.

    LYS   num me expertu's uspiam?

    OL   di melius faciant! sed crepuit ostium, exitur foras.

    LYS   di hercle me cupiunt seruatum.

    800 hymen ae eo hymen B, hymen et eo hymen VE[1], himen ac eo
himen E[c], himen ae eo himen J, hymenaeo hymen A
    806 etiam si A, etiam P, si etiam Leo offendam Ω, suffundam Leo
    808 hymen ae eo hymen P, hymenaeo hymen A

LYS + OL	Hymen Hymenaeus, o Hymen![28]	800

LYS How are you, my savior?

OL I'm so hungry that I'm past saving.

LYS But I'm in love.

OL But I don't care. Your love takes the place of food; I have intestines that have been rumbling from hunger for a long time already.

LYS Why on earth are those dawdlers delaying us so long inside now? The more of a hurry I'm in, the less progress is 805 made, as if on purpose.

OL What if I intone the wedding song again, in case they come out more quickly?

LYS I agree, and I'll support you in our shared wedding.

LYS + OL Hymen Hymenaeus, o Hymen!

LYS I'm dead, poor me! I can rupture myself from singing the wedding song; but there's no opportunity to rupture my- 810 self from the illness from which I want to be ruptured.

OL Seriously, if you were a stallion, you'd be untamable.

LYS How so?

OL You're very persistent.

LYS You haven't tried me out anywhere, have you?

OL May the gods forbid! (*pauses*) But the door has creaked, they're coming out.

LYS The gods want me saved.

---

[28] A ritual cry. The interpretation of *Hymen* as the name of a wedding god is secondary, but already occurs in early Greek.

IV. iv: CHALINVS. PARDALISCA. OLYMPIO.
LYSIDAMVS. CLEOSTRATA

PAR   iam oboluit Casinus procul.

815–16   sensim super attolle limen pedes, mea noua nupta;
           sospes iter incipe hoc, uti uiro tuo
           semper sis superstes,

819–20   tuaque ut potior pollentia sit uincasque uirum uictrixque
             sies,

821–22   tua uox superet tuomque imperium: uir te uestiat, tu ui-
             rum [de]spolies.
           noctuque et diu ut uiro subdola sis,
           opsecro, memento.

825 OL   malo maxumo suo hercle ilico, ubi tantillum peccassit.

LYS   tace.

OL   non taceo.

LYS   quae res?

OL   mala malae male monstrat.

LYS   facies tune hanc rem mi ex parata imparatam? id
           quaerunt, id uolunt, haec ut infecta faciant.

PAR   age Olympio, quando uis, uxo-

830   rem accipe hanc ab nobis.

OL   date ergo, daturae si umquam estis hodie uxorem.

LYS   abite intro.

CLEO   amabo, integrae atque imperitae huic
           impercito.

814 iam . . . procul *dedit Pardaliscae Leo*
815–16 mea *A, om. P*
821–22 despolies Ω, spolies *Müller*
827 tu‹n› *Lindsay*

*Enter PARDALISCA from the house of Lysidamus, followed
by CLEOSTRATA, MYRRHINA, and CHALINUS, the latter
veiled.*

PAR (*to the women*) He's already smelled our Casinus[29] in the
distance. (*to Chalinus*) Raise your feet above the thresh- 815
old gently, my new bride. Begin this journey safely, so
that you will always stand above your husband and so that 820
your power will be greater and you will have the upper
hand over your husband and be victorious, and so that
your voice and your command will be stronger. Your hus-
band shall clothe you, you shall plunder him. By night
and by day you shall trick your husband; remember that,
I beg you.

OL She'll pay a heavy price as soon as she commits the small- 825
est offense.

LYS Be quiet.

OL No, I won't.

LYS What's the matter?

OL The bad woman is showing her bad ways to a bad girl.

LYS Are you going to turn this business of mine from settled
to unsettled? That's what they're after, that's what they
want, to undo this.

PAR Go on, Olympio, since you wish it, take this wife of yours 830
from us.

OL Then give me my wife now, if you're ever going to give
her to me at all.

LYS (*to the women*) Go inside.

CLEO Please, be gentle with this innocent and inexperienced
girl.

----

[29] I.e. Casina with a masculine ending.

OL   futurum est.

PAR   ualete.

OL   ite iam.

LYS   ite.

CLEO   iam ualete.

835 LYS   iamne apscessit uxor?

OL   domi est, ne time.

LYS   euax!

nunc pol demum ego sum liber.

meum corculum, melculum, uerculum.

OL   heus tu,

malo, si sapis, cauebis;

mea est haec.

LYS   scio, sed meus fructus est prior.

840 OL   tene hanc lampadem.

LYS   immo ego hanc tenebo.

Venus multipotens, bona multa mihi

dedisti, huius quom copiam mi dedisti.

OL   o

corpusculum malacum!

mea uxorcula—quae res?

845 LYS   quid est?

OL   institit plantam

quasi luca bos.

LYS   tace sis,

nebula haud est mollis aeque atque huius pectus est.

OL   edepol papillam bellulam—ei misero mihi!

LYS   quid est?

832–33 amabo . . . impercito *dat Pardaliscae P, Cleostratae Seyffert*
841 multa bona mihi *A*, bonam uitam mihi *P*, bona multa mihi
Studemund   847 est pectus *A*, est *P*, pectus est *Leo*

OL	Yes.
PAR	Goodbye.
OL	(*again to the women*) Go now.
LYS	Go.
CLEO	Goodbye now.

Exeunt CLEOSTRATA, MYRRHINA, and PARDALISCA into the house of Lysidamus.

LYS	Has my wife left now?	835
OL	She's in the house, stop being afraid.	
LYS	Hurray! Now at last I'm free. (*to Chalinus*) My little sweetheart, my little honey, my little spring.	
OL	Hey, you, watch out for trouble if you're wise. She belongs to me.	
LYS	I know, but my enjoyment comes first.	
OL	Hold this torch. (*tries to hand it over*)	840
LYS	(*grabbing the bride*) No, this is what I'll hold. Mighty Venus, you gave me many good things when you gave me possession of her.	
OL	(*trying to fondle Chalinus*) Oh what a tender little body! My little wife—what on earth!	
LYS	What's the matter?	845
OL	She stamped on my foot like an elephant.	
LYS	Be quiet, will you? A cloud is not as soft as her breast.	
OL	(*trying to fondle again*) Yes, a pretty little nipple—dear me, poor me!	
LYS	What is it?	

	OL	pectus mi icit non cubito, uerum ariete.
850	LYS	quid tu ergo hanc, quaeso, tractas tam dura manu?
		at mihi, qui belle hanc tracto, non bellum facit.
	OL	uah!
	LYS	quid negoti est?
	OL	opsecro, ut ualentula est!
		paene exposiuit cubito.
	LYS	cubitum ergo ire uolt.
	OL	quin imus ergo?
	LYS	i belle, belliatula.

ACTVS V

V. i: MYRRHINA. PARDALISCA. CLEOSTRATA

855	MYR	acceptae bene et commode eximus intus
		ludos uisere huc in uiam nuptialis.
		numquam ecastor ullo die risi adaeque,
		neque hoc quod relicuom est plus risuram opinor.
	PAR	lubet Chalinum quid agat scire, nouom nuptum cum
		nouo marito.
860	MYR	nec fallaciam astutiorem ullus fecit
		poeta atque ut haec est fabre facta ab nobis.
	CLEO	optunso ore nunc peruelim progrediri
		senem, quo senex nequior nullus uiuit;
		nisi illum quidem
865		nequiorem arbitrare esse qui locum

864–65 ne *P*, n *A*, nisi *Brix uersus sic ego diuisi, alii aliter*

---

30 Pun on *belle* "prettily" and *bellum* "war."

31 *Nuptus* is a jocular formation; the verb, meaning "marry," is only used of women, but the ending is masculine.

OL   She hit me in the chest, not with her elbow, but with a
        battering ram.

LYS   Then why do you handle her with such a rough hand,   850
        please? But she doesn't attack me, since I handle her
        with tact.[30]

OL   Bah!

LYS   What's the matter?

OL   Please, what a strong little lady she is! She almost laid me
        out with her elbow.

LYS   Then she wants to get laid.

OL   Why don't we go then?

LYS   Go prettily, my pretty little creature.

*Exeunt LYSIDAMUS, OLYMPIO, and CHALINUS into the
house of Alcesimus.*

ACT FIVE

*Enter CLEOSTRATA, MYRRHINA, and PARDALISCA from
the house of Lysidamus.*

MYR   After we've been entertained well and pleasurably we're   855
        going outside here into the street to watch the wedding
        games. I've never, on any day, laughed as much, nor do I
        think I will laugh more during all the rest of my life.

PAR   I'd love to know what Chalinus is doing, the new he-
        bride[31] with the new husband.

MYR   No playwright has ever found a trick cleverer than this   860
        skillful one of ours.

CLEO   Now I'd love the old man to come out with his face bat-
        tered, the most worthless old man alive; unless you con-
        sider that chap worse who provided him with a place   865

103

praebet illi ⟨stupri⟩. ⟨te⟩ nunc praesidem
uolo hic, Pardalisca, esse, qui hinc exeat
eum ut ludibrio habeas.

PAR   lubens fecero et solens.

870–
71 MYR   *** spectato hinc omnia: intus quid agant ***.
              ***

PAR   pone me, amabo.

MYR   et ibi audacius licet
quae uelis libere proloqui.

PAR   tace,
uostra foris crepuit.

V. ii: OLYMPIO. MYRRHINA.
CLEOSTRATA. PARDALISCA

875 OL   nec quo fugiam neque ubi lateam neque hoc dedecus
     quo modo celem

scio, tantum erus atque ego flagitio superauimus nuptiis
     nostris,

ita nunc pudeo atque ita nunc paueo atque ita irridiculo
     sumus ambo.

sed ego insipiens noua nunc facio: pudet quem prius non
     puditum umquam est.

operam date, dum mea facta itero: est operae pretium
     auribus accipere,

880   ita ridicula auditu, iteratu ea sunt quae ego intus turbaui.

ubi intro hanc nouam nuptam deduxi, recta uia in con-
     claue abduxi.

---

866 stupri *add. Willcock* te *add. Valla*   870–71 *uersum, qui
sanari non potest, dat Myrrhinae Angelius, Cleostratae Bothe*

872–73 pone me amabo *dat Pardaliscae Angelius, Myrrhinae
Camerarius* et . . . proloqui *dat Myrrhinae Camerarius, Cleostratae
Lindsay*

for his affair. Now I want you to be in charge here,
Pardalisca, so that you make fun of whoever comes out
from here.

PAR I'll do so with pleasure and in my usual way.

MYR *** Watch everything from here: what they're doing in- 870
side ***.
***

PAR Stand behind me, please.

MYR And there you can more boldly and freely say what you
want.

PAR Be quiet, your door has creaked.

*Enter OLYMPIO from the house of Alcesimus, battered and
half-naked.*

OL I don't know where to flee, where to hide, or how to con- 875
ceal this disgrace: so much did master and I surpass our-
selves in disgrace during our wedding, so much am I
ashamed now, so much am I afraid now, and so much
have we both made fools of ourselves. But, stupid as I am,
I'm doing something new now: I, who never felt shame
before, am feeling shame now. Pay attention while I re-
count my deeds; it's worthwhile to take it in with your
ears: the mess I made inside is so funny to hear and 880
recount. When I led this new bride inside, I took her

---

872 loquere *add. Lindsay antequam Myrrhina loquitur*

874 uestra/uostra *AVJE*, nos *B¹*, nostra *B³* (*probante Lindsay qui
tace . . . crepuit Myrrhinae dat*)

878 puditum umquam est *P* (*septenarius*), puditumst umquam *A*
(*octonarius*)

sed tamen tenebrae ibi erant tamquam in puteo; dum
    senex abest "decumbe" inquam.
colloco, fulcio, mollio, blandior,
ut prior quam senex nup⟨tias perpetrem⟩.

885   tardus esse ilico coepi, quoniam ***
respecto identidem, ne senex ***.
illecebram stupri principio eam sauium posco,

888   reppulit mi manum, neque enim dare sibi
888ᵃ   sauium me siuit.

889–
90   enim iam magis ⟨insto⟩, iam appropero, magis iam lubet
    in Casinam irruere
cupio illam operam seni surrupere, forem obdo, ne senex
    me opprimeret.

CLEO agedum, tu adi hunc.

PAR   opsecro, ubi tua noua nupta est?

893–
95 OL perii hercle ego! manufesta res [est].

PAR   omnem [in] ordine rem
fateri ergo aequom est. quid intus agitur? quid agit

897–
98 Casina? satin morigera est?

OL   pudet dicere [me].

899–
900 PAR memora ordine, ut occeperas.

OL   pudet hercle.

PAR   age audacter ***.
⟨post⟩quam decubuisti, inde uolo memorare quid est
    factum ***
    ***.

OL   flagitium est.

884 nup⟨tias perpetrem⟩ *Schoell*
885–86 *desunt fines uersuum*   889–90 insto *add. Schoell*
893–95 est *del. Geppert* omnem in ordinem rem *BVE*, omnem
ordinem rem *J*, omnem ordine rem *Leo*

straight to a bedroom. But there was darkness in there
like in a dungeon. While the old man was away, I said,
"Lie down." I got her placed, supported her with pillows,
soothed her, and coaxed her, in order to consummate the
marriage before the old man. Then I began to slow down   885
since ***. I looked back again and again so that the old
man wouldn't ***. First I asked to give her a kiss, as an
enticement for sex. She pushed back my hand and didn't
let me give her a kiss. I became more insistent then, I   890
hurried to her then, I was keener to throw myself upon
Casina then. I wished to steal that job from the old man; I
bolted the door so that my old master wouldn't surprise
me.

CLEO *(to Pardalisca)* Go on, you approach him.

PAR *(to Olympio)* Please, where's your new bride?

OL I'm dead! It's all out.   895

PAR So it's only fair to confess everything one by one. What's
happening inside? What's Casina doing? Is she obedient
enough?

OL I'm ashamed to tell.

PAR Report one by one, as you began.   900

OL I'm really ashamed.

PAR Go on, boldly ***. After you lay down, from there I want
you to report what happened ***.

OL It's a disgrace.

---

896 aegum *B¹VE*, aegrum *B³*, actum *J*, aequum *Camerarius*
897–98 me *del. Schoell*
899–908 *uersus mutilati*
901 uam debuisti *BVE¹*, quam debuisti *JE³*, postquam decubuisti
Lambinus

PLAUTUS

PAR		cauebunt qui audierint faciant. ***
OL	*** hoc magnus est ⟨pudor⟩.	
PAR		⟨rem⟩ perdis. quin tu pergis?
OL		ubi ***

904–5 *** us suptus porro ***
***.

PAR quid?
OL babae!
PAR quid?
OL papae!
PAR *** est?
OL oh, erat maximum.
908 ⟨ferrum ne⟩ haberet metui: id quaerere occepi.
908ᵃ ***
909 dum gladium quaero ne habeat, arripio capulum.
910 sed quom cogito, non habuit gladium, nam esset frigidus.
PAR eloquere.
OL at pudet.
PAR num radix fuit?
OL non fuit.
PAR num cucumis?
OL profecto hercle ⟨istuc nescio sed⟩ non fuit quicquam
    holerum,
    nisi, quicquid erat, calamitas profecto attigerat num-
    quam.
    ita, quicquid erat, grande erat.
915–16 PAR quid fit denique? edisserta.
OL ibi appello, "Casina," inquam,
917–18 "amabo, mea uxorcula, quor uirum tuom sic me spernis?
    nimis tu quidem hercle immerito
920 meo mi haec facis, quia mihi te expetiui."

108

PAR   Those who hear it will be on their guard against doing it.
     ***

OL   *** I feel great shame about it.

PAR   You're losing the thread. Why don't you continue?

OL   When *** down below further ***. ***   905

PAR   What?

OL   Goodness!

PAR   What?

OL   Gracious!

PAR   *** is it?

OL   Oh, it was enormous. I was afraid that she'd have a sword.
     I began looking for it. *** While I was checking that she
     doesn't have a sword, I got hold of a hilt. But when I think 910
     about it, she didn't have a sword, because it would have
     been cold.

PAR   Tell us.

OL   But I'm ashamed.

PAR   Was it a radish?

OL   No, it wasn't.

PAR   A cucumber?

OL   I really don't know, but it wasn't any vegetable, ex-
     cept that, whatever it was, certainly no blight had ever
     touched it. Whatever it was, it was so well grown.

PAR   What happened in the end? Explain.   915

OL   Then I tried to seduce her. I said, "Casina, please, my
     little wife, why are you rejecting me, your husband, like
     this? Because I sought you for myself I don't deserve that 920

---

903 pudor *et* rem *add. Lindsay*   908 ferrum ne *add. Schoell*
   908ᵃ *lacunam indicant BJV*   912 *lacunam inter* hercle *et* non
indicant BV, istuc nescio sed *add. Leo*
   915–16 ubi appello Casinam inquit *P*, ibi a. "Casina" inquam *Bothe*

illa hau uerbum facit et saepit ueste id qui estis ‹mulie-
    res›.
ubi illum saltum uideo opsaeptum, rogo ut altero sinat
    ire.
uolo, ut obuortam, cubitis im ***
ullum †muttite† ***.

925   surgo, ut in eam in ***
atque illam in ***.

MYR   perlepide narrat ***.
OL   sauium ***
ita quasi saetis labra mihi compungit barba.

930   continuo in genua ut astiti,
930ᵃ   pectus mi pedibus percutit.
931   decido de lecto praecipes:
931ᵃ   supsilit, optundit os mihi.
932   inde foras tacitus profugiens
932ᵃ   exeo hoc ornatu quo uides,
933   ut senex hoc eodem poculo
933ᵃ   quo ego bibi biberet.

PAR   optume est.
sed ubi est palliolum tuom?
OL   hic intus reliqui.
935 PAR quid nunc? satin lepide adita est uobis manus?
OL   merito.
sed concrepuerunt fores. num illa me nunc sequitur?

V. iii: LYSIDAMVS. CHALINVS

LYS   maxumo ego ardeo flagitio
nec quid agam meis rebus scio,
nec meam ut uxorem aspiciam
940   contra oculis, ita disperii;
omnia palam sunt probra,

you do this to me." She didn't say a word and covered
with her dress that part because of which you are women.
When I saw that that entrance was blocked, I asked her to
let me enter through the other.[32] In order to turn her to-
ward me, I wanted *** with my elbows. *** any ***. I   925
rose in order to *** into her and *** her.

MYR He's telling it in such a lovely way ***.

OL *** a kiss. A beard punctured my lips like hogs' bristles.   930
No sooner had I got up onto my knees than she rammed
my chest with her feet. I fell off the bed head first. She
jumped up and battered my face. Fleeing quietly out
here, I came out in the outfit you see, so that the old man
should drink from this same cup I drank from.

PAR That's fantastic. But where's your cloak?

OL I left it inside here.

PAR Well then? Have you two been tricked neatly enough?   935

OL Yes, deservedly so. But the door has creaked. She isn't
following me, is she?

*Enter LYSIDAMUS from the house of Alcesimus, also battered
and half-naked, without his walking stick.*

LYS I'm burning with an enormous disgrace. I don't know
what I should do about my situation or how I should look
my wife into the eyes, so ruined am I. All my misdeeds   940

---

[32] I.e. the anus.

---

921 mulieres *add. Loman*   923–28 *desunt fines uersuum*
929 labram *P*, labra *Merula*   930 astuti *E¹*, astituti *BVE²*, ad-
stanti *J*, ut astiti *Seyffert*   931 praeceps *P*, praecipes *Seyffert*
932 praeficiens *BVE*, proficiens *J*, profugiens *Redslob*
941 nia *BVE¹*, quia *JE³*, omnia *Camerarius*

omnibus modis occidi miser.

*** ita manufesto faucibus teneor

*** nec quibus modis purgem scio me meae uxori

945   *** atque expalliatus sum miser,

*** clandestinae nuptiae.

*** censeo

*** mihi optumum est.

*** intro ad uxorem meam

950   sufferamque ei meum tergum ob iniuriam.

sed ecquis est qui homo munus uelit fungier pro me?

952–53   quid nunc agam nescio, nisi ut

improbos famulos imiter ac domo fugiam.

955–56   nam salus nulla est scapulis, si domum redeo.

†nugas istic dicere licet† uapulo hercle ego inuitus tamen

etsi malum merui.

959–60   hac dabo protinam ⟨me⟩ et fugiam.

CHAL   heus! sta ilico, amator.

961–62 LYS occidi! reuocor: quasi non audiam, abibo.

V. iv: CHALINVS. LYSIDAMVS. CLEOSTRATA.
MYRRHINA. OLYMPIO

CHAL ubi tu es, qui colere mores Massiliensis postulas?

nunc tu si uis subigitare me, proba est occasio.

965   redi sis in cubiculum; periisti hercle. age, accede huc
modo.

nunc ego tecum aequom arbitrum extra considium cap-
tauero.

LYS perii! fusti defloccabit iam illic homo lumbos meos.

943–49 *desunt initia uersuum in Palatinis*, A *abest*
945 quae *P*, atque *Geppert*
957 *nec sensus nec metrum satis constat*
959–60 me *add. Geppert*

are out, I've perished in every conceivable way, poor me.
*** like this I'm being held by the throat, red-handed ***
and I don't know how I can clear myself with my wife ***   945
and I've been robbed of my cloak, poor me. *** the fur-
tive wedding. *** I think *** is best for me. *** inside to
my wife and I'll offer her my back as compensation for   950
the injustice. (*to the audience*) But is there anyone who'd
like to take on this job for me? (*after a pause*) I don't
know what I should do now, except for imitating bad
slaves and fleeing from home: there's no salvation for my   955
shoulder blades if I return home. †One can call this rub-
bish there.† I'm getting a beating, against my will, even
though I've deserved a thrashing. I'll run off this way and   960
flee. (*turns to the right*)

*Enter CHALINUS from the house of Alcesimus, carrying the
cloak and walking stick of Lysidamus.*

CHAL Hey there! Lover, stop where you are.
LYS It's over with me! I'm being called back; I'll go away as if I
      didn't hear.
CHAL Where are you, you who wish to follow the customs of
      Marseille?[33] If you want to get me into bed now, you have
      a decent opportunity. Come back to the bedroom, will   965
      you? You're dead. Go on, just come here. Now I'll get
      a fair umpire with you, outside the regular bench of
      judges. (*raises Lysidamus' walking stick*)
LYS I'm dead! He'll smash my loins with his club now. I have

---

[33] The inhabitants of Marseille were considered effeminate (Athen.
Deipn. 12. 523c).

<table>
<tr><td></td><td>hac iter faciundum est, nam illac lumbifragium est ob-
uiam.</td></tr>
<tr><td>CLEO</td><td>iubeo te saluere, amator.</td></tr>
<tr><td>LYS</td><td>ecce autem uxor obuiam est:</td></tr>
</table>

        CLEO iubeo te saluere, amator.

970 nunc ego inter sacrum saxumque sum nec quo fugiam
     scio.
    hac lupi, hac canes: lupina scaeua fusti rem gerit;
    hercle opinor permutabo ego illuc nunc uerbum uetus:
    hac ibo, caninam scaeuam spero meliorem fore.

MYR quid agis, dismarite?

CLEO   mi uir, unde hoc ornatu aduenis?

975 quid fecisti scipione aut quod habuisti pallium?

PAR in adulterio, dum moechissat Casinam, credo perdidit.

LYS occidi!

CHAL   etiamne imus cubitum? Casina sum.

LYS   i in malam crucem!

CHAL non amas me?

CLEO   quin responde, tuo quid factum est pallio?

LYS Bacchae hercle, uxor—

CLEO   Bacchae?

LYS   Bacchae hercle, uxor—

MYR   nugatur sciens,

980 nam ecastor nunc Bacchae nullae ludunt.

LYS   oblitus fui,
    sed tamen Bacchae—

CLEO   quid, Bacchae?

975 scipionem Ω, scipione *Lambinus*
976 *Pardaliscae dat Camerarius*

  to turn this way: that way a loin wreck is facing me. (*turns away from Chalinus*)

CLEO My greetings, lover.

LYS Look, my wife is facing me. Now I'm between the altar 970 and the knife and don't know where to flee. On this side (*points to Chalinus*) there are wolves, on this side (*points to the women*) dogs.[34] The wolf omen does business with a club. I think I'll change that old proverb: I'll go this way, I hope the dog omen will be better.[35]

MYR How are you, bigamist?

CLEO My dear husband, where are you coming from with this getup? What did you do with your walking stick or the 975 cloak you had?

PAR He lost it in the act of adultery, I believe, while having sex with Casina.

LYS I'm dead!

CHAL (*calling after him*) Let's go to bed now! I'm Casina.

LYS Go and be hanged!

CHAL Don't you love me?

CLEO (*to her husband*) Answer me, what's happened to your cloak?

LYS Bacchants, my wife—

CLEO (*interrupting*) Bacchants?

LYS Bacchants, my wife—

MYR (*interrupting*) He's deliberately talking nonsense: no 980 Bacchants are reveling now.

LYS I'd forgotten, but still, Bacchants—

CLEO (*interrupting*) What, Bacchants?

---

[34] A proverb (attested also in Hor. *sat.* 2. 2. 64), meaning that he is threatened from all sides.   [35] He is changing the proverb by going towards one of the threatening alternatives.

LYS   sin id fieri non potest—

CLEO times ecastor.

LYS   egone? mentire hercle.

CLEO   nam palles male.

    n *** quid me ue *** us *** am me rogas?

    *** male r *** mihi

985   *** gratulor.

    *** qu *** senex.

LYS ho *** conspicillo ⟨quom⟩ conspexi uirginem

    *** unc Casinust ***

989–90 qui hic *** lem frus *** ram *** dis.

OL qui etiam me miserum famosum fecit flagitiis suis.

LYS non taces?

OL   non hercle uero taceo. nam tu maxumo

    me opsecrauisti opere Casinam ut poscerem uxorem mihi

994–95 tui amoris causa.

LYS   ego istuc feci?

OL   immo Hector Ilius.

LYS te quidem oppresset. feci ego istaec dicta quae uos dicitis?

CLEO rogitas etiam?

LYS   si quidem hercle feci, feci nequiter.

CLEO redi modo huc intro: monebo, siquidem meministi minus.

LYS hercle, opinor, potius uobis credam quod uos dicitis.

1000 sed, uxor, da uiro hanc ueniam ⟨mi⟩; Myrrhina, ora Cleostratam;

    si umquam posthac aut amasso Casinam aut occepso modo,

983–90 *uersus mutilati*

116

LYS   If that's impossible—

CLEO (*interrupting*) You really are afraid.

LYS   I? You're lying.

CLEO Well, you're terribly pale. *** what *** me *** you're
      asking me? *** badly *** to me *** I congratulate ***.   985
      *** old man ***.

LYS   *** when I spotted the girl clearly *** Casinus is *** who   990
      here ***.

OL   *** who even made an infamous man of me with his
      shameful acts.

LYS   Won't you be quiet?

OL   No, I won't: you begged me intensely to ask for Casina in
      marriage for the sake of your own love.   995

LYS   I did that?

OL   No, it was Hector of Troy.[36]

LYS   He'd have knocked you down for a start. (*to the women*)
      Did I do those things you say?

CLEO You even ask?

LYS   If I did them, I did wrong.

CLEO Just return in here: I'll remind you if you don't remember
      it well.

LYS   No, I think I'd rather believe what you say. But, my wife,   1000
      give this pardon to me, your husband; Myrrhina, ask
      Cleostrata for it. (*to Cleostrata again*) If I ever make love
      to Casina hereafter or if I only begin to do so, yes, as soon

---

[36] The greatest Trojan hero in the Iliad.

---

987 conspicillo ⟨quom⟩ conspexi uirginem *suppl. Tontini ex Os-*
berno, Uguccione, uestigiis litterarum in A
998 si quidem *P*, si qui *A*
1000 mi *add. Lindsay*

117

ne ut eam amasso, si ego umquam adeo posthac tale am-
    misero,

nulla causa est quin pendentem me, uxor, uirgis uerbe-
    res.

MYR censeo ecastor ueniam hanc dandam.

CLEO   faciam ut iubes.

1005   propter eam rem hanc tibi nunc ueniam minus grauate
        prospero,

hanc ex longa longiorem ne faciamus fabulam.

LYS non irata es?

CLEO   non sum irata.

LYS   tuaen fide credo?

CLEO   meae.

LYS lepidiorem uxorem nemo quisquam quam ego habeo
        hanc habet.

CLEO age tu, redde huic scipionem et pallium.

CHAL   tene, si lubet.

1010   mihi quidem edepol insignite facta est magna iniuria:

duobus nupsi, neuter fecit quod nouae nuptae solet.

V. v: PARDALISCA

PAR spectatores, quod futurum est intus, id memorabimus.

haec Casina huius reperietur filia esse ex proxumo

eaque nubet Euthynico nostro erili filio.

1015   nunc uos aequom est manibus meritis meritam merce-
        dem dare:

qui faxit, clam uxorem ducet semper scortum quod uolet;

uerum qui non manibus clare quantum poterit plauserit,

ei pro scorto supponetur hircus unctus nautea.

1002 *uersus suspectus*   1004 dandam ‹Cleostrata› *Lindsay*
1012–18 *dat Pardaliscae Schoell*

118

as I make love to her, if I ever become guilty of such a
deed hereafter, there's no reason why you shouldn't hang
me up and beat me with rods, my wife.

MYR I think he ought to be given this pardon.

CLEO (*to Myrrhina*) I'll do as you tell me. (*to Lysidamus*) Now 1005
I'm granting you this pardon less grudgingly for the sim-
ple reason that we shouldn't turn this long play into an
even longer one.

LYS You aren't angry?

CLEO No, I'm not angry.

LYS Can I trust your word?

CLEO Yes.

LYS Nobody has a more charming wife than I have.

CLEO (*to Chalinus*) Go on, you, return his walking stick and
cloak to him.

CHAL (*hands them over*) Take them if you like. Clearly a great 1010
injustice has been done to me: I married two men, but
neither did what one normally does to a newly wed
woman.

Exeunt ALL into the house of Lysidamus.
Enter PARDALISCA from the house of Lysidamus.

PAR Spectators, we'll tell you what's going to happen inside.
This Casina will be discovered to be the daughter of this
man from next door and she'll marry Euthynicus, our
master's son. Now it's right for you to give the deserving 1015
actors the deserved applause with your hands. The man
who does so shall always have the prostitute he wants be-
hind his wife's back. But the man who doesn't applaud us
with his hands clearly, as much as he can, shall always end
up with a goat, perfumed with bilgewater, in place of the
prostitute.

119

CISTELLARIA

INTRODUCTORY NOTE

For many plays of Plautus we have a complete and relatively secure text but know little about when they were first performed or what the Greek originals were called, let alone who had written them. For the *Cistellaria* the situation is the reverse. We know when it was first performed, who the Greek author was, and what his comedy was called, but the text of the Latin play is incomplete, though not beyond reconstruction.

The *Cistellaria* is a recognition play. It is named for the casket (*cistella*) where a rattle is kept, the recognition token of the girl Selenium. Selenium does not know that she is a freeborn citizen with respectable parents because she was raised by the procuress Melaenis. The comedy begins with a lunch to which Selenium has invited the young prostitute Gymnasium along with her unnamed mother. This scene was important enough for Menander, the author of the Greek original, to name his play for it; he called it *Synaristosai*, "Woman Lunching Together." For a long time it was unknown that Plautus' *Cistellaria* is based on the *Synaristosai*. There was a Menander fragment (fr. 337 Kassel-Austin) matching ll. 89–93 of the *Cistellaria*, but Hermogenes had quoted the Greek passage only as belonging to Menander, without stating which play it came from. Another Menander fragment (fr. 335 Kassel-Austin)

123

matches l. 18 of the Plautine play because in both passages Gymnasium's mother complains that she did not get enough wine to drink; and in this case it was known that the fragment came from the *Synaristosai*. But there were too many parallels to this second passage both in Latin and in Greek to allow scholars to make the connection between the two plays. Then a medieval letter was discovered in the Chalcidius codex of Bamberg, quoting fragment xiii of the *Cistellaria* as belonging to Plautus' *Synaristosae*. The anonymous medieval writer must have got his knowledge from a manuscript of Festus (who quotes the passage) that was not yet as damaged as the copies we have now, where the passage in question can only be restored fully because of our letter-writer. This chance discovery, then, established beyond doubt that Plautus had based his *Cistellaria* on Menander's *Synaristosai* and that the first Menander fragment mentioned above belongs to this same play by Menander. I should merely add that there is nothing unusual about the fact that Festus quotes a Plautine comedy under the name of the Greek original; he does the same with Plautus' *Mostellaria*, which he refers to by its Greek title *Phasma*, "The Ghost."

The reason why Selenium has invited Gymnasium and her mother is a sad one. Selenium has been cohabiting with her lover Alcesimarchus in a house which he rents in Sicyon, the city where the comedy is set. Alcesimarchus had promised to marry Selenium. In his absence on his father's country estate, it was discovered that his father, who remains unnamed, had decided that he should marry a distant relative from Lemnos. How this discovery was made is not known, since Alcesimarchus himself is at first unaware of the situation. We may assume that a servant had seen wedding preparations going on, which is the situation we find in Caecilius' *Synaristosae* (197–98 Ribbeck), another adaptation of Menander's comedy going back to a time when it was not yet considered inappropriate to use a Greek play that had already formed the basis of a Roman one. Melaenis has now told Selenium to come back immediately and Selenium wants to ask the procuress for permission to let Gymnasium stay at the house of Alcesimarchus to watch over it until he returns. The procuress grants her permission and Selenium leaves. Then the procuress and later the god Auxilium ("Help") give us the remaining background information. We learn that Selenium is the daughter of the Lemnian Demipho and his wife Phanostrata. She was conceived in Sicyon when Demipho, still a young man, raped Phanostrata. Demipho escaped to Lemnos and married there. He has a daughter from this marriage in Lemnos, who is the distant relative Alcesimarchus is supposed to marry. When Demipho's wife died, he went back to Sicyon and settled down there, marrying Phanostrata. He learned that Phanostrata had given birth to a daughter, but since she did not know who the father was, she gave her to her slave Lampadio to expose. Lampadio did expose her and observed that the girl was picked up by a woman. This woman was Gymnasium's mother, who gave the child to Melaenis. Demipho and Phanostrata are keen to recover their daughter and have asked Lampadio to find her.

What is now labeled the second act of the play is badly damaged. The archetype of the Palatine manuscripts lost several leaves between what is now l. 229 and l. 492; the number of lines lost, however, is far greater than this numbering might suggest. When the Ambrosian palimpsest

125

was discovered and deciphered in the nineteenth century, more of the text became available, but it also became apparent how much had been lost. Now the Ambrosian palimpsest has been examined again by W. Stockert with the help of the latest technology and new readings have been found, but even so, much remains illegible. At least we can now say with some certainty how much has been lost, because the quaternions are numbered and have a relatively constant number of lines per page. Thus we know how much has been lost because we know how many folios are missing, and if parts of a folio are illegible we know how many lines are missing in it. The standard line numbering today takes the extant pages of the Ambrosian palimpsest into account, even where some lines cannot be read, but does not take the lost folios into account.

Where folios are missing in the palimpsest, we can fill some gaps through the secondary tradition: ancient lexicographers and grammarians, who still had access to the complete text, preserve a number of quotations. Interestingly, before the palimpsest was examined no one even suspected that there was a gap in the Palatine manuscripts, and this despite the fact that the scholars who had worked on the *Cistellaria* include some of the most important classicists of all time. There were of course the fragments transmitted through the secondary tradition, but these were conveniently explained away by the great Scaliger, who assigned them to an otherwise unknown comedy called *Clitellaria,* "The Saddle Comedy."

But now we should turn to the action of the second act itself; I have indicated in the English translation how many lines are missing where and what their presumable content was, so that here we need not focus on reconstruction. The second act begins with the return of Alcesimarchus from his father's country estate, where he had been sent to do some work. Angry with himself that he was able to desert his girlfriend for almost a week, he tells his slave to insult him. He then goes to his rented house to see Selenium but finds Gymnasium instead, who tells him that he has to marry another woman and that Selenium has left him. Alcesimarchus is distraught and goes to find his father. Meanwhile, his father wants to go to Selenium to tell her to leave his son alone. He meets Gymnasium, whom he believes to be Selenium, and starts a tirade, but soon falls in love with this girl, who is enjoying making a fool of him. The decency of Alcesimarchus, who wants to marry Selenium and has purely honorable intentions, is thus not only in stark contrast with the behavior of Selenium's father, who is after all a rapist, but also with the behavior of his own father, who wants a quick affair with a prostitute whom he believes his own son to be having an affair with. However, Alcesimarchus' father does not get very far: Gymnasium's mother knows that Alcesimarchus is back in town and comes to fetch her daughter, the young man now being able to look after his own affairs. His father realizes that he was mistaken and leaves.

In the next scene Lampadio tells us about his search for the woman who had picked up Selenium; he went around various brothels and spotted some very ugly prostitutes. Then we see Alcesimarchus attempting to restore his good relationship with Selenium and Melaenis, but because of his impending marriage he is rejected. He runs off into his house when Lampadio reappears. He reports to Phanostrata that he has found Gymnasium's mother and that he has found out that Selenium was raised by Melaenis.

Melaenis, who has overheard this conversation, realizes that her game is up and that she has to bring Selenium back to her parents.

This is where the third act begins in our editions, but since these traditional divisions were established at a time when large portions of the play were not known to exist, they are only post-Plautine but in this case cannot even vaguely reflect act divisions in Menander.

Melaenis tells Selenium about her parentage and wants to take her back to Demipho and Phanostrata. They are accompanied by their servant Halisca, who carries the casket with the rattle that should enable her parents to recognize her. On their way they see Alcesimarchus holding a sword in his hands and apparently about to commit suicide. Selenium, followed by the other two women, rushes toward him to prevent him from doing so, and Alcesimarchus immediately takes Selenium into his house. The two other women follow, but in the tumult Halisca forgets the casket outside.

Lampadio finds the casket and shows it to Phanostrata, who recognizes it immediately. They see Halisca coming out and looking for the casket. After some discussion, they give her the casket in exchange for taking them to Selenium. Halisca and Phanostrata go into the house of Alcesimarchus, where Selenium and Melaenis are with the young man, and soon after they are joined by Demipho, who is taken there by Lampadio.

Thus the ending of the play is happy: Demipho and Phanostrata have found their daughter, and Alcesimarchus can marry a daughter of Demipho, as had been planned by his father, though not the one his father had had in mind.

One problem that I have thus far left to the side concerns ancient marriage laws. Alcesimarchus is a Sicyonian citizen; Selenium is believed to be the daughter of an unknown father and of Melaenis, a freedwoman and thus a noncitizen. Alcesimarchus has promised to marry Selenium, but could he actually do so? Not under Athenian law, which since Pericles' legislation of 451 permitted only citizen pairs to marry. Of course Alcesimarchus, being passionately in love, might have promised more than he could do, but when his father arranges a marriage for him, it is with Demipho's daughter from his Lemnian marriage, that is, with a fully Lemnian girl. How could this be? It is possible that Sicyonian law was different from Athenian law and that a male Sicyonian could marry a noncitizen and have citizen children with her, as was the case in Athens before 451. But it is also possible, as Brown suggests, that Menander did not set his play at Sicyon, but at Athens. Lemnos was an Athenian cleruchy and its inhabitants had Athenian citizenship, so that the marriage arranged by the father of Alcesimarchus would be unproblematic, as would be the marriage with Selenium after the discovery of her parentage. If we accept this hypothesis, the question remains why Plautus transferred the play to Sicyon, and this question has to remain unanswered. But there is no reason to assume that Plautus did not change locations, as he was happy to change names: from a mosaic at Mytilene depicting the opening scene of the *Synaristosai* we know that Selenium was called Plangon in Menander and that Gymnasium was called Pythias.

The date of the *Cistellaria* is almost certain. In l. 202 the hope is expressed that the Romans will conquer and punish the Carthaginians. The Second Punic War ended in 201, and nearly everyone agrees that the play must have been written before that. But we can be more precise. The date of the *Miles Gloriosus* is well known: it was first performed in 206 or 205. *Cist.* 190–93 and *Mil.* 99–101 as well as *Cist.* 89–93 and *Mil.* 104–8 are so close in content and structure that the lines of one play must be adaptations of those of the other. With regard to the first pair of passages, *Cist.* 193 fits the wider context much better than *Mil.* 101; and with regard to the second pair it has to be said that *Mil.* 105 does not fit at all, because it is simply not true that the soldier comes to be on close terms with the girl with whom he has fallen in love. Thus it seems that the passages in the *Miles* are based on the *Cistellaria* and not the other way round. The *Cistellaria* was first performed before 206 or 205. We can go even further. In the passage in which the Carthaginians are mentioned, Plautus also speaks of "allies, old and new" (l. 199) and of auxiliaries (l. 200). These could be references to ratification of the treaty of friendship with the Aetolian League in 209 and to the fact that many Iberians also joined Rome's forces around this time. Since 206 was an almost peaceful year, the *Cistellaria* was in all likelihood first performed between 209 and 207, which makes it one of the earliest Plautine plays.

SELECT BIBLIOGRAPHY

Editions and Commentaries

Stockert, W. (2009), *Titus Maccius Plautus: Cistellaria* (Sarsina and Urbino).

Thamm, G. (1971), *Zur Cistellaria des Plautus* (diss. Freiburg im Breisgau).

CISTELLARIA

Criticism

Bettini, M. (1987), "La stirpe di Iuno ovvero il metodo nella follia (Plauto *Cist.* 512–517)," in *Filologia e forme letterarie: Studi offerti a Francesco Della Corte*, vol. 2: *Letteratura Latina dalle origini ad Augusto* (Urbino), 27–40.

Brown, P. G. McC. (2005), "The Legal and Social Framework of Plautus' *Cistellaria*," in *Papers of the Langford Latin Seminar* 12: 53–70.

Fraenkel, E. (1932), "Das Original der Cistellaria des Plautus," in *Philologus* 87: 117–20.

Hartkamp, R. F., and Hurka, F. (eds.) (2004), *Studien zu Plautus' Cistellaria* (Tübingen).

Ludwig, W. (1970), "Die plautinische *Cistellaria* und das Verhältnis von Gott und Handlung bei Menander," in *Entretiens sur l'Antiquité Classique* 16: 43–96.

Raffaelli, R., and Tontini, A. (eds.) (2004), *Lecturae Plautinae Sarsinates VII: Cistellaria (Sarsina, 27 settembre 2003)* (Urbino).

Süss, W. (1935), "Zur Cistellaria des Plautus," in *Rheinisches Museum für Philologie* 84: 161–87.

——— (1938), "Nochmals zur Cistellaria des Plautus," in *Rheinisches Museum für Philologie* 87: 97–141.

Thierfelder, A. (1961), "De Plauti Cistellaria," in *Studi Urbinati di storia, filosofia e letteratura* 35: 113–17.

Woytek, E. (1971), "Ein Cistellariaproblem," in *Wiener Studien* 84: 110–22.

CISTELLARIA

ARGVMENTVM

Comprimit adulescens Lemnius Sicyoniam;
Is redit in patriam et gnatam generat nuptiis.
Sicyonia aeque parit puellam. hanc seruolus
Tulit atque exponit, et ex insidiis aucupat.
5　Eam sublatam meretrix alii detulit.
Lemno post rediens ducit quam compresserat
Lemnique natam spondet adulescentulo
Amore capto illius proiecticiae.
Requirens seruos reperit quam proiecerat.
10　Itaque lege et rite ciuem cognitam
Alcesimarchus, ut erat nactus, possidet.

arg. 4 tollit *P*, tulit *Schoell*
arg. 7 despondit *P*, spondet *Bothe*
arg. 10 itaque ⟨eam⟩ *Pylades sed* itāque *in huius modi uersibus fortasse ferendum*

THE CASKET COMEDY

PLOT SUMMARY

A young man from Lemnos raped a girl from Sicyon; he returned to his own country, married, and had a daughter. The girl from Sicyon also gave birth to a daughter. A slave took the daughter and abandoned her, and observed in hiding what happened. A prostitute picked her up and took her to another pros- 5
titute. The man later returned from Lemnos and married the woman he had raped; he betroths his daughter born in Lemnos to a young man who is deeply in love with that foundling girl. In the course of his search the slave finds the girl he had exposed. 10
And so, when she is recognized as a citizen according to law and custom, Alcesimarchus retains the girl whom he had already taken.

PERSONAE

SELENIVM meretrix
GYMNASIVM meretrix
LENA
AVXILIVM DEVS prologus
ALCESIMARCHVS adulescens
SERVOS
SENEX
LAMPADIO seruos
MELAENIS lena
PHANOSTRATA matrona
HALISCA ancilla
DEMIPHO senex

SCAENA

Sicyoni

CISTELLARIA

CHARACTERS

SELENIUM a girl about to become a prostitute; lost daughter of Demipho and Phanostrata
GYMNASIUM a prostitute; friend of Selenium
A PROCURESS Gymnasium's mother
THE GOD HELP speaker of the prologue
ALCESIMARCHUS a young man; in love with Selenium
A SERVANT slave of Alcesimarchus
AN OLD MAN father of Alcesimarchus
LAMPADIO a slave; works for Demipho and Phanostrata
MELAENIS a procuress; the supposed mother of Selenium
PHANOSTRATA a married woman; eager to find her daughter
HALISCA a female servant; works for Melaenis
DEMIPHO an old man; a Lemnian living in Sicyon

STAGING

The stage represents a street in Sicyon. On it there are three houses. The one on the left belongs to Melaenis, the one in the middle belongs to Demipho, and the one on the right is rented by Alcesimarchus. To the left the street leads to the countryside, to the right it leads to the city center.

135

ACTVS I

I. i: SELENIVM. GYMNASIVM. LENA

	SEL	quom ego antidhac te amaui et mi amicam esse creui,
		mea Gymnasium, et matrem tuam, tum id mihi hodie
		aperuistis, tu atque haec: soror si mea esses,
		qui magis potueritis mi honorem ire habitum,
5		nescio, nisi, ut meus est animus,
5ᵃ		fieri non posse arbitror; i-
6		ta omnibus relictis rebus
6ᵃ		mi frequentem operam dedistis.
7		eo ego uos amo et eo a me
7ᵃ		magnam inistis gratiam.
8	GYM	pol isto quidem nos pretio [tanti est] facile est frequen-
		tare
		tibi utilisque habere:
10		ita in prandio nos lepide ac nitide
		accepisti apud te, ut semper meminerimus.
	SEL	lubenti[que] edepol animo factum et fiet a me,
		quae uos arbitrabor uelle, ea ut expetessam.
14	LENA	quod ille dixit, qui secundo uento uectus
14ᵃ		est tranquillo mari,
15		uentum gaudeo . . . ecastor ad ted, ita hodie

1 anted hac *VE*, ante hac *BJ Varro*, antidhac *Pareus*
3 aperuistis *JK*, aperuisti *BVE*
4 potueritis *VJE*, potueris *B*
8 pretio facile est *P*, pretio ptanti est *Varro*

ACT ONE

*Enter SELENIUM, looking disheveled, along with GYMNA-
SIUM and the PROCURESS from the house of Alcesimarchus.*

SEL   I've always loved you and decided that you were my
     friend, my dear Gymnasium, and also your mother, but
     today you've revealed it, you and she: if you were my
     sister, I don't know how you two could have shown more
     regard for me; but to my mind, I think it would be impos- 5
     sible, seeing how you put everything aside and gave me
     your uninterrupted attention. That's why I love you and
     that's why I'm very grateful to you.

GYM It's easy for us to devote ourselves to you and be of service
     to you when you pay us so well: you received us so charm- 10
     ingly and pleasantly for lunch at your place that we'll
     always remember it.

SEL   It was a pleasure for me, and it will be one, to seek what I
     think you like.

PROC As the man said who traveled on a calm sea with good
     wind: I'm glad about the wind[1] . . . which carried me to 15

---

[1] A pun that is difficult to reproduce. *Ventum* is the accusative of
"wind," but can also be the participle of "to come" used to form an im-
personal passive.

---

12 que *del.* Pylades
13 arbitror *P,* arbitrabor *Camerarius*

15ᵃ   hic acceptae sumus

16   suauibus modis,

                nec nisi disciplina apud te fuit quicquam ibi quin mi pla-
                        ceret.

SEL   quid ita, amabo?

LENA   raro nimium dabat quod biberem, id merum
                      infuscabat.

19–20 GYM   amabo, hicine istuc decet?

LENA   iusque fasque est:
        nemo alienus hic est.

SEL   merito uostro amo uos,
        quia me colitis, [et] magni facitis.

LENA   decet pol, mea Selenium,
        hunc esse ordinem beneuolentis inter se
        beneque amicitia utier,

25   ubi istas uideas summo genere gnatas, summatis matro-
                nas,

        ut amicitiam colunt atque ut eam iunctam bene habent
                inter se.

        si idem istuc nos faciamus, si [idem] imitemur, ita tamen
                uix uiuimus

        cum inuidia summa. suarum opum nos uolunt esse indi-
                gentis.

29–30 nostra copia nil uolunt nos potesse
        suique omnium rerum nos indigere,
        ut sibi simus supplices.

        eas si adeas, abitum quam aditum malis, ita nostro ordini
        palam blandiuntur, clam, si occasio usquam est,

35   aquam frigidam subdole suffundunt.
        uiris cum suis praedicant nos solere,
        suas paelices esse aiunt, eunt depressum.
        quia nos libertinae sumus, et ego et tua mater, ambae

138

your place, what with the lovely reception we got, and
there was nothing I didn't like, apart from the way your
servant is trained.

SEL What do you mean, please?

PROC She didn't fill my cup often enough, and she ruined the
wine with water.[2]

GYM Please, is that appropriate here?   20

PROC It's right and proper: there's no stranger here.

SEL I'm fond of you two, and deservedly so, because you're
kind to me and appreciate me.

PROC My dear Selenium, people in our walk of life ought to
mean well with each other and to cultivate friendship,
when you see those highborn ladies, the married women   25
of the upper class, how they practise friendship and how
they are connected with each other by it. If we do the
same and imitate them, we still barely survive, and that
with their ill will. They want us to be dependent on their
support. They don't want us to be able to do anything   30
from our own means and to be dependent on them in ev-
erything, so that we're at their mercy. If you go to them,
you'd wish you'd gone away rather than gone to them,
seeing how they flatter people of our walk of life to their
faces, but in secret, if there's ever an opportunity, they 35
pour cold water over us on the sly. They say that we have
affairs with their husbands, they claim that we're their
mistresses, and they try to put us down. Because we're
freedwomen, I and your mother, we were both prosti-

[2] Drinking undiluted wine was considered bad style.

22 et *del. Spengel*
27 idem[2] *del. Lindsay*

meretrices fuimus: illa te, ego hanc mihi educaui

40   ex patribus conuenticiis. neque ego hanc superbiai
causa pepuli ad meretricium quaestum, nisi ut ne esuri-
rem.

SEL   at satius fuerat eam uiro dare nuptum potius.

LENA   heia!

haec quidem ecastor cottidie uiro nubit, nupsitque
hodie,

nubet mox noctu: numquam ego hanc uiduam cubare
siui.

45   nam si haec non nubat, lugubri fame familia pereat.

GYM   necesse est quo tu me modo uoles esse ita esse, mater.

LENA   ecastor hau me paenitet, si ut dicis ita futura es.

nam si quidem ita eris ut uolo, numquam hac aetate fies
semperque istam quam nunc habes aetatulam optinebis,

50   multisque damno et mi lucro sine meo saepe eris sump-
tu.

GYM   di faxint!

LENA   sine opera tua di horunc nil facere possunt.

GYM   equidem hercle addam operam sedulo; sed tu aufer is-
taec uerba.

meus oculus, mea Selenium, numquam ego te tristiorem
uidi esse. quid, cedo, te opsecro, tam abhorret hilaritu-
do?

55   nec munda adaeque es, ut soles (hoc sis uide, ut petiuit
suspiritum alte) et pallida es. eloquere utrumque nobis,
et quid tibi est et quid uelis nostram operam, ut nos scia-
mus.

noli, opsecro, lacrumis tuis mi exercitum imperare.

52 inter *P*, aufer *Ussing*

tutes; she brought you up for herself and I this girl here, from fathers met by chance. I didn't push her into prosti- 40 tution out of pride, only in order not to starve.

SEL   Still, it would have been better to give her in marriage to a man.

PROC Nonsense! She does marry a man, every day, and she married one today and will soon marry one tonight; I've never let her sleep alone. Yes, if she didn't marry, our 45 household would perish from sorrowful hunger.

GYM I have to be the way you want me to be, my mother.

PROC Well, I can't complain if you're going to be as you say: if you're going to be the way I want you to be, you'll never turn my age, you'll always keep that tender age you have now, and you'll often give loss to many and profit to me, 50 without any expenditure on my part.

GYM May the gods make it so!

PROC Without your help the gods can't do any of it.

GYM *(to her mother)* I'll give you my help eagerly; but do stop this topic now. *(to Selenium)* You apple of my eye, my dear Selenium, I've never seen you more melancholy. Tell me, please, why has cheerfulness shrunk back from you so much? You're not as neat as usual (just look how 55 she heaved a deep sigh) and you're pale. Tell us two things, what the trouble is and what you want our help for, so that we know. Please don't make me wear myself out because of your tears.

SEL	misera excrucior, mea Gymnasium: male mihi est, male maceror;
60	doleo ab animo, doleo ab oculis, doleo ab aegritudine.
	quid dicam, nisi stultitia mea me in maerorem rapi?
GYM	indidem unde oritur facito ut facias stultitiam sepelibilem.
SEL	quid faciam?
GYM	in latebras apscondas pectore penitissumo.
	tuam stultitiam sola facito ut scias sine aliis arbitris.
65 SEL	at mihi cordolium est.
GYM	quid? id unde est tibi cor? commemora opsecro;
	quod neque ego habeo nec quisquam alia mulier, ut perhibent uiri.
SEL	siquid est quod doleat, dolet; si autem non est . . . tamen hoc hic dolet.
GYM	amat haec mulier.
SEL	eho an amare occipere amarum est, opsecro?
GYM	namque ecastor Amor et melle et felle est fecundissumus;
70	gustui dat dulce, amarum ad satietatem usque oggerit.
SEL	ad istam faciem est morbus qui me, mea Gymnasium, macerat.
GYM	perfidiosus est Amor.
SEL	ergo in me peculatum facit.
GYM	bono animo es, erit isti morbo melius.
SEL	confidam fore,
	si medicus ueniat qui huic morbo facere medicinam potest.
75 GYM	ueniet.
SEL	spissum istuc amanti est uerbum "ueniet," nisi uenit.
	sed ego mea culpa et stultitia peius misera maceror,

SEL   I'm wretched and I'm being tortured, my dear Gymnasium: I'm feeling bad and I'm being tormented in a bad way. I feel pain in my heart, I feel pain in my eyes, I feel 60 pain in my sorrow. What should I say, except that I'm driven to sadness by my own silliness?

GYM Mind that you make your silliness ready for burial in the place from which it originates.

SEL   What should I do?

GYM Hide it in the darkness in your inmost heart. Make sure that you alone know your silliness without other witnesses.

SEL   But I have heartache. 65

GYM What? Where have you got a heart from? Tell me, please; it's something neither I nor any other woman have, so men say.

SEL   If I have anything to feel pain with, I feel pain; but if I don't . . . I still feel it here. (*puts her hand on her heart*)

GYM This woman's in love.

SEL   What! Falling in love isn't bitter, is it?

GYM To be sure, Love abounds in honey as well as in gall; if you 70 taste him, he gives you sweetness, but then he piles you up with bitterness till you're full.

SEL   The illness that's tormenting me is of that sort, my dear Gymnasium.

GYM Love is treacherous.

SEL   Yes, he's embezzling all I have.

GYM Take heart, that illness will get better.

SEL   I trust it will, if the doctor comes who can cure this illness.

GYM He will come. 75

SEL   That phrase "he will come" is a sluggish one for a lover, unless he does come. But I'm being tormented in a worse

143

quom ego illum unum mi exoptaui quicum aetatem de-
gerem.

LENA matronae magis conducibile est istuc, mea Selenium,
unum amare et cum eo aetatem exigere quoi nupta est
semel,

80 uerum enim meretrix fortunati est oppidi similluma:
non potest suam rem optinere sola sine multis uiris.

SEL hoc uolo agatis. qua accersitae causa ad me estis eloquar.
nam mea mater, quia ego nolo me meretricem dicier,
opsecuta est, gessit morem oranti morigerae mihi,

85 ut me, quem ego amarem grauiter, sineret cum eo
uiuere.

LENA stulte ecastor fecit. sed tu enumquam cum quiquam uiro
consueuisti?

SEL nisi quidem cum Alcesimarcho, nemine,
nec pudicitiam meam mi alius quisquam imminuit.

LENA opsecro,
quo is homo insinuauit pacto se ad te?

SEL per Dionysia

90 mater pompam me spectatum duxit. dum redeo domum,
conspicillo consecutust clanculum me usque ad fores.
inde in amicitiam insinuauit cum matre et mecum simul
blanditiis, muneribus, donis.

GYM mi istunc uellem hominem dari;
ut ego illum uorsarem!

SEL quid opust uerbis? consuetudine

95 coepi amare contra ego illum, et ill' me.

LENA o mea Selenium,
assimulare amare oportet. nam si ames, extemplo
melius illi multo quem ames consulas quam rei tuae.

88 meam mihi alius quisquam imminuit *P*, i. meam mihi q. a. *A*

144

way through my own fault and stupidity, since I hankered after that man alone in order to spend my life with him.

PROC It's more advisable for a matron, my dear Selenium, to love only one man and to spend her life with the man she has once been married to; but a prostitute closely resem- 80 bles a flourishing town: she cannot be successful alone, without many men.

SEL I want you two to pay attention. I'll tell you why you were sent for. Well, since I didn't want to be called a prostitute, my mother humored me and obeyed me, her pleading, obedient daughter, so that she allowed me to live with the 85 man I was madly in love with.

PROC She really behaved stupidly. But have you ever been intimate with any man?

SEL No, with no one, except for Alcesimarchus, and no one else has done damage to my chastity.

PROC Please, how did he come to be on close terms with you?

SEL During the festival of Dionysus[3] my mother took me to 90 watch the procession. While I was returning home he spied on me and followed me secretly up to the door. Then he came to be on friendly terms with my mother and with me at the same time through flattery, services, and gifts.

GYM I wish that man were given to me; how I'd manipulate him!

SEL What need is there for words? I started a relationship with him and began to return his love and he mine. 95

PROC My dear Selenium, you should only pretend to be in love: if you're in love for real, you immediately look after the one you love far better than after your own interests.

---

[3] An annual festival in honor of Bacchus.

SEL   at ille conceptis iurauit uerbis apud matrem meam
      me uxorem ducturum esse: ei nunc alia ducenda est do-
        mum,
100   sua cognata Lemniensis, quae habitat hic in proxumo.
      nam eum pater eius subegit. nunc mea mater irata est
        mihi,
      quia non redierim domum ad se, postquam hanc rem
        resciuerim,
      eum uxorem ducturum esse aliam.

LENA   nihil amori iniurium est.

SEL   nunc te amabo ut hanc hic ⟨unum⟩ triduom hoc solum
        sinas
105   esse et hic seruare apud me. nam ad matrem accersita
        sum.

LENA quamquam istuc mihi erit molestum triduom, et dam-
        num dabis,
      faciam.

SEL   facis benigne et amice. sed tu, Gymnasium mea,
      si me apsente Alcesimarchus ueniet, nolito acriter
      eum inclamare: utut erga me est meritus, mihi cordi est
        tamen.
110   sed, amabo, tranquille: ne quid quod illi doleat dixeris.
      accipias clauis: si quid tibi opus erit prompto, promito.
      ego uolo ire.

GYM   ut mi exciuisti lacrumas!

SEL   Gymnasium mea,
      bene uale.

GYM   cura te, amabo. sicine immunda, opsecro,
      ibis?

SEL   immundas fortunas aequom est squalorem sequi.
115 GYM amiculum hoc sustolle saltem.

SEL   sine trahi, quom egomet trahor.

SEL But he swore solemnly before my mother that he'd marry
me; now he has to marry another woman, his relative 100
from Lemnos, who lives here next door: his father forced
him. Now my mother's angry with me, on the grounds
that I didn't return home to her after finding out that he's
marrying another woman.

PROC All is fair in love and war.

SEL (*to the procuress*) Now please let your daughter stay
here, only for the next two days, and look after things 105
here at my place, because I've been summoned to my
mother.

PROC Although those next two days will be a nuisance to me
and you'll bring me loss of income, I'll do so.

SEL (*to the procuress*) That's really nice and friendly of you.
(*turning to Gymnasium*) But you, my dear Gymnasium,
don't abuse Alcesimarchus harshly, if he comes in my ab-
sence; however he's deserved of me, he's still dear to me. 110
But gently, please: don't say anything that could hurt him.
Take the keys: if you need to take anything, do so. (*hands
them over*) I want to go.

GYM How you've made me cry!

SEL My dear Gymnasium, farewell.

GYM Look after yourself, please. I beg you, do you insist on
going in such an unkempt state?

SEL It's appropriate if squalor follows such a messy fate.

GYM At least lift up this cloak of yours. (*tries to take it*) 115

SEL (*moving away*) Let it be dragged along because I myself
am being dragged along.

---

104 unum *add. Seyffert*
106 dabis Ω, dabit *Dousa*
109 in cordi *P*, mihi cordi *Camerarius*

147

GYM   quando ita tibi lubet, uale atque salue.

SEL   si possim uelim.

GYM   numquid me uis, mater, intro quin eam? ecastor mihi
uisa amare.

LENA   istoc ergo auris grauiter optundo tuas,
ne quem ames. abi intro.

GYM   numquid me uis?

LENA   ut ualeas.

GYM   uale.

I. ii: LENA

120 LENA idem mi est quod magnae parti uitium mulierum

quae hunc quaestum facimus: quae ubi saburratae su-
mus,

122   largiloquae extemplo sumus, plus loquimur quam sat est.

126   quin ego nunc quia sum onusta mea ex sententia

127   quiaque adeo me compleui flore Liberi,

128   magis libera uti lingua collibitum est mihi,

129   tacere nequeo misera quod tacito usus est.

123   nam ego illanc olim, quae hinc flens abiit, paruolam

124   puellam proiectam ex angiportu sustuli.

125   [adulescens quidam hic est apprime nobilis

130   Sicyone, summo genere; ei uiuit pater.

is amore misere hanc deperit mulierculam,

quae hinc modo flens abiit. contra amore eum haec per-
dita est.]

eam meae ego amicae dono huic meretrici dedi,

quae saepe mecum mentionem fecerat,

135   puerum aut puellam alicunde ut reperirem sibi,

126–29 *om. A, del. Ritschl, post 122 posuit Acidalius*
123 illa(m) *ego BVEJ,* ego illam *S,* ego illanc *Pareus*

GYM   Since you want it like this, farewell and be well.
SEL   If I could I'd like to.

Exit SELENIUM into the house of Melaenis.

GYM   Is there anything you want from me, mother, to keep me
      from going in? Goodness, she really seemed to be in love
      to me.
PROC That's why I drum it into you so intensely that you
      shouldn't be in love with anyone. Go in.
GYM   Do you want anything from me?
PROC Only that you keep well.
GYM   You too.

Exit GYMNASIUM into the house of Alcesimarchus.

PROC (*to the audience*) I have the same fault as most of the   120
      women in my line of business: once we've had our fill, we   122
      become chatterboxes immediately and talk more than is
      enough. Well, because now I'm supplied according to my   126
      wishes and because I've filled myself with the bouquet
      of Bacchus, I've taken a fancy to speaking more freely.   129
      Poor me, I can't be quiet about what one needs to be
      quiet about: the girl who went away crying, I picked her   123
      up from the alley a long time ago as a little tot that had
      been abandoned. [There's a certain young man here in   125
      Sicyon, of high rank and noble family, whose father is   130
      alive. He's crazy about this woman who went off crying a
      moment ago. She is crazy about him in turn.] I gave her
      as a present to my friend, the prostitute here (*points to
      the house of Melaenis*), who had often mentioned to me   135

125, 130–32 *del. Windischmann*

recens natum, eapse quod sibi supponeret.
ubi mi potestas primum euenit, ilico
feci eius ei quod me orauit copiam.
postquam eam puellam a me accepit, ilico
140 eandem puellam peperit quam a me acceperat,
sine opstetricis opera et sine doloribus,
item ut aliae pariunt quae malum quaerunt sibi.
nam amatorem aibat esse peregrinum sibi
suppositionemque eius facere gratia.
145 id duae nos solae scimus, ego quae illi dedi
et illa quae a me accepit, praeter uos quidem.
haec sic res gesta est. si quid usus uenerit,
meminisse ego hanc rem uos uolo. ego abeo domum.

I. iii: AVXILIVM

AVX utrumque haec, et multiloqua et multibiba, est anus.
150 satin uix reliquit deo quod loqueretur loci,
ita properauit de puellae proloqui
suppositione. quod si tacuisset, tamen
ego eram dicturus, deus, qui poteram planius.
nam mi est Auxilio nomen. nunc operam date,
155 ut ego argumentum hoc uobis plane perputem.
fuere Sicyoni iam diu Dionysia.
mercator uenit huc ad ludos Lemnius,
isque hic compressit uirginem, adulescentulus,
⟨ui⟩, uinolentus, multa nocte, in uia.
160 is ubi malam rem scit se meruisse, ilico
pedibus perfugium peperit, in Lemnum aufugit,
ubi habitabat tum. illa quam compresserat

154 auxilio est *P, transp. Camerarius*
159 ui *add. Pareus*

that I should find her a boy or a girl from somewhere, a
newborn, whom she could pretend to be her own child.
As soon as I got the opportunity, I supplied her at once
with what she asked me for. After receiving this girl from
me, she at once gave birth to the same girl she'd received   140
from me, without the help of a midwife and without la-
bor, the same way other women looking for trouble give
birth. She said she had a foreign lover and was introduc-
ing the girl into her family because of him. Apart from   145
you of course, only the two of us know this, I who gave
the girl to her and she who took her from me. This is how
it happened. If the occasion comes, I want you to remem-
ber it. I'm going home.

Exit the PROCURESS to the right.
Enter the god HELP from the right.

HELP This old woman is both a great gossip and a great drinker.   150
She has barely left me, the god, any subject to talk about,
seeing how she rushed into revealing the fraudulent in-
troduction of the girl into the family. If she'd kept quiet
about it, I would have told you nevertheless; being a god,
I'd have been able to do so more clearly: my name is   155
Help. Now pay attention that I may give you a clear out-
line of this plot. A long time ago there was a festival in
honor of Dionysus in Sicyon. A merchant from Lemnos
came to the games here and, being a very young lad,
raped a virgin girl here in the street, with violence,   160
drunk, and late at night. When he realized that he'd de-
served punishment, he immediately gave birth to an es-
cape with his feet and ran off to Lemnos, where he lived
at the time. The girl he'd raped gave birth to a daughter

151

decumo post mense exacto hic peperit filiam.
quoniam reum eius facti nescit qui siet,
165 paternum seruom sui participat consili,
dat eam puellam ei seruo exponendam ad necem.
is eam proiecit. haec puellam sustulit.
[ill' clam opseruauit seruos ⟨qui eam proiecerat⟩
quo aut quas in aedis haec puellam deferat.]
170 ut eampse uos audistis confiterier,
dat eam puellam meretrici Melaenidi,
eaque educauit eam sibi pro filia
bene ac pudice. tum illic autem Lemnius
propinquam uxorem duxit, cognatam suam.
175 ea diem suom obiit, facta morigera est uiro.
postquam ille uxori iusta fecit, ilico
huc commigrauit; duxit uxorem hic sibi
eandem quam olim uirginem hic compresserat,
et eam cognoscit esse quam compresserat;
180 illa illi dicit eius se ex iniuria
peperisse gnatam atque eam se seruo ilico
dedisse exponendam. ille extemplo seruolum
iubet illum eundem persequi, si qua queat
reperire quae sustulerit. ei rei nunc suam
185 operam usque assiduo seruos dat, si possiet
meretricem illam inuenire quam olim tollere,
quom ipse exponebat, ex insidiis uiderat.
nunc quod relicuom restat uolo persoluere
ut expungatur nomen, ne quid debeam.
190 adulescens hic est Sicyoni, ei uiuit pater.
is amore proiecticiam illam deperit
quae dudum flens hinc abiit ad matrem suam,

168–69 del. Degering

152

here after her ten months[4] were up. Since she didn't
know who the offender in this matter was, she took her   165
father's slave into her confidence and gave this girl to this
slave to expose her and leave her to die. He did expose
her. This woman picked the girl up. [That slave who'd
abandoned her observed secretly where and into which
house the woman was taking the girl.] As you've heard   170
her admit herself, she gave this girl to the prostitute
Melaenis, who brought her up well and chastely as her
own daughter. That man from Lemnos, on the other
hand, later married his neighbor, his relative. She passed   175
away and thus obliged her husband. After laying his wife
to rest, he moved here at once. He married the same
woman whom he'd once raped here when she was a vir-
gin, and he recognized that she was the one he'd raped.   180
She said to him that she gave birth to a daughter because
of his wrong deed and that she immediately gave her to a
slave to expose. Right away he had that same slave make a
search, to see if he could find out who picked her up.
Now the slave is incessantly giving his attention to this   185
task, to see if he can find that prostitute whom he'd once
seen from his hiding place pick up the girl when he had
exposed her. Now I want to pay off the remainder of my
debt so that my name may be crossed off your books
and I won't owe you anything. There's a young man here   190
in Sicyon, whose father is alive. He is crazy about that
abandoned girl who went off to her mother a moment

[4] Lunar months, thus slightly more than nine calendar months.

---

168 qui eam proiecerat *add. Camerarius*

et illa hunc contra, qui est amor suauissumus.
ut sunt humana, nihil est perpetuom datum.
195   pater adulescenti dare uolt uxorem; hoc ubi
mater resciuit, iussit accersi eam domum.
haec sic res gesta est. bene ualete et uincite
uirtute uera, quod fecistis antidhac;
seruate uostros socios, ueteres et nouos,
200   augete auxilia uostra iustis legibus,
perdite perduellis, parite laudem et lauream,
ut uobis uicti Poeni poenas sufferant.

ACTVS II

II. i: ALCESIMARCHVS

ALC   credo ego Amorem primum apud homines carnuficinam
        commentum.
    hanc ego de me coniecturam domi facio, ni foris quae-
        ram,
205   qui omnis homines supero, [atque] antideo cruciabilitati-
        bus animi.
    iactor [crucior], agitor, stimulor, uorsor
    in amoris rota, miser exanimor,
    feror, differor, distrahor, diripior,
209–
10   ita nubilam mentem animi habeo.
211–
12   ubi sum, ibi non sum, ubi non sum, ibi est animus: ita mi
        omnia sunt ingenia;
    quod lubet, non lubet iam id continuo,
214–
15   ita me Amor lassum animi ludificat,
    fugat, agit, appetit, raptat, retinet,
217   lactat, largitur: quod dat non

200 uostris *P*, uostra *Ussing*   205 atque *del. Hermann*

ago, crying; and she in turn is crazy about him, which is the sweetest kind of love. But that's how human life is: nothing is given for good. The young lad's father wants 195 to give him a wife. When the girl's mother found out about this, she commanded that her daughter be brought home. This is how it happened. Farewell and be victorious through true valor, as you've been so far. Protect your allies, old and new, increase your auxiliaries through just 200 laws, lay low your enemies, and earn laud and laurels, so that the conquered Carthaginians may suffer punishment at your hands.

Exit the God HELP to the right.

ACT TWO

Enter ALCESIMARCHUS from the left.

ALC   I believe it was Love who first devised torture among us men. I draw this inference from home, from my own experience—no need to look outside: I outdo and sur- 205 pass everyone in mental agony. I'm being thrown around, tossed around, pierced, turned on the wheel of love; poor me, I'm being destroyed, driven, driven apart, dragged apart, torn apart: so clouded is my mind. Where I am, 210 there I'm not, where I'm not, there my heart is; all my moods are like this. What I like I dislike at once: this is 215 how Love tricks me—I am mentally exhausted—how he puts me to flight, drives me off, lays hands on me, drags me back, holds me back, entices me, bestows on me.

206 *crucior del. Fleckeisen*

155

217ᵃ	dat; deludit:
218	modo quod suasit, ⟨id⟩ dissuadet,
219–20	quod dissuasit, id ostentat.
221–22	maritumis moribus mecum experitur: ita meum frangit
	amantem animum;
	nec, nisi quia miser non eo pessum,
	mihi ulla abest perdito permities.
225	ita pater apud uillam detinuit
	me hos dies sex ruri continuos,
	nec licitum interea est meam amicam
228–29	uisere: estne hoc miserum memoratu?
	***

FRAGMENTVM

230 i	ALC	nudiussextus
		***

II. ii: ALCESIMARCHVS. SERVOS

***

FRAGMENTVM

231	ALC	potine tu homo facinus facere strenuom?
ii	SER	aliorum affatim est
		qui faciant. sane ego me nolo fortem perhiberi uirum.
		***
233	SER	sed quid istuc?

218 id *add. Reiz*
221–22 experitur *SGE*³, expetitur *ceteri Palatini*
230–491 *deficiunt Palatini, A saepissime non legitur; inter 229 et 233 perierunt circiter 100 uersus*

156

What he gives he does not give, he tricks me. What he
just advised he advises against, what he advised against   220
he recommends. He handles me like the sea, to judge
from how he batters my lovesick heart to pieces. I'm de-
stroyed and lack no ruin, except that I don't sink to the
bottom, wretch that I am: my father kept me in the coun-   225
try, at our farm, for the last five days without interrup-
tion, and I didn't have a chance to see my girlfriend in the   229
meantime. Isn't this a sorry tale?

*At this point the transmission of the Palatine manuscripts stops;
it resumes at l. 492. The Ambrosian palimpsest contains parts of
the passage missing in the Palatine tradition, but in many places
the remaining parts are more or less illegible. Some fragments
have come down to us through the indirect tradition. Fr. i and ii
probably stood among the roughly one hundred lines that were
lost between ll. 229 and 231.[5] Fr. i still belongs to the preceding
scene. Fr. ii belongs to the following scene, in which Alcesimar-
chus asks his slave to insult him because he did not stay with his
girlfriend. Fr. ii may have stood directly before l. 233.*

ALC   five days ago   230 i
ALC   Can you do an energetic deed?   231
SER   There are plenty of others who will. I really don't wish to   ii
      be considered an energetic man.

SER   But what's that?   233

[5] Fr. i: Gloss. *Plaut. gramm.* iii. 58. 4, Plautus uses *nudiussextus* "five
days ago" in the *Cistellaria*. Fr. ii: Gell. 6. 7. 1–4, *affatim* "plenty" is
stressed on the first syllable because it is no longer analysed as two
words (*ad + fatim*).

	ALC	mala multa dici mihi uolo.
	SER	qua gratia?
	ALC	quia uiuo.
	SER	facile id quidem edepol possum, si tu uis.
	ALC	uolo.
235	SER	at enim ne tu exponas pugnos tuos in imperio meo.
	ALC	numquam edepol faciam.
	SER	fidem da.
	ALC	do, non facturum esse me.

ALC sed ego primum, tot qui ab amica abesse potuerim dies,
sum nihili.

SER   nihili hercle uero es.

ALC   quam ego amarem perdite,
quae me amaret contra.

SER   dignus hercle es infortunio.

240 ALC ei me tot tam acerba facere in corde!

SER   frugi numquam eris.

ALC praesertim quae coniurasset mecum et firmasset fidem.

SER nec deos neque homines aequom est facere tibi posthac
bene.

ALC quae esset aetatem exactura mecum in matrimonio.

SER compedis te capere oportet neque eas umquam ponere.

245 ALC quae mihi esset commendata et meae fide concredita.

SER hercle te uerberibus multum caedi oportere arbitror.

ALC quae mellillam me uocare et suauium solita est suom.

SER ob istuc unum uerbum dignu's deciens qui furcam feras.

ALC egomet fateor. sed quid auctor nunc mihi es?

---

238 . . idoroiaroperite *A*, quam ego amarem perdite *Leo*

---

[6] An instrument of torture used for slaves.

ALC I want a lot of harsh things to be said to me.

SER What for?

ALC Because I'm alive.

SER I can do that easily enough if you wish.

ALC I do.

SER But don't show your fists during my period of authority. 235

ALC I'll never do so.

SER Give me your word.

ALC I do: I won't do so. But first of all I'm worthless because I could endure being away from my girlfriend for so many days.

SER Yes, you are worthless.

ALC A girlfriend whom I love madly and who loves me in return.

SER You deserve trouble.

ALC The thought of me doing so many things to her which are 240 so bitter in her heart!

SER You'll never be a decent chap.

ALC Especially a girl who'd given me her oath and made a solemn promise.

SER It wouldn't be right if gods or men did you a good turn after this.

ALC Who was going to spend her life with me in marriage.

SER You ought to wear shackles and never be free of them.

ALC Who was put in my keeping and entrusted to my protec- 245 tion.

SER I think you should be beaten a lot.

ALC Who used to call me her honey and her kiss.

SER Because of that one word you deserve to carry the fork[6] ten times.

ALC I admit it. But what do you advise me now?

	SER	dicam tibi:
250		supplicium illi des, suspendas te, ne tibi suscenseat.
	ALC	quian *** a‹mi›cam *** le?
	SER	quid tu ergo ** i *** name *** te manuleo
		*** ue amica ne te caiet ***
		quid *** dari iussit pater
255		uu *** ss * o * er mihi
		saxi *** abduxi semel
		sanus ***
		nam *** qu *** n *** neu
		*** hoc r *** ‹di uo›stram fidem
260		qui * du *** q‹u›a‹m›qu‹am› exemeri‹t›
		inla *** rum *** rum *** maximum
		u * ll *** ‹exe›mpla *** ores
		sublestum *** claudito
		*** m *** om
265		ne quo *** ino *** sus est
266		*** es * sed quem *** a * s * in *** ni foras
266ᵃ		***

II. iii: ALCESIMARCHVS. GYMNASIVM. SERVOS

266ᵇ		***
267		*** m hercle cras ***
		censen tu es *** ar *** lu
		siquidem illaec ads ***
270		ubi eam u *** o * numquam * suma ***
		iam te moriri non sini *** ce ***
		semper sunt †situiut† uxor *** fec * idem.
	ALC	quid si am‹o›? ***
	GYM	*** non idi *** cinis est amor
		n *** du * u atque illam quam te amare intellego.
275	ALC	* c *** si conclusos uos me habere in carcere

SER   I'll tell you: give her satisfaction, hang yourself, so that   250
she won't be angry with you.

ALC   Because *** girlfriend ***?

SER   Then what do you *** you at the sleeve *** your girl-
friend so that she doesn't beat you *** what did your
father order to be given *** to me *** I took her away   255
once, sane *** for *** this *** gods, your protection, who   260
*** although he took out *** the biggest *** examples
*** unsound *** close *** so that nowhere *** is *** but   265
whom *** unless outside ***

*Around seventy lines have been lost between ll. 266 and 267.
After the tirade, Alcesimarchus goes to his house, where he finds
Gymnasium, who tells him of the wedding preparations for
him. Alcesimarchus believes that he is going crazy.*

*** really, tomorrow *** do you think *** if they ***   266b
when *** her *** never *** take *** now *** not *** for   –70
you to die *** they are always *** the wife *** the same
thing.

ALC   What if I'm in love? ***

GYM   *** not *** is love *** and the girl whom I see you're in
love with ***.

ALC   *** if for me to have you locked up in prison *** of love   275

---

251 a‹mi›cam *Schoell*
259 ‹di uo›stram *Schoell*
260 q‹u›a‹m›qu‹am› exemeri‹t› *Stockert*
262 ‹exe›mpla *scripsi*
266ᵃ–66ᵇ *duo folia (fere 70 uersus) desunt*
273 am‹o› *Schoell*

†tibitoteestd† ** amoris noctesque et dies
ni emortuos era *** miumo
mihi numquam quisquam creduit ⟨p⟩ostilla ⟨i⟩de⟨m⟩
non ese ** a *** em *** s.

GYM   immo maxumus.

280   nam qui amant stulte atque immodeste atque improbe,
*** nne *** †imecurc† *** e ne ament.
adduxtin ill *** †itmauoltiter†

ALC   un *** nus th *** he, ubi tu es?

SER   ecce me.

ALC   i, affer mihi arma, et loricam adducito.

285 SER   loricam adducam? sa *** ned ** ⟨add⟩ucere.

ALC   i, curre, equom affer.

SER   perii hercle, hic insanit miser.

ALC   abi atque hastatos multos, multos uelites,
multos cum multis—nil moror precario.
ubi sunt quae iussi?

SER   sanus hic non est satis.

290 GYM manu esse credo nocitum, quom illaec sic facit.

SER   utrum deliras, quaeso, an astans somnias,
qui equom me afferre iubes, loricam adducere,
multos hastatos, postid multos uelites,
multos cum multis? haec tu peruorsario

295   mihi fabulatu's.

ALC   dixin ego istaec, opsecro?

SER   modo quidem hercle haec dixisti.

ALC   non praesens quidem.

SER   praestigiator [es], siquidem hic non es atque ades.

GYM uideo ego te Amoris ualde tactum toxico,
adulescens; eo te magis uolo monitum.

278 ⟨p⟩ostilla ⟨i⟩de⟨m⟩ *Dunsch*   285 ⟨add⟩ucere *Lindsay*
297 es¹ *del. Studemund*

by night and day, unless *** dead *** may no one believe
me in this same thing after this *** not ***.

GYM No, the greatest: those who love in a stupid, immoderate, 280
and inappropriate way *** in order that they don't love.
*** did you bring ***?

ALC (*to his slave*) *** where are you?

SER Here I am.

ALC Go, bring me arms, and get me a breastplate.

SER I should get you a breastplate? *** get ***. 285

ALC Go, run, bring me a horse.

SER (*aside*) I'm ruined, he's mad, poor chap.

ALC Go and fetch many men with spears, many light-armed
soldiers, and many soldiers with many things—I'll accept
no entreaties. Where are the things I ordered?

SER (*to Gymnasium*) This man isn't in his right mind.

GYM Because he's behaving like this I believe he's been be- 290
witched.

SER (*to Alcesimarchus*) Are you mad or dreaming while
standing upright? You're telling me to bring you a horse,
get you a breastplate, many men with spears, then many
light-armed soldiers, and many soldiers with many things?
You've been prattling this sort of thing to me in a wrong- 295
headed way.

ALC Please, did I say these things?

SER Just now you said them.

ALC I wasn't present.

SER You're a wizard if you aren't here and yet are here.

GYM (*to Alcesimarchus*) I can see that you've been hit hard by
Love's poisoned shaft, young man. That's why I want to
warn you all the more.

	ALC	mone.
300	GYM	caue sis cum Amore tu umquam bellum sumpseris.
	ALC	quid faciam?
	GYM	ad matrem eius deuenias domum,

expurges, iures, ores blande per precem
eamque exores ne tibi suscenseat.

	ALC	expurigabo hercle omnia ad raucam rauim.
304ᵃ		***

II. iv: SENEX. GYMNASIVM

304ᵇ		***

FRAGMENTVM

305 iii 305ᵃ	SEN	prohibet diuitiis maxumis, dote altili atque opima. ***
306	SEN	mulierculam exornatulam ‹faci›e quidem hercle scita.

quamquam uetus cantherius sum, etiam nunc, ut ego
    opinor,
adhinnire equolam possum ego hanc, si detur sola soli.

	GYM	nimis opportune mi euenit rediisse Alcesimarchum;
310		nam sola nulla inuitior solet esse.
	SEN	me uocato

ne sola sis: ego tecum ‹ero, uolo› ego agere, ut tu agas
    aliquid.

	GYM	nimis lepide exconcinnauit hasce aedis Alcesimarchus.
	SEN	ut quo‹m Ven›us aggreditur, ‹place›t! lepidum est

amare semper.

304ᵃ–5ᵃ *duo folia (fere 70 uersus) perierunt*   306 ‹faci›e quidem
Fontaine   311 ero, uolo *add. Studemund*   313 quo‹m Ven›us
et ‹place›t *Leo*

---

7 Fr. iii: Non. p. 101 Lindsay: *altilis* can mean "rich."

ALC Do.

GYM Be careful, please, never to take up war against Love.   300

ALC What should I do?

GYM Go to her mother, to her home, apologize, swear an oath,
     ask her flatteringly through entreaty, and persuade her
     not to be angry with you.

ALC I'll apologize for everything till I'm completely hoarse.

*Around seventy lines have been lost between ll. 304 and 306.
Alcesimarchus and his servant go looking for the young man's
father. In the following scene, this old man comes to the house of
Alcesimarchus in order to tell Selenium that she should leave his
son alone. He meets Gymnasium and mistakes her for Selenium;
Gymnasium enjoys the misunderstanding. Fr. iii belongs to this
scene, but does not immediately precede l. 306.*[7]

OM   She's keeping him away from greatest wealth, a rich and   305
     fat dowry.   iii

OM   (*spotting Gymnasium*) A nicely made-up little woman of   306
     really pretty appearance. Although I'm an old hack, I
     think I could whinny to this little filly even now, if she
     were given to me when we're alone.

GYM (*pretending to be Selenium and not to see the old man*)
     It's a very convenient coincidence that Alcesimarchus
     has come back: usually no girl is less willing to be alone   310
     than me.

OM   (*aside*) Invite me so that you won't be alone: I'll be with
     you, I'll be busy keeping you busy.

GYM Alcesimarchus has embellished this house really prettily.

OM   (*aside*) How pleasant it is when Venus comes! Making
     love is always joyful.

GYM   uenerem meram haec aedes olent, quia amator expoliuit.
315 SEN   non modo ipsa lepida est, commode quoque hercle fabu-
          latur.
        sed quom dicta huius interpretor, haec hercle est, ut ego
          opinor,
        meum quae corrumpit filium. suspicio est eam esse,
        utpote quam numquam uiderim; de opinione credo.
        nam hasce aedis conductas habet meus gnatus, haec ubi
          astat:
320   hoc hanc eam esse opinio est; nam haec illum nominauit.
        quid si adeam atque appellem? mali damnique illecebra,
          salue.
GYM   qu *** nu *** e uapulabis.
SEN   neque *** a *** rreo *** uolo apud te.
        *** quaeret *** mer ***
325   lu *** uu ***
        *** fesn ***
        *** s *** s *** ulco
        *** ⟨pe⟩riclis
        ***
330   *** l ***.
GYM   intro abeo:
        nam meretricem astare in uia solam prostibuli sane est.
        *** d *** qu *** num me
        ** ssem *** meamque
        *** f ***
335   proh *** diu *** s * o ***
        ri * ds *** c ***
        as *** es * u *** s ***
        a *** ueal ***
        *** o *** il *** ep ***
340   neque ull *** cia *** a * i * s

166

GYM This house smells of pure passion because a lover has smartened it up.

OM *(aside)* Not only is she herself pretty, she also speaks in a   315
pleasant way. But as I understand her words, she's indeed
the one, I think, who is turning my son into a rake. It's
only my suspicion that she's the one, as I've never seen
her; I believe so from my conjecture: my son's renting
this house where she's standing. That's why I conjecture   320
that she's the one: she's named him. What if I approach
and address her? *(to Gymnasium)* You honeytrap full of
harm and damage, I give you my greetings.

GYM *** you'll get a beating.

OM Neither do I want *** at your place. *** he'll search for
*** dangers ***.   325–
30

GYM I'm going inside: for a prostitute to stand alone in the
street is really a sign of being a street whore. *** me ***   332
and my *** nor any *** good *** unless *** certainly   333–
44

---

328 ‹pe›riclis *Stockert*

bonu ***
en ***
***
nisi * unct * pr ***
345   ue ***
siu ** d *** sis ***
h *** fec ***
*** edic *** q ***
*** equidem *** pu *** o ***
350   a ***
* a *** ca *** ecesesl *** os ** e ***
*** face nunciam *** nc ***
no *** p * a *** sit *** s *** am ***
qu *** resea *** huc ***
355   qu ***
n *** quod *** um tuo ***
ne tu ** n ***
quae ub ***
359   *** ille *** ou *** mulier
359ª   ***
360   *** steram *** f *** omo
360ª   *** mihi opus ut
361   *** ‹co›lloqui *** s
apu *** ut * m ** i *** lus ego uolo quiduis.

SEN   uolo ex te scire, quicquid est m‹eus filiu›s qu‹od fecit›,
quid ego usquam male feci tibi ‹aut meu›s quisquam, id
        edisserta,
365   quam ob rem me meumque filium cum matre remque
        nostram
habes perditui et praedatui?

GYM   miser errat, ut ego dixi.
lepida est materies, ludam ego hunc, nam occasio uide-
        tur.

168

   *** now make *** to this place *** which *** your *** so ³⁵⁰
that you don't *** which *** that man *** woman *** it's 359
necessary for me to *** to speak *** I want whatever ***.

OM   I want to know from you whatever it is that my son's done,
what harm I or anyone of mine have ever done you, tell
me that, that you should use me, my son with his mother, 365
and our possessions as opportunities for destruction and
looting?

GYM   (*aside*) The poor chap's mistaken, as I said. The opportu-
nity is lovely, I'll make fun of him: it seems the right occa-

---

361 ⟨co⟩lloqui *Leo*
363 m⟨eus filiu⟩s qu⟨od fecit⟩ *Studemund*
364 ⟨aut meu⟩s *Seyffert*

potin operam ⟨in⟩ique equidem mala⟨m ut ne⟩ des in-
     nocenti?

SEN   sed ⟨opsecro⟩ te, nullusne est tibi amator alius quis-
     quam?

370 GYM nisi tuos modo unus filiust, quem quidem ego amem alius
     nemo est.

SEN   at ecc ***.

GYM   nil moror: damno sunt tui mi s⟨imil⟩es.

372 SEN quid f *** m?

GYM   uisne est is arbitratus?

372ᵃ   ***

FRAGMENTVM

373 GYM uos datores
iv
373ᵃ   negotioli bellissumi senices soletis esse.
      ***

368 ⟨in⟩ique . . . mala⟨m ut ne⟩ *Leo*
369 opsecro *add. Studemund*
371 s⟨imil⟩es *Schoell*
372ᵃ, 385–88 *fere uersus 55 exciderunt quia folium periit unum et
nonnulli uersus in sequenti folio legi non possunt*

---

8 Fr. iv: Prisc. *gramm.* ii. 111. 4–7, nouns in *-ium*, like *negotium*
"business," form the diminutive in *-iolum*; Prisc. *gramm.* ii. 279.18–280.
2, *senex* "old man" can have a plural *senices*. Fr. v: Prisc. *gramm.* ii. 387.
16–388. 6, *stipulari* takes *ab* + ablative, whether it means "exact a prom-
ise from someone" or "being asked to promise by someone." Fr. vi:
Prisc. *gramm.* ii. 107. 4–8, fifth-declension nouns like *res* "means"
form diminutives in *-ecula*. Fr. vii: Fest. p. 512. 6 Lindsay, *uegrandis*
means "tiny." Fr. viii: Non. p. 291–2 Lindsay, there is a feminine noun
cursura from *currere* "run." Fr. ix: Non. p. 802 L., *meminisse* "remem-

sion. *(to the old man)* Can't you stop being unfair and treating an innocent girl badly?

OM   But please, don't you have any other lover?

GYM   Apart from your only son, there's no one for me to love.   370

OM   But ***.

GYM   I don't care: people like you are my ruin.

OM   What ***?

GYM   Is that opinion tantamount to violence?

Between ll. 372 and 389 around fifty-five lines have been lost. Fr. iv still belongs to the preceding scene; Gymnasium has made the old man fall in love with her.[8] Then Gymnasium's mother comes to take her back since Alcesimarchus is back in town and can look after his house himself. In fr. v the procuress addresses the old man, who understands what has been going on and leaves. Fr. vi–viii are from the ensuing dialogue between the procuress and Gymnasium, unless fr. vi still belongs to the old man, who could be addressing the procuress. Fr. vii and viii clearly belong together. Gymnasium and her mother return to their house and Lampadio enters from the right, from his search for the woman whom he had seen picking up Selenium. In fr. ix he talks about good slaves remembering their duty and no doubt considers himself to be one of them. In fr. x–xii he describes what he saw during his search.

GYM   You old men usually give us the most pleasant little busi-   373
ness.   iv

ber" can take the accusative instead of the genitive. Fr. x: Non. p. 88 L., *mustulentus*, from *mustum* "fresh wine," means "smelling of fresh wine"; Non. p. 669 L., *uentus* can also mean "smell." Fr. xi: Non. p. 154 L., *excissatus* means "wounded." Fr. xii: Non. p. 279 L., "passage" can be masculine (*angiportus*) or neuter (*angiportum*).

II. v: LENA. GYMNASIVM

***

FRAGMENTA

374 v	LENA	me respondere postulas? iniurium est.
375		stipulari semper me ultro oportet a uiris.
		eum quaestum facio, nil uiris promittere.
vi	GYM	siquidem imperes pro copia, pro recula
vii	LENA	quin is, si itura es? nimium is uegrandi gradu.
viii	GYM	pol ad cubituram, mater, magis sum exercita
380		fere quam ad cursuram. eo sum tardiuscula.
380ᵃ		***

II. vi: LAMPADIO

380ᵇ		***
ix	LAM	meminere officium suom.
x	LAM	ita mustulentus uentus naris attigit
xi	LAM	capillo scisso atque excissatis auribus
384 xii	LAM	quae quasi carnuficis angiporta purigans
385– 88		***
389		*** rist
390		cu ***
		fuist *** llo modo
		uobo *** es negent
		*** a *** d ***
		*** guela ** qui teris
395		*** uero ** s ***
		*** ticulus fui
		*** us
		***
		u *** eras

172

PROC You expect me to give you my word in return? It's unfair.   374–
On the contrary, I should always exact promises from   75 v
men. That's my line of business, not to make any prom-
ises to men.

GYM if you should give orders in accordance with your wealth,   vi
your small means

PROC Why don't you go if you're going to go? You walk with   vii
such a tiny step.

GYM Goodness, my mother, I'm better trained in lying down   viii
than in running. That's why I'm a little slow.   380

LAM They remember their duty.   viii

LAM the way a breeze smelling of fresh wine has touched my   x
nostrils

LAM with torn hair and clipped ears   xi

LAM who, cleaning these passages as if they were an execu-   384
tioner's   xii

*** way *** they might deny *** you who rub *** but *** I was   385–
***   400

---

382 uentus *Non.* 669 *Lindsay*, aestus *Non.* 88 L.

173

400   ***

    qu ** sq ***
uel ***
quaeq *** m darent
** l ***.

FRAGMENTVM

405 **LAM** non quasi nunc haec sunt hic, limaces liuidae,
xiii
    febricul‹osae, m›iserae amicae, osseae,
diobolares, schoeniculae, miraculae,
cum extritis talis, cum todillis crusculis
***

410   qua ***
** qua ***
***

    qu ***
ti ***

415   am ***
pr * ms * h *** m loco
sus ***
*** l ***
m ***

420   at die illa ***
s *** qu ***
dei me omnes ***
illae ***
haec sustulit, post ***

425   circumcur‹saui› ***
o *** neq ***
qua *** disti *** ‹long›um loquor

428–
30   ***

174

Fr. xiii still belongs to Lampadio's monologue. The palimpsest is badly damaged here, but the traces of letters allow us to locate fr. xiii precisely. Lampadio is talking about ugly prostitutes.[9]

LAM   not the type that are here nowadays, livid slugs, fever-   405
ish, miserable wenches, bony, to be hired for two obols,   xiii
smelling of cheap ointment, freakish, with worn-down
ankles, with little legs the size of sparrows

   *** in the place *** but on that day *** may all the gods *   410–
me *** those *** she lifted her up, then *** I ran about   24
*** I've been talking for a long time *** is ***   425–
   425–
   35

The palimpsest is still barely legible, but somewhere here a new scene must have begun. Lampadio has by now returned to the forum and Alcesimarchus has reentered from the right and come to the house of Melaenis, where he apologizes to her and Selenium.

[9] The passage is quoted by several grammarians and lexicographers, e.g. Fest. p. 442. 7 Lindsay: Plautus calls some prostitutes *schoeniculae* because they use *schoenum*, the worst ointment.

---

406 febricul‹osae m›iserae *Schoell*
408 exteritis *A*, extertis *Festus*, extortis *Paulus, Priscianus, Osbernus*, extritis *Scaliger*
425 circumcur‹saui› *Suess*
427 ‹long›um *Suess*
428–48 *fol. 245v palimpsesti legi paene non potest*

431	*** est
432–35	***
436	qu ***
437	h ***
438–39	***

II. vii: SELENIVM. ALCESIMARCHVS. MELAENIS

440		***
441		*** us
		*** io
		tu ***
		c *** ogo
445		*** s
446		*** ⟨mise⟩ris modis.
447–48		***
449	SEL	molestus es.
450	ALC	meae issula sua ⟨aede⟩s egent. ad me ⟨sine ducam⟩.
	SEL	aufer manum.
	ALC	germana mea sororcula.
	SEL	repudio te fraterculum.
	ALC	tum tu igitur, mea matercula.
	MEL	repudio te puerculum.
	ALC	opsecro te—
	SEL	ualeas.
	ALC	—ut sinas—
	SEL	nil moror.
	ALC	—expurigare me.
	SEL	oppressas.
	ALC	sine dicam.
	MEL	satis sapit mi tuis periuriis.
455	ALC	†uer . . . sita sunt.†
	MEL	at nunc non potis est.

	*** in wretched ways. ***	440–46
SEL	You're a nuisance.	
ALC	My house is missing its mistress. Let me take her home. *(tries to grab Selenium)*	450
SEL	Take your hand off.	
ALC	My own dear little sister![10]	
SEL	I refuse to have you as my little brother.	
ALC	*(turning to Melaenis)* Well then, you, my dear little mother.	
MEL	I refuse to have you as my little boy.	
ALC	I beg you—	
SEL	*(interrupting)* Goodbye.	
ALC	—to let me—	
SEL	*(interrupting)* I don't care.	
ALC	—apologize. *(tries to grab Selenium again)*	
SEL	You're being violent.	
ALC	Let me speak.	
MEL	She's been taught sense enough by your false oaths.	

Exit SELENIUM into the house of Melaenis.

ALC	***	455
MEL	But now it isn't possible.	

[10] The terms "sister" and "brother" are used for lovers elsewhere as well, e.g. in Petronius 127. 1–2.

---

446 ‹mise›ris *scripsi*
449 *initium huius uersus in priore folio uidetur fuisse*
450 ‹aede›s . . . ‹sine ducam› *Leo*
454 o(pe)r(os)sa(m) *A*, oppressas *Leo*

ALC   supplicium uolo
        polliceri.

MEL   at mi aps te accipere non lubet.

ALC   em, om⟨nia⟩
        patior iur⟨e⟩.

MEL   ho⟩c illi uolup est nec tis misereri decet
        quemquam hominem.

ALC   inter *** us nep ***
        uerba dare ⟨ne⟩cesse.

460   non illata *** mator.

MEL   pol mi qui ⟨sanct⟩a [qui] frangant foedera
        eos *** enim u ** et me * e *** cerit
        iu *** quid lubet * sta quid *** uesto * c dabis.

ALC   at ⟨ego⟩ ne⟨c⟩ do nec te amittam hodie, nisi quae uolo
           tecum loqui
        das mihi operam.

465 MEL   potin ut mihi molestus ne sis?

ALC   quin id ⟨est no⟩men mihi,
        omnes mortales u⟨o⟩c⟨ant Mole⟩stu⟨m: eunde⟩m cons-
           picis.

MEL   quo ***

AL   ⟨o⟩psecro.

MEL   at frustra opsecras.
        *** rfu *** ui insanissumust,
        qui * sine omni *** †uetundie† suom.

ALC   dabo

470   ius iurandum *** n * u *** uum.

MEL   at ego nunc ⟨ab⟩ illo m⟨i caueo⟩ iure iurando ⟨tuo⟩;
        simile est ius iurandum amantum quasi ius confusicium.
        nescia *** su *** mu *** dest
        nono *** o mihi te nos *** †c snunde† *** s nugas agis

475   sia *** iu quaquam ma *** si
        non me *** res *** do *** †aisel†.

      178

ALC I want to promise satisfaction.

MEL But I have no interest in receiving any from you.

ALC There! I'm suffering all this deservedly.

MEL She's happy about that and no one ought to feel pity for you.

ALC Between *** necessary to trick. *** not brought in ***.   460

MEL To me, people who break sacred agreements, those *** and me *** what I like *** what *** you'll give.

ALC But I'm not giving it and I won't let you go today, unless you pay attention to what I want to say to you.

MEL Can't you stop being a nuisance to me?   465

ALC No, that's my name, all mortals call me Nuisance; and you're looking at him now.

MEL ***.

AL I entreat you.

MEL But you do so in vain. *** he's barking mad, he who * without any *** his ***.

ALC I'll swear an oath ***.   470

MEL But I am now on my guard against that oath of yours; a lover's oath is as insubstantial as oatmeal gruel.[11] *** to me, you * us *** you're talking rubbish *** any *** not me ***.   475

---

[11] A pun on the two meanings of *ius*: *ius iurandum* is an oath, while *ius confusicium* refers to a hotch-potch soup.

---

456 om‹nia› *Studemund*

457 iur‹e. MEL ho›c *Lindsay*   459 ‹ne›cesse *Leo*

460 ‹sanct›a [qui] *Leo*   463 at ‹ego› ne‹c› *Leo*

465 id ‹est no›men *Schoell*   466 u‹o›c‹ant Mole›stu‹m› *Schoell*   ‹eunde›m conspicis *Handley*

467 ‹o›psecro *Lindsay*

471 nunc ‹ab› illo m‹i caueo› iure iurando ‹tuo› *Leo*

ALC supplicium dabo a *** p * i ** atque illi * e
      quo modo eg⟨o⟩ *** ad medi *** ⟨mi⟩ser
      *** ss ***.

MEL   quia es nanctus nouam,
480   quaedam *** big *** s quaedam quasi tu nescias
      perg ***.

ALC   ⟨di⟩ deaeque illam perdant †pariter†
      pem *** m †usero† umquam, si hoc fallo.

MEL   nil moror
      *** ⟨fa⟩lsum fallis, eo te hac ignorat Fides.
      postremo, si mihi dedisses uerba, dis numquam dares.
485 ALC quin equidem illam ducam uxorem.

MEL   ducas, si di tib⟨i duint⟩.
      nunc hoc si tibi commodum est, quae * o ***.

ALC instruxi illi aurum atque ues⟨tem⟩ *** magis t ** ra ***.

MEL si quidem amabas, proin di ** omu ** t ** illi instrui.
      sed sino. iam hoc mihi responde quod ego te r⟨ogauero⟩.
490   ins⟨truxis⟩t⟨i⟩ ** eam ** †cepo * o * tenes† quia ** indu-
      ta * u ***
      tibi ita ut uoluisti quidem **.

ALC   ** ct * t *** os quod uolo.

MEL eo facetu's quia tibi alia est sponsa locuples Lemnia.
      habeas. nec nos factione tanta quanta tu sumus
      neque opes nostrae tam sunt ualidae quam tuae; uerum
      tamen
495   hau metuo ne ius iurandum nostrum quisquam culpitet:
      tu iam, si quid tibi dolebit, scies qua doleat gratia.

ALC di me perdant—

MEL   quodquomque optes, tibi uelim contingere.

ALC —si illam uxorem duxero umquam, mihi quam despon-
      dit pater!

ALC supplicium dabo a *** p * i ** atque illi * e
      quo modo eg⟨o⟩ *** ad medi *** ⟨mi⟩ser
      *** ss ***.

MEL   quia es nanctus nouam,

480   quaedam *** big *** s quaedam quasi tu nescias
        perg ***.

ALC   ⟨di⟩ deaeque illam perdant †pariter†
      pem *** m †usero† umquam, si hoc fallo.

MEL   nil moror
      *** ⟨fa⟩lsum fallis, eo te hac ignorat Fides.
      postremo, si mihi dedisses uerba, dis numquam dares.

485 ALC quin equidem illam ducam uxorem.

MEL   ducas, si di tib⟨i duint⟩.
      nunc hoc si tibi commodum est, quae * o ***.

ALC instruxi illi aurum atque ues⟨tem⟩ *** magis t ** ra ***.

MEL si quidem amabas, proin di ** omu ** t ** illi instrui.
      sed sino. iam hoc mihi responde quod ego te r⟨ogauero⟩.

490   ins⟨truxis⟩t⟨i⟩ ** eam ** †cepo * o * tenes† quia ** indu-
        ta * u ***
      tibi ita ut uoluisti quidem **.

ALC   ** ct * t *** os quod uolo.

MEL eo facetu's quia tibi alia est sponsa locuples Lemnia.
      habeas. nec nos factione tanta quanta tu sumus
      neque opes nostrae tam sunt ualidae quam tuae; uerum
           tamen

495   hau metuo ne ius iurandum nostrum quisquam culpitet:
      tu iam, si quid tibi dolebit, scies qua doleat gratia.

ALC di me perdant—

MEL   quodquomque optes, tibi uelim contingere.

ALC —si illam uxorem duxero umquam, mihi quam despon-
      dit pater!

ALC	I want to promise satisfaction.
MEL	But I have no interest in receiving any from you.
ALC	There! I'm suffering all this deservedly.
MEL	She's happy about that and no one ought to feel pity for you.
ALC	Between *** necessary to trick. *** not brought in ***.
MEL	To me, people who break sacred agreements, those *** and me *** what I like *** what *** you'll give.
ALC	But I'm not giving it and I won't let you go today, unless you pay attention to what I want to say to you.
MEL	Can't you stop being a nuisance to me?
ALC	No, that's my name, all mortals call me Nuisance; and you're looking at him now.
MEL	***.
AL	I entreat you.
MEL	But you do so in vain. *** he's barking mad, he who * without any *** his ***.
ALC	I'll swear an oath ***.
MEL	But I am now on my guard against that oath of yours; a lover's oath is as insubstantial as oatmeal gruel.[11] *** to me, you * us *** you're talking rubbish *** any *** not me ***.

The line numbers in the right margin: 460, 465, 470, 475.

[11] A pun on the two meanings of *ius*: *ius iurandum* is an oath, while *ius confusicium* refers to a hotch-potch soup.

---

456 om‹nia› *Studemund*

457 iur‹e. MEL ho›c *Lindsay*   459 ‹ne›cesse *Leo*

460 ‹sanct›a [qui] *Leo*   463 at ‹ego› ne‹c› *Leo*

465 id ‹est no›men *Schoell*   466 u‹o›c‹ant Mole›stu‹m› *Schoell*   ‹eunde›m conspicis *Handley*

467 ‹o›psecro *Lindsay*

471 nunc ‹ab› illo m‹i caueo› iure iurando ‹tuo› *Leo*

179

ALC   I'll give satisfaction *** and to her *** how I *** to ***
wretch that I am ***.

MEL   Because you've got hold of a new girl, a certain *** cer-   480
tain things, as if you didn't know ***.

ALC   May the gods and goddesses destroy her *** ever, if I de-
ceive you in this.

MEL   I don't care *** a deception you deceive, that's why Good
Faith does not recognize you in this. Finally, even if you'd
fooled me, you'd never fool the gods.

ALC   No, I will marry her.   485

MEL   Marry her, if the gods give her to you. Now if this is con-
venient to you, what ***.

ALC   I've provided gold and clothes for her *** more ***.

MEL   If you loved her, then *** her being fitted out. But never
mind. Now answer me what I'm asking you. You've fitted   490
her out *** because *** dressed *** to you as you wanted
***.

ALC   *** what I want.

MEL   What makes you witty is that you have another woman
engaged to you, the wealthy Lemnian. Have her. We
don't have as great connections as you, and our influence
isn't as great as yours; but still, I'm not afraid that anyone   495
will ever find fault with our oath. If anything hurts you,
you'll know right away why it does.

ALC   May the gods kill me—

MEL   (*interrupting*) I'd like you to get whatever you wish for.

ALC   —if I ever marry the girl my father engaged me to!

---

478 ⟨mi⟩ser *scripsi*   481 di *add. Schoell*
483 ⟨fa⟩lsum *Lindsay*   485 tib⟨i duint⟩ *Studemund*
487 ues⟨tem⟩ *F. Skutsch*   489 r⟨ogauero⟩ *Leo*
490 ins⟨truxis⟩t⟨i⟩ *Leo*   491 quidam *A*, quidem *Schoell*

PLAUTUS

MEL et me, si umquam tibi uxorem filiam dedero meam.
500 ALC patierin me periurare?
MEL   pol te aliquanto facilius
     quam me meamque rem perire et ludificari filiam.
     abi, quaere ubi iuri iurando tuo sit satias supsidi:
     hic apud nos iam, Alcesimarche, confregisti tesseram.
ALC face semel periclum.
MEL   feci saepe, quod factum queror.
505 ALC redde mi illam.
MEL   inter nouam rem uerbum usurpabo uetus:
     "quod dedi datum non uellem, quod relicuom est non
        dabo."
ALC non remissura es mihi illam?
MEL   pro me responsas tibi.
ALC non remittes?
MEL   scis iam dudum omnem meam sententiam.
ALC satin istuc tibi in corde certum est?
MEL   quin ne commentor quidem.
510 [non edepol istaec tua dicta nunc in auris recipio.
ALC non? hem, quid agis igitur?
MEL   animum aduorte iam, ut quid agam scias.]
ALC at ita me di deaeque, superi atque inferi et medioxumi,
     itaque me Iuno regina et Iouis supremi filia
     itaque me Saturnus eius patruos—
MEL   ecastor pater.
515 ALC —itaque me Ops opulenta, illius auia—

     502 abi P, alibi A   sit satias subsidii A, satis sit subsidii P
     510–11 om. A, del. Müller
     511 agas P, agam Rost

182

MEL   And me if I ever give you my daughter as your wife.

ALC   You'll let me swear a false oath?   500

MEL   Yes, a lot more easily than let me and my possessions per-
      ish and let my daughter be made a fool of. Go, find a place
      where there's plenty of support for your oath; here at
      our place you've already lost any claim to friendship,
      Alcesimarchus.

ALC   Try it once.

MEL   I've tried often, which I regret.

ALC   Give her back to me.   505

MEL   I'll apply the old proverb to a new situation: "I wish I
      hadn't given you what I gave and what's left I won't give
      you."

ALC   You aren't going to send her back to me?

MEL   You're answering for me.

ALC   You won't send her back?

MEL   You've known my decision for a while already.

ALC   Have you made up your mind about this?

MEL   I don't even think about it. [I'm not letting those words of   510
      yours get into my ears now.

ALC   You aren't? What's that? What are you doing then?

MEL   Pay attention now so that you know what I'm doing.]

ALC   But as truly as the gods and goddesses, the ones above
      and below and in the middle, and as truly as Juno, their
      queen and the daughter of Jupiter on high, and as truly as
      Saturn, her uncle—[12]

MEL   (*interrupting*) Goodness, her father.

ALC   —and as truly as opulent Ops, her grandmother—   515

[12] The correct relationships are as follows: Saturn and Ops are hus-
band and wife, and their children Jupiter and Juno are married to each
other.

MEL   immo mater quidem.
        Iuno filia et Saturnus patruos et pater Iuppiter?
ALC   tu me delenis, propter te haec pecco.
MEL   perge dicere.
ALC   anne etiam quid consultura sis sciam?
MEL   perge eloqui.
        non remittam. definitum est.
ALC   enim uero ita me Iuppiter
520   itaque me Iuno itaque Ianus ita—quid dicam nescio.
        iam scio. immo, mulier, audi, meam ut scias sententiam.
        di me omnes, magni minuti, et etiam patellarii,
        faxint ne ego dem ⟨uiuae⟩ uiuos sauium Selenio,
        nisi ego teque tuamque filiam aeque hodie optruncaue-
            ro,
525   poste autem cum primo luci cras nisi ambo occidero,
        et equidem hercle nisi pedatu tertio omnis efflixero,
        nisi tu illam remittis ad me. dixi quae uolui. uale.
MEL   abiit intro iratus. quid ego nunc agam? si redierit
        illa ad hunc, ibidem loci res erit: ubi odium occeperit,
530   illam extrudet, tum hanc uxorem Lemniam ducet do-
            mum.
        sed tamen ibo et persequar: amans ne quid faciat, cauto
            opust.
        postremo, quando aequa lege pauperi cum diuite
        non licet, perdam operam potius quam carebo filia.

---

516 summus Ω, pater *Bettini*   *uersum Melaenidi dedit Ussing*
522 minuti *AE³*, minutique *ceteri Palatini*
523 uiuae *add. Benoist*
526 perdat utertio *B*, perdat utercio *VE¹*, perdam te tercio *JE³*,
pedatu tertio *Turnebus*
531 amens *B¹*, amans *B³VJE*

MEL (*interrupting again*) No, her mother, surely. Juno the daughter, Saturn the uncle, and Jupiter the father?

ALC You're bewitching me, because of you I'm making these mistakes.

MEL Go on speaking.

ALC I should know your verdict, shouldn't I?

MEL Go on talking. I won't send her back. It's final.

ALC But as truly as Jupiter and as truly as Juno and as truly as   520
Janus[13] and as truly—I don't know what to say. Now I know. Listen, woman, so that you may know my decision. May all the gods, the great and the minor ones, and even the domestic ones, prevent me from giving a kiss to Selenium while we're both alive, if I don't butcher you and also your daughter today, if I don't kill you both after-   525
wards, tomorrow, at the crack of dawn, and if I don't exterminate you all in a third and final stage, unless you send her back to me. I've said what I wanted then. Goodbye.

Exit ALCESIMARCHUS into his house.

MEL He went inside in a rage. What should I do now? If she returns to him, things will be back to square one: when he's had enough of her, he'll throw her out, then he'll   530
marry that wife from Lemnos. But still I'll go and follow him; I need to be careful that our lover doesn't do anything stupid. And finally, since a poor person can't deal with a rich one on equal terms, I'd rather waste my effort than be without my daughter. But who is this who's di-

---

[13] The god of gates and doorways and thus also of beginnings.

sed quis hic est qui recta platea cursum huc contendit
suom?

535   et illud paueo et hoc formido, ita tota sum misera in
metu.

II. viii: LAMPADIO

LAM   anum sectatus sum clamore per uias,
miserrumam habui. ut illaec hodie quot modis
moderatrix ⟨linguae⟩ fuit atque immemorabilis!
quot illi blanditias, quid illi promisi boni,
540   quot ammoeniui fabricas, quot fallacias
in quaestione! uix exsculpsi ut diceret,
quia ei promisi dolium uini dare.

II. ix: PHANOSTRATA. LAMPADIO. MELAENIS

PHAN   audire uocem uisa sum ante aedis modo
mei Lampadisci serui.

LAM   non surda es, era:
545   recte audiuisti.

PHAN   quid agis hic?

LAM   quod gaudeas.

PHAN   quid id est?

LAM   hinc ex hisce aedibus paullo prius
uidi exeuntem mulierem.

PHAN   illam quae meam
gnatam sustulerat?

LAM   rem tenes.

PHAN   quid postea?

LAM   dico ei quo pacto eam ab hippodromo uiderim
550   erilem nostram filiam sustollere.
extimuit tum illa.

538 linguae *add. Ussing*

recting his course here straight up the street? I'm afraid   535
of one thing and scared of the other: I'm completely in
fear, poor me. (*steps aside*)

Enter LAMPADIO from the right, without noticing Melaenis.

LAM   I followed the old woman through the streets shouting
loudly and I gave her a very hard time. How and in how
many ways she controlled her tongue today and was un-
able to remember a thing! How much flattery I gave her,
how much good I promised her, how many tricks, how   540
many guiles I brought to bear while questioning her! I
barely wormed it out from her, and only because I prom-
ised to give her a vat of wine.

*Enter PHANOSTRATA from her house. MELAENIS remains in
the background.*

PHAN   Just now I seemed to hear the voice of my good slave
Lampadio in front of the house.

LAM   (*approaching her*) You aren't deaf, mistress: you heard   545
correctly.

PHAN   What are you doing here?

LAM   Something you'll be happy about.

PHAN   What's that?

LAM   A little earlier I saw a woman come out of this house.
(*points to the house of Alcesimarchus*)

PHAN   The one who'd picked up my daughter?

LAM   You've got it.

PHAN   What then?

LAM   I told her how I'd seen her pick up our mistress's daugh-   550
ter down by the racecourse. She got scared then.

MEL   iam horret corpus, cor salit.
       nam mihi ab hippodromo memini afferri paruolam
       puellam eamque me mihi supponere.

PHAN age perge, quaeso. animus audire expetit

555   ut gesta res sit.

MEL   utinam audire non queas.

555ᵃ   ***

556 LAM pergo illa⟨m onerare⟩ dictis: "illaec ted anus
       fortu⟨nis ex secundis ad mi⟩seras uocat.
       nam illaec tibi nutrix est, ne matrem censeas.
       ego te reduco et reuoco ad ⟨summas⟩ ditias,

560   ubi tu locere in luculentam familiam,
       und' tibi talenta magna uiginti pater
       det dotis; non enim hic ubi ex Tusco modo
       tute tibi indigne dotem quaeras corpore."

PHAN an, amabo, meretrix illa est quae illam sustulit?

565 LAM immo [meretrix] fuit; sed ut sit, de ea re eloquar.
       iam perducebam illam ad me suadela mea:
       anus ei amplexa est genua plorans, opsecrans
       ne deserat se: eam suam esse filiam,
       seque eam peperisse sancte adiurabat mihi.

570   "istanc quam quaeris," inquit, "ego amicae meae
       dedi, quae educaret eam pro filiola sua;
       et uiuit," inquit. "ubi ea est?" inquam extempulo.

PHAN seruate di me, opsecro!

555ᵃ *lacunam indicauit Guyet*
556 illa⟨m onerare⟩ *Schoell*
557 fortu⟨nis ex secundis ad mi⟩seras *Schoell*
559 uoco *P*, reuoco *Pylades*   summas *add. Brix*
565 meretrix *del. Bothe*

MEL (*aside*) My body's shaking now, my heart's jumping up and down: I remember that I was brought a little girl from the racecourse and that I pretended that she was my own child.

PHAN Continue, please. I'm burning to hear how things hap- 555 pened.

MEL (*aside*) Would that you couldn't hear!
      ***

LAM I continued to weigh her down with my words: "That old woman is inviting you from a good fortune to a wretched one; she's your nurse, in case you believe she's your mother. I'm taking and inviting you back to greatest wealth, where you'll be placed into a splendid family, 560 from where your father will give you twenty Attic talents of dowry; that's definitely not the case here, where you'd earn your dowry yourself with your body, in a manner unworthy of yourself, in the Tuscan way."[14]

PHAN Please, is the woman who picked her up a prostitute?

LAM No, but she was; but I'll tell you what things are like. I was 565 already winning her over to my side with my persuasive speech; the old woman clasped her knees, crying and entreating her not to leave her: she gave me a solemn oath that she was her daughter, and that she'd given birth to her. "The girl you're looking for," she said, "I gave to a 570 friend of mine to bring up as her own daughter; and she's alive," she said. "Where is she?" I asked at once.

PHAN Save me, gods, I implore you!

[14] The Tuscans were believed to come from Lydia, where it was not considered shameful for a woman to acquire her dowry through prostitution (Herodotus 1. 93). The shopping district *Vicus Tuscus* in Rome had a bad reputation.

MEL   at me perditis.

PHAN quoi illam dedisset exquisisse oportuit.

575 LAM quaesiui, et dixit meretrici Melaenidi.

MEL meum elocutust nomen, interii ⟨oppido⟩!

LAM ubi elocuta est, ego continuo [anum] interrogo;
       "ubi habitat?" inquam, "duce ac demonstra mihi."
       "auecta est," inquit, "peregre hinc habitatum."

MEL   obsipat

580   aquolam.

LAM   "quo auecta est, eo sequemur. sicine
       agis nugas? periisti hercle, ni ⟨mi dixeris
       ubi habitet nunc." non hercle⟩ hoc longe destiti
       instare usque adeo donec se adiurat anus
       iam mihi monstrare.

PHAN   at non missam oportuit.

585 LAM seruatur. sed illaec se quandam aibat mulierem
       suam beneuolentem conuenire etiam prius,
       commune quacum id esset sibi negotium.
       et scio uenturam.

MEL   me indicabit, et suas

589–90   ad meas miserias †alias faciem consciam.†

PHAN quid nunc uis facere me?

LAM   intro abi atque animo bono es.
       uir tuos si ueniet, iube domi opperirier,
       ne ⟨in⟩ quaestione mihi sit, si quid eum uelim.
       ego ad anum recurro rursum.

PHAN   Lampadio, opsecro,

595   cura.

LAM   perfectum ego hoc dabo negotium.

PHAN deos teque spero.

LAM   eosdem ego . . . uti abeas domum.

190

MEL	(*aside*) Yet you're ruining me.	
PHAN	You ought to have inquired who she'd given her to.	
LAM	I did inquire and she said to the prostitute Melaenis.	575
MEL	(*aside*) He's let out my name, I'm completely ruined!	
LAM	When she'd spoken, I questioned her at once; "Where does she live?" I said. "Take me there and show me." "She's gone away," she said, "to live abroad."	
MEL	(*reviving, aside*) She's sprinkling a little water onto me.	580
LAM	"We'll follow her wherever she went. Are you trying to fool me like this? You're dead unless you tell me where she lives now." I didn't stop insisting on this until the old woman swore that she'd show her to me right away.	
PHAN	But you shouldn't have let her go.	
LAM	She's being watched. But she said she was already going to meet a certain woman, a friend of hers, who was also affected by this business. And I know she'll come.	585
MEL	(*aside*) She'll tell on me and †****† her wretchedness to mine.	590
PHAN	What do you want me to do now?	
LAM	Go inside and take heart. If your husband comes, tell him to wait at home, so that I don't have to look for him if I want him for anything. I'm rushing back to the old woman.	
PHAN	Lampadio, please take care of it.	595
LAM	I'll sort this business out properly.	
PHAN	I put my hope in the gods and you.	
LAM	I also put mine in them . . . that you'll go home.	

---

576 oppido *add.* Pylades   577 anum *del.* Acidalius
581–82 mi dixeris ubi habitet nunc. non hercle *add.* Schoell
589–90 *alii alio modo uersum sanare uolunt*
593 in *add.* Camerarius

191

MEL   adulescens, asta atque audi.

LAM   men, mulier, uocas?

MEL   te.

LAM   quid negoti est? nam occupatus sum ampliter.

MEL   quis istic habitat?

LAM   Demipho, dominus meus.

600 MEL   nempe istic est qui Alcesimarcho filiam

         suam despondit in diuitias maxumas?

LAM   is ipsust.

MEL   eho tu, quam uos igitur filiam

         nunc quaeritatis alteram?

LAM   ego dicam tibi:

         non ex uxore natam uxoris filiam.

605 MEL   quid istuc est uerbi?

LAM   ex priore muliere

         nata, inquam, meo ero est filia.

MEL   certe modo

         huius, quae locuta est, quaerere aibas filiam.

LAM   huius ergo quaero.

MEL   quo modo igitur, opsecro,

         haec est prior quae nupta nunc est?

LAM   conteris

610   tu tua me oratione, mulier, quisquis es.

         medioxumam quam duxit uxorem, ex ea

         nata est haec uirgo Alcesimarcho quae datur.

         ea uxor diem obiit. iam scis?

MEL   teneo istuc satis.

         sed ego illud quaero confragosum, quo modo

615   prior posterior sit et posterior sit prior.

LAM   prius hanc compressit quam uxorem duxit domum,

         prius grauida facta est priusque peperit filiam;

         eam postquam peperit, iussit paruam proici:

Exit PHANOSTRATA into Demipho's house.

MEL (*coming forward*) Young man, stop and listen.

LAM Are you calling me, woman?

MEL Yes.

LAM What's the matter? I'm very busy.

MEL Who lives there? (*points to Demipho's house*)

LAM Demipho, my master.

MEL Do you mean the one who promised to give his daughter 600
to Alcesimarchus in marriage, into great wealth?

LAM That's the one.

MEL Hey there, then what other daughter are you looking for
now?

LAM I'll tell you: his wife's daughter, who wasn't born from his
wife.

MEL What sort of statement is that? 605

LAM My master's daughter, I'm telling you, was born from an
earlier woman.

MEL Just now you certainly said you were looking for the
daughter of the woman who spoke.

LAM Yes, that's the one whose daughter I'm looking for.

MEL Then how is she an earlier woman, please? She's married
to him now.

LAM You're wearing me out with your talk, woman, whoever 610
you are. The girl who is being given to Alcesimarchus was
born from the woman he married in between. This wife
passed away. Do you understand it now?

MEL I've understood it well enough. But I'm asking you about
that difficult point, how the earlier one is the later one 615
and the later one is the earlier one.

LAM Before he married her, he raped her, she got pregnant,
and she gave birth to a daughter. After she gave birth
to her, she ordered the little one to be abandoned; I was

193

ego eam proieci. alia mulier sustulit.
620 ego inspectaui. erus hanc duxit postibi.
eam nunc puellam filiam eius quaerimus.
quid nunc supina sursum caelum conspicis?

MEL i nunciam istuc quo properabas, nil moror.
nunc intellexi.

LAM   dis hercle habeo gratiam,
625 nam ni intellexes, numquam, credo, amitteres.

MEL nunc mihi bonae necessust esse ingratiis,
quamquam esse nolo. rem palam esse intellego:
nunc egomet potius hanc inibo gratiam
ab illis quam illaec me indicet. ibo domum,
630 atque ad parentes redducam Selenium.

ACTVS III

III. i: MELAENIS. SELENIVM

MEL rem elocuta sum tibi omnem; sequere hac me, Selenium,
ut eorum quoiam esse oportet te sis potius quam mea.
quamquam inuita te carebo, animum ego inducam ta-
men
ut illud <quod minus meam> quam tuam in rem bene
conducat consulam.
635 nam hic crepundia insunt, quibuscum te illa olim ad me
detulit,
quae mihi dedit, parentes te ut cognoscant facilius.
accipe hanc cistellam, Halisca. agedum pulta illas fores.
dic me orare ut aliquis intus prodeat propere ocius.

619 alia *P*, aliena *Schoell*
631 sequerem mea *B¹*, sequere me mea *B³JE³*, sequere hac me
Seyffert
634 quod minus meam *add. Seyffert*

the one who did so. Another woman picked her up.
I observed it. My master married this woman afterward.   620
We're now looking for this girl, her daughter. Why are
you looking up to heaven now, bent backward?

MEL Now do go where you were in such a hurry to get to, I'm
not delaying you. Now I've understood.

LAM Thank heavens! If you hadn't understood, you'd never   625
have let me go, I believe.

Exit LAMPADIO to the right.

MEL Now I need to be good against my wishes, even though I
don't want to. I understand that the matter's out: now I'd
rather get the thanks for this from them than have her tell
on me. I'll go home and restore Selenium to her parents.   630

Exit MELAENIS into her house.

ACT THREE

*Enter MELAENIS from her house, carrying a casket, followed
by SELENIUM and HALISCA. They walk toward Demipho's
house.*

MEL I've told you the whole story; follow me this way, Sele-
nium, so that you may belong to those who you should
belong to rather than to me. Although I'm reluctant to be
separated from you, I'll bring myself to look after your in-
terests rather than my own: in here is the rattle with   635
which the woman who gave you to me brought you to me,
so that your parents might recognize you more easily.
Take this casket, Halisca. (*hands it over*) Go on, knock at
that door. Say that I'm asking for someone to come out
quickly and promptly.

195

III. ii: ALCESIMARCHVS. SELENIVM. MELAENIS

639–40   ALC   recipe me ad te, Mors, amicum et beneuolum.

SEL   mater mea,
periimus miserae.

ALC   utrum hac me feriam an ab laeua latus?

MEL   quid tibi est?

SEL   Alcesimarchum non uides? ferrum tenet.

ALC   ecquid agis? remorare. lumen linque.

SEL   amabo, accurrite,
ne se interemat.

ALC   o Salute mea salus salubrior,

645   tu nunc, si ego uolo seu nolo, sola me ut uiuam facis.

MEL   hau uoluisti istuc seuerum facere.

ALC   nil mecum tibi,
mortuos tibi sum: hanc ut habeo certum est non amit-
     tere;
nam hercle iam ad me agglutinandam totam decretum
     est dare.
ubi estis, serui? occludite aedis pessulis, repagulis

650   ilico. hanc ego tetulero intra limen.

MEL   abiit, apstulit
mulierem. ibo, persequar iam illum intro, ut haec ex me
     sciat
eadem, si possum tranquillum facere ex irato mihi.

650 ibo *P*, ilico *Ussing*

Enter ALCESIMARCHUS from his house, carrying a sword and not noticing anyone.

ALC Receive me unto thee, o Death, your friend and well- 640
     wisher.
SEL My dear mother, we're dead, poor us.
ALC Should I strike my side here or on the left?
MEL (*to Selenium*) What's wrong with you?
SEL Can't you see Alcesimarchus? He's holding a sword.
ALC Won't you do something? You're delaying. Leave the
     light.
SEL (*to Melaenis and Halisca*) Please, come to my aid, so that
     he doesn't kill himself!

All three women rush toward him; Halisca drops the casket in the process.

ALC (*spotting Selenium and grabbing her*) O my salvation,
     more saving than Salvation herself! You alone now make 645
     me stay alive, whether I want to or not.
MEL You didn't mean to do that harsh deed.
ALC I have nothing to do with you, to you I'm dead. Now that
     I have this girl, I'm resolved not to let go of her: it's my
     decision to glue her entirely onto me. (*into the house*)
     Where are you, slaves? Lock the house with bolts and
     door-bars at once. I'll carry this girl inside the threshold. 650

Exeunt ALCESIMARCHUS and SELENIUM into his house.

MEL He's left, he's taken the woman away. I'll go, I'll follow
     him in right now, so that he may learn the same things
     from me; maybe I can turn him from angry to calm.

Exeunt MELAENIS and HALISCA into the house of Alcesimarchus.

197

ACTVS IV

IV. i: LAMPADIO. PHANOSTRATA

LAM nullam ego me uidisse credo magis anum excruciabilem
quam illaec est: quae dudum fassa est mihi, quaene in-
fitias eat?

655 sed eccam eram uideo. sed quid hoc est, haec quod cis-
tella hic iacet
cum crepundiis? nec quemquam conspicor alium in uia.
faciundum est puerile officium: conquiniscam ad cistu-
lam.

PHAN quid agis, Lampadio?

LAM   haec cistella numnam hinc ab nobis domo est?
nam hinc ab ostio iacentem sustuli.

PHAN   quid nuntias

660 super anu?

LAM   scelestiorem in terra nullam esse alteram;
omnia infitiari eam, quae dudum confessa est mihi!
nam hercle ego ‹ quam › illam anum irridere me ut sinam,
satiust mihi
quouis exitio interire.

PHAN   di, opsecro uostram fidem!

LAM quid deos opsecras?

PHAN   seruate nos.

LAM   quid est?

PHAN   crepundia

665 haec sunt, quibuscum tu extulisti nostram filiolam ad ne-
cem.

LAM sanane es?

661 infitiare ea *BVE*, infitiare *JK*, infitiari eam *Pontanus*
662 quam *add. Seyffert*

ACT FOUR

Enter LAMPADIO from the right.

LAM   I don't think I've seen an old woman deserving torture
      more than that one does: is she denying what she con-
      fessed to me a moment ago?   655

Enter PHANOSTRATA into her doorway.

      But look, I can see my mistress. But what's this? This cas-
      ket is lying here with a rattle. And I can't see anyone else
      in the street. Now I have to do a boy's part: I'll bend over
      and pick up the casket. (*does so*)

PHAN How are things, Lampadio?

LAM   This casket isn't from here, from our home, is it? I picked
      it up from here, by the door, where it lay.

PHAN What news have you about the old woman?   660

LAM   That there isn't any more crooked creature on earth; she
      denies everything she confessed to me a while ago! It's
      better for me to die any kind of death than to let that old
      woman poke fun at me.

PHAN (*looking at the casket*) Gods, I implore your protection!

LAM   Why are you imploring the gods?

PHAN Save us!

LAM   What's the matter?

PHAN (*taking the casket*) This is the rattle with which you ex- 665
      posed our little daughter to let her die.

LAM   Are you in your right mind?

PHAN   haec sunt profecto.

LAM   pergin?

PHAN   haec sunt.

LAM   si mihi
alia mulier istoc pacto dicat, dicam esse ebriam.

PHAN non ecastor falsa memoro.

LAM   nam, opsecro, unde haec gentium?
aut quis deus obiecit hanc ante ostium nostrum, quasi
670   dedita opera, in tempore ipso?

PHAN   Spes mihi sancta subueni.

IV. ii: HALISCA. LAMPADIO. PHANOSTRATA

HAL   nisi quid mi opis di dant, disperii, neque unde auxilium
        expetam habeo.
        itaque ⟨et⟩ petulantia mea me animi miseram habet ⟨et
        nequitia angit⟩.
        quae in tergum meum ne ueniant male formido,
        si era mea ⟨me⟩ sciat tam socordem esse quam sum.
675   quamne in manibus tenui atque accepi hic ante aedis
        cistellam, ubi ea sit nescio, nisi ut opinor
        loca haec circiter mi excidit.
        mei homines, mei spectatores, facite indicium, si quis ui-
        dit,
        quis eam apstulerit quisu' sustulerit et utrum hac an illac
        iter institerit.
680   non sum scitior quae hos rogem aut quae fatigem,
        qui semper malo muliebri sunt lubentes.
        nunc uestigia hic si qua sunt noscitabo.
        nam si nemo hac praeter iit, postquam intro abii,
        cistella hic iaceret. quid hic? perii, opinor,
685   actum est, ilicet me infelicem et scelestam!

672 et *et* et nequitia angit *add. Schoell*   674 me *add. Leo*

PHAN This really is the one.

LAM Are you going to carry on?

PHAN This is the one.

LAM If any other woman were to speak to me like this, I'd say she's drunk.

PHAN Honestly, I'm not telling lies.

LAM Where on earth does it come from, please? Or what god threw it in front of our door, as if on purpose, right in the 670 nick of time?

PHAN Holy Hope, come to my help!

Enter HALISCA from the house of Alcesimarchus, without noticing anyone.

HAL Unless the gods give me their help, I'm dead, and I don't have anyone to seek help from: my own heedlessness makes me wretched in my heart and my uselessness distresses me. I'm terribly afraid that this might have consequences for my back, if my mistress finds out that I'm as careless as I am. I don't know where the casket is which I 675 held in my hands and received here in front of the house, but I believe it got lost around this area. (*to the audience*) My dear people, my dear spectators, if anyone has seen it, disclose to me who picked it up or who took it away and whether he went this way or that. (*to herself again*) I'm 680 none the wiser for asking or pestering these people, who always take pleasure in the misfortune of women. Now I'll find out if there are any footprints here. Well, if nobody had passed this way after I went in, the casket would still lie here. What's here? I'm ruined, I think, it's over, it's 685

		nulla est, neque ego sum usquam. perdita perdidit me.
		sed pergam ut coepi tamen, quaeritabo.
688		nam et intus paueo et foris formido,
688ᵃ		ita nunc utrubique metus me agitat,
689		ita sunt homines misere miseri.
690		ille nunc laetus est, quisquis est, qui illam habet,
		quae neque illa illi quicquam usui et mi [esse] potest:
		sed memet moror quom hoc ago setius.
		Halisca, hoc age, ad terram aspice et despice,
		oculis inuestiges, astute augura.
695	LAM	era.
	PHAN	hem! [LAM est. PHAN] quid est?
	LAM	haec est.
	PHAN	quis ⟨est⟩?
	LAM	quoi haec excidit cistella.
	PHAN	certe eccam; locum signat, ubi ea excidit: apparet.
	HAL	sed is hac iit, hac socci uideo
		uestigium in puluere, persequar hac.
699		in hoc iam loco cum altero constitit. hic
699ᵃ		meis turba oculis modo se obiecit:
700		nec prorsum iit hac: hic stetit, hinc il-
700ᵃ		lo exiit. hic concilium fuit.
701		ad duos attinet, liquidum est. attat!
701ᵃ		singulum uestigium uideo.
702		sed is hac abiit. contemplabor. hinc huc iit, hinc nusquam abiit.
		actam rem ago. quod periit, periit: meum corium ⟨cum⟩ cistella.
		redeo intro.

691 esse *del. Seyffert*
695 [LAM est. PHAN] *del. Camerarius*   quis ⟨est⟩ *Spengel*

all up with me, unhappy and wretched me! It's nowhere,
and I'm nowhere too. The girl who got lost has made me
get lost. But still, I'll continue as I began, I'll search. Yes,
inside I'm afraid and outside I'm scared, seeing how fear
is driving me mad on both sides and seeing how terri-
bly wretched human beings are. That man who has it is 690
happy now, whoever he is, though it can't be of any use to
him and it can be to me. But I'm delaying myself because
I'm doing this so slowly. Halisca, pay attention, look at
the ground and look down, examine the street with your
eyes, practice augury cleverly. (*stoops down*)

LAM Mistress. 695

PHAN Yes, what is it?

LAM This is her.

PHAN Who is it?

LAM The one who dropped the casket.

PHAN Look at her, it certainly is! She's marking the place where
she dropped it: it's obvious.

HAL (*examining the ground*) But he went this way, along here
I can see the mark of a shoe in the dust; I'll follow this
way. In this place now he stopped with another person.
Here my eyes met with a fracas a moment ago. He didn't 700
continue on this way: he stood here, from here he went
there. Here there was a gathering. It concerns two, that's
obvious. Aha! I can see a single footprint. But he went
away this way. I'll examine it. From here he went here,
from here he never went away. (*pauses*) I'm doing some-
thing that's already done. What's gone is gone: my back
along with the casket. I'm going back inside. (*goes to-
ward the door of the house of Alcesimarchus*)

---

703 cum *add.* Pius

PHAN   mulier, ⟨mane⟩, mane. sunt qui uolunt te conuentam.

705   HAL   quis me reuocat?

LAM   bona femina et malus masculus uolunt te.

HAL   ⟨bona femina et malus masculus uolunt me?⟩ postremo
ille

plus qui uocat scit quod uelit quam ego quae uocor. re-
uortor.

ecquem uidisti quaerere hic, amabo, in hac regione

cistellam cum crepundiis, quam ego hic amisi misera?

710   nam dudum ut accucurrimus ad Alcesimarchum, ne se

uita interemeret, tum ⟨eam mihi opi⟩nor excidisse.

LAM   cistellam haec mulier ⟨perdidit. tace⟩amus, era, parum-
per.

HAL   disperii misera! quid ego [eae] erae dicam? quae me
opere tanto

seruare iussit, qui suos Selenium parentes

715   facilius posset noscere, quae erae [meae] supposita est
parua,

quam quaedam meretrix ei dedit.

LAM   nostram haec rem fabulatur,

hanc scire oportet filia tua ubi sit, signa ut dicit.

HAL   nunc eam uolt suae matri et patri, quibus nata est, red-
dere ultro.

mi homo, opsecro, alias res geris, ego tibi meas res man-
do.

---

704 mane *add. F. Skutsch*
706 bona . . . me *add. Lindsay*
708–22 *secl. Langen et Thierfelder*
711 ⟨eam mihi opi⟩nor *Leo*
712 ⟨perdidit. tace⟩amus *Leo*
713 eae *del. Guyet*   715 meae *del. Bothe*

PHAN Wait, wait, my woman. There are people who want to meet you.

HAL Who is calling me back? 705

LAM A good woman and a bad man want to speak to you.

HAL (*aside*) A good woman and a bad man want to speak to me? Well, after all, the man who is calling me knows better what he wants than I who am being called. I'm returning. (*to Lampadio*) Did you see anyone looking for a casket with a rattle here, in this area, please? Poor me, I lost it here. I believe I dropped it a short while ago, when 710 we were running toward Alcesimarchus to stop him committing suicide.

LAM (*to Phanostrata*) This woman's the one who lost the casket. Let's be quiet for a bit, my mistress.

HAL (*still to Lampadio*) Dear me, I'm ruined! What should I say to my mistress? She told me so strictly to watch over it so that Selenium could recognize her parents more easily 715 with it, the girl who was introduced into my mistress's family when she was little, whom a certain prostitute gave her.

LAM (*to Phanostrata*) She's talking about our business, she ought to know where your daughter is, judging from the indications she's giving.

HAL (*still to Lampadio*) Now she wants to take the initiative in returning her to her mother and father, to whom she was born. My good man, please, you aren't paying attention, I'm entrusting you with my affairs.

720 LAM istuc ago, atque istic mihi cibus est, quod fabulare,
           sed inter rem agendam istam erae huic respondi quod ro-
              gabat.
           nunc ad te redeo: si quid est opus, dice et impera tu.
           quid quaeritabas?
     HAL   mi homo et mea mulier, uos saluto.
     PHAN et nos te. sed quid quaeritas?
     HAL   uestigium hic requiro,
725   qua aufugit quaedam ⟨ac pluribus m⟩aestit⟨iam dat.⟩
     LAM   quid id? quidnam est?
     HAL alienum ⟨concinnat malum⟩ et maerorem familiarem.
     LAM mala merx, era, haec et callida est.
     PHAN   ecastor ita uidetur.
     LAM imitatur nequam bestiam et damnificam.
     PHAN   quamnam, amabo?
     LAM inuoluolum, quae in pampini folio intorta implicat se:
730   itidem haec exorditur sibi intortam orationem.
           quid quaeritas?
     HAL   cistellula hinc mi, adulescens, euolauit.
     LAM in cauea latam oportuit.
     HAL   non edepol praeda magna.
     LAM mirum quin grex uenalium in cistella infuerit una.
     PHAN sine dicat.
     LAM   si dicat quidem.
     PHAN   age loquere [tu] quid ibi infuerit.
735 HAL crepundia una.
     LAM   est quidam homo qui illam ait se scire ubi sit.

       721 rem agendam istam *P*, rem istam agendam *Gulielmius*
       725 ⟨ac pluribus m⟩aestit⟨iam dat⟩ *Leo*
       726 concinnat malum *add. Schoell*
       728 quin nam *BVJ*, quid nam *E*, quamnam *Camerarius*
       732 caueam *P*, cauea *Pylades*   734 tu *del. Leo*

LAM *(finally turning to Halisca)* I *am* paying attention to your   720
    affairs, and what you say is meat and drink to me, but
    while sorting out your business I replied to a question of
    my mistress here. Now I'm returning to you; if you need
    anything, tell me and command me. What were you look-
    ing for?

HAL My dear man and my dear woman, my greetings to you.

PHAN And ours to you. But what are you looking for?

HAL I'm trying to find a footprint here, where something's dis-   725
    appeared and is creating sadness for many.

LAM What's that? What on earth is it?

HAL It'll bring trouble to others and sadness to our household.

LAM My mistress, this woman's a bad piece of work and a sly
    one.

PHAN Yes, that's what she seems like.

LAM She's imitating a wicked animal that causes loss.

PHAN Which one, please?

LAM The caterpillar, the animal which twists around and rolls
    itself up in a vine leaf; in the same way this woman is be-   730
    ginning a twisted speech. *(to Halisca)* What are you look-
    ing for?

HAL A casket flew away from me from here, young man.

LAM It should have been carried in a cage.

HAL There was no great booty in it.

LAM It would be odd if there wasn't a whole group of slaves in
    that one casket.

PHAN Let her speak.

LAM If only she would!

PHAN *(to Halisca)* Come on, say what was inside.

HAL Only a rattle.   735

LAM There's a certain man who says he knows where the cas-
    ket is.

HAL   at pol ille a quadam muliere, si eam monstret, gratiam
       ineat.

LAM   at sibi ille quidam uolt dari mercedem.

HAL   at pol illa quaedam,
       quae illam cistellam perdidit, quoidam negat esse quod
       det.

LAM   at enim ille quidam o⟨peram bonam magis⟩ expetit
       quam argentum.

740 HAL   at pol illi quoidam mulieri nulla opera gratuita est.

PHAN commodule quaedam. tu tibi nunc prodes. confitemur
       cistellam habere.

HAL   at uos Salus seruassit! ubi ea nunc est?

PHAN saluam eccam. sed ego rem meam magnam confabulari
       tecum uolo: sociam te mihi adopto ad meam salutem.

745 HAL   quid istuc negoti est? aut quis es?

PHAN   ego sum illius mater,
       quae haec gestitauit.

HAL   hicine tu ergo habitas?

PHAN   hariolare.
       sed quaeso, ambages, mulier, mitte atque hoc age.
       eloquere, unde haec sunt tibi, cito, crepundia.

HAL   mea haec erilis gestitauit filia.

750 LAM   mentiris, nam mea gestitauit, non tua.

PHAN ne obloquere.

LAM   taceo.

PHAN   mulier, perge dicere.
       ubi ea est quae gestitauit?

HAL   hic in proxumo.

753 PHAN istic quidem edepol mei uiri habitat gener.

739 o⟨peram bonam magis⟩ *Seyffert*

741 commodo loquel(l)am *BVEK*, commoda loquelam *J*, commo-
dule quaedam *Leo* (*cf. Rud. 468*)   tua(m) *P*, tu *Ussing*

HAL   But if he were to show it, he'd receive thanks from a certain woman.

LAM   But that certain man wants to be given a reward.

HAL   But that certain woman who lost that casket says she doesn't have anything to give to the certain man.

LAM   But that certain man is looking for a favor rather than money.

HAL   But with that certain woman no favor goes without a re-   740
ward.

PHAN Nice of that certain woman! You're doing yourself a good turn now. We admit that we have the casket.

HAL   May Salvation keep you both safe! Where is it now?

PHAN (*producing it*) It's safe, look. But I want to talk with you about a matter of the utmost importance to me. I take you as my partner in securing my salvation.

HAL   What business is that? Or who are you?   745

PHAN I'm the mother of the girl who used to wear this.

HAL   So do you live here? (*points to Demipho's house*)

PHAN You're prophesying. But please, woman, stop beating about the bush and pay attention. Tell me quickly where you got this rattle from.

HAL   The daughter of my mistress used to wear it.

LAM   You're lying: the daughter of *my* mistress, not of yours,   750
used to wear it.

PHAN Stop interrupting.

LAM   I'm silent.

PHAN My good woman, continue speaking. Where's the girl who used to carry it?

HAL   Here next door. (*points to the house of Alcesimarchus*)

PHAN My husband's future son-in-law lives there.

753ᵃ   ***

754   PHAN   ne obloquere rursus. perge porro dicere.

755   quot annos nata dicitur?

    HAL   septemdecim.

    PHAN   mea est.

    LAM   ea est: u⟨t numer⟩us annorum attulit.

    HAL   quid? qua⟨esti partem dimidiam⟩ quaero meam.

    LAM   at po⟨l ego, quom duo as⟩sunt, quaero tertiam.

    PHAN   quod quaeritabam, filiam inueni meam.

760   HAL   aequom est ⟨reponi⟩ per fidem quod creditum est,

     ne bene merenti sit malo benignitas.

     nostra haec alumna est, tua profecto filia:

     era reddidura est tuam tibi, et ea gratia

     domo profecta est. ceterum ex ipsa, opsecro,

765   exquaeritote: ego serua sum.

    PHAN   aequom postulas.

    HAL   illius ego istanc esse malo gratiam.

     sed istanc cistellam te opsecro ut reddas mihi.

    PHAN   quid fit, Lampadio?

    LAM   quod tuom est teneas tuom.

    PHAN   at me huius miseret.

    LAM   sic faciundum censeo:

770   da isti cistellam et intro abi cum istac simul.

    PHAN   tibi auscultabo. tene tu cistellam tibi,

     abeamus intro. sed quid ⟨est⟩ nomen tuae

     dominae?

    HAL   Melaenis.

    PHAN   i prae, iam ego te sequar.

    753ᵃ *lacunam indicauit Lambinus*   754 ne obloquere rursus
Lampadioni dant B¹JKE³, Phanostratae dat Palmerius
    756 u⟨t numer⟩us *Camerarius*   757 qua⟨esti partem dimi-
diam⟩ *Schoell*   758 po⟨l ego, quom duo as⟩sunt *Ussing*

***

PHAN (*to Lampadio*) Stop interrupting again. (*to Halisca*)
Speak on. How old do they say she is?   755

HAL Seventeen.

PHAN She's mine.

LAM It's her, to judge from the number of years.

HAL Well then? I'm looking for my half of the reward.

LAM But I, since we're three, am looking for a third.

PHAN I've found what I'd been looking for: my daughter.

HAL It's only fair that what's been entrusted in good faith   760
should be returned, so that a woman doing you a good
turn doesn't get a bad one in return. She's our foster child
and indeed your daughter. My mistress is going to return
your girl to you, and she's set out from home for that very
reason. Please ask her the rest in person: I'm just a slave.   765

PHAN Fair enough.

HAL I'd rather *she* gets the credit for this. But I ask you to re-
turn that casket to me.

PHAN What to do, Lampadio?

LAM Keep as yours what belongs to you.

PHAN But I'm sorry for her.

LAM This is what I think ought to be done: give her the casket   770
and go inside along with her.

PHAN I'll follow your advice. (*to Halisca*) You, take the casket.
Let's go inside. But what's the name of your mistress?

HAL Melaenis.

PHAN Go in front, I'll follow you at once.

*Exeunt HALISCA and PHANOSTRATA into the house of
Alcesimarchus; LAMPADIO waits outside.*

---

760 reponi *add. Leo*   763 et redditura *P*, era redditura
Trappes-Lomax per litteras   772 est *add. Bothe*

ACTVS V

v. i: DEMIPHO. LAMPADIO

DEM quid hoc negoti est, quod omnes homines fabulantur per
      uias

775 mi esse filiam inuentam? et Lampadionem me in foro
      quaesiuisse aiunt.

LAM   ere, unde is?

DEM   ex senatu.

LAM   gaudeo
      tibi mea opera liberorum esse amplius.

DEM   enim non placet.
      nil moror aliena mi opera fieri pluris liberos.
      sed quid istuc est?

LAM   propera ire intro huc ad affinem tuom,

780 filiam tuam iam cognosces intus. ibidem uxor tua est.
      abi cito.

DEM   praeuorti hoc certum est rebus aliis omnibus.

v. ii: GREX

GREX ne exspectetis, spectatores, dum illi huc ad uos exeant:
      nemo exibit, omnes intus conficient negotium.
      ubi id erit factum, ornamenta ponent; postidea loci

785 qui deliquit uapulabit, qui non deliquit bibet.
      nunc quod ad uos, spectatores, relicuom relinquitur,
      more maiorum date plausum postrema in comoedia.

ACT FIVE

Enter DEMIPHO from the right.

DEM   What's this business that everybody's talking about in every street that my daughter has been found? And they say 775
      Lampadio has been looking for me in the forum.

LAM   Master, where are you coming from?

DEM   From the senate.

LAM   I'm happy that you now have more children through my efforts.

DEM   I don't like it. I don't care for getting more children through another's efforts. But what is it?

LAM   Quickly go in here to your relative by marriage. (*points to the house of Alcesimarchus*) You'll recognize your daugh- 780
      ter inside at once. Your wife's also there. Off with you, quickly!

DEM   I'm resolved to sort this out before anything else.

Exeunt DEMIPHO and LAMPADIO into the house of Alcesimarchus.
Enter the whole TROUPE.

TROUPE   In case you're waiting, spectators, for those people to come out here to you, no one will come out, they'll all sort out their business inside. When this is done, they'll put away their costumes. Then anyone who made a mistake 785
will get a beating and anyone who made no mistake will get a drink. Now what remains for you, spectators, is this: following the custom of your forefathers give us your applause at the end of the comedy.

PLAUTUS

FRAGMENTA INCERTAE SEDIS

xiv malum aufer, bonum mi opus est.
xv summatim
xvi benigniter

FRAGMENTA DVBIA

xvii scrattae, scrupipedae, strittabillae, sordidae
xviii cistellam mi offers cum crepundiis.

Fragments xiv–xvi belong to our comedy, but are difficult to lo-
cate precisely.[15] *It is unclear whether fr. xvii and xviii belong to*
our play as well.[16] *If they do, fr. xvii must come from Lampadio's*
monologue in which he reports what types of prostitutes he saw
during his search for Gymnasium's mother. The meaning of fr.
xviii would make it go well with the later parts of the play where
the casket and rattle make their appearance, but here the text is
complete again and the line does not seem to fit in anywhere.

Take away the bad one, I need a good one.	xiv
summarily	xv
benevolently	xvi
wretched, bony, tottering, dirty women	xvii
You're bringing me a casket with a rattle.	xviii

[15] Fr. xiv: Non. p. 773 Lindsay, *mihi opus est* "I need" can take the accusative instead of the ablative. Fr. xv: Gloss. *Plaut. gramm.* iii. 58. 4, Plautus uses the word *summatim*. Fr. xvi: Gloss. *Plaut. gramm.* iii. 58. 5, Plautus uses the word *benigniter*.

[16] Fr. xvii: quoted by Varro *ling.* 7. 65 as being "in the same place," which could refer to the *Cistellaria*; but Gell. 3. 3. 6 assigns the verse to the *Neruolaria*. Fr. xviii: Fulg. *serm. ant.* 124. 9–11 Helm glosses *cistella* as *capsella* "little container," but says about the provenance of the line only that it comes from Plautus.

CURCULIO

INTRODUCTORY NOTE

The *Curculio* is easily overlooked: with its little more than
seven hundred lines, it is Plautus' shortest comedy, and
with its array of stock characters and stock scenes, it ap-
pears entirely unremarkable at first sight. Phaedromus is
the ordinary love-sick young man; Planesium is the chaste
girl who is enslaved; Cappadox is an evil pimp; and Thera-
pontigonus Platagidorus is the standard boastful soldier.
The eponymous hero of the play, Curculio ("Weevil"), is a
typical hanger-on, clever and always hungry. Many motifs
of the comedy can also hardly be described as out of the
ordinary: there is a running-slave scene in ll. 280–98
(although strictly speaking the runner, Curculio, is not
a slave) and a recognition scene in ll. 635–58, in which
Planesium turns out to be freeborn and the sister of Thera-
pontigonus. Nevertheless, the *Curculio* is not a boring
play. There are certain innovations; for instance, the motif
of the *paraclausithyron*, the song in front of the door of
one's beloved, makes its first appearance in Latin literature
here (ll. 147–55). More important, because the play is so
short, it is unusually fast-paced, and this speed is only pos-
sible because of its particularly neat and clear plot con-
struction. That does not mean that there are no incon-
sistencies or oddities at all; I shall look at some below,

because they seem to show us how Plautus adapted and shortened his Greek original.

The play begins at night. Phaedromus, accompanied by his witty slave Palinurus, goes to the house of the pimp Cappadox to meet his beloved Planesium behind the pimp's back. Cappadox himself is not around: he usually sleeps in the temple of Aesculapius, the god of healing, as he suffers from a liver disease and hopes to be cured by divine intervention. Phaedromus tells Palinurus that Planesium does not yet work as a prostitute and that he cannot afford to buy her. For this reason he sent his hanger-on, Curculio, to Caria, where he is supposed to borrow money from a friend of Phaedromus.

Incidentally, this Caria can hardly be the region Caria, which is in what is now Turkey; our play is situated in Epidaurus, and the hanger-on is supposed to travel to Caria and back in four days (ll. 206–7). What is more, the Caria of our play is described as a town with a market (l. 336), and later in the play (l. 443) the real Carians are mentioned among distant peoples. Perhaps the Plautine city Caria is Calauria on the Peloponnesus.

When Phaedromus arrives at the pimp's door, he sprinkles some wine in front of it. The doorkeeper, the old woman Leaena, who is always keen on drink, smells it and comes out quickly. In exchange for a jug of wine she brings out Planesium. The ensuing conversation between Phaedromus and his girl would be romantic were it not for the constant interruptions by Palinurus, who in this respect resembles Sosia in the *Amphitruo* or the hanger-on Peniculus in the *Menaechmi*.

Planesium has to leave at daybreak, which is when the pimp returns. On his way back he meets Palinurus and then a cook working for Phaedromus. The cook interprets the pimp's dream, which indicates that Aesculapius does not want to heal him. At this point Curculio returns and tells Phaedromus that his friend did not have any money to spare. However, his news is not entirely negative. He met a soldier, Therapontigonus Platagidorus, and dined with him. It transpired that the soldier has an agreement with Cappadox and the banker Lyco. He deposited money at the banker's and this sum is meant to be given to Cappadox in exchange for Planesium. Curculio managed to steal the soldier's signet ring. Now he has Phaedromus write a letter to the banker and seal it with that ring.

Curculio then goes to the banker in disguise and claims to be the soldier's freedman Summanus. He convinces him partly through his behavior and partly through the seal on the letter. The banker takes Curculio to Cappadox, where the pimp receives his money and Curculio gets the girl.

The soldier arrives not much later and goes to the banker to get the money for Planesium. Naturally, he gets very angry when the banker refuses to pay on the grounds that he has already given the money to his freedman Summanus. Next Therapontigonus goes to see Cappadox, who informs him that his freedman Summanus has taken the girl away. Only at this point does the soldier realize that it was Curculio who tricked him.

In the meantime, Curculio went to Phaedromus and handed over the girl. She saw the ring Curculio had stolen from the soldier and recognized it as her father's signet ring. She asked him for it because it could help her to find her family. Curculio, however, thought that she simply

wanted to steal a beautiful ring and ran away with it. Phae-
dromus manages to catch Curculio. He says that the ring
belongs to the soldier, who arrives at this very point.
When he sees all three together, Phaedromus, Curculio,
and Planesium, he demands the girl. Planesium asks him
where he got his ring and he says it used to be worn by his
father. Planesium and Therapontigonus realize that they
are brother and sister, and the soldier promises to betroth
his sister to Phaedromus. Therapontigonus has thus lost
his love but regained his sister. In the end he also regains
his money, since it is illegal to buy and sell freeborn girls;
for this reason the pimp had guaranteed to return Thera-
pontigonus' money to him should anyone claim the girl as
freeborn. He does so, but very unwillingly. The ending
of the play is thus happy in every respect: Phaedromus
and Planesium can marry, Therapontigonus has found his
sister, Curculio is promised free food for good, and the
wicked pimp has received a fair punishment.

We know neither the author nor the title of the Greek
play on which the *Curculio* was based, but it must have
been longer, since the Plautine comedy exhibits clear signs
of compression. First, it was standard practice in Greek
New Comedy, a practice normally followed by Plautus as
well, to state explicitly in a prologue which city the stage
represents, unless that city is Athens. The *Curculio* takes
place in Epidaurus, but we only learn this in l. 341. Either
Plautus omitted the Greek prologue or, if he translated it,
it was lost in the process of textual transmission. Similarly,
it is not immediately obvious why Phaedromus is so anx-
ious that he sends his hanger-on to get money from a
friend. This behavior would be more in line with an emer-

gency situation, and it seems likely there was such an emergency situation in the Greek original, where the soldier's arrival was presumably imminent and Phaedromus, well aware of having a rival, was forced to act quickly. Perhaps we can still see traces of the structure of the Greek original in the period of three days mentioned in l. 208 and the phrase "win with the highest bid" in l. 213; the former points to a deadline set by the pimp, who had probably promised Phaedromus not to sell the girl before it (see l. 458), and the latter implies a wealthy rival. When Plautus shortened the text he was working on, he obscured these plot elements. What is more, Plautus had no qualms about treating the encounter between Curculio and the soldier as friendly and intimate (ll. 338–50) without telling us why it should be thus; did the soldier and Curculio know each other from before? Again we get the feeling that something essential was lost when Plautus cut out what he deemed unimportant. However, despite such minor flaws, the play runs along smoothly and elegantly.

It is uncertain when the *Curculio* was first performed. The gold Philippics referred to in l. 440 do not occur in Greek New Comedy and hence cannot come from the original; they first became more widely known in Rome after Titus Quinctius Flaminius won the war against Macedonia in 194BC. The *rogitationes plurumas*, the "countless bills" against bankers mentioned to in ll. 509–11, could conceivably allude to a law presented to and accepted by the people by Marcus Sempronius Tuditanus in 193; this law stated that the same rules concerning moneylending should apply to Roman citizens and to the inhabitants of allied cities. The existence of other Plautine additions to the *Curculio* is more than doubtful. However, the amount of song in this play points in the same direction as the two allusions discussed: the later a play, the more song it contains, and since the *Curculio* seems to have an average amount, it probably belongs to the middle period of Plautus' work.

SELECT BIBLIOGRAPHY

Editions and Commentaries

Collart, J. C. (1962), *T. Maccius Plautus: Curculio; Plaute: Charançon; édition, introduction et commentaire* (Paris).

Lanciotti, S. (2008), *Titus Maccius Plautus: Curculio* (Urbino).

Monaco, G. (1969), *Plauto: Curculio* (Palermo).

Criticism

Bosscher, H. (1903), *De Plauti Curculione disputatio* (diss., Louvain).

Fantham, E. (1965), "The *Curculio* of Plautus: An Illustration of Plautine Methods in Adaptation," in *Classical Quarterly* NS 15: 84–100.

Legrand, Ph.-E. (1905), "Observations sur le 'Curculio,'" in *Revue des Études Anciennes* 7: 25–29.

Lefèvre, E. (1991), "Curculio oder Der Triumph der Edazität," in E. Lefèvre, E. Stärk, and G. Vogt-Spira (eds.), *Plautus Barbarus: Sechs Kapitel zur Originalität des Plautus* (Tübingen), 71–105.

Paratore, E. (1962), "*Antestor* nel *Curculio* e nel *Poenulus*," in *Dioniso* 36: 98–122.

Raffaelli, R., and Tontini, A. (eds.) (2005), *Lecturae Plautinae Sarsinates VIII: Curculio (Sarsina, 25 settembre 2004)* (Urbino).

Walsh, J. T. (2006), "Cato, Plautus, and the Metaphorical Use of *anulus*," in *Phoenix* 60: 133–39.

CVRCVLIO

ARGVMENTVM

Curculio missu Phaedromi it Cariam
Vt petat argentum. ibi eludit anulo
Riualem. scribit atque opsignat litteras.
Cognoscit signum Lyco, ubi uidit, militis.
5 **V**t amicam mittat pretium lenoni dedit.
Lyconem miles ac lenonem in ius rapit.
Ipsus sororem, quam peribat, repperit,
Oratu quoius Phaedromo nuptum locat.

PERSONAE

PALINVRVS seruos
PHAEDROMVS adulescens
LEAENA anus
PLANESIVM uirgo
CAPPADOX leno
COQVOS
CVRCVLIO parasitus
LYCO tarpezita
CHORAGVS
THERAPONTIGONVS miles

CURCULIO

PLOT SUMMARY

At the behest of Phaedromus, Curculio goes to Caria in order to
ask for money. There he tricks the rival of Phaedromus out of
his ring. He has Phaedromus write and seal a letter. When Lyco
sees the seal, he recognizes it as the soldier's. He gives the pimp 5
his payment so that he can send off the girlfriend. The soldier
drags Lyco and the pimp to court. He finds out that the girl he
was in love with is his sister. At her request he gives her in mar-
riage to Phaedromus.

CHARACTERS

PALINURUS a slave; belongs to Phaedromus
PHAEDROMUS a young man; loves Planesium
LEAENA an old woman; works in the pimp's establishment
PLANESIUM a young girl; owned by the pimp, but chaste
CAPPADOX a pimp; very ill
COOK works for Phaedromus
CURCULIO a hanger-on; the main character of the play, got
his nickname ("Weevil") because of his appetite
LYCO a banker; of disreputable character
SUPPLIER OF COSTUMES only makes a brief appearance,
has no real role in the play
THERAPONTIGONUS a soldier; also loves Planesium

PLAUTUS

SCAENA

Epidauri

228

STAGING

The stage represents a street in Epidaurus. In its middle is the sanctuary of Aesculapius. To its left there is the pimp's house, in front of which stands an altar for Venus. To the right of the sanctuary of Aesculapius we find the house of Phaedromus. On this side, the street leads to the market. On the other side, it leads out of the city.

ACTVS I

I. i: PALINVRVS. PHAEDROMVS

PAL quo ted hoc noctis dicam proficisci foras
     cum istoc ornatu cumque hac pompa, Phaedrome?
PHAE quo Venus Cupidoque imperat, suadetque Amor:
     si media nox est siue est prima uespera,
5   si status, condictus cum hoste intercedit dies,
     tamen est eundum quo imperant ingratiis.
PAL at tandem, tandem—
PHAE   tandem es odiosus mihi.
PAL istuc quidem nec bellum est nec memorabile:
     tute tibi puer es, lautus luces cereum.
10 PHAE egon apicularum opera congestum non feram
     ex dulci oriundum melliculo dulci meo?
PAL nam quo te dicam ego ire?
PHAE   si tu me roges,
     dicam ut scias.
PAL   si rogitem, quid respondeas?
PHAE hoc Aesculapi fanum est.
PAL   plus iam anno scio.
15 PHAE huic proxumum illud ostium <est> oculissumum.
     salue, ualuistin?

11 melliculo *P*, melculo *testari uidetur Gloss. I Ansil. ME 434 L. si
huc attinet*
     15 est *add. Pylades*

ACT ONE

Enter PHAEDROMUS from his house, holding a candle, followed by some slaves, one with a jug of wine, and by PALINURUS.

PAL   Where should I say you're going out to at this time of night, with that dress and with this accompaniment, Phaedromus?

PHAE Where Venus and Cupid command me, and Love urges me to go. If it's midnight or early evening, if a court date   5 firmly settled on with your adversary from outside comes in between, one still has to go where they command despite oneself.

PAL   But see here, see here—

PHAE *(interrupting)* See here, you're getting on my nerves.

PAL   That isn't a pretty sight or one to talk about: you're playing your own slave, and elegantly turned out you light your candle.

PHAE Shouldn't I bring to my sweet little honey the product of   10 the bees' industry coming from stores of sweet?

PAL   Where on earth should I say you're going?

PHAE If you were to ask me, I'd tell you so you know.

PAL   If I were to ask you, what would you reply?

PHAE This is the shrine of Aesculapius. *(points to it as they approach it)*

PAL   I've known that for more than a year already.

PHAE Next to it is that door most dear. *(still at a distance from   15 the pimp's door)* Greetings, have you been well?

231

PAL	ostium occlusissumum,
	caruitne febris te heri uel nudiustertius
	et heri cenauistine?
PHAE	deridesne me?
PAL	quid tu ergo, insane, rogitas ualeatne ostium?
20	PHAE	bellissumum hercle uidi et taciturnissumum,
	numquam ullum uerbum muttit: quom aperitur tacet,
	⟨et⟩ quom illa noctu clanculum ad me exit tacet.
PAL	numquid tu quod te aut genere indignum sit tuo
	facis aut inceptas facinus facere, Phaedrome?
25		num tu pudicae quoipiam insidias locas
	aut quam pudicam esse oportet?
PHAE	nemini;
	nec me ille sirit Iuppiter!
PAL	ego item uolo.
	ita tuom conferto amare semper, si sapis,
	ne id quod ames populus si sciat, tibi sit probro.
30		semper curato ne sis intestabilis.
32	PHAE	quid istuc est uerbi?
PAL	caute ut incedas uia:
31		quod amas amato testibus praesentibus.
33	PHAE	quin leno hic habitat.
PAL	nemo hinc prohibet nec uotat
	quin quod palam est uenale, si argentum est, emas.
35		nemo ire quemquam publica prohibet uia;
	dum ne per fundum saeptum facias semitam,
	dum ted apstineas nupta, uidua, uirgine,
	iuuentute et pueris liberis, ama quidlubet.

22 et *add. Lindsay in apparatu*
26 esse oportet *P, transp. Pylades*
31–32 *transp. Bothe*

232

PAL   Door most shut, did the fever spare you yesterday or the
      day before[1] and did you have dinner yesterday?

PHAE Are you mocking me?

PAL   Then why do you ask if the door is well, you idiot?

PHAE It's the most charming and most silent door I've ever   20
      seen, it never utters a single word: when it's opened it's
      silent and when she comes out to me secretly at night it's
      silent.

PAL   Are you doing anything that's unworthy of you or your
      family, or are you beginning to do anything of this sort,
      Phaedromus? Are you setting a trap for any chaste   25
      woman, or one who ought to be chaste?

PHAE Certainly not; Jupiter above forbid!

PAL   I wish so too. If you're smart, always handle your love in
      such a way that if the people know the object of your love
      it isn't a disgrace for you. Always make sure you can call 30
      on someone to testify.

PHAE What do you mean?

PAL   Tread carefully on your road: love what you love in the
      presence of your testifiers.[2]

PHAE Well, a pimp lives here.

PAL   Nobody stops or prevents you from buying from here
      what's openly for sale, if you have the money. Nobody   35
      forbids anyone to go on a public road. So long as you
      don't take a path through a fenced property, so long as
      you stay away from the married woman, the widow, the
      virgin, the youth, and freeborn boys, love whatever you
      like.

[1] The fever referred to is probably malaria, hence the intermissions.

[2] *Testis* can mean "witness" as well as "testicle." Adulterers could be
castrated.

PHAE lenonis hae sunt aedes.

PAL   male istis euenat!

40 PHAE qui?

PAL   quia scelestam seruitutem seruiunt.

PHAE obloquere.

PAL   fiat maxume.

PHAE   etiam taces?

PAL   nempe obloqui me iusseras.

PHAE   at nunc uoto.
       ⟨sed⟩ ita uti occepi dicere: ei ancillula est.

PAL   nempe huic lenoni qui hic habitat?

PHAE   recte tenes.

45 PAL   minus formidabo, ne excidat.

PHAE   odiosus es.
       eam uolt meretricem facere. ea me deperit,
       ego autem cum illa facere nolo mutuom.

PAL   quid ita?

PHAE   quia proprium facio: amo pariter simul.

PAL   malus clandestinus est amor, damnum est merum.

50 PHAE est hercle ita ut tu dicis.

PAL   iamne ea fert iugum?

PHAE tam a me pudica est quasi soror mea sit, nisi
       si est osculando quippiam impudicior.

PAL   semper tu scito, flamma fumo est proxuma;
       fumo comburi nil potest, flamma potest.

39 eueniat *P*, euenat *Muretus*
43 id uti *B*, induti *VE*, indutias *E³*, inducias *K*, . . . as *J*, sed ita uti *Reiz*

---

³ *Obloquere* can be an indicative, which is the meaning Phaedromus intends, but also an imperative, which is Palinurus' malevolent interpretation.

234

CURCULIO

PHAE This is the house of a pimp.
PAL Bad luck to it!
PHAE Why?   40
PAL Because it serves in scandalous slavery.
PHAE (*annoyed*) That's it, interrupt me.[3]
PAL Yes, by all means.
PHAE Won't you be quiet now?
PAL But you told me to interrupt you.
PHAE But now I forbid you. But as I was about to say: he has a
      slave girl.
PAL You mean the pimp who lives here?
PHAE You've got it.
PAL Then I'll be less afraid of losing it.   45
PHAE You're getting on my nerves. He wants to turn her into a
      prostitute. She is madly in love with me, but I don't want
      to return her love.[4]
PAL How is that?
PHAE Because I want to keep it for my very own: I love her just
      as much.
PAL A secret love affair is bad, it's pure loss.
PHAE Yes, it's just as you say.   50
PAL Does she already carry the yoke?
PHAE From me she's as chaste as if she were my sister, unless
      she's somewhat less chaste from kissing.
PAL Always keep this in mind: flame is the next thing to
      smoke. Nothing can be burned by smoke, but anything

[4] Pun on the two meanings of *mutuom*: Phaedromus jokes that he
does not want the girl's love "on loan," i.e. for a short time only, but
Palinurus thinks he means he does not want to love her "mutually,"
which is a more natural interpretation of his master's words.

235

55   qui e nuce nuculeum esse uolt, frangit nucem:
        qui uolt cubare, pandit saltum sauiis.
PHAE   at illa est pudica necdum cubitat cum uiris.
PAL   credam, pudor si quoiquam lenoni siet.
PHAE   immo ut illam censes? ut quaeque illi occasio est
60   surrupere se ad me, ubi sauium oppegit, fugit.
        id eo fit, quia hic leno, ‹hic qui› aegrotus incubat
        in Aesculapi fano, is me excruciat.
PAL   quid est?
PHAE   alias me poscit pro illa triginta minas,
        alias talentum magnum; nec quicquam queo
65   aequi bonique ab eo impetrare.
PAL   iniuriu's
        qui quod lenoni nulli est id ab eo petas.
PHAE   nunc hinc parasitum in Cariam misi meum
        petitum argentum a meo sodali mutuom.
        quod si non affert, quo me uortam nescio.
70 PAL si deos salutas, dextrouorsum censeo.
PHAE   nunc ara Veneris haec est ante horunc fores;
        me inferre Veneri uoui iaientaculum.
PAL   quid? ‹te› antepones Veneri iaientaculo?
PHAE   me, te atque hosce omnis.
PAL   tum tu Venerem uomere uis.
75 PHAE cedo, puere, sinum.
PAL   quid facturu's?
PHAE   iam scies.
        anus hic solet cubare custos ianitrix,
        nomen Leaenae est, multibiba atque merobiba.

        61 hic qui *add.* Leo
        73 te *add.* Müller, an te pones *Pontanus*

can be burned by flame. He who wants to eat the kernel 55
from a nut breaks the nut. He who wants to sleep with a
woman opens up her passage with kisses.

PHAE But she's chaste and doesn't sleep with men yet.

PAL I'd believe it if any pimp had chastity.

PHAE On the contrary; what do you think she's like? Whenever
she has the opportunity, she comes over to me furtively, 60
and when she's planted a kiss on me, she runs away. It
happens like that because this pimp is torturing me, the
sick man who sleeps in the sanctuary of Aesculapius.

PAL How so?

PHAE At one time he demands thirty minas for her from me, at
another, an Attic talent, and I can't get anything decent or 65
just out of him.

PAL It's unfair of you to demand from him what no pimp has.

PHAE Now I sent my hanger-on off to Caria to ask a friend of
mine to lend me the money. If he doesn't bring it, I don't
know where to turn to.

PAL If you're greeting the gods, I should think to the right. 70
(points to the altar of Venus)

PHAE Now there's this altar of Venus in front of their door. I
vowed to offer myself a breakfast to Venus.

PAL What? You'll offer yourself a breakfast to Venus?[5]

PHAE Yes, myself, yourself, and all these here.

PAL Then you want Venus to vomit.

PHAE Boy, give me the jug. (takes it from him) 75

PAL What are you going to do?

PHAE You'll know in a moment. Normally an old woman sleeps
here, the guardian and keeper of the door. Her name is
Leaena. She's a great drinker of undiluted wine.

---

[5] Phaedromus uses *me* as subject accusative, Palinurus deliberately
misunderstands it as object.

PAL   quasi tu lagoenam dicas, ubi uinum Chium
      solet esse.
PHAE   quid opust uerbis? uinosissuma est;
80   eaque extemplo ubi‹ubi› uino has conspersi fores,
      de odore adesse me scit, aperit ilico.
PAL   eine hic cum uino sinus fertur?
PHAE   nisi neuis.
PAL   nolo hercle, nam istunc qui fert afflictum uelim;
      ego nobis [af]ferri censui.
PHAE   quin tu taces?
85   si quid super illi fuerit, id nobis sat est.
PAL   quisnam istic fluuiust quem non recipiat mare?
PHAE sequere hac, Palinure, me ad fores, fi mi opsequens.
PAL   ita faciam.
PHAE   agite bibite, festiuae fores;
      potate, fite mihi uolentes propitiae.
90 PAL uoltisne oliuas, [aut] pulpamentum, [aut] capparim?
PHAE exsuscitate uostram huc custodem mihi.
PAL   profundis uinum: quae te res agitant?
PHAE   sine.
      uiden ut aperiuntur aedes festiuissumae?
      num muttit cardo? est lepidus.
PAL   quin das sauium?
95 PHAE tace, occultemus lumen et uocem.
PAL   licet.

80 ubi *P*, ubiubi *Lindsay*, ubi ego *Guyet*
84 afferri *P*, ferri *Bentley*
90 aut *utrumque del. Muretus*

PAL As if you were calling her a bottle which is usually full of wine from Chios.[6]

PHAE What need is there for words? She's a great lover of wine. 80
Whenever I sprinkle this door with wine, she immediately knows from the smell that I'm here and opens straightaway.

PAL Is this jug of wine being brought for *her*?

PHAE Unless you object.

PAL I do object: I want to see the person carrying it struck down. I thought it was being brought for us.

PHAE Why won't you be quiet? If she leaves any, that's enough 85
for us.

PAL What river is there which the sea cannot swallow up?

PHAE Palinurus, follow me this way to the door, be obedient to me.

PAL Yes, I will.

PHAE (*sprinkling some wine*) Go on, drink, dearest door; imbibe and be favorable and well-disposed toward me.

PAL (*also addressing the door*) Would you like olives, meat, or 90
capers?

PHAE (*still to the door*) Wake up and send out your guardian here to me.

PAL (*to Phaedromus*) You're pouring out wine; what's wrong with you?

PHAE Let it be. Can't you see how the dearest house is opening up? Is the hinge muttering? No, it's lovely.

PAL Why don't you give it a kiss?

PHAE Be quiet, let's conceal the light and our voices. 95

PAL Okay. (*they step back*)

---

[6] Island in the Aegean Sea, largest exporter of Greek wine in antiquity. There is a pun on *Leaena* and *lagoena* "bottle."

I. ii: LEAENA. PHAEDROMVS. PALINVRVS

96	LEAE	flos ueteris uini meis naribus obiectust,
96ᵃ 97 97ᵃ		eius amor cupidam me huc prolicit per tenebras. ubiubi est, prope me est. euax, habeo!
98		salue, anime mi, Liberi lepos.
98ᵃ		ut ueteris uetus tui cupida sum!
99		nam omnium unguentum odor prae tuo nautea est,
100		tu mihi stacta, tu cinnamum, tu rosa,
101– 2 103– 4 105		tu crocinum et casia es, tu telinum, nam ubi tu profusu's, ibi ego me peruelim sepultam. sed quom adhuc naso odos opsecutust meo, da uicissim meo gutturi gaudium. nil ago tecum: ubi est ipsus? ipsum expeto tangere, inuergere in me liquores tuos, sine, ductim. sed hac abiit, hac persequar.
110	PHAE	sitit haec anus.
	PAL	quantillum sitit?
	PHAE	modica est, capit quadrantal.
110ᵃ	PAL	pol ut praedicas, uindemia haec huic anu non satis est soli.
110ᵇ		canem esse hanc quidem magis par fuit: sagax nasum habet.
	LEAE	amabo,
111		quoia uox sonat procul?
	PHAE	censeo hanc appellandam anum.
113		adibo. redi et respice ad me, Leaena.
113ᵃ	LEAE	imperator quis est?

---

[7] Bacchus, the god of wine.

[8] A *quadrantal* is a cubic foot.

Enter LEAENA from the pimp's house, sniffing.

LEAE My nostrils have been offered the flowery scent of old
 wine. Love for him is driving my eager self out here
 through the darkness. Wherever he is, he's close to me.
 (*kneels down at the door, sniffing*) Hurray, I have him!   98
 Greetings, my life, lure of Liber.[7] How I, an old one, am
 keen on you, another old one! Yes, the smell of all per-
 fumes is puke compared with yours, you are my myrrh,   100
 you my cinnamon, you my rose, you my saffron and my
 cassia, you my ointment of fenugreek: where you are
 poured out, there I desire to be buried. (*pauses and*   105
 stands up again) But while the only thing so far has been
 that the smell has satisfied the desires of my nose, now
 give joy to my gullet in turn. I have no business with you;
 where is he himself? I desire to touch you yourself, dear
 jug, to pour your liquid contents into me in great gulps.
 (*following the scent like a bloodhound*) But he went away
 this way, I'll follow him this way.

PHAE (*to Palinurus*) This old woman's thirsty.   110

PAL How small is her thirst?

PHAE She's moderate, she'll take in an amphora.[8]

PAL Seriously, the way you're talking, this year's harvest of
 grapes isn't enough for this old woman alone. It would
 have been more appropriate for her to be a dog: she has a
 keen nose.

LEAE Please, whose voice sounds in the distance?

PHAE (*to Palinurus*) I think I should to address this old woman.
 I'll approach her. (*to Leaena*) Come back and look at me,
 Leaena.

LEAE Who is in command?

241

114	PHAE	uinipollens lepidus Liber,
115		tibi qui screanti, siccae, semisomnae
		affert potionem et sitim sedatum it.
	LEAE	quam longe a med abest?
	PHAE	lumen hoc uide.
	LEAE	grandiorem gradum ergo fac ad me, opsecro.
119	PHAE	salue.
	LEAE	egon salua sim, quae siti sicca sum?
	PHAE	at
119ᵃ		iam bibes.
	LEAE	diu fit.
120	PHAE	em tibi, anus lepida.
	LEAE	salue, oculissume homo.
	PAL	age, effunde hoc cito in barathrum, propere prolue cloa-
		cam.
	PHAE	tace. nolo huic male dici.
	PAL	faciam igitur male potius.
	LEAE	Venus, de paulo paululum hoc tibi dabo hau lubenter.
		nam tibi amantes propitiantes uinum dant potantes
125		omnes [homines], mihi hau saepe [e]ueniunt tales here-
		ditates.
126–27	PAL	hoc uide ut ingurgitat impura in se merum auariter, fau-
		cibus plenis.
128–29	PHAE	perii hercle! huic quid primum dicam nescio.
	PAL	em istuc, quod mi dixti.
130	PHAE	quid id est?
	PAL	periisse ut te dicas.
	PHAE	male tibi di faciant!

123 hic *P*, hoc *S*
125 homines *del. Camerarius* eueniunt *P*, ueniunt *Lindsay*, eue-
nunt *Fleckeisen*

PHAE Lovely Liber, lord of liquor, who is bringing drink to you, 115
a hawking, dry, drowsy creature, and who is going to
quench your thirst.

LEAE How far is he away from me?

PHAE Look at this light. (*holds it up*)

LEAE Then take bigger steps toward me, please. (*the men approach her and stop in front of her*)

PHAE Be well.

LEAE I should be well, even though I'm dry?

PHAE But you'll drink in a moment.

LEAE It's a long time coming.

PHAE (*handing over the jug*) Here you are, my charming old 120
lady.

LEAE (*to Phaedromus*) Hello, dearest of all men.

PAL (*to Leaena*) Go on, pour it into the pit quickly and flush
the sewer fast.

PHAE (*to Palinurus*) Be quiet. I don't want harsh words spoken
to her.

PAL Then I'll rather *do* harsh things.

LEAE (*sprinkling a few drops on the altar*) Venus, from the little I have I'll give you this very little portion, and not with
pleasure: all lovers trying to seek your favor and drinking
give you wine, but such legacies don't often come to me. 125

PAL (*to Phaedromus*) Look at that, how the filthy creature's
pouring undiluted wine into herself greedily, her maws
full.

PHAE I'm really done for! I don't know what I shall say to this
woman first.

PAL Well, the very thing you said to me.

PHAE What's that? 130

PAL Say to her that you're done for.

PHAE May the gods treat you badly!

	PAL	dic isti.
131	LEAE	ah!
	PAL	quid est? ecquid lubet?
	LEAE	lubet.
	PAL	etiam mihi quoque stimulo fodere lubet te.
131ᵃ	PHAE	tace.
	PAL	noli, taceo. ecce autem bibit arcus, pluet credo
		hercle hodie.
132	PHAE	iamne ego huic dico?
	PAL	quid dices?
	PHAE	me periisse.
	PAL	age dice.
	PHAE	anus, audi.
		hoc uolo scire te: perditus sum miser.
	LEAE	at pol ego oppido seruata.
135		sed quid est? quid lubet perditum dicere
		te esse?
	PHAE	quia id quod amo careo.
	LEAE	Phaedrome mi, ne plora, amabo.
		tu me curato ne sitiam, ego tibi quod amas iam huc addu-
		cam.
139	PHAE	tibine ego, si fidem seruas mecum,
139ᵃ		uineam pro aurea statua statuam,
140		quae tuo gutturi sit monumentum.
141		qui me in terra aeque fortuna-
141ᵃ		tus erit, si illa ad me bitet,
142		Palinure?

PAL   Yes, tell her that.

LEAE   (*loudly*) Ah!

PAL   (*to Leaena*) What is it? Do you like it?

LEAE   I do like it.

PAL   And *I* would like to poke you with a cattle prod.

PHAE   Be quiet. (*hits him*)

PAL   Don't! I'm quiet. (*after a short pause*) But look, the rainbow is drinking, I do think it'll rain today.[9]

PHAE   Shall I tell her now?

PAL   What will you tell her?

PHAE   That I'm done for.

PAL   Go on, tell her.

PHAE   Old lady, listen. I want you to know this: I'm done for, poor me.

LEAE   But *I* am completely saved. But what is it? Why do you 135
wish to say you're done for?

PHAE   Because I lack what I love. (*sobs*)

LEAE   My dear Phaedromus, stop crying, please. You make sure
that I'm not thirsty and I shall bring here at once what
you love.

PHAE   Yes, if you keep your word towards me, I'll set up a vineyard for you instead of a golden statue, as a monument to 140
your gullet. (*to Palinurus*) Who on earth will be as fortunate as me if she comes to me, Palinurus?

Exit LEAENA into the pimp's house; she closes the door again.

[9] The rainbow was believed to suck up liquid on the ground and
transport it back to heaven, hence Statius' *imbrifer arcus* "rain-bringing
rainbow" (*Theb.* 7. 427).

PAL   edepol qui amat, si eget, misera affligitur aerumna.
PHAE non ita res est, nam confido parasitum hodie aduenturum
      cum argento ad me.
PAL   magnum inceptas, si id exspectas quod nusquam est.
145 PHAE quid si adeam ad fores atque occentem?
PAL   si lubet, nec uoto nec iubeo,
      quando ego te uideo immutatis moribus esse, ere, atque
        ingenio.
PHAE pessuli, heus pessuli, uos saluto lubens,
      uos amo, uos uolo, uos peto atque opsecro,
      gerite amanti mihi morem, amoenissumi,
150   fite causa mea ludii barbari,
      sussilite, opsecro, et mittite istanc foras
      quae mihi misero amanti ebibit sanguinem.
      hoc uide ut dormiunt pessuli pessumi
      nec mea gratia commouent se ocius!
155   re specio nihili meam uos gratiam facere.
      st, tace, tace!
PAL   taceo hercle equidem.
PHAE   sentio sonitum.
      tandem edepol mihi morigeri pessuli fiunt.

I. iii: LEAENA. PALINVRVS. PLANESIVM. PHAEDROMVS
LEAE placide egredere et sonitum prohibe forium et crepitum
      cardinum,
      ne quae hic agimus erus percipiat fieri, mea Planesium.
160   mane, suffundam aquolam.

142 misera adficitur *P*, misera adfligitur *F. Skutsch*, afficitur misera
Goetz
156 sed *P*, st *Muretus*

PAL   Truly, he who is in love is struck by miserable sorrow if
       he's without money.
PHAE   It's not like that; I trust that my hanger-on will come to
       me today with the money.
PAL   You're in for great riches if you wait for what doesn't exist
       anywhere.[10]
PHAE   What if I approach the door and sing it a song?   145
PAL   If you want to, I neither forbid you nor tell you to do so,
       master, since I can see that your habits and character
       have changed.
PHAE   (*singing enticingly*) Bolts, hey, bolts, I greet you gladly, I
       love you, I want you, I desire you, and I beseech you,
       obey me in my love, most charming bolts. Become for-   150
       eign dancers for my sake, jump up, please, and send out
       the woman who drinks up my blood, miserable lover that
       I am. (*pauses and steps back*) Look at that, how the basest
       bolts are sleeping and won't move any more quickly for
       my sake! I can see from how you behave that you don't   155
       care about my goodwill toward you. (*pauses and turns to
       Palinurus*) Hush, be quiet, be quiet!
PAL   I for one am quiet.
PHAE   I can hear a sound. At long last the bolts are becoming
       obedient to me.

LEAENA opens the door a little.

LEAE   Come out quietly and prevent any noise of the door and
       any creaking of the hinges so that master doesn't hear
       what we're doing here, my dear Planesium. Wait, I'll   160
       pour a little water underneath. (*does so*)

[10] A hanger-on with money.

PAL   uiden ut anus tremula medicinam facit?
eapse merum condidicit bibere, foribus dat aquam quam
    bibant.

PLA ubi tu es qui me conuadatu's Veneriis uadimoniis?
sisto ego tibi me et ⟨te⟩ mihi contra itidem ut sistas sua-
    deo.

PHAE assum; nam si apsim, hau recusem quin mi male sit, mel
    meum.

165 PLA anime mi, procul ⟨a me⟩ amantem abesse hau consenta-
    neum est.

PHAE Palinure, Palinure!

PAL   eloquere, quid est quod Palinurum uoces?

PHAE est lepida.

PAL   nimis lepida.

PHAE   sum deus.

PAL   immo homo hau magni preti.

PHAE quid uidisti aut quid uidebis magis dis aequiparabile?

PAL male ualere te, quod mi aegre est.

PHAE   male mi morigeru's, tace.

170 PAL ipsus se excruciat qui homo quod amat uidet nec potitur
    dum licet.

PHAE recte obiurgat. sane hau quicquam est magis quod cu-
    piam iam diu.

PLA tene me, amplectere ergo.

163 te *add.* Schoell
165 a me *add.* Mueller

---

11 Parody of legal language; the *uadimonium* is a guarantee that the
defendant will appear in court.

PAL   (*to Phaedromus*) Can you see how this doddery old woman is practicing the medical profession? She herself has learned to drink undiluted wine, but to the door she gives water to drink.

The door opens further. Enter PLANESIUM from the pimp's house. LEAENA disappears.

PLA   Where are you who have summoned me to the court of Venus?[11] I present myself to you and I advise you likewise to present yourself to me.

PHAE   I'm here; if I were away, I wouldn't protest against having a hard time, my honey.

PLA   My sweetheart, it isn't acceptable that my lover should be   165 standing at a distance from me.

PHAE   Palinurus, Palinurus!

PAL   Tell me, what is it you're calling Palinurus for?

PHAE   She's lovely.

PAL   Terribly lovely.

PHAE   I'm a god.

PAL   No, a man of little worth.

PHAE   What have you seen or what will you see that's more comparable to the gods?

PAL   (*ignoring the second half of the sentence*) That you're in a bad way, which I'm sorry about.

PHAE   You're obeying me in a bad way, be quiet.

PAL   He who sees what he loves and doesn't take advantage   170 while he may merely tortures himself.

PHAE   (*turning to Planesium*) He's right to scold me. Yes, there hasn't been anything this long time which I'd prefer.

PLA   Hold me, embrace me, then.

249

PHAE   hoc etiam est quam ob rem cupiam uiuere.
      quia te prohibet erus, clam [ero] potior.

PLA   prohibet? nec prohibere quit
      nec prohibebit, nisi mors meum animum aps te abalie-
      nauerit.

175 PAL   enim uero nequeo durare quin ego erum accusem
      meum:
      nam bonum est pauxillum amare sane, insane non bo-
      num est;
      uerum totum insanum amare, hoc est . . . quod meus erus
      facit.

PHAE   sibi sua habeant regna reges, sibi diuitias diuites,
      sibi honores, sibi uirtutes, sibi pugnas, sibi proelia:

180   dum mi apstineant inuidere, sibi quisque habeant quod
      suom est.

PAL   quid tu? Venerin peruigilare te uouisti, Phaedrome?
      nam hoc quidem edepol hau multo post luce lucebit.

PHAE   tace.

PAL   quid, taceam? quin tu is dormitum?

PHAE   dormio, ne occlamites.

PAL   tuquidem uigilas.

PHAE   at meo more dormio: hic somnust mihi.

185 PAL   heus tu, mulier, male mereri de immerente inscitia est.

PLA   irascere, si te edentem hic a cibo abigat.

PAL   ilicet!
      pariter hos perire amando uideo, uterque insaniunt.
      uiden ut misere moliuntur? nequeunt complecti satis.
      etiam dispertimini?

173 ero *del. Guyet*

PHAE (*grabbing her*) This, this is why I desire to live. Because your master keeps you away from me, I have you secretly.

PLA He keeps me away from you? He can't keep me away from you and he won't, unless death deprives you of my heart.

PAL I really can't help complaining about my master: yes, it is 175 good to be a little bit in love sanely, but being insanely in love is not good. But being completely insanely in love, that's . . . what my master is.

PHAE Let the kings have their kingdoms, the rich their riches; let them have their honors, their feats, their fights, their battles: so long as they refrain from envying me, let every 180 man have what is his.

PAL (*turning to Phaedromus*) What do you say? Did you vow to hold an all-night vigil for Venus, Phaedromus? Yes, not much later it'll be clear day.

PHAE Be quiet.

PAL What? I should be quiet? Why don't you go home to sleep?

PHAE I am sleeping, so don't shout.

PAL No, you're awake.

PHAE But I'm sleeping in my own way. This is sleep for me.

PAL (*to Planesium*) Hey there, woman, it's stupid to treat a 185 man badly who isn't treating you badly.

PLA You'll be angry if he drives you away from your food while you're eating.

PAL (*to the audience*) Hopeless! I can see that both alike are dying from love, both are mad. Can you see how wretchedly they're laboring? They can't embrace each other enough. (*to the lovers*) Will you get away from each other?

251

PLA   nulli [est] homini perpetuom bonum:

190   iam huic uoluptati hoc adiunctum est odium.

PAL   quid ais, propudium?

tun etiam cum noctuinis oculis "odium" me uocas?

ebriola persolla, nugae.

PHAE   tun meam Venerem uituperas?

quod quidem mi polluctus uirgis seruos sermonem
serat?

at ne tu hercle cum cruciatu magno dixisti id tuo.

195   em tibi male dictis pro istis, dictis moderari ut queas.

PAL   tuam fidem, Venus noctuuigila!

PHAE   pergin etiam, uerbero?

PLA   noli, amabo, uerberare lapidem, ne perdas manum.

PAL   flagitium probrumque magnum, Phaedrome, experge-
facis:

bene monstrantem pugnis caedis, hanc amas, nugas me-
ras.

200   hoccin fieri, ut immodestis hic te moderes moribus?

PHAE auro contra cedo modestum amatorem: a me aurum
accipe.

PAL   cedo mihi contra aurichalco quoi ego sano seruiam.

PLA   bene uale, ocule mi, nam sonitum et crepitum claustro-
rum audio,

aeditumum aperire fanum. quo usque, quaeso, ad hunc
modum

205   inter nos amore utemur semper surrupticio?

189 est *seclusi*
193 quod quidem *corruptum uidetur*

---

12 *Lapis* "stone" is also a metaphor for someone stupid.
13 Greek *oreichalcos* "mountain-copper" became Latin *aurichal-*

PLA   (*to Phaedromus*) No man has constant happiness. With   190
this pleasure this pest is connected now.

PAL   (*to Planesium*) What do you say, you slut? You with your
owl eyes are calling me a pest? You drunken little person,
you trash.

PHAE (*to Palinurus*) Are you finding fault with my Venus?
Should a slave sacrificed to the rods give me cheeky talk?
Seriously, saying that will cost you dearly. (*hitting him*) 195
Take this for your bad words so you can keep your words
in check.

PAL   (*to Planesium*) Your protection, Venus of the nightly
wake!

PHAE Are you continuing, you criminal? (*hits him again*)

PLA   (*to Phaedromus*) Please, don't hit a stone[12] so you don't
hurt your hand.

PAL   You're committing a very shameful and disgraceful
crime, Phaedromus: you knock down the man giving you
sound advice and love this girl, pure trash. Can this really 200
be happening, that you conduct yourself with immoder-
ate conduct here?

PHAE Give me a moderate lover against his weight in gold and
receive the gold from me.

PAL   Give me someone sane against his weight in gold-
copper[13] so I can be a slave to him.

PLA   (*looking at the temple of Aesculapius*) Goodbye, my dar-
ling: I can hear the grating sound of the bolts, the tem-
ple overseer is opening the temple. How much longer,
please, will we always conduct our love affair in secret? 205

cum: the first element "mountain" was not understood and changed to
the Latin word for gold. In Plautus the term refers to a mythical metal
of great value.

PHAE minime, nam parasitum misi nudiusquartus Cariam
    petere argentum, is hodie hic aderit.

PLA   nimium consultas diu.

PHAE ita me Venus amet, ut ego te hoc triduom numquam
    sinam

    in domo esse istac, quin ego te liberalem liberem.

210 PLA facito ut memineris. tene etiam, prius quam hinc abeo,
    sauium.

PHAE siquidem hercle mihi regnum detur, numquam id potius
    persequar.

    quando ego te uidebo?

PLA   em istoc uerbo uindictam para:

    si amas, eme, ne rogites, facito ut pretio peruincas tuo.

    bene uale.

PHAE   iamne ego relinquor? pulchre, Palinure, occidi.

215 PAL ego quidem, qui et uapulando et somno pereo.

PHAE   sequere me.

ACTVS II

II. i: CAPPADOX. PALINVRVS

CAP migrare certum est iam nunc e fano foras,
    quando Aesculapi ita sentio sententiam
    ut qui me nihili faciat nec saluom uelit.
    ualetudo decrescit, accrescit labor;

220   nam iam quasi zona liene cinctus ambulo,

---

14 *Liberalis* means "worthy of freedom," but also "pretty."

PHAE Not at all: three days ago I sent my hanger-on to Caria in order to fetch money. He'll be back today.

PLA You deliberate far too long.

PHAE As truly as Venus may love me, I shall never let you remain in that house for two more days; rather, I'll give you the freedom you deserve.[14]

PLA Make sure you remember. Have a kiss, too, before I leave 210 you.

PHAE If in fact I was offered a kingdom, I'd never take it by preference to you. (*they kiss*) When will I see you?

PLA There you go: because of what you've just said secure my freedom: if you love me, buy me and don't just ask for me, but make sure you win with the highest bid. Farewell.

Exit PLANESIUM into the pimp's house.

PHAE Am I already being left alone? Palinurus, I've perished nicely.

PAL No, *I* have, who am dying from the beating and lack of 215 sleep.

PHAE Follow me.

Exeunt PHAEDROMUS and PALINURUS into their house, followed by the slaves.

ACT TWO

Enter CAPPADOX from the sanctuary of Aesculapius.

CAP I'm resolved to leave the sanctuary now since I feel that it's the decision of Aesculapius that he couldn't care less for me and that he doesn't want me to be well. My health is decreasing, my suffering is increasing: I'm now walk- 220

geminos in uentre habere uideor filios.
nil metuo nisi ne medius dirrumpar miser.

PAL si recte facias, Phaedrome, auscultes mihi
atque istam exturbes ex animo aegritudinem.

225 paues parasitus quia non rediit Caria:
afferre argentum credo; nam si non ferat,
tormento non retineri potuit ferreo
quin reciperet se huc esum ad praesepem suam.

CAP quis hic est qui loquitur?

PAL   quoiam uocem ego audio?

230 CAP estne hic Palinurus Phaedromi?

PAL   quis hic est homo
cum collatiuo uentre atque oculis herbeis?
de forma noui, de colore non queo
nouisse. iam iam noui: leno est Cappadox.
congrediar.

CAP   salue, Palinure.

PAL   o scelerum caput,

235 salueto. quid agis?

CAP   uiuo.

PAL   nempe ut dignus es?
sed quid tibi est?

CAP   lien enicat, renes dolent,
pulmones distrahuntur, cruciatur iecur,
radices cordis pereunt, hirae omnes dolent.

PAL tum te igitur morbus agitat hepatiarius.

240 CAP facile est miserum irridere.

PAL   quin tu aliquot dies
perdura, dum intestina exputescunt tibi,
nunc dum salsura sat bona est: si id feceris,
uenire poteris intestinis uilius.

ing around constricted tightly by my spleen as if by a belt,
I seem to have twin sons in my belly. I don't fear anything
except that I might burst in the middle, poor wretch that
I am.

Enter PALINURUS from Phaedromus' house.

PAL (*into the house*) If you did the right thing, Phaedromus,
you'd listen to me and throw this sorrow of yours out of
your mind. You're afraid because your hanger-on hasn't   225
returned from Caria. I believe he's bringing the money: if
he weren't bringing it, he couldn't be prevented by an
iron fetter from returning here to his stable to eat.

CAP Who is this man who is talking?

PAL Whose voice can I hear?

CAP   Isn't this Palinurus, the slave of Phaedromus?   230

PAL Who is this chap with a well-stuffed belly and eyes as
green as grass? From his figure I know him, but from his
color I don't know him. Now I know him: it's the pimp
Cappadox. I'll go up to him. (*does so*)

CAP Hello, Palinurus.

PAL O you dreadful criminal, hello. How are you?   235

CAP I'm alive.

PAL In the way you deserve, I suppose? But what's your prob-
lem?

CAP My spleen is killing me, my kidneys hurt, my lungs are
being torn apart, my liver is in agony, the deepest part of
my heart is dying, all my intestines ache.

PAL Then you must suffer from a liver disease.

CAP It's easy to mock a poor wretch.   240

PAL Just wait some more days while your intestines are rot-
ting away, now while the pickling is good enough. If you
do that, you can be sold for less than your own intestines.

CAP	lien dierectust.
PAL	ambula, id lieni optumum est.
245 CAP	aufer istaec, quaeso, atque hoc responde quod rogo.
	potin coniecturam facere, si narrem tibi
	hac nocte quod ego somniaui dormiens?
PAL	uah! solus hic homo est qui sciat diuinitus.
	quin coniectores a me consilium petunt:
250	quod eis respondi, ea omnes stant sententia.

II. ii: COQVOS. PALINVRVS. CAPPADOX. PHAEDROMVS

CO	Palinure, quid stas? quin depromuntur mihi
	quae opus sunt, parasito ut sit paratum prandium
	quom ueniat?
PAL	mane sis, dum huic conicio somnium.
CO	tute ipse, si quid somniasti, ad me refers.
255 PAL	fateor.
CO	abi, deprome.
PAL	age tu interea huic somnium
	narra: meliorem quam ego sum suppono tibi.
	nam quod scio omne ex hoc scio.
CAP	operam ut det.
PAL	dabit.
CAP	facit hic quod pauci, ut sit magistro opsequens.
	da mi igitur operam.
CO	tam etsi non noui, dabo.
260 CAP	hac nocte in somnis uisus sum uiderier
	procul sedere longe a me Aesculapium,
	neque eum ad me adire nec me magni pendere
	uisum est.
CO	item alios deos facturos scilicet:

CAP My spleen is bust.

PAL Go for a walk, that's best for the spleen.

CAP Please leave this aside now and answer my question. Can 245
you interpret if I tell you what I dreamed about in my
sleep last night?

PAL Bah! (*points to himself*) This man's the only one who
knows through divine inspiration. In fact, even the sooth-
sayers ask me for advice. Whatever reply I give them, 250
that advice they all abide by.

Enter the COOK from Phaedromus' house.

CO Palinurus, what are you standing around for? Why aren't
the things being fetched which I need so that the hanger-
on will have a lunch ready when he comes?

PAL Please wait while I'm interpreting a dream for this chap.

CO You yourself come to me if you have a dream.

PAL I admit it. 255

CO Go fetch the things.

PAL (*to Cappadox*) Go on, you tell this fellow your dream in
the meantime; I leave you a substitute who is a better
man than I am: everything I know I know from him.

CAP If only he'd make the effort.

PAL He will. (*moves back to Phaedromus' house, but stays in
the door and observes*)

CAP (*aside*) This chap does what few people do: he obeys his
teacher. (*to the cook*) Make an effort for me, then.

CO I will, even though I don't know you.

CAP Last night I seemed to see in my dreams that Aesculapius 260
was sitting at a great distance from me, and it seemed
that he didn't approach me and didn't care much for me.

CO Naturally the other gods will behave in the same way:

259

		sane illi inter se congruont concorditer.
265		nihil est mirandum melius si nil fit tibi,
		namque incubare satius te fuerat Ioui,
		auxilio tibi qui in iure iurando fuit.
	CAP	siquidem incubare uelint qui periurauerint,
		locus non praeberi potis est in Capitolio.
270	CO	hoc animum aduorte: pacem ab Aesculapio
		petas, ne fort' tibi eueniat magnum malum,
		quod in quiete tibi portentum est.

CAP   bene facis.
        ibo atque orabo.

CO   quae res male uortat tibi!

PAL   pro di immortales, quem conspicio? quis illic est?

275   estne hic parasitus qui missust in Cariam?
        heus Phaedrome, exi, exi, exi, inquam, ocius!

PHAE quid istic clamorem tollis?

PAL   parasitum tuom
        uideo currentem ellum usque in platea ultuma.
        hinc auscultemus quid agat.

PHAE   sane censeo.

---

267 qui tibi auxilio *P*, a. t. q. *Trappes-Lomax per litteras*

they completely agree among each other. It's not surpris- 265
ing if you aren't getting any better: it would have been
better if you'd slept in Jupiter's temple, who helped you
when you gave an oath.

CAP Well, if all who had given false oaths wanted to sleep
in his temple, there wouldn't be enough space on the
Capitoline hill.[15]

CO Mark my words: seek peace from Aesculapius, so that 270
you won't by chance end up with the great disaster you
were shown during your rest.

CAP Thank you. I'll go and pray.

Exit CAPPADOX into the shrine of Aesculapius.

CO (*aside*) May this turn out badly for you!

Exit the COOK into Phaedromus' house.

PAL (*still standing in the door*) Immortal gods, who can I see?
Who is that man? Isn't this the hanger-on who was sent to 275
Caria? Hey there, Phaedromus, come out, come out,
come out, I'm telling you, hurry up!

Enter PHAEDROMUS from his house, followed by some slaves.

PHAE What are you shouting for there?

PAL Look there, I can see your hanger-on running at the far-
thest end of the street. Let's listen from here what he's
up to.

PHAE Yes, good idea.

---

[15] The Roman hill with the most famous temple of Jupiter.

261

II. iii: CVRCVLIO. PHAEDROMVS. PALINVRVS

280 CVR   date uiam mihi, noti [atque] ignoti, dum ego hic officium
meum
facio: fugite omnes, abite et de uia secedite,
ne quem in cursu capite aut cubito aut pectore offendam
aut genu.
ita nunc subito, propere et celere obiectum est mihi ne-
gotium,
⟨nusquam⟩ quisquam est tam opulentus, qui mi opsistat
in uia,
285   nec strategus nec tyrannus quisquam neque agoranomus
nec demarchus nec comarchus nec cum tanta gloria,
quin cadat, quin capite sistat in uia de semita.
tum isti Graeci palliati, capite operto qui ambulant,
qui incedunt suffarcinati cum libris, cum sportulis,
290   constant, conferunt sermones inter sese drapetae,
opstant, opsistunt, incedunt cum suis sententiis,
quos semper uideas bibentes esse in thermopolio,
ubi quid surrupuere: operto capitulo calidum bibunt,
tristes atque ebrioli incedunt: eos ego si offendero,
295   ex unoquoque eorum crepitum exciam polentarium.
tum isti qui ludunt datatim serui scurrarum in uia,
et datores et factores omnis subdam sub solum.
proin sese domi contineant, uitent infortunio.

PHAE   recte hic monstrat, si imperare possit. nam ita nunc mos
uiget,
300   ita nunc seruitium est: profecto modus haberi non po-
test.

280 atque *del. Bentley*
284 nec quisquamst *BEK*, ne quisquam est *VJ*, nusquam quis-
quamst *Lange*

Enter CURCULIO from the left, apparently in great haste, without noticing anyone.

CUR   Make way for me, known and unknown, while I'm doing   280
my duty here: flee, all of you, go away and get off the
streets, so that while running I don't hit anyone with my
head, my elbow, my chest, or my knee. So suddenly, fast,
and quickly has this business now been thrown my way,
that there's no one anywhere so rich that he could afford
to block my way, not a general, not a despot, not a mar-   285
ket inspector, not a district magistrate, not a village su-
perintendent, not anyone with such great fame: no, he'll
fall, drop from the sidewalk and stand on his head in
the street. Then those Greeks in their cloaks, who wan-
der around with their heads covered, who prance about
stuffed with books and food baskets, who stop and pala-   290
ver among each other, those runaway slaves, who stand in
your way and block your path, who prance about with
their clever sayings, whom you can always see drinking in
the tavern when they've stolen something; with their
heads covered they drink mulled wine and prance about
with a grave expression and drunk. If I meet them, I'll   295
drive the barley-fed farts out of every single one of them.
Then those slaves of the city bon vivants, who play ball in
the street, I'll put all the throwers and players under the
ground. So let them stay at home and avoid a thrashing.

PHAE   He gives good orders, if only he had authority. Yes, nowa-
days this is the custom, nowadays this is what the slave   300
class is like: it is indeed impossible to keep them under
control.

CVR ecquis est qui mihi commonstret Phaedromum genium
    meum?
    ita res subita est, celeriter mi hoc homine conuento est
    opus.
PAL te ille quaerit.
PHAE   quid si adeamus? heus Curculio, te uolo.
CVR quis uocat? quis nominat me?
PHAE   qui te conuentum cupit.
305 CVR hau magis cupis quam ego te cupio.
PHAE   o mea opportunitas,
    Curculio exoptate, salue.
CVR   salue.
PHAE   saluom gaudeo
    te aduenire. cedo tuam mi dexteram. ubi sunt spes meae?
    eloquere, opsecro hercle.
CVR   eloquere, te opsecro, ubi sunt meae?
PHAE quid tibi est?
CVR   tenebrae oboriuntur, genua inedia succidunt.
310 PHAE lassitudine hercle credo.
CVR   retine, retine me, opsecro.
PHAE uiden ut expalluit? datin isti sellam, ubi assidat, cito
    et aqualem cum aqua? properatin ocius?
CVR   animo male est.
PAL uin aquam?
CVR   si frustulenta est, da, opsecro hercle, opsorbeam.
PAL uae capiti tuo!
CVR   opsecro hercle, facite uentum ut gaudeam.
315 PAL maxume.
CVR   quid facitis, quaeso?

CUR Is there anyone who can show me Phaedromus, my good
     spirit? It's an emergency, I need to meet him quickly.

PAL He's looking for you.

PHAE (*to Palinurus*) How about approaching him? (*loudly*)
     Hey, Curculio, I want to speak to you.

CUR Who is calling me? Who is naming me?

PHAE Someone who wants to meet you.

CUR (*noticing Phaedromus*) You don't want to meet me more   305
     than I want to meet you.

PHAE O my Opportunity, longed-for Curculio, my greetings to
     you.

CUR And mine to you.

PHAE I'm happy that you've arrived safely. Give me your right
     hand. Where are my hopes? Tell me, I beg you.

CUR (*appearing to faint*) Tell me, I beg *you*, where are mine?

PHAE What's wrong with you?

CUR Darkness is spreading over me, my knees are giving way
     under me through lack of food.

PHAE From exhaustion, no doubt.   310

CUR Hold me, hold me please. (*Phaedromus does so*)

PHAE (*to Palinurus*) Can you see how he's turned pale? (*to
     slaves*) Won't you give him a chair to sit on, quickly, and a
     bowl of water? Won't you hurry faster? (*the slaves bring a
     chair and water*)

CUR I feel faint.

PAL Do you want water?

CUR If it's full of morsels, do please give it to me to gulp it
     down.

PAL Curse you!

CUR Please, give a joyous air to my arrival.

PAL Certainly. (*he and the slaves fart loudly*)   315

CUR What are you doing, please?

265

PAL	uentum.

PAL   uentum.

CVR   nolo equidem mihi

fieri uentulum.

PHAE   quid igitur [uis]?

CVR   esse, ut uentum gaudeam.

PAL   Iuppiter te dique perdant!

CVR   perii, prospicio parum,

gramarum habeo dentes plenos, lippiunt fauces fame,

ita cibi uaciuitate uenio lassis lactibus.

320 PHAE iam edes aliquid.

CVR   nolo hercle aliquid: certum quam aliquid mauolo.

PAL   immo si scias reliquiae quae sint!

CVR   scire nimis lubet

ubi sient, nam illis conuentis sane opus est meis dentibus.

PHAE pernam, abdomen, sumen, sueris, glandium . . .

CVR   ain tu omnia haec?

in carnario fortasse dicis.

PHAE   immo in lancibus,

325   quae tibi sunt parata, postquam scimus uenturum.

CVR   uide

ne me ludas.

PHAE   ita me amabit quam ego amo ut ego hau mentior.

sed quod te misi, nihilo sum certior.

CVR   nihil attuli.

PHAE perdidisti me.

CVR   inuenire possum, si mi operam datis.

postquam tuo iussu profectus sum, perueni in Cariam,

330   uideo tuom sodalem, argenti rogo uti faciat copiam.

scires uelle gratiam tuam, noluit frustrarier,

316 uis *del. Bentley*
323 suis *P*, sueris *genetiuo casu Scaliger, accusatiuo Ernout*

PAL   Producing air.[16]

CUR   I don't want a puff of air being produced for me.

PHAE What do you want then?

CUR   I want to eat so that my arrival has a joyous air for me.

PAL   May Jupiter and the gods ruin you!

CUR   I'm done for, I can barely see, I have teeth full of rheum, my throat is bleary from hunger: I come with intestines exhausted from emptiness of food.

PHAE You'll eat something in a minute.   320

CUR   I don't want *something*: I prefer a definite thing to just something.

PAL   Well, if you knew what leftovers there are!

CUR   I'm very keen to know *where* they are: they really need to meet my teeth.

PHAE Ham, tripe, udder, pork chops, sweatbread . . .

CUR   All these things, you say? Perhaps you're telling me they're hanging from the meat rack.

PHAE No, on the platters; these things were prepared for you 325 after we knew you were coming.

CUR   Make sure you aren't making fun of me.

PHAE As truly as the woman I love will love me, I'm not lying. But as for the mission I sent you on, I'm no less in the dark.

CUR   I didn't bring anything.

PHAE You've ruined me.

CUR   I can find something if you assist me. (*pauses briefly*) After I left at your request, I arrived in Caria, saw your 330 chum, and asked him to provide you with the money. It was obvious that he wanted to please you, he didn't want

---

[16] *Ventum* is ambiguous; Curculio uses it as past participle of *uenire* "come," Palinurus interprets it as accusative of *uentus* "wind, fart."

ut decet uelle hominem amicum amico atque opitularier:
respondit mihi paucis uerbis, atque adeo fideliter,
quod tibi est item sibi esse, magnam argenti . . . inopiam.

335 PHAE perdis me tuis dictis.

     CVR   immo seruo et seruatum uolo.

postquam mihi responsum est, abeo ab illo maestus ad
    forum
med illo frustra aduenisse. forte aspicio militem.
aggredior hominem, saluto adueniens. "salue," inquit
    mihi,
prendit dexteram, seducit, rogat quid ueniam Cariam;

340 dico me illo aduenisse animi causa. ibi me interrogat,
ecquem in Epidauro Lyconem tarpezitam nouerim.
dico me nouisse. "quid? lenonem Cappadocem?" annuo
uisitasse. "sed quid eum uis?" "quia de illo emi uirginem
triginta minis, uestem, aurum; et pro is decem coacce-
    dunt minae."

345 "dedistin tu argentum?" inquam. "immo apud tarpezi-
    tam situm est
illum quem dixi Lyconem, atque ei mandaui, qui anulo
meo tabellas opsignatas attulisset, ut daret
operam ut mulierem a lenone cum auro et ueste abduce-
    ret."
postquam hoc mihi narrauit, abeo ab illo. reuocat me i-
    lico,

350 uocat me ad cenam; religio fuit, denegare nolui.
"quid si abeamus, [ac] decumbamus?" inquit. consilium
    placet:
"nec diem decet [me] morari, nec nocti nocerier."
"omnis res parata est." "et nos, quibus paratum est, assu-
    mus."
postquam cenati atque appoti, talos poscit sibi in ma-
    num,

268

to trick you, just as a friend should want to please and
support a friend. He answered me in a few words, and
entirely without pretence, that money-wise he has the
same that you have, a great . . . lack.

PHAE You're ruining me with your words. 335

CUR No, I'm saving you and I want you saved. After receiving
this answer, I went away from him to the market, sad that
I'd gone there for nothing. By chance I saw a soldier. I ap-
proached him and greeted him. "Hello," he said to me;
he grabbed my right hand, took me aside, and asked me
why I'd come to Caria. I said I'd come there to enjoy my- 340
self. Then he asked me if I knew some banker in Epi-
daurus called Lyco. I said I did. "What about a pimp
Cappadox?" I gave him a nod to show that I'd often
seen him. "But what do you want from him?" "Because I
bought a girl from him for thirty minas, and ten minas
more for her clothes and jewelry." "Have you given him 345
the money?" I asked. "No, it's with that banker I was talk-
ing about, Lyco, and I told him to make sure that the man
who brought tablets sealed with my ring should take the
woman away from the pimp together with her jewelry
and clothes." After he told me this, I made as if to leave
him. He called me back at once and invited me to dinner; 350
it would have been against my principles, so I didn't want
to refuse. "What if we go and lie down?" he asked. I liked
the plan: "It isn't right to delay the day, and it isn't right to
waste the night." "Everything's prepared." "And we, for
whom it's prepared, are present." After we ate and drank

---

344 his *P*, is *Camerarius* coaccedunt *P*, eo accedunt *Baehrens*,
accedunt *Guyet* 345 dedisti *P*, dedistin *Fleckeisen*
351 adeamus *P*, abeamus *Brant* ac *del. Reiz* 352 memo-
rari *VJE¹*, me morari *BE³*, morari *Scaliger*, demorari *Lindsay*

355   prouocat me in aleam, ut ego ludam: pono pallium;
        ill' suom amiculum opposiuit, inuocat Planesium.
PHAE meosne amores?
CVR   tace parumper. iacit uolturios quattuor.
        talos arripio, inuoco almam meam nutricem . . . Herculem,
        iacto basilicum; propino magnum poclum: ille ebibit,
360   caput deponit, condormiscit. ego ei subduco anulum,
        deduco pedes de lecto clam, ne miles sentiat.
        rogant me serui quo eam: dico me ire quo saturi solent.
        ostium ubi conspexi, exinde me ilico protinam dedi.
PHAE laudo.
CVR   laudato quando illud quod cupis effecero.
365   eamus nunc intro ut tabellas consignemus.
PHAE   num moror?
CVR atque aliquid prius opstrudamus, pernam, sumen, glandium.
        haec sunt uentris stabilimenta, pane et assa bubula,
        poculum grande, aula magna, ut satis consilia suppetant.
        tu tabellas consignato, hic ministrabit, ego edam.
370   dicam quem ad modum conscribas. sequere me hac intro.
PHAE   sequor.

356 animulum *B¹VE¹*, anulum *B³E³JK*, amiculum *Leo*

he asked for dice and challenged me to play a game. I 355
staked my cloak; he staked his mantle against it and in-
voked Planesium.

PHAE (*interrupting*) My beloved?

CUR Be quiet for a moment. He threw four vultures.[17] I
grabbed the dice, invoked my blessed nurse . . . Hercu-
les,[18] and threw the royal throw. I proposed a toast with a
great goblet. He emptied it, put down his head and fell 360
asleep. I removed the ring from him and quietly moved
my feet from the couch so that the soldier wouldn't no-
tice. The servants asked me where I was going. I said I
was going where those who are full normally go. As soon
as I spotted the door, I immediately ran off.

PHAE I praise you.

CUR Praise me once I've achieved what you long for. Now let's 365
go inside in order to seal the tablets.

PHAE Am I responsible for any delay?

CUR And let's first gulp something down, ham, tripe, and
sweatbread. These stabilize the stomach, bread and roast
beef, a large goblet, a big pot, so that we have sufficient
wisdom. You seal the tablets, this chap (*points to Palinu-*
rus) will wait on me, I shall eat. I'll tell you how you are to 370
write them. Follow me inside this way.

PHAE I'm following you.

Exeunt CURCULIO, PHAEDROMUS, PALINURUS, and the
slaves into Phaedromus' house.

[17] A throw of low value, as opposed to the high royal throw.
[18] Not only known as a great hero, but also as a great eater.

PLAUTUS

ACTVS III

III. i: LYCO. CVRCVLIO. CAPPADOX

LYCO   beatus uideor: subduxi ratiunculam,
      quantum aeris mihi sit quantumque alieni siet:
      diues sum, si non reddo eis quibus debeo;
      si reddo illis quibus debeo, alieni ampliust.
375   uerum hercle uero quom belle recogito,
      si magis me instabunt, ad praetorem sufferam.
      habent hunc morem plerique argentarii
      ut alius alium poscant, reddant nemini,
      pugnis rem soluant, si quis poscat clarius.
380   qui homo mature quaesiuit pecuniam,
      nisi eam mature parsit, mature esurit.
      cupio aliquem ⟨mi⟩ emere puerum qui usurarius
      nunc mihi quaeratur. usus est pecunia.
CVR   nil tu me saturum monueris. memini et scio.
385   ego hoc effectum lepide tibi tradam. tace.
      edepol ne ego hic me intus expleui probe,
      et quidem reliqui in uentre cellae uni locum,
      ubi reliquiarum reliquias reconderem.
      quis hic est operto capite qui Aesculapium
390   salutat? attat, quem quaerebam! sequere me.
      simulabo quasi non nouerim. heus tu, te uolo!
LYCO unocule, salue.
CVR   quaeso, deridesne me?

---

374 plus alieni est *P*, alieni ampliust *Lindsay in apparatu, uersum del. Bothe*   382 mi *add. Bentley*
    389 qui operto capite *P, transp. Bothe*

---

[19] Roman magistrate with mainly judicial functions.

ACT THREE

Enter LYCO from the right.

LYCO I seem prosperous: I've done the reckoning of how much money I have and how much debt I have. I'm rich if I don't return the money to those whom I owe something; if I do return it to those whom I owe something, the debt is greater. But seriously, when I think it through nicely, 375 if they push me harder, I'll go to the praetor[19] for arbitration. Most bankers have this custom of demanding money from each other, repaying nothing to anyone, and settling financial matters with their fists if anyone should make his demands too vociferously. A man who has made 380 money quickly goes hungry quickly unless he's saved it quickly. I wish to buy myself a slave boy whom I could acquire as a catamite to be lent out on interest now: I need money.

Enter CURCULIO from Phaedromus' house, sporting an eye patch and carrying a letter. He is followed by a slave boy.

CUR *(into the house)* Don't remind me when I'm full. I remember and know. I'll sort this out in a lovely way for 385 you. Be quiet. *(to himself)* Honestly, I filled myself properly inside here, and I left place for one room in my belly where I can store the remains of the remains. *(pauses)* Who is that greeting Aesculapius with covered head? 390 Goodness, the very man I was looking for! *(to slave boy)* Follow me. I'll pretend not to know him. *(loudly, to Lyco)* Hey, you there, I want to speak to you!

LYCO Hello, one-eyed man.

CUR Tell me, are you poking fun at me?

LYCO de Coculitum prosapia te esse arbitror,
      nam i sunt unoculi.

CVR   catapulta hoc ictum est mihi

395   apud Sicyonem.

LYCO   nam quid id refert mea,
      an aula quassa cum cinere effossus siet?

CVR superstitiosus hicquidem est, uera praedicat;
      nam illaec catapultae ad me crebro commeant.
      adulescens, ob rem publicam hoc intus mihi

400   quod insigne habeo, quaeso ne me incomities.

LYCO licetne inforare, si incomitiare hau licet?

CVR non inforabis me quidem, nec mi placet
      tuom profecto nec forum nec comitium.
      sed hunc quem quaero commonstrare si potes,

405   inibis a me solidam et grandem . . . gratiam.
      Lyconem quaero tarpezitam.

LYCO   dic mihi,
      quid eum nunc quaeris? aut quoiati's?

CVR   eloquar.
      ab Therapontigono Platagidoro milite.

LYCO noui edepol nomen, nam mihi istoc nomine,

410   dum scribo, expleui totas ceras quattuor.
      sed quid Lyconem quaeris?

CVR   mandatum est mihi
      ut has tabellas ad eum ferrem.

LYCO   quis tu homo es?

CVR libertus illius, quem omnes Summanum uocant.

---

394 hi *P Varro*, i *Camerarius*   401 non *P*, haud *Bentley*

---

[20] Fabulous giants whose name means "round-eye."
[21] Greek city in the northern Peloponnesus.

274

LYCO I take it you come from the lineage of Cyclopes:[20] they
      are one-eyed.

CUR   I was hit here by a missile at Sicyon.[21]   395

LYCO What do I care whether this is true or whether it was
      knocked out by a broken pot of ashes?

CUR   (aside) He's a prophet, he's telling the truth: such missiles
      often wind their way toward me. (to Lyco) Young man, as
      for the fact that I got this wound in me in defense of my   400
      country, I ask you not to bug me in public.

LYCO Can I bugger you in your privates if I can't bug you in
      public?[22]

CUR   You certainly won't bugger me in my privates, and I really
      don't like your public or your privates. But if you can
      show me the man I'm looking for, you'll earn my solid and 405
      great . . . gratitude. I'm looking for the banker Lyco.

LYCO Tell me, why are you looking for him now? Or where are
      you from?

CUR   I'll tell you. I'm coming from the soldier Theraponti-
      gonus Platagidorus.

LYCO (aside) Yes, I know the name: while I was writing down   410
      that name, I filled four entire wax tablets with it. (to Cur-
      culio) But why are you looking for Lyco?

CUR   I was told to bring these tablets to him.

LYCO Who are you?

CUR   His freedman, whom all men call Summanus.[23]

---

[22] *Incomitiare* "annoy" comes from *comitium*, the public assembly
place. Lyco creates a pun with *inforare* "drill a hole/bugger" as if that
word came from *forum* "market."

[23] A title of Jupiter in his function as protector of houses from light-
ening. The Latin pun is based on an etymologically wrong derivation
from *summanare* "to pee on."

LYCO Summane, salue. qui Summanu's? fac sciam.
415 CVR   quia uestimenta ⟨mea⟩, ubi obdormiui ebrius,
          summano, ob eam rem me omnes Summanum uocant.
LYCO alibi te meliust quaerere hospitium tibi:
          apud me profecto nihil est Summano loci.
          sed istum quem quaeris ego sum.
CVR   quaeso, tune is es,
420   Lyco tarpezita?
LYCO   ego sum.
CVR   multam me tibi
          salutem iussit Therapontigonus dicere,
          et has tabellas dare me iussit.
LYCO   min?
CVR   ita.
          cape, signum nosce. nostin?
LYCO   quidni nouerim?
          clupeatus elephantum ubi machaera diligit.
425 CVR   quod isti scriptum est, id te orare iusserat
          profecto ut faceres, suam si uelles gratiam.
LYCO concede, inspiciam quid sit scriptum.
CVR   maxume,
          tuo arbitratu, dum auferam aps te id quod peto.
LYCO "miles Lyconi in Epidauro hospiti
430   suo Therapontigonus Platagidorus plurumam
          salutem dicit."
CVR   meus hic est, hamum uorat.
LYCO "tecum oro et quaeso, qui has tabellas afferet
          tibi, ut ei detur quam istic emi uirginem,
          quod te praesente isti egi teque interprete,
435   et aurum et uestem. iam scis ut conuenerit:
          argentum des lenoni, huic des uirginem."
          ubi ipsus? quor non uenit?

LYCO Hello, Summanus. How come you're Summanus? Let
me know.

CUR Because whenever I'm drunk, I sure act like some anus. 415
For that reason all men call me Summanus.

LYCO It's better if you look for hospitality elsewhere: at my
house there's definitely no place for Summanus. But I am
the man you're looking for.

CUR Please, is it you, the banker Lyco? 420

LYCO Yes, that's me.

CUR Therapontigonus told me to give you his best wishes, and
he told me to give these tablets to you.

LYCO To me?

CUR Yes. Take them, examine the seal. (*hands them over*) Do
you recognize it?

LYCO Why shouldn't I? Where a man with a shield is cutting an
elephant in two with his sword.

CUR He told me to ask you to do what's written there if you 425
wanted his gratitude.

LYCO Step aside, I'll look at what's written.

CUR By all means, just as you like, so long as I take away from
you what I seek.

LYCO "The soldier Therapontigonus Platagidorus gives his 430
warmest greetings to his host in Epidaurus, Lyco."

CUR He's mine, he's swallowing the fishhook.

LYCO "I ask you and request from you that the girl I bought at
your place be given to the man who brings these tablets
to you—business I transacted there in your presence and
with you as go-between— and also the jewelry and cloth- 435
ing. You already know how it was agreed: you are to give
the money to the pimp and you are to give the girl to this
man." Where's the man himself? Why hasn't he come?

---

415 mea *add.* Fleckeisen   424 diligit *Nonius*, dessicit *P*

CVR	ego dicam tibi:

quia nudiusquartus uenimus in Cariam
ex India; ibi nunc statuam uolt dare auream
440   solidam faciundam ex auro Philippo, quae siet
septempedalis, factis monumentum suis.

LYCO quam ob rem istuc?

CVR dicam. quia enim Persas, Paphlagonas,
Sinopas, Arabas, Caras, Cretanos, Syros,
Rhodiam atque Lyciam, Perediam et Perbibesiam,
445   Centauromachiam et Classiam, Vnomammiam,
Libyamque, ⟨et⟩ oram omnem Conterebromniam,
dimidiam partem nationum usque omnium
subegit solus intra uiginti dies.

LYCO uah!

CVR quid mirare?

LYCO quia enim in cauea si forent
450   conclusi, itidem ut pulli gallinacei,
ita non potuere uno anno circumirier.
credo hercle te esse ab illo: [nam] ita nugas blatis.

CVR immo etiam porro, si uis, dicam.

LYCO nil moror.
sequere hac, te apsoluam qua aduenisti gratia.
455   atque eccum uideo. leno, salue.

CAP di te ament.

446 et *add. Bothe*
452 nam *del. Langen*

---

[24] Paphlagonia is in what is northern Turkey today. Sinope is a city
on the Black Sea. Caria is a region in southwest Turkey, next to Lycia.
Peredia and Perbibesia are made-up names punning on food and drink.
Centauromachia and Unomammia are also made up and pun on mythi-

CUR   I'll tell you why: three days ago we came from India to Caria. There he wants to have a golden statue made now,   440 a solid one of Philippic gold, which should be seven feet high, as a monument for his feats.

LYCO   Why's that?

CUR   I'll tell you. Because within twenty days he single-handedly subjected the Persians, the Paphlagonians,[24] the inhabitants of Sinope, the Arabs, the Carians, the Cretans, the Syrians, Rhodes and Lycia, Gobbleonia and Booziania, Centaurobattaglia and Classia, Onenipplea-   445 nia, Libya, and the entire coast of Wineknockoutia, in short, half of all nations on earth.

LYCO   Bah!

CUR   What are you surprised about?

LYCO   Because even if they were locked up in a cage like little   450 chicks, one couldn't walk around them in a single year. Yes, I do believe you come from him: you're talking such rubbish.

CUR   Well, if you want me to, I'll tell you even more.

LYCO   I couldn't care less. Follow me this way, I'll settle the business you've come here for.

Enter CAPPADOX from the shrine of Aesculapius.

LYCO   Look, I can see our man. Pimp, hello.   455

CAP   May the gods love you.

cal fights with centaurs (half horse, half man) and Amazons (female warriors who cut off their right breasts so as not to impede javelin-throwing). On this interpretation Classia remains an unclear name; others have taken it to mean "fleet" (like *classis*). Conterebromnia is an invented toponym containing the words "wear down" and Bromius, an alternative name of the god of wine.

279

LYCO	quid hoc quod ad te uenio?
CAP	dicas quid uelis.
LYCO	argentum accipias, cum illo mittas uirginem.
CAP	quid quod iuratus sum?
LYCO	quid id refert tua,

459–60   dum argentum accipias?

CAP	qui monet quasi adiuuat.
	sequimini.
CVR	leno, caue mora in te sit mihi.

ACTVS IV

IV. i: CHORAGVS

CHO   edepol nugatorem lepidum lepide hunc nanctust Phae-
        dromus.

halophantam an sycophantam magis ess' dicam nescio.
ornamenta quae locaui metuo ut possim recipere;

465   quamquam cum istoc mihi negoti nihil est: ipsi Phae-
        dromo

credidi; tamen asseruabo. sed dum hic egreditur foras
commonstrabo quo in quemque hominem facile inue-
        niatis loco,

ne nimio opere sumat operam si quem conuentum uelit,
uel uitiosum uel sine uitio, uel probum uel improbum.

470   qui periurum conuenire uolt hominem ito in comitium;
qui mendacem et gloriosum, apud Cloacinae sacrum,
dites, damnosos maritos sub basilica quaerito.

---

461 in te sit mora *P, transp. Müller*

[25] The Comitium, the place where certain magistrates could assemble the people on specified days.

280

LYCO What about the matter I'm coming to you for?

CAP Tell me what you want.

LYCO Take your money and send the girl off with that man. (*points to Curculio*)

CAP What about the oath I gave?

LYCO What does that matter to you so long as you receive your   460
money?

CAP He who advises helps, so to speak. Follow me.

CUR Pimp, make sure you don't delay me.

Exeunt CAPPADOX, LYCO, and CURCULIO with his slave-boy into the house of Cappadox.

ACT FOUR

Enter the SUPPLIER OF COSTUMES from the market.

SUP Goodness, it's a charming swindler that Phaedromus has
charmingly got hold of. I don't know whether I should say
he's more of a trickster or of a prankster. I'm afraid I
might not be able to get back the costumes I hired out; al-   465
though I have no business with that chap: I entrusted
them to Phaedromus himself. Still, I'll be on my guard.
But until he comes out I'll show in which place you can
easily find which sort of person, so that no one labors too
laboriously if he wants to meet someone, be it a man of
vice or a man without vice, be it a worthy or a worthless
character. Anyone who wants to meet a perjurer should   470
go to the assembly place.[25] Anyone who wants to meet a
liar and a braggart must look for him at the temple of Ve-
nus Cloacina, and anyone who wants to meet rich and

ibidem erunt scorta exoleta quique stipulari solent;
symbolarum collatores apud forum piscarium.

475   in foro infumo boni homines atque dites ambulant;
in medio propter canalem, ibi ostentatores meri;
confidentes garrulique et maleuoli supra lacum,
qui alteri de nihilo audacter dicunt contumeliam
et qui ipsi sat habent quod in se possit uere dicier.

480   sub ueteribus, ibi sunt qui dant quique accipiunt fae-
      nore.

pone aedem Castoris, ibi sunt subito quibus credas male.
in Tusco uico, ibi sunt homines qui ipsi sese uenditant.
in Velabro uel pistorem uel lanium uel haruspicem
uel qui ipsi uortant uel qui aliis ubi uorsentur praebeant.

485   [dites, damnosos maritos apud Leucadiam Oppiam.]
sed interim fores crepuere: linguae moderandum est
      mihi.

477 supra lacum *ferendum est si est quasi una uox*
485 uersum *secl. Camerarius*

26 Venus presided over the *Cloaca Maxima*, the Roman system of
sewers; her shrine was in the Forum. The reference to the colonnaded
hall is unclear; it cannot be the Basilica Porcia because that was inaugu-
rated in the year of Plautus' death.

27 The *lacus Curtius*, a hole in the ground in the Roman Forum, at
one time filled with water.

28 South side of the Forum. The temple of Castor is also in the
Forum.

29 Between the Forum and the Velabrum, which is another market
situated between the Capitoline and Palatine hills.

married wasters must look below the colonnaded hall.[26]
In the same place there will also be grown-up prostitutes
and men who ask for formal guarantees from prospective
debtors. Those who contribute to shared meals are on
the fish market. At the lower end of the market decent   475
and wealthy people stroll around; in the middle part
of the market next to the open drain are the mere show-
offs. Arrogant, overtalkative, and malevolent people are
above the Lake,[27] ones who boldly insult their neighbor
for no good reason and who have enough that could in all
truth be said about themselves. Below the Old Shops[28]   480
there are those who give and receive on interest. Behind
the temple of Castor there are those whom you shouldn't
trust quickly. In the Tuscan Quarter[29] there are those
people who sell themselves. In the Velabrum you can
meet the miller or the butcher or the soothsayer or those
who turn or give others the opportunity to turn.[30] [Rich 485
and married wasters at the house of Leucadia Oppia.[31]]
But meanwhile the door has creaked: I have to keep my
tongue in check.

Exit the SUPPLIER OF COSTUMES to the market.

[30] The meaning of l. 484 is obscure. It has been suggested that
uortere and *uorsari* mean "to trick financially," but it has also been
argued that they refer to homosexual intercourse; if the latter is correct,
l. 484 fits well with l. 482 and the syntactically awkward l. 483 ought to
be deleted.

[31] Probably Leucadia, freedwoman of Oppius, ran a brothel in the
Forum.

IV. ii: CVRCVLIO. CAPPADOX. LYCO

CVR   i tu prae, uirgo: non queo quod pone me est seruare.
     et aurum et uestem omnem suam esse aiebat quam haec
       haberet.

CAP   nemo it infitias.

CVR   at tamen meliusculum est monere.

490 LYCO memento promisisse te, si quisquam hanc liberali
     causa manu assereret, mihi omne argentum redditum iri,
     minas triginta.

CAP   meminero, de istoc quietus esto.
     et nunc idem dico.

CVR   et ‹quidem› [com]meminisse ego haec uolam te.

CAP   memini, et mancupio tibi dabo.

CVR   egon ab lenone quicquam
495   mancupio accipiam, quibus sui nihil est nisi una lingua
     qui abiurant si quid creditum est? alienos mancupatis,
     alienos manu emittitis alienisque imperatis,
     nec uobis auctor ullus est nec uosmet estis ulli.
     item genus est lenonium inter homines meo quidem ani-
       mo
500   ut muscae, culices, cimices pedesque pulicesque:
     odio et malo et molestiae, bono usui estis nulli,
     nec uobiscum quisquam in foro frugi consistere audet;
     qui constitit, culpant eum, conspicitur, uituperatur,
     eum rem fidemque perdere, tam etsi nil fecit, aiunt.

505 LYCO edepol lenones meo animo nouisti, lusce, lepide.

CVR   eodem hercle uos pono et paro: parissumi estis hibus:

487 proę *VE¹*, pre *JKE²*, pro ę *B¹*, pro de *B³*, *uel* prode?
493 et commeminisse *P*, et quidem meminisse *Leo*

*Enter CURCULIO with Planesium and his slave boy, CAPPA-
DOX, and LYCO from the pimp's house.*

CUR   You go in front, girl; I can't watch over what's behind me.
     (*to Cappadox*) He said that all the jewelry and clothes
     she has belong to her.

CAP   No one denies it.

CUR   But still it's better to remind you.

LYCO (*to Cappadox*) Remember that you promised that if any- 490
     one should claim the girl as free, all the money would be
     returned to me, thirty minas.

CAP   I shall remember, be calm on that front. Now I still say
     the same.

CUR   And *I* shall want you to remember this, too.

CAP   I do remember it, and I'll hand her over to you formally.

CUR   I should take anything formally from a pimp? They have 495
     nothing of their own except for the bare tongue with
     which they swear off if anything's been entrusted to
     them. You don't own the ones you formally sell, you don't
     own the ones you set free, you don't own the ones you or-
     der around, no one sells to you with authority, and you
     don't sell with authority to anyone. In my opinion the
     class of pimps is among men like flies, gnats, bedbugs, 500
     lice, and fleas: you're a pest, a pain, and a nuisance, and
     you aren't of any use to anybody. Nobody decent dares to
     stand beside you on the market; if anyone does, people
     find fault with him, he's seen and rebuked, and they say
     he's throwing away his money and reputation, even if he
     hasn't done anything.

LYCO You really do know your pimps well in my opinion, One- 505
     eye.

CUR   I put you in the very same category and consider you

  hi saltem in occultis locis prostant, uos in foro ipso;
  uos faenori, hi male suadendo et lustris lacerant homi-
   nes.
  rogitationes plurumas propter uos populus sciuit,
510 quas uos rogatas rumpitis: aliquam reperitis rimam;
  quasi aquam feruentem frigidam esse, ita uos putatis
   leges.
LYCO tacuisse mauellem.
CAP   hau male meditate maledicax es.
CVR indignis si male dicitur, male dictum id esse dico,
  uerum si dignis dicitur, bene dictum est meo quidem
   animo.
515 ego mancupem te nil moror nec lenonem alium quem-
   quam.
  Lyco, numquid uis?
LYCO   bene uale.
CVR   uale.
CAP   heus tu! tibi ego dico.
CVR eloquere, quid uis?
CAP   quaeso ut hanc cures ‹ut› bene sit isti.
  bene ego istam eduxi meae domi et pudice.
CVR   si huius miseret,
  ecquid das qui bene sit?
CAP   malum.
CVR   tibi opust [hoc] qui te procures.
520 CAP quid stulta ploras? ne time, bene hercle uendidi ego te;
  fac sis bonae frugi sies, sequere istum bella belle.

---

517 ut *add. Pylades* 519 hoc *del. Pylades*

---

[32] Boiling water can hurt, cold water cannot. Bankers behave as if
the laws had no power over them.

equals: you're just the same as these. They at least offer
their services in hidden places, but you do so in the very
market. You tear people to pieces with your interest,
they do so by encouraging people to behave badly and
through brothels. The people have passed countless bills
because of you, which you break as soon as they've been   510
passed; you always find some loophole. As if boiling wa-
ter were cold, that's how you consider laws.[32]

LYCO (*aside*) I wish I'd kept quiet.

CAP (*to Curculio*) You're not badly prepared for a tirade.

CUR (*to Cappadox*) If you speak badly about people who don't
deserve it, then I say it's badly spoken. But if you speak
badly about people who do deserve it, it's well spoken in
my opinion. I don't care for you as an agent, nor for any   515
other pimp for that matter. (*to the banker*) Lyco, do you
want anything?

LYCO Goodbye.

CUR Bye. (*turns to go*)

CAP (*to Curculio*) Hey you! I'm talking to you.

CUR (*stopping*) Tell me, what do you want?

CAP I ask you to make sure that all goes well for her. I brought
her up well and chastely in my house.

CUR If you feel pity for her, are you giving her anything from
which all will go well for her?

CAP A thrashing.

CUR *You* need that to look after yourself with.

CAP (*to Planesium*) What are you crying for, stupid woman?   520
Stop being afraid, I've sold you well.[33] Make sure you're a
good girl, please, follow him prettily, my pretty one.

---

[33] *Bene* "well" is ambiguous: it can refer to the high price she
fetched, but it can also indicate that the man she has been sold to is de-
cent.

LYCO Summane, numquid nunciam me uis?

CVR   uale atque salue,
     nam et operam et pecuniam benigne praebuisti.

LYCO salutem multam dicito patrono.

CVR   nuntiabo.

525 LYCO numquid uis, leno?

CAP   istas minas decem, qui me procurem,
     dum melius sit mi, des.

LYCO   dabuntur, cras peti iubeto.

CAP quando bene gessi rem, uolo hic in fano supplicare.
     nam illam minis olim decem puellam paruolam emi,
     sed eum qui mi illam uendidit numquam postilla uidi;

530   periisse credo. quid id mea refert? ego argentum habeo.
     quoi homini di sunt propitii, lucrum ei profecto obiciunt.
     nunc rei diuinae operam dabo. certum est bene me
     curare.

IV. iii: THERAPONTIGONVS. LYCO

THER non ego nunc mediocri incedo iratus iracundia,
     sed eapse illa qua excidionem facere condidici oppidis.

535   nunc nisi tu mi propere properas dare iam triginta minas,
     quas ego apud te deposiui, uitam propera ponere.

LYCO Summanus, do you want anything from me now?

CUR Farewell and be well: you were most accommodating with your effort and money.

LYCO Give my best regards to your patron.

CUR I shall.

Exit CURCULIO with Planesium and slave boy, apparently to the left; they make a detour and enter the house of Phaedromus.

LYCO Do you want anything, pimp?   525

CAP Yes, give me those ten minas with which I can look after myself till I feel better.

LYCO You'll receive them, send for them tomorrow.

Exit LYCO to the right.

CAP Since I've been successful, I want to express my gratitude here in the sanctuary; I bought that woman as a little girl for ten minas a long time ago, but afterward I never saw the man who sold her; I believe he's died. What do I   530
care? I have the money. Him to whom the gods are well-disposed they really shower with profit. Now I'll see to the sacrifice. I'm resolved to look after myself well.

Exit CAPPADOX into the shrine of Aesculapius.
Enter THERAPONTIGONUS with a slave boy and LYCO from the market.

THER I am walking along, not enraged with some minor rage now, but with that very same rage through which I've learned to level entire towns. Unless you're quick now to   535
quickly give me the thirty minas I left at your place, be quick to leave your life.

LYCO non edepol nunc ego te mediocri macto infortunio,
sed eopse illo quo mactare soleo quoi nil debeo.

THER ne te mi facias ferocem aut supplicare censeas.

540 LYCO nec tu me quidem umquam subiges redditum ut reddam
tibi,
nec daturus sum.

THER   idem ego istuc quom credebam credidi,
te nihil esse redditurum.

LYCO   quor nunc a me igitur petis?

THER scire uolo quoi reddidisti.

LYCO   lusco liberto tuo,
is Summanum se uocari dixit, ei reddidi.

545 qui has tabellas opsignatas attulit, quas tu mihi [tabel-
las]—

THER quos tu mihi luscos libertos, quos Summanos somnias?
nec mihi quidem libertus ullust.

LYCO   facis sapientius
quam pars lenonum, libertos qui habent et eos deserunt.

THER quid nunc?

LYCO   quod mandasti feci, tui honoris gratia,

550 tuom qui signum ad me attulisset, nuntium ne sper-
nerem.

THER stultior stulto fuisti qui is tabellis crederes.

LYCO quis res publica et priuata geritur, nonne is crederem?
ego abeo, tibi res soluta est recte. bellator, uale.

THER quid, ualeam?

LYCO   at tu aegrota aetatem, si lubet, per me quidem.

545 tabellas[2] *del. Camerarius*

LYCO I am not inflicting some minor misfortune on you now, but the very same misfortune I habitually inflict on someone to whom I owe nothing.

THER Don't act the wild man to me or think that I'll entreat you.

LYCO Neither will you ever force me to return to you what's already been returned, nor will I give it to you.   540

THER When I trusted you with that money, I trusted that the very same thing would happen, that you wouldn't return anything.

LYCO Then why do you demand it from me now?

THER I want to know who you returned it to.

LYCO To your one-eyed freedman. He said he was called Summanus. I returned it to him. He brought me these sealed   545
tablets (shows them) which you—

THER (interrupting) What one-eyed freedmen, what Summanuses are you dreaming about? I for one don't have any freedman.

LYCO You act more wisely than part of the pimps, who do have freedmen and then leave them in the lurch.

THER What now?

LYCO I've done what you instructed me to do, out of regard for you: I didn't reject the messenger who brought your seal   550
to me.

THER You were more stupid than stupidity itself to trust these tablets.

LYCO Shouldn't I have trusted the documents through which public and private business is conducted? I'm going away, you've been paid correctly. Farewell, warrior.

THER What, I should fare well?

LYCO Then be ill for the rest of your life if you wish, I couldn't care less.

555 THER quid ego nunc faciam? quid refert me fecisse regibus
　　　　ut mi oboedirent, si hic me hodie umbraticus deriserit?

IV. iv: CAPPADOX. THERAPONTIGONVS

CAP quoi homini di sunt propitii, ei non esse iratos puto.
　　　postquam rem diuinam feci, uenit in mentem mihi,
　　　ne tarpezita exulatum abierit, argentum ut petam,
560　ut ego potius comedim quam ille.
THER　　　　　　　　　　　　　　　　iusseram saluere te.
CAP Therapontigone Platagidore, salue; saluos quom aduenis
　　　in Epidaurum, hic hodie apud me . . . numquam delinges
　　　salem.
THER bene uocas, uerum locata res est . . . ut male sit tibi.
　　　sed quid agit meum mercimonium apud te?
CAP　　　　　　　　　　　　　　　　nil apud me quidem,
565　ne facias testis, neque equidem debeo quicquam.
THER　　　　　　　　　　　　　　　　　　quid est?
CAP quod fui iuratus, feci.
THER　　　　　　　　　　　　reddin an non uirginem,
　　　prius quam te huic meae machaerae obicio, mastigia?
CAP uapulare ego te uehementer iubeo: ne me territes.
　　　illa abducta est, tu auferere hinc a me, si perges mihi
570　male loqui, profecto, quoi ego nisi malum nil debeo.
THER min malum minitare?

Exit LYCO to the right.

THER What should I do now? What's the point of having forced   555
kings to obey me if this liver of a sheltered life has the
laugh of me today?

Enter CAPPADOX from the shrine of Aesculapius.

CAP   (*to himself*) With him to whom the gods are well-dis-
posed I don't think they are angry. After I offered sacri-
fice, it occurred to me to demand my money for fear that
the banker might have gone into exile, so that I eat it up   560
rather than he.

THER I gave my greetings to you.

CAP   Therapontigonus Platagidorus, my greetings. Since
you've arrived safely in Epidaurus, here at my place to-
day you'll . . . never have as much as a lick of salt.

THER Thanks for the invitation, but I've already arranged . . . to
give you a tough time. But what about my merchandise at
your place?

CAP   Not at *my* place. No need to bring any witnesses, and I   565
for one don't owe you anything.

THER What's that?

CAP   I did what I'd sworn.

THER Are you returning the girl to me or not before I throw you
in front of this sword of mine, you good-for-nothing?
(*draws his sword*)

CAP   I tell you to get a good beating: don't try to scare me. The
girl has been *led* away, and you will be *carried* away from
me if you continue to insult me, mark my words; I owe   570
you nothing except a beating.

THER Are you threatening me with a beating?

CAP   atque edepol non minitabor, sed dabo, [mihi]
     si perges molestus esse.

THER   leno minitatur mihi,
     meaeque pugnae proeliares plurumae optritae iacent?
     at ita me machaera et clupeus *** ⟨meus⟩
575   bene iuuent pugnantem in acie: nisi mi uirgo redditur,
     iam ego te faciam ut hinc formicae frustillatim differant.

CAP   at ita me uolsellae, pecten, speculum, calamistrum
         meum
     bene me amassint meaque axitia linteumque extersui,
     ut ego tua magnufica uerba neque istas tuas magnas mi-
         nas
580   non pluris facio quam ancillam meam quae latrinam
         lauat.
     ego illam reddidi qui argentum a te attulit.

THER   quis is est homo?

CAP   tuom libertum sese aiebat esse Summanum.

THER   meum?
     attat! Curculio hercle uerba mihi dedit, quom cogito.
     is mihi anulum surrupuit.

CAP   perdidistin tu anulum?
585   miles pulchre centuriatus est expuncto in manipulo.

THER ubi nunc Curculionem inueniam?

CAP   in tritico facillume,
     uel quingentos curculiones pro uno faxo reperias.
     ego abeo, uale atque salue.

571–72 mihi² *del. Müller* (*an ad insequentem uersum pertinet?* mi si
perges ess' molestus *haud displicet*)
574 *altera pars uersus deest* meus *add. Lindsay*
576 hic *P*, hunc *Osbernus*, hinc *Lanciotti in apparatu*
582 esse aiebat sese *P, transp. Camerarius*

CAP   And I won't just threaten you, but I'll give you one if you
      continue to be a nuisance.

THER A pimp is threatening me, and my large number of mili-
      tary exploits lie trampled on in the dust? But as truly as
      my sword and shield *** may support me well when I   575
      fight in the field: unless the girl is returned to me, I'll
      make sure this instant that ants will carry you away here
      in pieces.

CAP   But as truly as my depilatory tweezers, comb, mirror,
      curling tongs, makeup pot, and bath towel may love me
      well: I don't care about those pompous words and those
      great threats of yours any more than about the slave girl   580
      who cleans my loo. I returned the girl to the man who
      brought the money from you.

THER Who is that man?

CAP   He said he was your freedman Summanus.

THER Mine? Goodness! Curculio has really tricked me when I
      think about it. He made off with my ring.

CAP   You gave up your ring? The soldier is well marshaled in a   585
      buggered brigade.[34]

THER Where should I now find Curculio, this weevil?

CAP   Very easily in the wheat; I bet you'll even find five hun-
      dred weevils instead of one. I'm off, farewell and be well.

Exit CAPPADOX to the right.

[34] Pun on the two meanings of *anulus* "ring/anus": the soldier is
mocked for losing his ring/being the passive partner in anal sex. Hence
he fits into a military unit of 140–200 "buggered" men.

THER   male uale, male sit tibi!

       quid ego faciam? maneam an abeam? sicin mi esse os
       oblitum?

590   cupio dare mercedem qui illunc ubi sit commonstret
       mihi.

ACTVS V

V. i: CVRCVLIO

CVR   antiquom poetam audiui scripsisse in tragoedia

       mulieres duas peiores esse quam unam. res ita est.

       uerum mulierem peiorem quam haec amica est Phae-
       dromi

       non uidi neque audiui, nec pol dici nec fingi potest

595   peior quam haec est: quae ubi me habere hunc conspica-
       ta est anulum

       rogat unde habeam. "quid id tu quaeris?" "quia mi quae-
       sito est opus."

       nego me dicere. ut eum eriperet, manum arripuit mordi-
       cus.

       uix foras me abripui atque effugi. apage istanc cani-
       culam!

V. ii: PLANESIVM. PHAEDROMVS. CVRCVLIO.
THERAPONTIGONVS

PLA   Phaedrome, propera.

PHAE   quid properem?

PLA   parasitum ne amiseris.

600   magna res est.

---

595 quam haec est *P*, *del. Pylades* (*qui* med hunc habere *seruat*)
med *B*, met *VE¹*, me *JKE^c* hunc habere *P*, *transp. Gruterus*

THER Fare badly, may you have a bad time! What shall I do? Shall I wait or go away? Is it possible that I've been tricked like this? I wish to give a reward to the man who 590 shows me where that person is. (*steps aside with slave boy*)

ACT FIVE

Enter CURCULIO from Phaedromus' house, running and carrying a ring in his hands.

CUR I've heard that an ancient poet wrote in a tragedy that two women are worse than one. That is true. But I haven't seen or heard of a woman worse than this girlfriend of Phaedromus is, and a woman worse than she is 595 can't be mentioned or invented: when she saw that I have this ring, she asked me where I got it from. "Why are you asking me this?" "Because I need to ask." I refused to tell her. She snatched my hand, biting me in the process, in order to pull it off. I hardly managed to get outside and run off. Away with that little bitch!

Enter PLANESIUM and PHAEDROMUS from his house.

PLA Phaedromus, hurry up.
PHAE Hurry up with what?
PLA Don't lose your hanger-on. Something big is at stake. 600

CVR	nulla est mihi, nam quam habui apsumpsi celeriter.
PHAE	teneo. quid negoti est?
PLA	rogita unde istunc habeat anulum.
	pater istum meus gestitauit.
CVR	at mea . . . matertera.
PLA	mater ei utendum dederat.
CVR	pater tuos rursum tibi.
PLA	nugas garris.
CVR	soleo, nam propter eas uiuo facilius.

605   quid nunc?

PLA	opsecro, parentes ne meos mi prohibeas.
CVR	quid ego? sub gemmane apstrusos habeo tuam matrem
	et patrem?
PLA	libera ego sum nata.
CVR	et alii multi qui nunc seruiunt.
PHAE	enim uero irascor.
CVR	dixi equidem tibi unde ad me hic peruenerit.
	quotiens dicendum est? elusi militem, inquam, in alea.

610   THER   saluos sum, eccum quem quaerebam. quid agis, bone
                uir?

CVR	audio.
	si uis tribus bolis uel in chlamydem.
THER	quin tu is in malam crucem
	cum bolis, cum bulbis? redde etiam argentum aut uirgi-
	nem.

603 uo is *B*, uois *VE¹*, tuos *E³*, tuus *JK*
605 quid nunc *Planesio dedit Ribbeck*
612 bulbis *BVK*, bullis *JE*

298

CUR   Nothing is at stake with me: I've used up quickly everything I ever had.[35]

PHAE *(to Planesium, grabbing Curculio)* I've got him. What's the matter?

PLA   Ask him where he has that ring from. My father used to wear it.

CUR   But also my . . . aunt.

PLA   His mother gave it to him to use.

CUR   And your father in turn to you.

PLA   You're talking nonsense.

CUR   That's my habit: because of it I live more easily. What 605
now?

PLA   Please, don't keep my parents from me.

CUR   I'm doing what? Am I keeping your mother and father tucked away under the precious stone?

PLA   I was born free.

CUR   And so were many others who are slaves now.

PHAE I'm really getting angry.

CUR   I told you where I got the ring from. How often do you need to be told? I say, I tricked a soldier in a game of dice.

THER *(approaching with slave boy)* I'm safe, look, the very man 610
I was trying to find. How are you, my good man?

CUR   I'm listening. Three throws of dice, if you like—*(eyeing him)* well, for your cloak.

THER Why don't you go to the hangman with your dice and with your dishes?[36] Give me back the money or the girl now.

---

[35] Pun on the meanings of *res*: Planesium means "matter," Curculio, "wealth."

[36] Lit. "with your throws and with your onions." The *bulbi* do not only come up because they sound similar to *boli*, but also because the latter can mean "choice morsels" as well as "throws of the dice."

CVR   quod argentum, quas tu mihi tricas narras? quam tu uir-
       ginem
       me reposcis?

THER   quam ab lenone abduxti hodie, scelus uiri.

615   CVR   nullam abduxi.

THER   certe eccistam uideo.

PHAE   uirgo haec libera est.

THER   mean ancilla libera ut sit, quam ego numquam emisi
       manu?

PHAE   quis tibi hanc dedit mancupio? aut unde emisti? fac
       sciam.

THER   ego quidem pro istac rem solui ab tarpezita meo:
       quam ego pecuniam quadruplicem aps te et lenone aufe-
       ram.

620   PHAE   qui scis mercari furtiuas atque ingenuas uirgines,
       ambula in ius.

THER   non eo.

PHAE   licet te antestari?

THER   non licet.

PHAE   Iuppiter te, miles, perdat, intestatus uiuito;
       at ego, quem licet, te. accede huc.

THER   seruom antestari?

CVR   uide.

624–
25   em ut scias me liberum esse! ergo ambula in ius.

THER   em tibi!

CVR   o ciues, ciues!

THER   quid clamas?

PHAE   quid tibi istum tactio est?

THER   quia mi lubitum est.

622 male *P*, miles *Leo*

CUR   What money, what nonsense are you telling me about?
      What girl are you demanding back from me?
THER The one you took away from the pimp today, you crimi-
      nal.
CUR   I didn't take any away.   615
THER Of course you did, I can see her here.
PHAE This girl is free.
THER My slave girl should be free? I've never freed her.
PHAE Who sold her to you? Or where did you buy her? Let me
      know.
THER I paid for her from my banker's. This money I'll take away
      from you and the pimp, fourfold.
PHAE You who know how to buy stolen freeborn girls, go to   620
      court.
THER I'm not going.
PHAE (still to the soldier) Can you testify?
THER No, I can't.
PHAE May Jupiter ruin you, soldier; live without your testicles[37]
      then. (to Curculio) But I, who can, take you as my wit-
      ness. Come here. (touches his ear[38])
THER A slave acting as witness?
CUR   Watch out. Here, so that you know that I'm free! (hits   625
      him) Go to court then.
THER Here, one for you! (hits back)
CUR   O citizens, citizens!
THER What are you shouting for?
PHAE What did you touch this chap for?
THER Because I felt like it.

[37] Lat. testis can mean "witness" as well as "testicle."
[38] The ordinary procedure in engaging a witness.

PHAE	accede huc tu, ego illum tibi dedam, tace.
PLA	Phaedrome, opsecro, serua me.
PHAE	tamquam me et genium meum.
	miles, quaeso ⟨te⟩ ut mihi dicas unde illum habeas anu-
	lum,

630   quem parasitus hic te elusit.

PLA	per tua genua te opsecro,
	ut nos facias certiores.
THER	quid istuc ad uos attinet?
	quaeratis chlamydem et machaeram hanc unde ad me
	peruenerit.
CVR	ut fastidit gloriosus!
THER	mitte istum, ego dicam omnia.
CVR	nihil est quod ille dicit.
PLA	fac me certiorem, opsecro.

635 THER ego dicam, surge. hanc rem agite atque animum aduor-
       tite.

       pater meus habuit Periplanes, Planesium.
       is prius quam moritur mihi dedit tamquam suo,
       ut aequom fuerat, filio—

PLA	pro Iuppiter!
THER	et isti me heredem fecit.
PLA	⟨o⟩ Pietas mea,

640   serua me, quando ego te seruaui sedulo.
       frater mi, salue.

THER	qui credam ego istuc? cedo,
	si uera memoras, quae fuit mater tua?
PLA	Cleobula.
THER	nutrix quae fuit?

629 te *add. Becker*

PHAE (*to Curculio*) You, come here, I shall hand him over to
      you, be quiet.

PLA   Phaedromus, please, save me!

PHAE (*to Planesium*) Just like myself and my vital spirit. (*to
      Therapontigonus*) Soldier, I ask you to tell me where you
      got that ring from which my hanger-on tricked you out of.   630

PLA   I implore you by your knees, do let us know. (*prostrates
      herself*)

THER What business of yours is this? You might as well ask
      where I got this cloak and sword from.

CUR   How this pompous person is giving himself airs!

THER (*to Phaedromus*) Hand this chap over (*points to Curcu-
      lio*) and I'll tell you everything.

CUR   What he's saying amounts to nothing.

PLA   Do let me know, I implore you.

THER (*to Planesium*) I shall tell you. Rise. (*she obeys; to all*) Lis-   635
      ten carefully and pay attention. (*to Planesium*) My father
      Periplanes had it, Planesium. Before he died he gave it to
      me, since I was his son, as was appropriate—

PLA   (*interrupting*) O Jupiter!

THER And with it he made me his heir.

PLA   O my dear goddess of filial love, preserve me, since I've   640
      preserved you eagerly. (*to Therapontigonus*) My dear
      brother, greetings.

THER Why should I believe this? Tell me, if you speak the truth,
      who was your mother?

PLA   Cleobula.

THER Who was your nurse?

---

636 Planesium *uocatiuus plerisque editoribus post imperatiuum
pluralem suspectus aut ineptus uidetur*

   639 iste *P*, isti *Bothe* o *add.* ς

PLA   Archestrata.

644–45   ea me spectatum tulerat per Dionysia.
postquam illo uentum est, iam, ut me collocauerat,
exoritur uentus turbo, spectacla ibi ruont,
ego pertimesco: [tum] ibi me nescioquis arripit
timidam atque pauidam, nec uiuam nec mortuam.

650   nec quo me pacto apstulerit possum dicere.

THER   memini istanc turbam fieri. sed tu dic mihi,
ubi is est homo qui te surrupuit?

PLA   nescio.
uerum hunc seruaui semper mecum una anulum;
cum hoc olim perii.

THER   cedo ut inspiciam.

CVR   sanan es,

655   quae isti committas?

PLA   sine modo.

THER   pro Iuppiter!
hic est quem ego tibi misi natali die.
tam facile noui quam me. salue, mea soror.

PLA   frater mi, salue.

PHAE   deos uolo bene uortere
istam rem uobis.

CVR   et ego nobis omnibus:

660   tu ut hodie adueniens cenam des sororiam,
hic nuptialem cras dabit. promittimus.

PHAE   tace tu.

CVR   non taceo, quando res uortit bene.
tu istanc desponde huic, miles. ego dotem dabo.

THER   quid dotis?

CVR   egone? ut semper, dum uiuat, me alat.

665   uerum hercle dico.

PLA   Archestrata. She'd taken me to watch the festival of Dio- 645
     nysus. After we'd arrived there and she'd put me in my
     seat, a whirlwind arose immediately and the seats col-
     lapsed. I began to be terrified. Someone snatched me
     there, a trembling and fearful girl, neither alive nor dead. 650
     And I can't tell how he carried me off.

THER I remember that panic arising. But you, tell me, where is
     the man who snatched you?

PLA   I don't know. But I've always kept this ring with me. (*pro-*
     duces ring) With this ring I got lost back then.

THER Give it to me so I can examine it. (*she hands it over*)

CUR   (*to Planesium*) Are you in your right mind, giving it to this 655
     person?

PLA   Just let him have it.

THER O Jupiter! This is the one I sent you on your birthday. I
     know it as well as myself. Greetings, my dear sister.

PLA   My dear brother, greetings.

PHAE I wish that the gods may bless you in this.

CUR   And I wish that they may bless us all: (*to the soldier*) you 660
     are to provide the sister-finding dinner on your arrival
     today and he (*points to Phaedromus*) will provide the
     wedding dinner tomorrow. We accept the invitation.

PHAE Be quiet, you.

CUR   I won't be quiet since things are going well. Betroth the
     girl to this man, soldier. I'll give the dowry.

THER What dowry?

CUR   I? That she shall always feed me as long as I live. Yes, I'm 665
     speaking the truth.

---

648 tum *del. Kampmann*

THER   me lubente feceris.

    et leno hic debet nobis triginta minas.

PHAE quam ob rem istuc?

THER   quia ille ita repromisit mihi:

    si quisquam hanc liberali asseruisset manu,

    sine controuorsia omne argentum reddere.

670   nunc eamus ad lenonem.

  CVR   laudo.

PHAE   hoc prius uolo,

    meam rem agere.

THER   quid id est?

PHAE   ut mihi hanc despondeas.

  CVR quid cessas, miles, hanc huic uxorem dare?

THER si haec uolt.

  PLA   mi frater, cupio.

THER   fiat.

  CVR   bene facis.

PHAE spondesne, miles, mi hanc uxorem?

THER   spondeo.

675 CVR et ego hoc idem unum: spondeo.

THER   lepide facis.

676–78   sed eccum lenonem, incedit, thesaurum meum.

           V. iii: CAPPADOX. THERAPONTIGONVS.
                PHAEDROMVS. PLANESIVM

679 CAP argentariis male credi qui aiunt, nugas praedicant:

680   nam et bene et male credi dico; id adeo ego hodie exper-
        tus sum.

    non male creditur qui numquam reddunt, sed prorsum
        perit.

    uel ille decem minas dum soluit, omnis mensas transiit.

    postquam nil fit, clamore hominem posco: ille in ius me
        uocat;

THER You'll do me a pleasure. And the pimp here owes us thirty minas.

PHAE What for?

THER Because he promised me that if anyone claimed this girl as free, he would return the entire price without any argument. Now let's go to the pimp. 670

CUR Excellent idea.

PHAE First I want to sort out my business.

THER What's that?

PHAE Betroth this lady to me.

CUR Soldier, what are you hesitating to give her to him as his wife?

THER If she wants it.

PLA My dear brother, I desire it.

THER So be it.

CUR Thank you.

PHAE Soldier, do you betroth this girl to me as my wife?

THER Yes, I betroth her.

CUR And I do the very same thing: I betroth her. 675

THER Charming of you. (*turning around*) But look at the pimp, here he comes, my treasure.

Enter CAPPADOX from the right.

CAP People who say bankers are ill trusted talk nonsense: I 680 say they are trusted both well and ill. What's more, I've experienced this myself today. Money is not ill trusted to those who never return it, but perishes completely. For instance, while that Lyco was trying to pay me the ten minas, he went around all the banks. After nothing came of it, I demanded my money from him by shouting. He

---

667 ille *P*, illic *Fleckeisen*   682 uelut *P*, uel ille *Leo*

pessume metui ne mihi hodie apud praetorem solueret.
685   uerum amici compulerunt: reddit argentum domo.
nunc domum properare certum est.

THER   heus tu, leno, te uolo!
CVR   et ego te uolo.
CAP   at ego uos nolo ambos.
THER   sta sis ilico.
CVR   atque argentum propere propera uomere.
CAP   quid mecum est tibi?
aut tibi?
THER   quia ego ex te hodie faciam pilum catapultarium
690   atque ita te neruo torquebo, itidem ut catapultae solent.
CVR   delicatum te hodie faciam, cum catello ut accubes,
ferreo ego dico.
CAP   at ego uos ambo in robusto carcere
ut pereatis.
THER   collum opstringe, abduce istum in malam crucem.
CVR   quicquid est, ipse ibit potius.
CAP   pro deum atque hominum fidem!
695   hocin pacto indemnatum atque intestatum me abripi?
opsecro, Planesium, et te, Phaedrome, auxilium ut feras.
PLA   frater, opsecro te, noli hunc indemnatum perdere.
bene et pudice me domi habuit.

687 et . . . uolo *dedit Phaedromo P, Curculioni Lanciotti*
688 atque . . . uomere *dedit Phaedromo P, Curculioni Lanciotti*
691–92 delicatum . . . dico *dedit militi P, Curculioni Lanciotti,*
Phaedromo Pistoris
693 collum . . . crucem *dat militi P, Phaedromo Leo*
694 quicquid . . . potius *dat Phaedromo P, Curculioni Lanciotti,*
Therapontigono Leo
697 condempnatum *P,* indemnatum *Pius*

called me to court. I was terribly afraid that he would pay
me at the praetor's today.[39] But his friends coerced him. 685
He returned the money out of his own. Now I'm resolved
to rush home.

THER *(approaching)* Hey, you, pimp, I want to speak to you!

CUR And *I* want to speak to you.

CAP But I don't want to speak to either of you.

THER Stop at once, will you?

CUR And be quick to spit out the money quickly.

CAP *(to the soldier)* What business have I with you? *(to Cur-
culio)* Or with you?

THER Because I'll turn you into the missile of a catapult today 690
and tie you up with a twisted rope in the same way as cat-
apults do.[40]

CUR I'll turn you into a fop today, so that you will sleep with a
little dog, I mean a dog collar, an iron one.[41]

CAP But I shall put you both into a solid cell so that you perish.

THER *(to slave boy)* Put a noose round his neck, drag him off to
the gallows.

CUR Whatever it is, he'll prefer to go by himself.

CAP In the name of all that's sacred on heaven and earth! That 695
I should be dragged off in this way without sentence and
without witnesses against me! I implore you, Planesium,
and you, Phaedromus, bring me help!

PLA My brother, I beg you, don't kill this man without sen-
tence. He looked after me well and chastely at his house.

---

[39] There he might perjure himself and get away without paying or
with paying little.

[40] A *neruos* can be the rope in a catapult or an apparatus for binding
and torturing prisoners.

[41] A pun on *catellus* "puppy" and *catella* "little chain."

THER   hau uoluntate id sua:
       Aesculapio huic habeto, quom pudica es, gratiam;

700   nam si is ualuisset, iam pridem quoquo posset mitteret.

PHAE animum aduortite ⟨hoc⟩, si possum hoc inter uos compo-
            nere.
       mitte istunc. accede huc, leno. dicam meam sententiam,
       siquidem uoltis quod decrero facere.

THER   tibi permittimus.

CAP   dum quidem hercle ita iudices, ne quisquam a me argen-
            tum auferat.

705 THER quodn' promisti?

CAP   qui promisi?

PHAE   lingua.

CAP   eadem nunc nego.
       dicendi, non rem perdendi gratia haec nata est mihi.

PHAE nihil agit, collum opstringe homini.

CAP   iam iam faciam ut iusseris.

THER quando uir bonus es, responde quod rogo.

CAP   roga quod lubet.

THER promistin, si liberali quisquam hanc assereret manu,

710   te omne argentum redditurum?

CAP   non commemini dicere.

THER quid? negas?

CAP   nego hercle uero. quo praesente? quo in loco?

CVR   me ipso praesente et Lycone tarpezita.

CAP   non taces?

CVR   non taceo.

CAP   non ego te flocci facio; ne me territes.

THER me ipso praesente et Lycone factum est.

    701 hoc *add. Langen*

THER Not out of his free will: be grateful to Aesculapius here
for being chaste: if this chap had been well, he'd long   700
have sent you wherever he could.

PHAE Pay attention if I can settle this between you. (*to Thera-
pontigonus' slave boy*) Let go of him. (*to Cappadox*)
Pimp, come here. (*to all*) I'll pronounce my judgment, if
indeed you're willing to do what I decide.

THER We leave it to you.

CAP So long as you don't judge in such a way that anyone takes
money away from me.

THER The money you promised?   705

CAP How did I promise it?

PHAE With your tongue.

CAP With the very same I deny it now. My tongue was born to
me for the sake of speaking, not for the sake of ruining
my property.

PHAE He's trying to fool us. (*to slave boy*) Tie his neck.

CAP No, I'll do as you command this minute.

THER Since you're a good man, reply to what I ask you.

CAP Ask what you like.

THER Didn't you promise that if anyone claimed this woman as
free you would return the entire money?   710

CAP I don't remember saying it.

THER What? You deny it?

CAP I do indeed deny it. In whose presence? In what place?

CUR In my very own presence and that of the banker Lyco.

CAP Won't you be quiet?

CUR No, I won't.

CAP I don't give a damn about you; don't try to scare me.

THER It happened in my very own presence and that of Lyco.

712–13 me . . . tarpezita *et non taceo Curculioni dat* B³, *militi dant*
VEK

PHAE   satis credo tibi.
715   nunc adeo, ut tu scire possis, leno, meam sententiam:
        libera haec est, hic huius frater est, haec autem huius
           soror,
        haec mihi nubet: tu huic argentum redde. hoc iudicium
           meum est.
THER tu autem in neruo iam iacebis, nisi mi argentum redditur.
CAP   hercle istam rem iudicasti perfidiose, Phaedrome.
720   et tibi oberit et te, miles, di deaeque perduint.
        tu me sequere.
THER   quo sequar te?
CAP   ad tarpezitam meum
        ad praetorem. nam inde rem soluo omnibus quibus
           debeo.
THER ego te in neruom, haud ad praetorem hinc rapiam, ni ar-
           gentum refers.
CAP   ego te uehementer perire cupio, ne tu [me] nescias.
725 THER itane uero?
CAP   ita hercle uero.
THER   noui ego hos pugnos meos.
CAP   quid tum?
THER   "quid tum" rogitas? hisce ego, si tu me irritaueris,
        placidum te hodie reddam.
CAP   age ergo, recipe.
THER   ⟨at⟩ actutum.
CAP   licet.
PHAE tu, miles, apud me cenabis. hodie fient nuptiae.
CVR   quae res bene uortat mi et uobis! spectatores, plaudite.

716 illius soror *P*, huius s. *Luchs*   724 me *del. Guyet*
  727 at *et notam personae add. Ussing*
  729 *uersum militi dedit P, Curculioni dedi ego, Phaedromo con-*
tinuauit Seyffert

312

PHAE (*to Therapontigonus*) I believe you fully. (*to pimp*) And 715
now so you can know my opinion, pimp: this girl is free,
this man is her brother, this girl in turn is his sister, and
this girl will marry me. You return the money to him
(*points to the soldier*). This is my judgment.

THER (*to Cappadox*) You'll sit in prison in a minute unless I'm
given back my money.

CAP You've really been a treacherous judge in this matter,
Phaedromus. You shall rue it, and as for you, soldier, may 720
the gods and goddesses ruin you. Follow me, you.

THER Where should I follow you?

CAP To my banker, to the praetor: from that account I pay all
those I owe something.

THER I'll drag you off to jail, not to the praetor, unless you re-
turn the money.

CAP Just so you know, I very much wish that you come to a
sticky end.

THER Indeed? 725

CAP Yes indeed.

THER I know these fists of mine. (*bares his arms*)

CAP So what?

THER You're asking me "so what"? If you provoke me, I'll pacify
you with them today.

CAP Go on then, receive your money.

THER But at once.

CAP Okay.

PHAE You, soldier, will dine at my place. The wedding will take
place today.

CUR May this turn out well for me and you! Spectators, give us
your applause.

EPIDICUS

INTRODUCTORY NOTE

The *Epidicus* is one of several comedies named after a clever slave who helps his young master to trick the head of the household. The head of household in our play is a former Athenian soldier called Periphanes. Periphanes has a daughter, Telestis, with Philippa, a woman he loves. But Philippa is not his wife and does not live with him; Telestis was conceived in Epidaurus and born in Thebes, and Periphanes has not seen her since she was a baby, though Epidicus has been sent occasionally to see Philippa and Telestis. Telestis was taken prisoner in a war between Athens and Thebes and is now being brought to Athens. Philippa immediately contacted Periphanes to tell him that she is also coming to Athens in order to find her daughter.

We are told very little about the affair between Periphanes and Philippa, not even whether it took place before or after he married another woman in Athens. Periphanes never got along with his Athenian wife, who died some time ago but left him a son, Stratippocles. Periphanes is afraid of confessing his old affair and still-existing love to his son, even though his pompous but not very intelligent friend Apoecides tells him that there is nothing to be ashamed of.

Stratippocles is far less successful as a soldier than his

father but has an equally complex love life. Just as Periph-
anes wants to keep his affair a secret from his son, Stratip-
pocles does not want to confide in his father. Before he
took part in the war against Thebes, Stratippocles fell in
love with a girl called Acropolistis. He asked Epidicus
by post to procure her for him behind his father's back.
So Epidicus told Periphanes that Acropolistis is his daugh-
ter. Periphanes, unaware that he was being tricked, gave
Epidicus thirty minas, with which he then bought the girl
for the old man. But while abroad, Stratippocles lost inter-
est in Acropolistis and fell in love with another girl, a pris-
oner of war. This girl is Telestis, the half-sister he was
never told about. Stratippocles borrowed forty minas from
a moneylender and bought her, but never slept with her.

Our play begins when Stratippocles returns from
abroad and asks Epidicus for help since his useless friend
Chaeribulus cannot provide him with the necessary
money. Epidicus comes up with a clever plan. He goes to
Periphanes and tells him that his son wants to buy a music
girl. Periphanes prefers his son to marry a woman from a
good family and wants to get rid of this music girl. Epidicus
recommends buying the girl and selling her to a certain
soldier who is in love with her. Periphanes gives Epidicus
fifty minas and asks his friend Apoecides to make sure that
everything is done properly. Apoecides, however, being
as lazy and unintelligent as Chaeribulus, does not watch
Epidicus, who hires an unnamed music girl cheaply and
gives the rest of the money to Stratippocles, who pays off
his debt to the money-lender. In order not to arouse the
suspicion of the old men, Epidicus instructs the pimp from
whom he had bought Acropolistis to say, should he be
asked, that he has received fifty minas for a music girl. The

pimp had only received thirty minas for Acropolistis, but agrees to play along because he thinks that Epidicus wants to sell her off for a higher sum. Should the old men ask, they will of course believe that the pimp is talking about the unnamed music girl, not about Acropolistis.

It had been Periphanes' plan to hire a music girl to take part in a sacrifice he wanted to make. Epidicus makes the old men believe that he has bought Stratippocles' girl-friend and is bringing her home, but that she has been tricked into believing that she is just coming for the sacrifice. Epidicus instructs the girl to tell the truth, that is, that he has hired her for the sacrifice. The old men take her statement as proof that she has been tricked by Epidicus. Since Periphanes believes the music girl to be a disreputable character, he puts her up in a different room from Acropolistis, his supposed daughter.

Naturally, Epidicus' deception can only last for a limited time. A soldier has heard that the girl he loves, Acropolistis, is in Periphanes' house and comes to buy her. Periphanes is happy at the opportunity to sell his son's girl-friend to his rival. But because Periphanes believes Acropolistis to be his daughter, he presents the soldier with the unnamed music girl. The soldier tells him that this is not the girl he loves. She cannot conceal the situation any longer and says that she is free and cannot be sold anyway, as she had claimed all along. She also says truthfully that she does not know where Acropolistis is. Periphanes realizes that the girl was speaking the truth all along and angrily sends her off.

The next person to arrive is Philippa. She finds Periphanes and they recognize each other. She is distraught because she has not found her daughter. Periphanes tells her not to worry and brings out the supposed daughter, Acropolistis. Of course Philippa notices instantly that this is not Telestis and Acropolistis admits lying to Periphanes.

Periphanes and Apoecides now go looking for Philippa's daughter, but also for Epidicus, who is to be punished severely. Epidicus is preparing to flee, but then meets Stratippocles' new girlfriend and realizes who she is. He tells Telestis and a crestfallen Stratippocles that they have the same father. Then he confronts the old men. When Periphanes understands that Epidicus has secured his daughter for him, anger changes to gratitude and he sets the slave free.

The central figure of the play is of course its eponymous hero, Epidicus. The audience admires his boldness, fears for his safety when the old men are looking for him, and rejoices when he becomes a freedman. However, the ending of the play remains somewhat unsatisfactory. Will Periphanes and Philippa marry? Under Athenian law this is not possible because Philippa is not a citizen. She can only be an unofficial life-partner, which is perhaps all that Periphanes wants after his unhappy experience of marriage. Will Stratippocles follow Epidicus' insensitive suggestion and become the lover of Acropolistis again? Such fickleness may not endear Stratippocles to us, but would certainly be in keeping with his character. But would he actually be allowed to see her again after her insolent behavior toward his father? If Terence's *Phormio* is anything to go by, he would probably be given permission to go back to her; in Terence's play the harsh father wants to forbid his son to have a girlfriend but must relent when rebuked by his wife, who reminds him that his son has only one girlfriend while he, the father, had two wives.

The uncertainties with which the comedy ends are such that a number of scholars came to the conclusion that Plautus must have changed the Greek original considerably, the idea being that a Greek author would not have allowed so many loose ends and so much frustration on the part of Stratippocles. Since we know neither the name of the Greek original nor that of its author, all such theories must remain speculative. One theory of this kind, first advocated by Dziatzko in 1899–1900, has won relatively widespread acceptance. According to Dziatzko, it is likely that in the Greek original Stratippocles married his half-sister. Marriage between half-siblings of the same father was legal in Athens and would have tied up most of the loose ends: Stratippocles' frustration would not even have arisen, both siblings would be happily married to partners from a good background, and Periphanes' worries about his son's inappropriate liaisons would disappear immediately. Since a Roman audience would not have approved of such a marriage, however, Plautus had to change the ending, which as a consequence became somewhat unsatisfactory and would have become even more so had Plautus not given such emphasis to the successful slave Epidicus.

To this theory one can object that while marriages between half-siblings were legal in Athens, they were certainly not the norm. And if there is a family crisis early on in a Greek comedy, the order that is restored is not merely legal but normative as well. This makes it highly unlikely that there ever was a Greek play in which half-siblings married each other, just as homosexual relationships, while not taboo in ancient Greece, were certainly not considered appropriate endings to comedies. Perhaps the legal argument against a marriage between Stratippo-

cles and Telestis in the Greek original of the *Epidicus*
is even more important: half-sister marriage was allowed
in Athens but only between Athenian nationals. Since
Telestis is no more an Athenian citizen than her mother, a
Greek playwright could hardly write a convincing ending
involving the marriage between Stratippocles and Telestis.

We do not know when the *Epidicus* was first staged.
The play is mentioned in the *Bacchides* (ll. 214–15), but
the *Bacchides* is one of Plautus' last comedies, so this does
not help us much. In ll. 349–51 Epidicus mentions parri-
cides. This may be a reference to Lucius Hostius, reput-
edly the first parricide at Rome, who became notorious af-
ter the Second Punic War, which ended in 201. We can
further narrow down the period in which the *Epidicus*
must have been staged for the first time if the list of expen-
sive women's dresses in ll. 222–235 is an allusion to the re-
peal of the *lex Oppia*, a law against luxury given up in 195.
The frequency and length of sung passages points in the
same direction. The *Epidicus* contains fewer long verses
than average, but a higher number of senarii and, more
important, a higher number of songs. The *Epidicus* thus
seems to belong to Plautus' middle or late period.

SELECT BIBLIOGRAPHY

Editions and Commentaries

Ammendola, G. (1917), *Plauto: Epidico* (Città di Castello).
Duckworth, G. E. (1940), *T. Macci Plauti Epidicus: Edited
with Critical Apparatus and Commentary, in Which*

EPIDICUS

Is Included the Work of the Late Arthur L. Wheeler (Princeton and London).

Gray, J. H. (1893), *T. Macci Plauti Epidicus* (Cambridge).

Criticism

Auhagen, U. (ed.) (2001), *Studien zu Plautus' Epidicus* (Tübingen).

Dziatzko, K. (1899 and 1900), "Der Inhalt des Georgos von Menander," in *Rheinisches Museum für Philologie* 54: 497–525 and 55: 104–11.

Keyes, C. W. (1940), "Half-Sister Marriage in New Comedy and the *Epidicus*," in *Transactions of the American Philological Association* 71: 217–29.

Raffaelli, R., and Tontini, A. (eds.) (2006), *Lecturae Plautinae Sarsinates IX: Epidicus (Sarsina, 24 settembre 2005)* (Urbino).

EPIDICVS

ARGVMENTVM

Emit fidicinam, filiam credens, senex
Persuasu serui, atque conducticiam
Iterum pro amica ei subiecit filii.
Dat erili argentum. eo sororem destinat
5 **I**mprudens iuuenis. compressae ac militis
Cognoscit opera sibi senex os sublitum—
Vt ille amicam, haec quaerebat filiam—
Sed inuenta gnata seruolum emittit manu.

PERSONAE

EPIDICVS seruos
THESPRIO seruos
STRATIPPOCLES adulescens
CHAERIBVLVS adulescens
APOECIDES senex
PERIPHANES senex
SERVOS
MILES

arg. 2 conductam *P*, conducticiam *Pylades*, conductam alteram *Leo*
arg. 5 *uel* atque

EPIDICUS

PLOT SUMMARY

Persuaded by his slave, an old man bought a lyre girl in the belief that she is his daughter, and again the slave tricked him by palming off a hired woman as his son's girlfriend. The slave gives the money to his master's son. With it the young man buys his sister without knowing it. With the help of a woman he had 5 raped and of a soldier, the old man realizes that he has been tricked—just as the soldier was looking for his girlfriend, the woman was looking for her daughter—but when his daughter is discovered, he frees his slave.

CHARACTERS

EPIDICUS a slave; the clever main character of the play
THESPRIO a slave; accompanied his young master to war
STRATIPPOCLES a young man; master of Epidicus and Thesprio
CHAERIBULUS a young man; close friend of Stratippocles
APOECIDES an old man; close friend of Periphanes
PERIPHANES an old man; father of Stratippocles and a former soldier
A SLAVE works for Periphanes
A SOLDIER rich and pompous

FIDICINA
PHILIPPA mulier
ACROPOLISTIS fidicina
DANISTA
TELESTIS uirgo

SCAENA

Athenis

EPIDICUS

A MUSIC GIRL plays the lyre
PHILIPPA a woman; comes to Athens to find her daughter
Telestis
ACROPOLISTIS a music girl; impudent
A MONEYLENDER has lent money to Stratippocles
TELESTIS a young girl; half-sister of Stratippocles

STAGING

The stage represents a street in Athens. To the left it leads to the
harbor, to the right to the city center. There are two houses on-
stage. The one on the left belongs to Periphanes, the one on the
right to Chaeribulus.

ACTVS I

I. i: EPIDICVS. THESPRIO

EPI heus, adulescens!

THES quis properantem me reprehendit pallio?

EPI familiaris.

THES fateor, nam odio es nimium familiariter.

EPI respice uero, Thesprio.

THES oh,
Epidicumne ego conspicor?

5 EPI satis recte oculis uteris.

THES salue.

EPI di dent quae uelis.
uenire saluom gaudeo.

THES quid ceterum?

EPI quod eo assolet:
cena tibi dabitur.

THES spondeo—

EPI quid?

THES —me accepturum, si dabis.

9 EPI quid tu agis? ut uales?

9ᵃ THES exemplum adesse intellego.

9ᵇ EPI eugae!

10 corpulentior uidere atque habitior.

THES huic gratia.

11 EPI quam quidem te iam diu

11ᵃ perdidisse oportuit.

EPIDICUS

ACT ONE

Enter THESPRIO from the left, clearly in a rush, followed by EPIDICUS.

EPI Hey there, young man! (*grabs his cloak from behind*)

THES Who is holding me back by my cloak when I'm in a rush?

EPI One of the family.

THES I admit it: you're being tedious in a very familiar way.

EPI But do look back, Thesprio.

THES (*turning round*) Oh, do I see Epidicus?

EPI Your eyesight is pretty normal.   5

THES Hello.

EPI May the gods give you what you wish for. I'm happy you've returned safely.

THES What about the rest?

EPI What's normally added to this: you'll be given a dinner.

THES I promise—

EPI (*interrupting*) What?

THES —to accept if you give me one.[1]

EPI How are you? Are you well?

THES I realize that my model is here.

EPI Excellent! You seem stouter and heavier.   10

THES Thanks to this one (*lifts up his left hand*).

EPI You ought to have lost it long ago.[2]

---

[1] The normal expectation is that Thesprio should promise a dinner in return.   [2] A punishment for thieves.

12	THES	minus iam furtificus sum quam antehac.
	EPI	quid ita?
	THES	rapio propalam.
	EPI	di immortales te infelicent, ut tu es gradibus grandibus!
		nam ut apud portum te conspexi, curriculo occepi sequi:
15		uix adipiscendi potestas modo fuit.
	THES	scurra es.
	EPI	scio
		te esse equidem hominem militarem.
	THES	audacter quam uis dicito.
	EPI	quid agis? perpetuen ualuisti?
	THES	uarie.
	EPI	qui uarie ualent,
		capreaginum hominum non placet mihi nec pantheri-
		num genus.
	THES	quid tibi uis dicam nisi quod est?
	EPI	ut illae res? responde.
	THES	probe.
20	EPI	quid erilis noster filius?
	THES	ualet pugilice atque athletice.
	EPI	uoluptabilem mihi nuntium tuo aduentu apportas, Thes-
		prio.
		sed ubi est is?
	THES	aduenit simul.
	EPI	ubi is ergo est? nisi si in uidulo
		aut si in melina attulisti.
	THES	di te perdant!
	EPI	te uolo . . .
		percontari: operam da, opera reddetur tibi.

19 obstenia *A*, respon *B¹VJE¹*, respondi *B³*, respondeti *E²*, respon-
detis *E³*, responde *Goetz*

THES I'm less of a sneakerthief than I was.

EPI How so?

THES I rob people openly.

EPI May the immortal gods make you unhappy! How big
your steps are! When I spotted you at the harbor, I began
to follow you at a run. I barely managed to get hold of 15
you.

THES You're a real townie.

EPI Well, I know that *you* are a military man.

THES You can say that however boldly you wish.

EPI How are you? Have you been well throughout?

THES Checkered.

EPI I don't like those of checkered health, the roe-deer or
panther type of person.[3]

THES What do you want me to tell you if not the facts?

EPI How have things been there? Answer me.

THES Fine.

EPI What about our master's son? 20

THES He's as healthy as a boxer and an athlete.

EPI You're bringing me joyful news on your arrival, Thesprio.
But where is he?

THES He arrived at the same time.

EPI Then where is he? Unless you brought him in your travel-
ing bag or your wallet.

THES May the gods ruin you!

EPI No, you . . . I want to ask: make an effort for me, the effort
will be returned to you.

---

[3] Reference to the marks left on the skin by beatings.

25	THES	ius dicis.
	EPI	me decet.
	THES	iam tu autem nobis praeturam geris?
	EPI	quem dices digniorem esse hominem hodie Athenis alte-
		rum?
27	THES	at unum a praetura tua,
27a		Epidice, abest.
	EPI	quidnam?
	THES	scies:
28		lictores duo, duo ulmei
28ᵃ		fasces uirgarum.
	EPI	uae tibi!
29		sed quid ais?
	THES	quid rogas?
29ᵃ	EPI	ubi arma sunt Stratippocli?
30	THES	pol illa ad hostis transfugerunt.
	EPI	armane?
	THES	atque equidem cito.
30ᵃ	EPI	serione dicis tu?
31	THES	serio, inquam: hostes habent.
	EPI	edepol facinus improbum!
	THES	at iam ante alii fecerunt idem.
		erit illi illa res honori.
	EPI	qui?
	THES	quia ante aliis fuit.
		Mulciber, credo, arma fecit quae habuit Stratippocles:
35		trauolauerunt ad hostis.

28 uiminei *BE*, uimin ei *J*, inminei *V*, ulmei *Hermann*
30 quidem *P*, equidem *Luchs*

THES	You speak like a judge.	25
EPI	I ought to.[4]	
THES	But can we say that you're already holding the praetor-ship?[5]	
EPI	Who else in Athens will you say deserves it more today?	
THES	Yet one thing is missing from your praetorship, Epidicus.	
EPI	What's that?	
THES	You'll know: two lictors and the two bundles of elm rods.[6]	
EPI	Curse you! But what do you say?	
THES	What do you ask?	
EPI	Where are the arms of Stratippocles?	
THES	They flew over to the side of the enemy.	30
EPI	His arms?	
THES	Yes, and they did so quickly.	
EPI	Are you saying that in earnest?	
THES	In earnest, yes: the enemy have them.	
EPI	A shocking deed!	
THES	But others have done so before. It'll be an honor for him.	
EPI	How so?	
THES	Because it was one for others before.[7] I believe Mul-ciber[8] made the arms Stratippocles had: they flew over to the enemy.	35

[4] A pun; the name Epidicus is related to ἐπιδικάζειν, the verb used when an official adjudicates the claim to an inheritance.

[5] The main duties of the praetor have to do with the law and legal proceedings.   [6] The lictors accompany officials, carrying bundles of rods as sign of their executive powers. Lictors help the officials, but Thesprio refers to people punishing Epidicus.

[7] The Greek poets Archilochus and Alcaeus famously gave up their shields and fled.   [8] An epithet of Vulcan ("the one who smelts"); things made by Vulcan had magical properties.

EPI	tum ille prognatus Theti
	sine perdat: alia apportabunt ei Nerei filiae.
	id modo uidendum est, ut materies suppetat scutariis,
	si in singulis stipendiis is ad hostis exuuias dabit.
THES	supersede istis rebus iam.
EPI	tu ipse ubi lubet finem face.
40 THES	desiste percontarier.
EPI	loquere ipse: ubi est Stratippocles?
THES	est causa qua causa simul mecum ire ueritust.
EPI	quidnam id est?
THES	patrem uidere se neuolt etiam nunc.
EPI	quapropter?
THES	scies.
	quia forma lepida et liberali captiuam adulescentulam
	de praeda mercatust.
EPI	quid ego ex te audio?
THES	hoc quod fabulor.
45 EPI	quor eam emit?
THES	animi causa.
EPI	quot illic homo animos habet?
	nam certo, prius quam hinc ad legionem abiit domo
	ipsus mandauit mi ab lenone ut fidicina,
	quam amabat, emeretur sibi. id ei impetratum reddidi.
THES	utquomque in alto uentust, Epidice, exim uelum uorti-
	tur.
50 EPI	uae misero mihi, male perdidit me!
THES	quid‹nam› istuc? quid[nam] est?

47 ipse *P*, ipsus *Bothe*
50 quid istuc quidnam est *P*, quidnam istuc? quid est *Camerarius*

EPI   Then let that son of Thetis lose them: the daughters of Nereus will bring him others.[9] One only has to make sure that there is enough raw material for the shield makers, if he gives spoils to the enemy on each and every campaign.

THES   Steer clear of these things now.

EPI   Make an end to them yourself when you like.

THES   Stop questioning me.   40

EPI   Then speak yourself: where is Stratippocles?

THES   There's a reason why he was afraid to come along with me.

EPI   What on earth is this?

THES   He doesn't want to see his father yet.

EPI   Why not?

THES   You shall know the reason. He bought a captive girl with lovely looks appropriate for a free lady from the booty.

EPI   What must I hear from you?

THES   What I'm saying.

EPI   Why did he buy her?   45

THES   To make his heart happy.

EPI   How many hearts does he have? Before he went away to the army, he certainly told me himself to buy him a lyre girl he was in love with from a pimp. I've sorted this out for him.

THES   One turns the sail according to how the wind is on the sea, Epidicus.

EPI   Bad luck to me, poor wretch! He's killed me completely!   50

THES   How so? What is it?

[9] The weapons of the great hero Achilles, son of Thetis, were also made by Hephaestus/Vulcan. Thetis was one of the fifty daughters of Nereus.

	EPI	quid? istanc quam emit, quanti eam emit?
	THES	uili.
	EPI	haud istuc te rogo.
52	THES	quid igitur?
	EPI	quot minis?
52ᵃ	THES	tot: quadraginta minis.
53		id adeo argentum ab danista apud Thebas sumpsit fae-nore
		in dies minasque argenti singulas nummis.
	EPI	papae!
55	THES	et is danista aduenit una cum eo, qui argentum petit.
	EPI	di immortales, ut ego interii basilice!
	THES	quid iam? aut quid est,
57		Epidice?
	EPI	perdidit
57ᵃ		me.
	THES	quis?
	EPI	ille qui arma perdidit.
58	THES	nam quid ita?
	EPI	quia cottidie ipse ad me ab legione epistulas
		mittebat—sed taceam optumum est,
60		plus scire satiust quam loqui
60ᵃ		seruom hominem. ea sapientia est.
61	THES	nescio edepol quid [tu] timidu's; trepidas, Epidice: ita uoltu tuo
		uideor uidere commeruisse hic me apsente in te aliquid mali.
	EPI	potin ut molestus ne sies?
	THES	abeo.
	EPI	asta, abire hinc non sinam.

61 tu *del. Lindsay*   uoltum tuum *BVEJ*, uoltu tuo *Wheeler*

336

EPI	Well then? This woman he bought, how much did he buy her for?
THES	Cheaply.
EPI	That's not what I'm asking you.
THES	What are you asking then?
EPI	For how many minas?
THES	For so many: for forty minas. Yes, and he took that money from a moneylender in Thebes on interest, one coin for each mina per day.[10]
EPI	Whew!
THES	And this moneylender who is demanding the money has come here with him.
EPI	Immortal gods, how I've perished completely!
THES	How so? What is it, Epidicus?
EPI	He has annihilated me.
THES	Who?
EPI	The man who has annihilated his arms.
THES	How so?
EPI	Because he himself sent me letters from the army on a daily basis—(*aside*) but I'd better be quiet. It's better if a slave knows more than he says. That is wisdom.
THES	I really don't know why you're afraid. You're shaking, Epidicus: I seem to see on your face that you've committed some offense here in my absence.
EPI	Can you kindly not annoy me?
THES	I'm off. (*turns to go*)
EPI	(*grabbing him*) Stand there, I shan't let you go away.

(Lines 55, 60 marked in margin)

[10] If the coin referred to is a sesterce piece, the interest rate is 0.25% per day (91% per annum).

64	THES	quid nunc me retines?
	EPI	amatne istam quam emit de praeda?
	THES	rogas?
64ᵃ		***
64ᵇ		***
65		deperit.
	EPI	degitur
65ᵃ		corium de tergo meo.
66	THES	plusque amat quam te umquam amauit.
	EPI	Iuppiter te perduit!
67	THES	mitte nunciam,
67ᵃ		nam ille me domum
68		uotuit uenire, ad Chaeribulum iussit huc in proxumum;
69		ibi manere iussit, eo uen-
69ᵃ		turust ipsus.
	EPI	quid ita?
	THES	dicam:
70		quia patrem prius conuenire
70ᵃ		se non uolt nec conspicari,
71		quam id argentum, quod debetur
71ᵃ		pro illa, dinumerauerit.
72	EPI	eu edepol res turbulentas!
	THES	mitte me ut eam nunciam.
	EPI	haecine ubi scibit senex,
		puppis pereunda est probe.
75	THES	quid istuc ad me attinet,
		quo tu intereas modo?
77	EPI	quia perire solus nolo,
77ᵃ		te cupio perire mecum,
78		beneuolens cum beneuolente.
	THES	ab-
78ᵃ		i in malam rem maxumam a me
79		cum istac condicione.

THES	What are you keeping me back for now?	
EPI	Does he love that girl he bought from the spoils?	
THES	You ask? *** He's crazy about her.	65
EPI	The skin's being removed from my back.	
THES	And he loves her more than he's ever loved you.	
EPI	May Jupiter ruin you!	
THES	Let me go now: he forbade me to come home and told me to go to Chaeribulus here next door. He told me to wait there, he'll come there himself.	
EPI	Why is that?	
THES	I'll tell you why: he doesn't want to meet or see his father until he's paid the money owed for her.	70
EPI	Goodness, a messy situation!	
THES	Let me go now.	
EPI	When the old man knows about this, the ship will have to perish properly.	
THES	What does it matter to me how you die?	75
EPI	Because I don't want to perish alone, I'm keen on you perishing with me, a friend with a friend.	
THES	Go away from me and be hanged on those terms.	

64a–64b *duo uersus in A exstitisse uidentur*
65 detegetur *P*, degetur *Ec*, degitur *Nonius*
67a–68 uetuit domum *P, transp. O. Skutsch*

	EPI	i sane . . .
79ª		siquidem festinas magis.
80	THES	numquam hominem quemquam conueni unde abierim
		lubentius.
	EPI	illic hinc abiit. solus nunc es. quo in loco haec res sit uides
		Epidice: nisi quid tibi in tete auxili est, apsumptus es.
		tantae in te impendent ruinae: nisi suffulcis firmiter,
		non potes supsistere: itaque in te irruont montes mali.
85		neque ego nunc
85ª		quo modo
86		me expeditum ex impedito faciam, consilium placet.
87		ego miser
87ª		perpuli
88		meis dolis senem ut censeret suam sese emere filiam:
89		is suo
89ª		filio
90		fidicinam emit, quam ipse amabat, quam abiens man-
		dauit mihi.
90ª		si sibi nunc
90ᵇ		alteram
91		ab legione abduxit animi causa, corium perdidi.
92		nam ubi senex
92ª		senserit
93		sibi data esse uerba, uirgis dorsum depoliet meum.
94		at enim tu
94ª		praecaue.
95		at enim . . . bat enim! nihil est istuc. plane hoc corruptum
		est caput.
96		nequam homo es,
96ª		Epidice.
97		qui lubido est male loqui? quia tute tete deseris.
98		quid faciam?
98ª		men rogas?

340

EPI No, you go . . . if you're in such a rush. (*lets go of him*)

THES (*aside*) I've never met anyone I left more eagerly. 80

Exit THESPRIO into the house of Chaeribulus.

EPI He's left. Now you're alone. You can see in what state this situation is, Epidicus: unless you have some help for yourself in yourself, you're finished. Such a great disaster is looming above you: unless you prop it up firmly, you can't stand your ground; mountains of trouble are collapsing onto you. And I don't have a decent plan now to 85 make myself safe instead of unsafe. Poor me! With my guiles I prevailed on the old man to think he was buying his own daughter; he bought a lyre girl for his son, the 90 one the son himself was in love with and instructed me to buy when he was leaving. If he's now carried off a second one for himself from the army for his pleasure, I've ruined my skin: when the old man realizes that he's been fooled, he'll polish my back with rods. But be on your guard. Oh well . . . oh hell! It's no use. This head of mine is 95 clearly ruined. You're a good-for-nothing, Epidicus. Why do you wish to insult yourself? Because you're deserting yourself. What should I do? Are you asking me? Before

---

90 amat *P*, amabat *Guyet*
93 despoliet *BVJE²* (dispoliet *E*), depoliet *Palmerius*
97 tu te te d. *B*, tute d. *EJ*, tute tedeseris *V*, tute tete d. *Seyffert*

tuquidem antehac aliis solebas dare consilia mutua.

100   aliquid aliqua reperiundum est. sed ego cesso ire obuiam
adulescenti, ut quid negoti sit sciam. atque ipse illic est.
tristis est. cum Chaeribulo incedit aequali suo.
huc concedam, orationem unde horum placide perse-
quar.

I. ii: STRATIPPOCLES. CHAERIBVLVS. EPIDICVS

STRA   rem tibi sum elocutus omnem, Chaeribule, atque admo-
dum

105   meorum maerorum atque amorum summam edictaui
tibi.

CHAE   praeter aetatem et uirtutem stultus es, Stratippocles.
idne pudet te, quia captiuam genere prognatam bono
in praeda es mercatus? quis erit uitio qui id uortat tibi?

STRA   qui inuident omnis inimicos mi illoc facto repperi;

110   at pudicitiae eius numquam nec uim nec uitium attuli.

CHAE   iam istoc probior meo quidem animo es, quom in amore
temperes.

STRA   nihil agit qui diffidentem uerbis solatur suis;
is est amicus, qui in re dubia re iuuat, ubi re est opus.

CHAE   quid tibi me uis facere?

STRA   argenti dare quadraginta minas,

115   quod danistae detur, unde ego illud sumpsi faenore.

CHAE   si hercle haberem, ⟨pollicerer⟩.

STRA   nam quid te igitur retulit
beneficum esse oratione, si ad rem auxilium emortuom
est?

111 es meo quidem animo *P, transp. Bothe,* [es] m. q. a. *Mueller*
116 pollicerer *add. Mueller*

this you used to give advice to others on loan. Something 100
has to be found somehow. But I'm slow in approaching
the young chap to find out what's the matter. (*looking
around*) And that's him. He's depressed. He's walking
along with his companion Chaeribulus. I'll walk over
here, from where I'll follow their talk at my ease. (*steps
aside*)

Enter STRATIPPOCLES and CHAERIBULUS from the left.

STRA I've told you the entire matter, Chaeribulus, and I've
made the entire load of my afflictions and affections 105
known to you.

CHAE You're stupid beyond what your youth and bravery would
make me accept, Stratippocles. Are you ashamed be-
cause you bought a captive girl born in a good family in
the booty? Who will there be who'd find fault with you
for that?

STRA With this deed I've found as enemies all those who envy
me. But I've never done any damage or disgrace to her 110
chastity.

CHAE To my mind at least you're already more honorable be-
cause you restrain yourself in your love.

STRA A man who consoles someone in despair with his words
doesn't do anything useful; that man is a friend who in
a difficult situation helps with deeds, when deeds are
needed.

CHAE What do you want me to do for you?

STRA To give me forty silver minas that can be given to the 115
moneylender, from whom I took that sum on interest.

CHAE If I had it, I'd promise it.

STRA So what was the point of you being generous in your
speech if your help is dead when it comes to action?

343

CHAE quin edepol egomet clamore differor, difflagitor.

STRA malim istius modi mi amicos forno mersos quam foro.

120   sed operam Epidici nunc me emere pretio pretioso
        uelim.

    quem quidem ego hominem irrigatum plagis pistori
        dabo,

    nisi hodie prius comparassit mihi quadraginta minas

    quam argenti fuero elocutus ei postremam syllabam.

EPI   salua res est: bene promittit, spero seruabit fidem.

125   sine meo sumptu paratae iam sunt scapulis symbolae.

    aggrediar hominem. aduenientem peregre erum suom
        Stratippoclem

    impertit salute seruos Epidicus.

STRA   ubi is est?

EPI   adest.

    saluom huc aduenisse—

STRA   tam tibi istuc credo quam mihi.

EPI   benene usque ualuisti?

STRA   a morbo ualui, ab animo aeger fui.

130 EPI quod ad me attinuit, ego curaui: quod mandasti ‹tu› mihi

    impetratum est. empta ancilla est, quod tute ad me lit-
        teras

    missiculabas.

STRA   perdidisti omnem operam.

EPI   nam qui perdidi?

STRA quia meo nec cara est cordi nec placet.

EPI   quid retulit

    mihi tanto opere te mandare et mittere ad me epistulas?

119 furno mensos *P*, furno mersos *F*, furno occensos *Usener*
130 tu *add. Mueller*, mandauisti mihi *Bentley*
131 empta est ancilla *P, transp. Camerarius*

CHAE But I myself am being subjected to loud harassment and demands.

STRA I'd prefer friends of your sort being baked up to being bankrupt. Well, I'd like to buy the services of Epidicus 120 now for a precious price. I'll irrigate him with blows and hand him over to the miller unless he gets me forty minas today before I've pronounced the last syllable of the sum.

EPI *(with sarcasm)* The matter's safe: he's making good promises, I hope he'll keep his word. Without any ex- 125 pense on my part contributions[11] have already been prepared for my shoulder blades. I'll approach him. *(loudly)* The slave Epidicus bestows his greetings on his master Stratippocles upon his arrival from abroad.

STRA Where is he?

EPI *(stepping up)* He's present. That you have arrived safely—

STRA *(interrupting)* I believe you in this as much as myself.

EPI Have you been well throughout?

STRA Physically, yes, mentally, no.

EPI I've taken care of my duty. What you told me to do has 130 been achieved. The slave girl's been bought, which was why you kept sending me letters.

STRA You've wasted all your efforts.

EPI How come I've wasted them?

STRA She isn't dear to my heart and I don't love her.

EPI What was the point of commanding me so much and sending letters to me?

---

[11] A *symbola* "contribution" is a share each person participating in a joint banquet pays.

345

135 STRA illam amabam olim, nunc iam alia cura impendet pectori.
    EPI hercle miserum est ingratum esse homini id quod facias
        bene.
        ego quod bene feci male feci, quia amor mutauit locum.
    STRA desipiebam mentis quom illa scripta mittebam tibi.
    EPI men piacularem oportet fieri ob stultitiam tuam,
140   ut meum tergum tuae stultitiae subdas succidaneum?
    CHAE quid istic uerba facimus? huic homini opust quadraginta
        minis
        celeriter calidis, danistae quas resoluat, et cito.
    EPI dic modo: unde auferre me uis? quo a tarpezita peto?
    STRA und' lubet. nam ni ante solem occasum e lo⟨culis afferes⟩
145   meam domum ne imbitas: tu te in pistrinum ⟨conferas⟩.
    EPI facile tu istuc sine periclo et cura, corde libero
        fabulare; noui ego nostros: mihi dolet quom ego uapulo.
    STRA quid tu nunc? patierin ut ego me interimam?
    EPI   ne feceris.
        ego istuc accedam periclum potius atque audaciam.
150 STRA nunc places, nunc ego te laudo.
    EPI   patiar ego istuc quod lubet.
    STRA quid illa fiet fidicina igitur?
    EPI   aliqua res reperibitur,
        aliqua ope exsoluam, extricabor aliqua.
    STRA   plenus consili es.
        noui ego te.

144 e lo⟨culis afferes⟩ *Lindsay*
145 conferas *add. Lindsay*

STRA   I used to love her long ago, but now another love over-   135
       hangs my breast.

EPI   It really is wretched if the good you do someone is not re-
       ceived with thanks. The good I did turned bad because
       your love has changed its place.

STRA   I wasn't in my right mind when I sent you those letters.

EPI   Should I be the atonement for your stupidity, so that you   140
       subject my back as a substitute sacrifice[12] for your stu-
       pidity?

CHAE   Why are we making empty words here? He needs forty
       hot minas fast, to pay to the moneylender, and quickly.

EPI   Just tell me: where do you want me to take it from?
       Which banker should I seek it from?

STRA   From wherever you like: unless you bring it to me from
       the cash box before sunset, don't come into my house;   145
       carry yourself to the mill.

EPI   You say that easily, without danger and worry, and with a
       free heart. I know our torturers: I feel the pain when I get
       a beating.

STRA   (melodramatically) What now? Can you bear that I kill
       myself?

EPI   Don't do that. Rather, I shall take on that bold and dan-
       gerous deed.

STRA   Now I'm happy with you, now I praise you.   150

EPI   I'll bear what you like.

STRA   Then what'll happen with that lyre girl?

EPI   Something will be found, I'll rescue you with some re-
       source, I'll get you out of it in some way.

STRA   You're full of counsel. I know you.

---

[12] If the first sacrificial animal is not considered acceptable to the
gods, a substitute is slaughtered.

EPI   est Euboicus miles locuples, multo auro potens,
           qui ubi tibi istam emptam esse scibit atque hanc adduc-
             tam alteram,
155   continuo te orabit ultro ut illam tramittas sibi.
         sed ubi illa est quam tu adduxisti tecum?

STRA   iam faxo hic erit.

CHAE quid hic nunc agimus?

STRA   eamus intro huc ad te, ut hunc hodie diem
         luculentum habeamus.

EPI   ite intro, ego de re argentaria
         iam senatum conuocabo in corde consiliarium,
160   quoi potissumum indicatur bellum, unde argentum aufe-
            ram.
         Epidice, uide quid agas, ita res subito haec obiecta est
            tibi;
         non enim nunc tibi dormitandi nec cunctandi copia est.
         adeundum. senem oppugnare certum est consilium
            mihi.
         ibo intro atque adulescenti dicam nostro erili filio,
165   ne hinc foras exambulet neue obuiam ueniat seni.

ACTVS II

II. i: APOECIDES. PERIPHANES

166 AP   plerique homines, quos quom nil refert pudet,
166ᵃ   ubi pudendum est ibi eos deserit pudor,
167   quom usust ut pudeat.

       158 luculentum *A*, luculente *P*
       166 plerique homines Ω, *transp. Spengel*

EPI   There's a wealthy soldier from Euboea who owns a lot of
      gold. As soon as he knows that the first girl has been
      bought by you and that this second has been brought
      here, he'll ask you of his own accord to send the first over   155
      to him. But where's that girl you brought with you?

STRA I'll make sure she's here soon.

CHAE What are we doing here now?

STRA Let's go inside here to you so as to enjoy this day today.

EPI   (*to both*) Go inside, I'll immediately convene a delibera-
      tive session of the senate in my heart about the money
      business, whom I should declare war on and where I   160
      should take the money from.

*Exeunt STRATIPPOCLES and CHAERIBULUS into the lat-
ter's house.*

EPI   Epidicus, watch what you're doing: this matter has so
      suddenly been thrown your way. Now you don't have the
      time to be sleepy or to hesitate. You have to take him on.
      It's my definite plan to attack the old man. I'll go in and
      tell our young chap, master's son, not to walk out and not   165
      to meet the old man.

Exit EPIDICUS into the house of Chaeribulus.

ACT TWO

*Enter APOECIDES and PERIPHANES from the latter's house,
walking slowly toward the forum.*

AP   Most people who are ashamed when there's no point are
      deserted by their sense of shame when there is some-
      thing to be ashamed of, when it's necessary to feel shame.

349

is adeo tu es. quid est quod pudendum siet,

genere gnatam bono pauperem domum

170   ducere te uxorem?

171–
72   praesertim eam, qua ex tibi commemores hanc quae

    domi est filiam prognatam.

PER   reuereor filium.

AP   at pol ego te credidi

uxorem, quam tu extulisti, pudore exsequi,

175   quoius quotiens sepulcrum uides, sacruficas

ilico . . . Orco hostiis, neque adeo iniuria,

quia licitum est eam tibi uiuendo uincere.

PER   oh!

Hercules ego fui, dum illa mecum fuit;

nec sexta aerumna acerbior Herculi quam illa mihi

    obiecta est.

180 AP   pulchra edepol dos pecunia est.

PER   quae quidem pol non marita est.

II. ii: EPIDICVS. PERIPHANES. APOECIDES

EPI   st!

tacete, habete animum bonum.

183–
84
185   liquido exeo foras auspicio, aui sinistra;

acutum cultrum habeo, senis qui exenterem marsup-

    pium.

sed eccum ipsum ante aedis conspicor ⟨erum meum

    atque⟩ Apoecidem,

qualis uolo uetulos duo.

iam ego me conuortam in hirudinem atque eorum exsu-

    gebo sanguinem,

189   senati qui columen cluent.

186 erum meum atque *add. Goetz*

189ᵃ *lacunam indicauit Mueller*

You belong to precisely this category. What's there to be
ashamed of when you marry a poor woman born in a   170
good family? Especially the woman from whom you say
this daughter you have at home was born to you.

PER I respect my son's feelings.

AP But I thought you had regard for your wife, whom you
buried. Whenever you see her tomb, you immediately   175
sacrifice victims . . . to Orcus,[13] and quite rightly so, be-
cause you got the better of her by living longer.

PER Oh! I was a Hercules as long as she was with me. The
sixth labor of Hercules[14] wasn't harsher than the one that
was thrown my way.

AP A dowry is beautiful money.   180

PER Yes, if it comes without the wife.

*Enter EPIDICUS from the house of Chaeribulus, unseen by the
two old men.*

EPI (*into the house to the young men*) Hush! Be quiet, take
heart. I'm coming out with a clear omen, with the bird on
my left. I have a sharp knife which I'll disembowel the   185
old man's wallet with. (*to himself*) But look, I can see my
master himself and Apoecides in front of the house, two
old men of the sort I want. Now I'll turn myself into a
leech and suck out the blood of these men, who are
known as pillars of the senate.

---

[13] To the god of the Underworld rather than for the deceased wife.
[14] His struggle with Hippolyta.

189ª	⟨PER⟩ ***
	⟨AP⟩ ***
190	continuo ut maritus fiat.
PER	laudo consilium tuom.
	nam ego illum audiui in amore haerere apud nescioquam fidicinam,
	id ego excrucior.
EPI	di hercle omnes me adiuuant, augent, amant:
	ipsi hi quidem mi dant uiam, quo pacto ab se argentum auferam.
	age nunciam orna te, Epidice, et palliolum in collum conice
195	itaque assimulato quasi per urbem totam hominem quaesiueris.
	age, si quid agis. di immortales! utinam conueniam domi
	Periphanem, per omnem urbem quem sum defessus quaerere:
	per medicinas, per tonstrinas, in gymnasio atque in foro,
	per myropolia et lanienas circumque argentarias.
200	rogitando sum raucus factus, paene in cursu concidi.
PER	Epidice!
EPI	Epidicum quis est qui reuocat?
PER	ego sum Periphanes.
AP	et ego Apoecides sum.
EPI	et egoquidem sum Epidicus. sed, ere, optuma uos uideo opportunitate ambo aduenire.
PER	quid rei est?
EPI	mane, ⟨mane,⟩ sine respirem quaeso.
PER	immo acquiesce.
EPI	animo male est.

191 amorem *P*, amore *Camerarius*   204 mane *add. Weise*

PER   ***

AP   *** that he should get married at once.   190

PER   I praise your advice. I've heard that he is fixated on a love affair with some lyre girl or other. I'm in agony about this.

EPI   (*aside*) All the gods are helping, blessing, and loving me. They themselves are giving me a way to take the money away from them. Go on now, Epidicus, prepare yourself and throw your cloak round your neck. (*does so*) Like this 195 pretend that you've been looking for the chap throughout the whole city. If you're going to do something, do it. (*loudly, running past the two old men toward the house of Periphanes*) Immortal gods! I hope I can find Periphanes at home. I'm exhausted from looking for him through the entire town: through the clinics, through the barbers' shops, in the gymnasium and in the forum, through the perfume stalls and the butchers' shops and around the banks. I've become hoarse from asking, I al- 200 most collapsed as I ran.

PER   Epidicus!

EPI   (*pretending not to see them*) Who is it that's calling back Epidicus?

PER   I am Periphanes.

AP   And I am Apoecides.

EPI   (*turning toward them*) And I am Epidicus. But, master, I can see that you two are coming just in the nick of time.

PER   What's the matter?

EPI   Wait, wait, let me catch some breath, please.

PER   Yes, relax.

EPI   I'm feeling sick.

205	AP	recipe anhelitum.
	PER	clementer, requiesce.
	EPI	animum aduortite.
		a legione omnes remissi sunt domum Thebis.
	AP	⟨quis hoc⟩
		dicit factum?
	EPI	ego ita factum esse dico.
	PER	scin tu istuc?
	EPI	scio.
	PER	qui tu scis?
	EPI	quia ego ire uidi milites plenis uiis;
		arma referunt et iumenta ducunt.
	PER	nimis factum bene!
210	EPI	tum captiuorum quid ducunt secum! pueros, uirgines,
		binos, ternos, alius quinque; fit concursus per uias,
		filios suos quisque uisunt.
	PER	hercle rem gestam bene!
	EPI	tum meretricum numerus tantus quantum in urbe omni
		fuit
		obuiam ornatae occurrebant suis quaequae amatoribus,
215		eos captabant. id adeo qui maxume animum aduorterim?
		pleraeque eae sub uestimentis secum habebant retia.
		quom ad portam uenio, atque ego illam illi uideo praesto-
		larier
		et cum ea tibicinae ibant quattuor.
	PER	quicum, Epidice?
	EPI	cum illa quam tuos gnatus annos multos deamat, deperit,
220		ubi fidemque remque seque teque properat perdere;
		ea praestolabatur illum apud portam.
	PER	uiden ueneficam?

---

206 quis hoc *add. Camerarius*   207 scit *BEV*, sic *E³J*, dicit *Reiz*

| AP | Get your breath back. | 205 |

PER Gently, calm down.

EPI Pay attention, you two. Everybody's been sent home from military service in Thebes.

AP Who says so?

EPI I say so.

PER Do you know that for a fact?

EPI I do.

PER How do you know?

EPI Because I saw the soldiers walking down packed streets. They're bringing back arms and leading beasts of burden.

PER Excellent!

EPI Then the amount of captives they're bringing along with them! Boys, girls, two each, three each, another one five. There's a running to and fro throughout the streets, they all want to see their sons. 210

PER Fantastic!

EPI Then the entire number of prostitutes in town all rushed toward their lovers, made up nicely. They were trying to catch them. How did I know that? Most of them had nets with them under their dresses. When I came to the gate, I saw her waiting for him, and four flute girls were walking along with her. 215

PER With whom, Epidicus?

EPI With that woman with whom your son's been madly and crazily in love for many years and at whose place he's been quick to ruin his reputation and property, and himself and you. She was waiting for him at the gate. 220

PER Can you see the witch?

	EPI	sed uestita, aurata, ornata ut lepide, ut concinne, ut noue!
	PER	quid erat induta? an regillam induculam an mendiculam?
	EPI	impluuiatam, ut istaec faciunt uestimentis nomina.
225	PER	utin impluuium induta fuerit?

EPI   quid istuc tam mirabile est?
quasi non fundis exornatae multae incedant per uias.
at tributus quom imperatus est, negant pendi potis:
illis quibus tributus maior penditur, pendi potest.
quid istae quae uesti quotannis nomina inueniunt noua?
230   tunicam rallam, tunicam spissam, linteolum caesicium,
indusiatam, patagiatam, caltulam aut crocotulam,
supparum aut . . . subnimium, ricam, basilicum aut exoticum,
cumatile aut plumatile, carinum aut cerinum—gerrae maxumae!
cani quoque etiam ademptum est nomen.

PER   qui?
EPI   uocant Laconicum.
235   haec uocabula auctiones subigunt ut faciant uiros.

AP   quin tu ut occepisti loquere?
EPI   occepere aliae mulieres
duae sic post me fabulari inter sese—ego apscessi sciens
paulum ab illis, dissimulabam earum operam sermoni dare;
nec satis exaudibam, nec sermonis fallebar tamen,
240   quae loquerentur.

---

15 *Impluuiata* refers to a moiré dress (Non. 879 Lindsay), but looks as if it came from *impluuium* "basin."

16 Thus the interpretation in Non. p. 880 Lindsay.

EPI   But how nicely, how elegantly, how stylishly she was dressed, bejeweled, and made up!

PER   What did she wear? The royal or the beggarly dress?

EPI   The marbled[15] dress, as those women invent names for their clothes.

PER   How come she was wearing marble?   225

EPI   Why is that so strange? As if there weren't many women walking through the streets wearing entire estates. But when the taxes are levied, the men say they can't pay; but they can pay those women who are paid higher taxes. What about those women who find new names for their dresses every year? The sheer tunic, the thick tunic, the   230 small embroidered apron, the outer dress, the bordered dress, the marigold[16] or the saffron dress, the mini-shawl or . . . the maxi-shawl,[17] the hooded dress, the queen's or the foreign dress, the water-colored or the dishwater-colored dress, the nut-brown or the waxen dress—complete nonsense! One name's even been taken from a dog.

PER   How so?

EPI   They speak of the "Spartan."[18] These terms force hus-   235 bands to hold auctions.

AP   Why don't you talk the way you began?

EPI   Two other women began to talk among each other like this behind me—I deliberately went away from them a little and pretended not to pay attention to their conversation; I couldn't hear perfectly, but I didn't miss the gen-   240 eral drift of their conversation.

---

[17] *Supparus* "shawl" is mockingly analysed as *sub + parum* "under + too little," which enables the comic formation *subnimius* "under + too much."   [18] *Laconicus* "Spartan" can be used with ellipsis of its headnoun in the meaning "Spartan dress" (a thin garment) or "Spartan dog" (a breed used for hunting).

PER	id lubido est scire.
EPI	ibi illarum altera

dixit illi quicum ipsa ibat—

PER	quid?
EPI	tace ergo, ut audias—

postquam illam sunt conspicatae, quam tuos gnatus de-
perit:

"quam facile et quam fortunate euenit illi, opsecro,
mulieri quam liberare uolt amator!" "quisnam is est?"

245 inquit altera illi. ibi illa nominat Stratippoclem
Periphanei filium.

PER	perii hercle! quid ego ex te audio?
EPI	hoc quod actum est. egomet postquam id illas audiui lo-

qui,
coepi rursum uorsum ad illas pauxillatim accedere,
quasi retruderet hominum me uis inuitum.

PER	intellego.
250 EPI	ibi illa interrogauit illam: "qui scis? quis id dixit tibi?"

"quin hodie allatae tabellae sunt ad eam a Stratippocle,
eum argentum sumpsisse apud Thebas ab danista fae-
nore,
id paratum et sese ob eam rem id ferre."

PER	certo ego occidi!
EPI	haec sic aibat; sic audiuisse ex eapse atque epistula.
255 PER	quid ego faciam? nunc consilium a te expetesso, Apoe-

cides.

AP	reperiamus aliquid calidi, conducibilis consili.

nam illequidem aut iam hic aderit, credo hercle, aut iam
adest.

EPI	si aequom siet

me plus sapere quam uos, dederim uobis consilium
catum
quod laudetis, ut ego opino, uterque—

PER I'd like to hear about it.

EPI Then one of them said to the woman she was walking
     with—

PER (*interrupting*) What?

EPI Be quiet then so that you hear it—after they saw the
     woman your son is madly in love with, she says: "Please,
     how easily and happily things work out for a woman her
     lover wants to free!" "Who on earth is he?" the other one 245
     asks her. Then the first names Stratippocles, the son of
     Periphanes.

PER I'm dead! What must I hear from you?

EPI The facts. After I heard them talk about this, I began to
     approach them backward, gradually, as if the crowd were
     pushing me back against my will.

PER I understand.

EPI Then the second asks the other: "How do you know? 250
     Who told you this?" "Well, today she was brought a letter
     from Stratippocles, saying that he'd taken money at in-
     terest from a moneylender in Thebes, that it was ready,
     and that he was bringing it for that purpose."

PER I'm certainly dead!

EPI This was what she said; she said she'd heard this from the
     woman herself and the letter.

PER What should I do? Now I'm seeking your advice, Apoe- 255
     cides.

AP   Le's find some fresh, expedient plan: either he will be
     back in a moment, I believe, or he is back already.

EPI If it were proper for me to be wiser than you, I'd give you
     a smart plan you'd both praise, as I think—

---

253 cedo *B*, cede *J*, *om. E*, certo *Kampmann*
254 abse *BEJ*, ex eapse *Kampmann*

	PER	ergo ubi id est, Epidice?
260	EPI	—atque ad eam rem conducibile.
	AP	quid istuc dubitas dicere?
	EPI	uos priores esse oportet, nos posterius dicere,
		qui plus sapitis.
	PER	heia uero! age dice.
	EPI	at deridebitis.
	AP	non edepol faciemus.
	EPI	immo si placebit utitor,
		consilium si non placebit, reperitote rectius.
265		mi istic nec seritur nec metitur, nisi ea quae tu uis uolo.
	PER	gratiam habeo; fac participes nos tuae sapientiae.
	EPI	continuo arbitretur uxor tuo gnato atque ut fidicinam
		illam quam is uolt liberare, quae illum corrumpit tibi,
		ulciscare atque ita curetur, usque ad mortem ut seruiat.
270	AP	fieri oportet.
	PER	facere cupio quiduis dum id fiat modo.
	EPI	em!
		nunc occasio est faciundi, prius quam in urbem adue-
		nerit,
		sicut cras hic aderit, hodie non uenit.
	PER	qui scis?
	EPI	scio
		quia mihi alius dixit qui illinc uenit mane hic affore.
	PER	quin tu eloquere: quid faciemus?
	EPI	sic faciundum censeo,
275		quasi tu cupias liberare fidicinam animi gratia
		quasique ames uehementer tu illam.
	PER	quam ad rem istuc refert?

PER	(*interrupting*) Then where is it, Epidicus?	
EPI	—and expedient for this matter. (*pauses*)	260
AP	Why are you hesitating to tell us about it?	
EPI	*You* ought to come first, *we* ought to speak later.[19] You are wiser.	
PER	Come off it! Go on, tell us.	
EPI	But you'll laugh at me.	
AP	Honestly, we shan't.	
EPI	(*to Periphanes*) Well, if you like my plan, use it; (*to both*) if you don't like it, find a better one. (*to Periphanes*) The sowing and reaping isn't done for me here, but I want what you want.	265
PER	Thank you; share your wisdom with us.	
EPI	A wife should be decided on for your son at once, and as for that lyre girl whom he wants to free and who is corrupting him, you should take revenge on her and organize things so that she's a slave till death.	
AP	It ought to be seen to.	270
PER	I'm keen to do anything so long as it's seen to.	
EPI	There you are! Now's the chance to see to it, before he arrives in town; in fact, he'll be back tomorrow, but isn't coming today.	
PER	How do you know?	
EPI	I know because someone else who came from there told me he'd be back in the morning.	
PER	Tell me: what shall we do?	
EPI	I think you ought to act as if you yourself desired to free the lyre girl for your enjoyment and as if you yourself were madly in love with her.	275
PER	What's the point of that?	

---

[19] I.e. free men are more important.

EPI   rogas?

ut enim praestines argento, prius quam ueniat filius,
atque ut eam te in libertatem dicas emere—

PER   intellego.

EPI ubi erit empta, ut aliquo ex urbe amoueas; nisi quid tua
      est

280   secus sententia.

PER   immo docte!

EPI   quid tu autem, Apoecides?

AP quid ego iam nisi te commentum nimis astute intellego?

EPI iam igitur amota ei fuerit omnis consultatio
nuptiarum, ne grauetur quod uelis.

PER   uiue sapis

et placet.

EPI   tum tu igitur calide quicquid acturu's age.

285 PER rem hercle loquere.

EPI   et repperi haec te qui apscedat suspicio.

PER sine me scire.

EPI   scibis, audi.

AP   sapit hic pleno pectore.

EPI opus est homine qui illo argentum deferat pro fidicina;
nam te nolo neque opus facto est.

PER   quid iam?

EPI   ne te censeat

fili causa facere—

PER   docte!

EPI   —quo illum ab illa prohibeas:

290   ne qua ob eam suspicionem difficultas euenat.

PER quem hominem inueniemus ad eam rem utilem?

279–80 tua secus sententia est *P, transp. Weise*
282 erit *BEJ*, fuerit *Lindemann*

EPI   You ask? You are to buy her for money before your son
        comes and you are to say that you buy her in order to free
        her—

PER   (*interrupting*) I understand.

EPI   When she's bought, you have to remove her somewhere
        out of the city; unless you have a different opinion.   280

PER   No, that's brilliant!

EPI   What about you, Apoecides?

AP   What about me, except that I realize that you've thought
        this out incredibly cleverly.

EPI   Then any qualms about marrying will be removed along
        with her, so that he won't resist your wishes.

PER   You're wonderfully smart and I like it.

EPI   Then do in hot haste whatever you're going to do.

PER   Yes, you're right.   285

EPI   And I've found a way to make any suspicion in that matter
        go away from you.

PER   Let me know.

EPI   You shall, listen.

AP   This chap pours wisdom from a heart that's full of it.

EPI   (*to Periphanes*) We need someone to bring the money for
        the lyre girl there: I don't want you to do it and there's no
        need for you to do it.

PER   How so?

EPI   So that he doesn't think you're doing this on account of
        your son—

PER   (*interrupting*) Smart!

EPI   —so that you can keep him away from her; so that no dif-   290
        ficulty can arise because of this suspicion.

PER   What man will we find who can be useful for this busi-
        ness?

EPI		hic erit optumus,
	hic poterit cauere recte, iura qui et leges tenet.	
PER	Epidico habeas gratiam.	
EPI		sed ego istuc faciam sedulo:
	ego illum conueniam atque adducam huc ad te, quoia est, fidicinam	
295	atque argentum ego cum hoc feram.	
PER		quanti emi potest minimo?
EPI		illane?
	ad quadraginta fortasse eam posse emi minimo minis.	
	uerum si plus dederis referam, nihil in ea re captio est.	
	atque id non decem occupatum tibi erit argentum dies.	
PER	quidum?	
EPI	quia enim mulierem alius illam adulescens deperit,	
300	auro opulentus, magnus miles Rhodius, raptor hostium,	
	gloriosus: hic emet illam de te et dabit aurum lubens.	
	face modo, est lucrum hic tibi amplum.	
PER		deos quidem oro.
EPI		impetras.
AP	quin tu is intro atque huic argentum promis? ego uisam ad forum.	
	Epidice, eo ueni.	
EPI		ne abitas prius quam ego ad te uenero.
305 AP	usque opperiar.	
PER		sequere tu intro.
EPI		i numera, nil ego te moror.

294 fidicina *BEJ*, fidicinam *Schredinger*
299 illam alius *BEJ*, *transp. Bothe*

EPI   (*pointing to Apoecides*) This one will be best, this one can
       be on his guard all right, since he understands the laws
       and statutes.

PER   (*to Apoecides*) You should thank Epidicus.

EPI   But this is what I'll do eagerly: I'll meet him and bring
       the lyre girl here to you, to whom she belongs. And I'll   295
       bring the money together with this man here (*points to
       Apoecides*).

PER   What's the lowest price she can be bought for?

EPI   That woman? Perhaps she can be bought for forty minas
       at the lowest. But if you give me more I'll return it, there's
       no trick in this. And this money won't even be tied up for
       as long as ten days.

PER   How so?

EPI   Because another young man is madly in love with that
       woman, rich in gold, a great soldier from Rhodes, who   300
       ravages the enemy and is boastful: he will buy her from
       you and give you the gold with pleasure. Just do it, there's
       a fat profit in here for you.

PER   I'm praying to the gods for it.

EPI   Your prayer is answered.

AP   (*to Periphanes*) Why don't you go inside and get the
       money for him? I'll visit the forum. (*turning to the slave*)
       Epidicus, meet me there.

EPI   Don't go away before I meet you.

AP   I'll be waiting throughout.   305

Exit APOECIDES to the right.

PER   Follow me inside, you.

EPI   Go count it, I'm not delaying you at all.

Exit PERIPHANES into his house.

II. iii: EPIDICVS

EPI   nullum esse opinor ego agrum in agro Attico
aeque feracem quam hic est noster Periphanes:
quin ex occluso atque opsignato armario
decutio argenti tantum quantum mi lubet.
310   quod pol ego metuo si senex resciuerit
ne ulmos parasitos faciat quae usque attondeant.
sed me una turbat res ratioque, Apoecidi
quam ostendam fidicinam aliquam conducticiam.
atque id quoque habeo: mane me iussit senex
315   conducere aliquam fidicinam sibi huc domum,
dum rem diuinam faceret, cantaret sibi;
ea conducetur atque ei praemonstrabitur
quo pacto fiat subdola aduorsus senem.
ibo intro, argentum accipiam ab damnoso sene.

ACTVS III

III. i: STRATIPPOCLES. CHAERIBVLVS

320 STRA exspectando exedor miser atque exenteror
quo modo mi Epidici blanda dicta euenant.
nimis diu maceror: sitne quid necne sit
scire cupio.

CHAE   per illam tibi copiam
copiam parare aliam licet: sciui equidem in principio
ilico
325   nullam tibi esse in illo copiam.

STRA   interii hercle ego!

CHAE apsurde facis qui angas te animi; si hercle ego illum semel
prendero,
numquam irridere nos illum inul-
tum sinam seruom hominem.

EPI I don't think that any land in this Attic land is as fertile as this Periphanes of ours. I shake out as much money as I like from his locked and sealed cabinet. I'm really afraid 310 that if the old man finds out about this, he might turn elm rods into hangers-on to lick me to the bone. But one matter and concern troubles me, how I can show Apoecides some hired lyre girl. (*pauses*) And I also have a solution to this problem: early in the morning the old man told me to 315 hire some lyre girl to come here to him to his house, to sing for him while he offers sacrifice. She'll be hired and shown how to trick the old man. I'll go inside and receive the money from the old prodigal.

Exit EPIDICUS into the house of Periphanes.

ACT THREE

Enter STRATIPPOCLES and CHAERIBULUS from the latter's house.

STRA Poor me, I'm being consumed and disemboweled from 320 waiting to see how Epidicus' flattering words will turn out for me. I've been tormented far too long: I desire to know if there's any result or not.

CHAE As far as aid from him is concerned, you can look for aid elsewhere: I knew right from the beginning that there's 325 no aid for you in him.

STRA I'm dead!

CHAE It's odd of you to be so anxious in your mind. If I ever get hold of him, I'll never let that slave laugh at us without punishment.

367

STRA   quid illum facere uis qui, tibi quoi diuitiae domi maxu-
      mae sunt,

330   is nummum nullum habes nec soda-

330ᵃ   li tuo in te copia est.

331 CHAE si hercle habeam pollicear lubens, uerum aliquid aliqua
      aliquo modo

      alicunde ab aliqui aliqua tibi spes est fore mecum fortu-
      nam.

STRA   uae tibi, muricide homo!

CHAE   qui tibi lubet mi male loqui?

STRA   quipp' tu mi aliquid aliquo modo alicunde ab aliquibus
      blatis

335   quod nusquam est, neque ego id immitto in auris meas,

      nec mihi plus adiumenti habes quam ill' qui numquam
      etiam natust.

III. ii: EPIDICVS. STRATIPPOCLES. CHAERIBVLVS

EPI   fecisti iam officium tuom, me meum nunc facere oportet.

      per hanc curam quieto tibi licet esse . . . hoc quidem iam
      periit:

339   ne quid tibi hinc in spem referas,

339ᵃ   oppido hoc pollinctum est;

340   crede modo mi: sic ego ago,

340ᵃ   sic egerunt nostri.

341   pro di immortales, mi hunc diem dedistis luculentum!

      ut facilem atque impetrabilem! sed ego hinc migrare
      cesso,

      ut importem in coloniam hunc ‹meo› auspicio commea-
      tum.

329 ferre *BE¹*, fere *J¹*, facere *E³J²*
336 ades *BE*, des *J*, habes *Leo*   343 meo *add. Pylades*

STRA What do you want *him* to do? You, who have enormous
      riches at home, don't have a single coin for your chum 330
      and he doesn't have any assistance in you.

CHAE If I had anything, I'd promise it happily, but you have
      some hope to have a fortune with me, something, some-
      how, in some way, from somewhere, from someone.

STRA Curse you, you coward![20]

CHAE Why do you wish to insult me?

STRA Because you're waffling about something somehow from
      somewhere from some people, which doesn't exist any- 335
      where. I won't lend you my ears for this; you don't have
      any more help for me than someone who's never been
      born.

*Enter EPIDICUS from the house of Periphanes, with a wallet
hanging from his neck.*

EPI   (*into the house*) You've already done your duty, now I
      ought to do mine. As far as that worry is concerned, you
      can be calm . . . (*aside, lifting up the wallet*) you have lost
      this already: don't put any hopes into seeing any of it
      again, it's all laid out for burial. Just believe me: that's 340
      how I do things, that's how my ancestors used to do
      things. Immortal gods, this is a beautiful day you've given
      me! How easy and successful! But I'm wasting time when
      I should be setting off to bring these supplies to the
      settlement under my own auspices. I'm wasting my time

---

[20] *Muricidus* is glossed as "coward, idiot, lazybones" by Paul. Fest.
p. 112 Lindsay. It could be a by-form of *murcidus* or a translation of
μυοκτόνος "mouse-slayer" or τοιχωρύχος "wall-digger," the former an
insult to a soldier, the latter a general insult referring to stealing.

mihi cesso quom sto. sed quid hoc? ante aedis duos soda-
lis

345   erum et Chaeribulum conspicor. quid hic agitis? accipe
hoc sis.

STRA quantum hic inest?

EPI   quantum sat est et plus satis: superfit.
decem minis plus attuli quam tu danistae debes.
dum tibi ego placeam atque opsequar meum tergum
flocci facio.

STRA nam quid ita?

EPI   quia ego tuom patrem faciam parenticidam.

350 STRA quid istuc est uerbi?

EPI   nil moror uetera et uolgata uerba.
peratum ductarent: ego follitum ductitabo.
nam leno omne argentum apstulit pro fidicina, ego re-
solui.
[manibus his denumeraui, pater suam natam quam esse
credit.]
nunc iterum ut fallatur pater tibique auxilium apparetur

355   inueni: nam ita suasi seni atque hanc habui orationem
ut quom rediisses ne tibi eius copia esset.

STRA   eugae!

EPI ea iam domi est pro filia.

STRA   ⟨iam⟩ teneo.

EPI   nunc auctorem
dedit mi ad hanc rem Apoecidem, is apud forum manet
me
quasi qui a me caueat.

351 ductare at *P*, ductarent *Leo*   353 *uersum secl. Ritschl*
355 inueniam *BEJ*, inueni nam *Saracenus*
357 iam *add. Brix*
359 quasi quae amaret *BEJ*, quasi qui a me *Buecheler*

by standing around. (*looks around*) But what's that? I can 345
see the two chums before the house, master and Chae-
ribulus. (*to both*) What are you doing here? (*handing
over the wallet to Stratippocles*) Take this please.

STRA How much is in here?

EPI As much as is enough and more than enough: there's an
excess. I brought ten minas more than you owe the mon-
eylender. So long as I please and obey you I care little
about my back.

STRA How so?

EPI Because I'll turn your father into a parenticide.

STRA What sort of word is that? 350

EPI I don't care for old and common words. People would
carry a parricide off in a bag, but I shall carry your father
off in a wallet:[21] the pimp took away all the money for the
lyre girl; I paid him. [I counted it out with these hands of
mine for the girl your father believes to be his daughter.]
Now I've found another way to trick your father and to
help you: I advised the old man like this and gave him a 355
talk to the effect that when you returned you shouldn't
have access to her.

STRA Excellent!

EPI She's now at home as his daughter.

STRA I got it now.

EPI Now he's given me Apoecides as a supervisor for this
business. He's waiting for me in the forum, with the idea
of being on his guard against me.

---

[21] *Parricidae* "murderers of close kinsmen, especially of parents"
were sewn into sacks and drowned. *Parenticida*, a comic formation, has
a similar meaning; the form of punishment is of course also comic.

STRA	hau male.
EPI	iam ipse cautor captust.

360 ipse in meo collo tuos pater cruminam collocauit;
    is adornat, adueniens domi extemplo ut maritus fias.

STRA uno persuadebit modo, si illam quae adducta est mecum
    mi adempsit Orcus.

EPI   nunc ego hanc astutiam institui.
    deueniam ad lenonem domum egomet solus, eum [ego]
        docebo,

365   si qui ad eum adueniant, ut sibi esse datum argentum
        dicat
    pro fidicina, argenti minas se habere quinquaginta—
    quippe ego qui nudiustertius meis manibus denumeraui
    pro illa tua amica quam pater suam filiam esse retur:
    ibi leno sceleratum caput suom imprudens alligabit,

370   quasi pro illa argentum acceperit quae tecum adducta
        nunc est.

CHAE uorsutior es quam rota figularis.

EPI   iam ego parabo
    aliquam dolosam fidicinam, nummo conducta quae sit,
    quae se emptam simulet, quae senes duo docte ludifice-
        tur.
    eam ducet simul Apoecides ad tuom patrem.

STRA   ut parate!

375 EPI eam permeditatam, meis dolis astutiisque onustam
    mittam. sed nimis longum loquor, diu me estis demorati.
    haec scitis iam ut futura sint. abeo.

STRA   bene ambulato.

361 ueniens *BEJ*, adueniens *Camerarius*
364 ego *del. Pylades*
365 si quid . . . adueniam *P*, si qui . . . adueniant *Camerarius*

372

STRA Not bad.

EPI Now the guard has been gulled himself. Your father put 360
the wallet onto my neck in person. He's getting ready so
that when you arrive home you can immediately get mar-
ried.

STRA There's only one way he'll persuade me: if Orcus takes
away the girl from me who was brought here together
with me.

EPI Now I've prepared the following trick. I'll go to the
pimp's house alone and coach him to say, if any people 365
should come to him, that he's received the money for
the lyre girl, that he has fifty silver minas—because two
days ago I counted the money out with my own hands for
that girlfriend of yours your father believes to be his
daughter: then the pimp will swear by his criminal head
without knowing what he's doing, as if he'd received the 370
money for the woman who's now been brought along
with you.

CHAE You're up to more turns than a potter's wheel.

EPI I'll get some clever lyre girl now, one who can be hired for
a sesterce. She will pretend to have been bought and
trick the two old men cleverly. Apoecides will take her
with him to your father.

STRA How well prepared!

EPI I'll send her well rehearsed, loaded with my tricks and 375
wiles. But I've been talking far too much, you've delayed
me for too long. Now you know how this is going to hap-
pen. I'm off.

STRA Have a successful journey.

Exit EPIDICUS to the right.

CHAE nimis doctus ille ‹est› ad male faciendum.

STRA   me equidem certo
       seruauit consiliis suis.

CHAE   abeamus intro hinc ad me.

380 STRA atque aliquanto lubentius quam aps te sum egressus
       intus:

       uirtute atque auspicio Epidici cum praeda in castra
       redeo.

III. iii: PERIPHANES. APOECIDES. SERVOS

PER non oris causa modo homines aequom fuit
       sibi habere speculum ubi os contemplarent suom,
       sed qui perspicere possent [cor sapientiae,
385   igitur perspicere ut possint] cordis copiam;
       ubi id inspexissent, cogitarent postea
       uitam ut uixissent olim in adulescentia.
       fuit conducibile hoc quidem mea sententia.
       uel [quasi] ego[met], qui dudum fili causa coeperam
390   ego me excruciare animi, quasi quid filius
       meus deliquisset med erga aut [quasi] non pluruma
       malefacta mea essent solida in adulescentia.
       profecto deliramus interdum senes.
       sed meus sodalis it cum praeda Apoecides.
395   uenire saluom mercatorem gaudeo.
       quid fit?

AP   di deaeque te adiuuant.

PER   omen placet.

---

378 est *add. Camerarius*
384–85 cor . . . possint *secl. Geppert*
388 *post* 393 *in* BEJ, *huc transp. Brix*
389 uel [quasi] ego[met] *Guyet*
391 quasi *del. Ritschl*

CHAE He's very clever when it comes to making mischief.

STRA He certainly saved *me* with his stratagems.

CHAE Let's go inside to me.

STRA Yes, and I'll do so a lot more happily than I went out from   380
you: through the bravery of Epidicus and under his lead-
ership I return to the camp with booty.

*Exeunt STRATIPPOCLES and CHAERIBULUS into the lat-
ter's house.*
Enter PERIPHANES from his house.

PER It would be good if people had mirrors not just for the
sake of their faces, so as to look at their faces in them, but
also mirrors with which they could see into [the heart of
their wisdom, so that they could see into] the resources of   385
their hearts; after examining them, they could then think
about how they lived their lives long ago in their youth.
That would be useful in my opinion. Take me, for in-
stance: not long ago I'd begun to torture myself because   390
of my son, as if my son had wronged me in some way or as
if my own misdeeds throughout my youth hadn't been
countless. Yes, we old men are sometimes really mad.
(*looks around*) But my companion Apoecides is coming
along with the booty.   395

Enter APOECIDES from the right with a MUSIC GIRL.

PER I'm happy that the merchant is returning safely. How are
things?

AP The gods and goddesses are helping you.

PER I like the omen.

AP	quin omini omnes suppetunt res prospere.
	sed tu hanc iube sis intro abduci.
PER	heus! foras
	exite huc aliquis. duce istam intro mulierem.
400	atque audin?
SER	quid uis?
PER	caue siris cum filia
	mea copulari hanc nec conspicere. iam tenes?
	in aediculam istanc sorsum concludi uolo.
	diuortunt mores uirgini longe ac lupae.
AP	docte et sapienter dicis. num⟨quam⟩ nimis potest
405	pudicitiam quisquam suae seruare filiae.
	edepol ne istam ⟨in ipso⟩ tempore gnato tuo
	sumus praemercati.
PER	quid iam?
AP	quia dixit mihi
	iam dudum se alius tuom uidisse hic filium:
	hanc edepol rem apparabat.
PER	plane hercle hoc quidem est.
410 AP	ne tu habes seruom graphicum et quantiuis preti,
	non carust auro contra. ut ille fidicinam
	fecit nesciret esse sese emptam tibi!
	ita ridibundam atque hilaram huc adduxit simul.
PER	mirum hoc qui potuit fieri.
AP	te pro filio
415	facturum dixit rem esse diuinam domi,
	quia Thebis saluos redierit.

398 lubens *B*, iubes *EJ*, iube sis *Gruterus*
404 num *P*, numquam *Fleckeisen*   406 tempore *P* (*cum rasura
post* istam *in B*), in ipso tempore *Redslob*, temperi *Guyet*
412 nescire esse *BEJ*, nesciret esse sese *Brix*

AP   What's more, everything supports the omen successfully.
But please have her taken inside.

PER   (*into his house*) Hey! Someone come out here.

Enter a SLAVE from the house of Periphanes.

PER   Take that woman inside. And can you hear me?   400

SLAVE   What do you want?

PER   Make sure you don't let this person come into contact
with my daughter or see her. Do you understand now? I
want her to be locked up in a separate little room. The
habits of a virgin are very different from those of a whore.

Exeunt the SLAVE and the MUSIC GIRL into the house.

AP   You're speaking intelligently and wisely. No one can ever
guard his daughter's chastity too closely. Honestly, we've   405
bought this woman just in time before your son got a
chance.

PER   How so?

AP   Because someone else told me that he saw your son here
some time ago already: he was getting ready for this.

PER   Yes, that's obvious.

AP   You really have an exquisite slave, worth any price, worth   410
his weight in gold. How he made sure that the lyre girl
didn't know that she'd been bought for you! He brought
her along here laughing and cheerful.

PER   It's strange how this could happen.

AP   He said you were going to offer sacrifice at home for your   415
son because he returned safely from Thebes.

PER	rectam institit.
AP	immo ipsus illi dixit conductam esse eam
	quae hic amministraret ad rem diuinam tibi.
	[facturum hoc dixit rem ess' diuinam tibi domi.]
420	ego illic me autem sic assimulabam: quasi
	stolidum, combardum me faciebam.
PER	immo ita decet.
AP	res magna amici apud forum agitur, ei uolo
	ire aduocatus.
PER	at quaeso, ubi erit otium,
	reuortere ad me extemplo.
AP	continuo hic ero.
425 PER	nil homini amico est opportuno amicius:
	sine tuo labore quod uelis actum est tamen.
	ego si allegassem aliquem ad hoc negotium
	minus hominem doctum minusque ad hanc rem cal- lidum,
	os sublitum esset, itaque me albis dentibus
430	meus derideret filius meritissumo.
435	sed quis illic est quem huc aduenientem conspicor
	suam qui undantem chlamydem quassando facit?

III. iv: MILES. PERIPHANES

MIL	caue praeterbitas ullas aedis quin roges,
	senex hic ubi habitat Periphanes Plothenius.
	incertus tuom caue ad me rettuleris pedem.
PER	adulescens, si istunc hominem quem tu quaeritas
	tibi commonstrasso, ecquam aps te inibo gratiam?

416 recte *P*, rectam *Lambinus*
419 *uersum del.* Acidalius
435 hic *BEJ*, illic *Seyffert*
438 Platenius *P*, Plothenius *Petitus (etiam in 448)*

PER   That was the line to take.

AP   Yes, he himself told her that she was hired to assist you here in your sacrifice. [He said you were going to offer sacrifice for yourself at home.] But I pretended to be 420 stupid and daft there.

PER   Yes, that's appropriate.

AP   An important case of a friend is being dealt with in the forum and I want to go as a supporter for him.

PER   But please, when you have leisure, come back to me at once.

AP   I'll be back soon.

Exit APOECIDES to the right.

PER   A friend in need is a friend indeed. What you want done 425 is done, without any effort on your part. If I'd employed someone less smart in this business and less clever in this matter, I'd have been fooled: my son would laugh at 430 me, showing me his white teeth, and I'd fully deserve it. (*looks around*) But who is this I can see coming here? He 435 makes his cloak move like a wave by shaking it.

Enter the SOLDIER from the left, accompanied by a slave boy.

SOL   Make sure you don't pass any house without asking where old Periphanes of Plothea[22] lives here. Make sure you don't carry your foot back to me when you're not certain.

PER   (*approaching the soldier*) Young man, if I show you the 440 man you're looking for, will I earn some gratitude from you?

[22] A deme in Attica.

	MIL	uirtute belli armatus promerui ut mihi
		omnis mortalis agere deceat gratias.
	PER	non repperisti, adulescens, tranquillum locum
445		ubi tuas uirtutes explices ut postulas.
		nam strenuiori deterior si praedicat
		suas pugnas, de illius illae fiunt sordidae.
		sed istum quem quaeris Periphanem Plothenium
		ego sum, si quid uis.
	MIL	nemp' quem in adulescentia
450		memorant apud reges armis, arte duellica
		diuitias magnas indeptum?
	PER	immo si audias
		meas pugnas, fugias manibus demissis domum.
	MIL	pol ego magis unum quaero meas quoi praedicem
		quam illum qui memoret suas mihi.
	PER	hic non est locus;
455		proin tu alium quaeras quoi centones sarcias.
431		atque haec stultitia est me illi uitio uortere
432		egomet quod factitaui in adulescentia,
433		quom militabam: pugnis memorandis meis
434		eradicabam hominum auris, quando occeperam.
456	MIL	animum aduorte ut quod ego ad te aduenio intellegas.
		meam amicam audiui te esse mercatum.
	PER	attatae!
		nunc demum scio ego hunc qui sit: quem dudum Epi-
		dicus
		mihi praedicauit militem. adulescens, ita est
460		ut dicis, emi.
	MIL	uolo te uerbis pauculis
		si tibi molestum non est.

431–34 *post 455 posuit Acidalius*

380

SOL   Through valor in war I have in arms earned the right that
all mortals should give me thanks.

PER   Young man, you haven't found a quiet place for expound- 445
ing your feats as you wish: if a lesser man tells a braver
one about his battles, they look poor in comparison. But
the man you're looking for, Periphanes of Plothea, it's
me, if you want anything.

SOL   You mean the one who people say acquired great wealth 450
in his youth in the service of kings for his arms and art of
war?

PER   Yes, if you heard about my battles, you'd flee home with
your hands stretched out.[23]

SOL   I'm looking for someone I can tell about mine rather than
someone who tells me about his.

PER   Here is not the right place. So look for someone else to 455
make your patchworks for.[24] (*aside*) But it would be plain 431
stupidity to find fault with him for doing what I regularly
did in my own youth, when I was a soldier: by telling
people about my fights I tore out their ears whenever I
began.

SOL   Pay attention so that you understand why I've come to 456
you. I've heard that you bought my girlfriend.

PER   (*aside*) Goodness! Now at last I know who he is: the sol-
dier Epidicus was telling me about a while ago. (*to the
soldier*) Young man, it's just as you say, I did buy her. 460

SOL   I want to speak to you briefly if you don't mind.

[23] Like a runner, one before, one behind.
[24] Metaphor for telling and embellishing stories.

PER		non edepol scio

molestum necne sit, nisi dicis quid uelis.

MIL mi illam ut tramittas, argentum accipias.

PER   adest?

MIL nam quid ego apud te uera parcam proloqui?

465 ego illam uolo hodie facere libertam meam
mihi concubina quae sit.

PER   te apsoluam breui:
argenti quinquaginta mi illa empta est minis;
si sexaginta mihi denumerantur minae,
tuas possidebit mulier faxo ferias;

470 atque ita profecto ut eam ex hoc exoneres agro.

MIL estne empta mi istis legibus?

PER   habeas licet.
conciliauisti pulchre. heus! foras educite
quam introduxistis fidicinam. atque etiam fides,
ei quae accessere, addam tibi dono gratiis.

III. iv a: PERIPHANES. MILES. FIDICINA

475 PER age accipe hanc sis.

MIL   quae te intemperiae tenent?
quas tu mi tenebras trudis? quin tu fidicinam
produci intus iubes?

PER   haec ergo est fidicina.
hic alia nulla est.

MIL   non mihi nugari potes.
quin tu huc producis fidicinam Acropolistidem?

480 PER haec inquam est.

MIL   non haec inquam est. non nouisse me
meam rere amicam posse?

474 tibi addam *P, transp. Brix*

382

PER   I don't know if I mind or not unless you tell me what you want.

SOL   Hand her over to me, and take the money.

PER   Is it at hand?

SOL   Yes; why should I be economical with the truth toward you? I want to make her my freedwoman today so that   465 she can be my concubine.

PER   I'll keep it short for you: she was bought for me for fifty silver minas. If I'm paid sixty minas, I'll let the woman occupy your spare time; and all this on condition that you   470 remove her from this land.

SOL   Is she mine on those terms?

PER   You can have her. You've made a fine bargain. (*into the house*) Hey there! Bring out the lyre girl you took in. (*to the soldier again*) And I'll also give you the lyre that came with her as a present, for free.

Enter slaves with the MUSIC GIRL.

PER   (*to the soldier*) Go on, take her if you will.   475

SOL   What madness has come over you? What trick are you shoving off on me? Why won't you have the lyre girl brought out?

PER   Well, this *is* the lyre girl. There isn't any other here.

SOL   You can't impose on me. Why won't you bring out here the lyre girl Acropolistis?

PER   I'm telling you, this is her.   480

SOL   And I'm telling you, this is not her. Do you think I don't know my own girlfriend?

PER   hanc, inquam, filius
       meus deperibat fidicinam.

MIL   haec non est ea.

PER   quid? non est?

MIL   non est.

PER   unde haec igitur gentium est?
       equidem hercle argentum pro hac dedi.

MIL   stulte datum
485   reor, peccatum largiter.

PER   immo haec ea est.
       nam seruom misi qui illum sectari solet
       meum gnatum: is ipse hanc destinauit fidicinam.

MIL   em istic homo te articulatim concidit, senex,
       tuos seruos.

PER   quid? "concidit"?

MIL   sic suspicio est,
490   nam pro fidicina haec cerua supposita est tibi.
       senex, tibi os est sublitum plane et probe.
       ego illam requiram iam ubi ubi est.

PER   bellator, uale.
       eugae, eugae! Epidice, frugi es, pugnauisti, homo es,
       qui me emunxisti mucidum, minimi preti.
495   mercatus te hodie est de lenone Apoecides?

FID   fando ego istunc hominem numquam audiui ante hunc
           diem
       nec me quidem emere quisquam ulla pecunia
       potuit: plus iam sum libera quinquennium.

---

[25] An allusion to Medea and Pelias. Medea tricked the daughters of
Pelias into believing that they would rejuvenate their father if they cut
him to pieces and boiled him, which of course did not work.

PER   I'm telling you, my son was madly in love with this lyre girl.

SOL   This isn't her.

PER   What? It isn't her?

SOL   It isn't her.

PER   Then where on earth does this one come from? I paid for her.

SOL   I think that it was stupid of you to pay and that you made a   485
big mistake.

PER   No, this is her: I sent the slave who always accompanies
that son of mine. He himself bought this lyre girl.

SOL   Well, that man, your slave, has cut you to pieces limb by
limb, old man.[25]

PER   What? He's "cut me to pieces"?

SOL   That's my suspicion: this hind has been substituted for   490
the lyre girl.[26] Old man, you've been tricked plainly and
properly. I'll find her now wherever she is.

Exit SOLDIER to the right.

PER   (*calling after him*) Warrior, goodbye. (*to himself*) Bravo!
Bravo! Epidicus, you're a decent chap, you've fought,
you're a man; I was a sniffling, worthless creature and you
wiped my nose.[27] (*to the music girl*) Did Apoecides buy   495
you from the pimp today?

MUS   I've never heard that man being mentioned before this
day and no one could have bought me for any money: I've
been free for more than five years.

[26] An allusion to Iphigenia. She was supposed to be sacrificed on the
altar of Artemis, but Artemis replaced her with a hind.

[27] Metaphor for tricking someone.

	PER	quid tibi negoti est meae domi igitur?
	FID	audies.
500		conducta ueni ut fidibus cantarem seni,
		dum rem diuinam faceret.
	PER	fateor me omnium
		hominum esse Athenis Atticis minimi preti.
		sed tu nouistin fidicinam Acropolistidem?
	FID	tam facile quam me.
	PER	ubi habitat?
	FID	postquam libera est
505		ubi habitet dicere admodum incerte scio.
	PER	eho an libera illa est? quis eam liberauerit
		uolo scire, si scis.
	FID	id quod audiui [iam] audies.
		Stratippoclem aiunt Periphanei filium
		apsentem curauisse ut fieret libera.
510	PER	perii hercle, si istaec uera sunt, planissume:
		meum exenterauit Epidicus marsuppium.
	FID	haec sic audiui. numquid me uis ceterum?
	PER	malo cruciatu ut pereas atque abeas cito.
	FID	fides non reddis?
	PER	nec fides nec tibias.
515		propera sis fugere hinc si te di amant.
	FID	abiero.
		flagitio cum maiore post reddes tamen.
	PER	quid nunc? qui in tantis positus sum sententiis
		eamne ego sinam impune? immo etiam si alterum
		tantum perdundum est, perdam potius quam sinam
520		me impune irrisum esse, habitum depeculatui.

507 iam *A*, *deest in BEJ*   518–20 *uersus non feruntur in A*
520 depeculatum *BEJ*, depeculatui *Buecheler*

PER Then what's your business in my house?

MUS You shall hear it. I came because I was hired to play the 500
lyre for an old man while he was offering sacrifice.

PER I admit that of all men in Attic Athens I'm worth the least.
But do you know a lyre girl called Acropolistis?

MUS As well as myself.

PER Where does she live?

MUS Now that she's free I can't say with any certainty where 505
she lives.

PER What? She's free? I want to know who freed her, if you
know.

MUS You shall hear what I have heard. People say that Stratip-
pocles, the son of Periphanes, took care in his absence
that she should be freed.

PER If that's true, it's absolutely plain that I've perished. 510
Epidicus has disemboweled my wallet.

MUS That's what I've heard. Is there anything else you want
from me?

PER Yes, go away quickly and die a painful death.

MUS Won't you return my lyre to me?

PER Neither your lyre nor your flute! Be quick to run off if the 515
gods love you, will you?

MUS I'm off. You'll return it later nevertheless, under greater
and louder demands.

*Exit the MUSIC GIRL to the right, the slaves disappear in the
house again.*

PER What now? Should I let her off without punishment, I,
whose name is often to be seen as proposer of such im-
portant decrees? No, even if I had to waste the same sum
all over again, I'd rather waste it than let myself be made 520

ei! sic data esse uerba praesenti palam!
ac me minoris facio prae illo, qui omnium
legum atque iurum fictor, condictor cluet;
is etiam sese sapere memorat: malleum
525 sapientiorem uidi excusso manubrio.

ACTVS IV

IV. i: PHILIPPA. PERIPHANES

PHIL siquid est homini miseriarum quod miserescat, miser ex
animo est.
id ego experior, quoi multa in unum locum con-
fluont quae meum pectus pulsant
simul: multiplex ‹me› aerumna exercitam habet,
530 paupertas, pauor territat mentem animi,
neque ubi meas collocem spes habeo mi usquam muni-
tum locum.
ita gnata mea hostium est potita neque ea nunc ubi sit
scio.
533 PER quis illaec est mulier timido
533ᵃ pectore peregre adueniens
534 quae ipsa se miseratur?
PHIL in his
534ᵃ dictust locis habitare mihi
535 Periphanes.
PER me nominat haec;
535ᵃ credo ego illi hospitio usus uenit.
536 PHIL peruelim mercedem dare qui
536ᵃ monstret eum mi hominem aut ubi habitet.
537 PER noscito ego hanc, nam uideor nescio ubi
537ᵃ mi uidisse prius.
538 estne ea an non ea est quam animus retur meus?

a laughingstock and be cheated without punishing him.
Dear me! To be tricked like this, in person and publicly!
And yet my case is not as bad as the case of that chap who
has a reputation for being the maker and framer of all
laws and legal principles. He even says that he's clever.
I've seen a hammer cleverer than him, and that with its   525
handle knocked off.

ACT FOUR

Enter PHILIPPA from the left, without noticing anyone.

PHIL If humans are in misery that deserves commiseration,
they are truly miserable. I am experiencing this: many
things that beat my breast at the same time are flowing
together in one place. Manifold toil is keeping me agi-
tated, poverty and fear are terrifying my inmost heart,   530
and I don't have a safe place where I could put my hopes:
my daughter has been captured by the enemy and I don't
know where she is now.

PER Who is that woman coming from abroad with fear in her
breast, who is pitying herself?

PHIL I was told that Periphanes lives in this area.   535

PER She's naming me. I think she's in need of hospitality.

PHIL I'd like to give a reward to the person who shows me that
man or where he lives.

PER I'm trying to recognize her because I seem to have seen
her somewhere or other before. Is she the one or is she
not the one my heart thinks she is?

---

529 me *add. Gulielmus*
537ᵃ me *P,* mi *Lindemann*

539	PHIL	di boni! uisitaui ‹hunc an non› antidhac?
539ᵃ		***
540	PER	certo ea est ***
540ᵃ		quam in Epidauro ***
540ᵇ		pauperculam memini comprimere.
541	PHIL	plane hicine est qui
541ᵃ		mihi in Epidauro uirgini primus
541ᵇ		pudicitiam pepulit.
542	PER	quae meo compressu peperit
542ᵃ		filiam quam domi nunc habeo.
543		quid si adeam—
	PHIL	hau scio an congredias—
543ᵃ	PER	—si haec ea est.
	PHIL	—sin is est homo, sicut
544		anni multi dubia dant.
544ᵃ	PER	longa dies meum incertat animum.
545		sin ea est quam incerte autumo,
545ᵃ		hanc congrediar astu.
546	PHIL	muliebris adhibenda mi malitia nunc est.
	PER	compellabo.
	PHIL	orationis aciem contra conferam.
	PER	salua sis.
	PHIL	salutem accipio mi et meis.
	PER	quid ceterum?
	PHIL	saluos sis: quod credidisti reddo.
	PER	haud accuso fidem.
550		nouin ego te?
	PHIL	si ego te noui, animum inducam ut tu noueris.
	PER	ubi te uisitaui?
	PHIL	inique iniuriu's.
	PER	quid iam?

---

539 hunc an non *add. Geppert*   539ᵃ *lacuna sanari non potest*

PHIL (*noticing Periphanes*) Good gods! Have I seen this man before or not? ***

PER Certainly this is the poor girl *** whom in Epidaurus ***   540
I remember forcing to lie with me.

PHIL Certainly this is the man who first drove away my chastity in Epidaurus when I was still a virgin.

PER The woman whom I slept with and who gave birth to the daughter I have at home now. What if I go to her—

PHIL Perhaps you should approach him—

PER —if she is the one.

PHIL —if he is the man; in fact, the many years are giving me doubts.

PER The long passage of time makes my mind uncertain. I'll   545
approach her cleverly, to see if she is the one I'm talking about without being sure of it.

PHIL Now I have to use my woman's cunning.

PER I'll address her.

PHIL I'll arm my tongue against him.

PER (*loudly*) Greetings.

PHIL I accept your greetings for me and my family.

PER What else?[28]

PHIL Greetings: I'm returning what you lent me.

PER I don't find fault with your reliability. Don't I know you?   550

PHIL If I know you, I'll persuade myself that you know me.

PER Where have I seen you?

PHIL You're very unjust.

PER How so?

---

[28] Philippa's greeting is incomplete.

540–40ª *desunt fines uersuum*
541ᵇ pepulit *P*, perpulit *A*
543 congrediar *P*, congredias *Nonius*

PHIL   quia
       tuae memoriae interpretari me aequom censes.
PER   commode
       fabulata es.
PHIL   mira memoras ***.
PER   em istuc rectius.
       meministin?
PHIL   memini id quod memini.
PER   at in Epidauro—
PHIL   ah! guttula
555   pectus ardens mi aspersisti.
PER   —uirgini pauperculae
       tuaeque matri me leuare paupertatem?
PHIL   tun is es
       qui per uoluptatem tuam in me aerumnam opseuisti
         grauem?
PER   ego sum. salue.
PHIL   salua sum quia te esse saluom sentio.
PER   cedo manum.
PHIL   accipe. aerumnosam et miseriarum compotem
560   mulierem retines.
PER   quid est quod uoltus turbatur tuos?
PHIL   filiam quam ex te suscepi—
PER   quid eam?
PHIL   —eductam perdidi.
       hostium est potita.
PER   habe animum lenem et tranquillum. tace.
       domi meae eccam saluam et sanam. nam postquam au-
         diui ilico
       e meo seruo illam esse captam, continuo argentum dedi
565   ut emeretur. ille eam rem adeo sobrie et frugaliter
       accurauit ut . . . ut ad alias res est impense improbus.

PHIL Because you think it's fair that I should play interpreter
      to your memory.

PER   You have a point.

PHIL You're making a strange admission ***.

PER   Yes, that's more like it. Do you remember?

PHIL I remember what I remember.

PER   But do you remember that in Epidaurus—

PHIL (*interrupting*) Ah! You've sprinkled a drop on my burn-   555
      ing breast.

PER   —I eased the poverty of you, a poor girl, and of your
      mother?

PHIL Are you the one who sowed great distress in me through
      your pleasure?

PER   Yes, I am. Be well.

PHIL I am well because I realize that you are well.

PER   Give me your hand.

PHIL Take it. (*he grabs it*) You're holding a woman in distress
      and afflicted by sorrows.   560

PER   What is the reason that your expression is troubled?

PHIL The daughter I had by you—

PER   (*interrupting*) What about her?

PHIL —I brought her up and then lost her. She has been cap-
      tured by the enemy.

PER   Be calm and peaceful. Be quiet. Look, she's in my house,
      safe and sound: after I heard from my slave that she'd
      been taken captive, I immediately gave him money so   565
      she could be bought. He sorted this matter out just as
      soberly and decently as . . . as he's awfully bad in other
      matters.

---

553 Periphane *in A fuisse suspicatur Studemund* (*sed Philippa Peri-
phanem primum cognoscit in 556–557*)

560 te turbat *P*, turbatur *Duckworth*

PHIL   fac uideam, si mea, si saluam ⟨me⟩ uis.

PER   eho! istinc, Canthara,
iube Telestidem huc prodire filiam ante aedis meam,
ut suam uideat matrem.

PHIL   remigrat animus nunc demum mihi.

IV. ii: ACROPOLISTIS. PERIPHANES. PHILIPPA

570 ACR   quid est, pater, quod me exciuisti ante aedis?

PER   ut matrem tuam
uideas, adeas, aduenienti des salutem atque osculum.

ACR   quam meam matrem?

PER   quae exanimata exsequitur aspectum tuom.

PHIL   quis istaec est quam tu osculum mi ferre iubes?

PER   tua filia.

PHIL   haecine?

PER   haec.

PHIL   egone osculum huic dem?

PER   quor non, quae ex te nata sit?

575 PHIL   tu homo insanis.

PER   egone?

PHIL   tune.

PER   quor?

PHIL   quia ego hanc quae siet
nec scio nec noui neque ego hanc oculis uidi ante hunc
diem.

PER   scio quid erres: quia uestitum atque ornatum immutabi-
lem
habet haec ***

567 sim—seisaluam *A*, si me uis *P*, si mea si saluam me uis *Lindsay*
568 Acropolistidem Ω, Telestidem *Valla et Camerarius*
578–79 *duo uersus in A fuisse constat, unus uersus lacuna non indi-
cata inuenitur in P*

PHIL Let me see her, if she is mine, if you want me safe.

PER (*into the house*) Hey there! Canthara, have my daughter
Telestis come out here in front of the house, so that she
can see her mother.

PHIL Now at last my spirits are returning.

*Enter ACROPOLISTIS with an old maid from the house of
Periphanes.*

ACR Why is it, father, that you called me out in front of the 570
house?

PER So that you can see your mother, go to her, and greet and
kiss her on her arrival.

ACR What mother of mine?

PER The one who is almost dead while seeking to behold you.

PHIL Who is that woman you're asking to give me a kiss?

PER Your daughter.

PHIL This woman?

PER Yes, this woman.

PHIL I should give her a kiss?

PER Why not, since she was born from you?

PHIL You're mad. 575

PER I?

PHIL Yes, you.

PER Why?

PHIL Because I don't know or recognize who she is and I
haven't set eyes on her before this day.

PER I know why you're mistaken: because she has a different
dress and get-up ***

PHIL   *** aliter catuli longe olent, aliter sues.
580   ne ego me ⟨nego⟩ nosse ⟨hanc quae sit⟩.
PER   pro deum atque hominum fidem!
       quid? ego lenocinium facio qui habeam alienas domi
       atque argentum egurgitem domo prorsus? quid tu, quae patrem
       tuom uocas me atque osculare, quid stas stupida? quid taces?
ACR   quid loquar uis?
PER   haec negat se tuam esse matrem.
ACR   ne fuat
585   si non uolt: equidem hac inuita tamen ero matris filia;
       non med istanc cogere aequom est meam esse matrem si neuolt.
PER   quor me igitur patrem uocabas?
ACR   tua istaec culpa est, non mea.
       non patrem ego te nominem, ubi tu tuam me appelles filiam?
       hanc quoque etiam, si me appellet filiam, matrem uocem.
590   negat haec filiam me suam esse: non ergo haec mater mea est.
       postremo haec mea culpa non est: quae didici dixi omnia;
       Epidicus mi fuit magister.
PER   perii! plaustrum perculi.
ACR   numquid ego ibi, pater, peccaui?
PER   si hercle te umquam audiuero
       me patrem uocare, uitam tuam ego interimam.
ACR   non uoco.
595   ubi uoles pater esse ibi esto; ubi noles ne fueris pater.
PHIL   quid? ⟨si⟩ ob eam rem hanc emisti quia tuam gnatam ratu's,
       quibus de signis agnoscebas?

PHIL   *** Puppies smell very differently from pigs. Seriously,   580
       I'm telling you that I don't know who she is.

PER   By all that's sacred in heaven and on earth! What? Am I
       turning myself into a brothel-keeper, keeping women
       in my house that don't belong here and pouring forth
       money? (to Acropolistis) What about you, who call me
       your father and kiss me? What are you standing here like
       an idiot? What are you silent for?

ACR   What do you want me to say?

PER   This lady denies being your mother.

ACR   She needn't be if she doesn't want to: I for one shall still   585
       be my mother's daughter, even against this woman's will.
       It wouldn't be fair of me to force her to be my mother if
       she doesn't want to be.

PER   Then why did you call me father?

ACR   That's your fault, not mine. Shouldn't I address you as fa-
       ther when you call me daughter? I'd also call this woman
       mother if she addressed me as daughter. She denies that   590
       I'm her daughter: then she isn't my mother. Finally, this
       isn't my fault. Everything I've said I was taught. Epidicus
       was my teacher.

PER   I'm dead! I've upset the applecart.

ACR   Have I done anything wrong there, father?

PER   If I ever hear you again call me father, I'll take your life.

ACR   I won't. When you want to be my father, be it; when you   595
       don't want to be my father, don't be.

PHIL   (to Periphanes) Well then? If you bought her because
       you thought she's your daughter, by which signs did you
       recognize her?

---

580 nego *et* hanc quae sit *add. Leo*
596 si *add. Studemund*

PER   nullis.

PHIL   qua re filiam
credidisti nostram?

PER   seruos Epidicus dixit mihi.

PHIL quid si seruo aliter uisum est, non poteras nouisse, opse-
    cro?

600 PER quid ego, qui illam ut primum uidi, numquam uidi pos-
    tea?

PHIL perii misera!

PER   ne fle, mulier. intro abi, habe animum bonum;
ego illam reperiam.

PHIL   hinc Athenis ciuis eam emit Atticus:
adulescentem equidem dicebant emisse.

PER   inueniam, tace.
abi modo intro atque hanc asserua Circam Solis filiam.
605 ego relictis rebus Epidicum operam quaerendo dabo:
si inuenio exitiabilem ego illi faciam hunc ut fiat diem.

ACTVS V

V. i: STRATIPPOCLES. EPIDICVS. DANISTA. TELESTIS

STRA male morigerus mi est danista, qui a me argentum non
    petit
neque illam adducit quae ⟨empta⟩ ex praeda ⟨est⟩. sed
    eccum incedit Epidicus.
quid illuc est quod illi caperrat frons seueritudine?

597–99 *uersus non feruntur in* A
608 quae est praeda *B*, que ex praeda *E*, quae ex praeda *J*, quae
⟨empta⟩ ex praeda ⟨est⟩ *Camerarius*

---

[29] The girl is compared to Circe because Circe practised magic
(hence this is an insult) and because she never knew her father.

PER By none whatsoever.

PHIL Why did you believe she's our daughter?

PER My slave Epidicus told me so.

PHIL What if the slave had a different impression, couldn't you
recognize her, please?

PER What should I have done? After seeing her for the first 600
time I never saw her again.

PHIL (*in tears*) I'm done for, poor me!

PER Stop crying, my woman. Go inside and cheer up. I shall
find her.

PHIL An Attic citizen here from Athens bought her. They said a
young man bought her.

PER I shall find her, be quiet. Just go inside and watch over
this Circe, daughter of the Sun.[29]

*Exit PHILIPPA into the house of Periphanes, followed by
ACROPOLISTIS and the maid.*

PER I'll leave everything aside and make an effort to find 605
Epidicus. If I find him, I'll make sure that this will be-
come his day of doom.

Exit PERIPHANES to the right.

ACT FIVE

Enter STRATIPPOCLES from the house of Chaeribulus.

STRA The moneylender humors me badly: he won't demand
the money from me and he won't bring the girl that was
bought from the spoils. But look, here comes Epidicus.
What's the reason that his forehead is wrinkled from
grave thoughts?

610 EPI   si undecim deos praeter sese secum adducat Iuppiter,
            ita non omnes ex cruciatu poterunt eximere Epidicum.
            Periphanem emere lora uidi, ibi aderat una Apoecides;
            nunc homines me quaeritare credo. senserunt, sciunt
            sibi data esse uerba.

STRA   quid agis, mea Commoditas?

EPI   quod miser.

615 STRA quid est tibi?

EPI   quin tu mi adornas ad fugam uiaticum
            prius quam pereo? nam per urbem duo defloccati senes
            quaeritant me, in manibus gestant copulas secum simul.

STRA habe bonum animum.

EPI   quippe ego quoi libertas in mundo sita est.

STRA ego te seruabo.

EPI   edepol me illi melius si nancti fuant.

620   sed quis haec est muliercula et ille rauastellus qui uenit?

STRA hic est danista, haec illa est autem quam [ego] emi de
            praeda.

EPI   haecine est?

STRA haec est. estne ita ut tibi dixi? aspecta et contempla, Epi-
            dice:
            usque ab unguiculo ad capillum summum est festiuissu-
            ma.
            estn' consimilis quasi quom signum pictum pulchre as-
            pexeris?

621 ego emi de *A*, emi ex *P*
622 ista *A*, *om. BEJ*, ita *Mueller*

---

30 Pun on the two meanings of *seruare*: Stratippocles means "pro-
tect," Epidicus, "guard in prison."

Enter EPIDICUS from the right.

EPI   (*to himself*) Even if Jupiter brought the other eleven 610
      gods in addition to himself, they'll all be unable to save
      Epidicus from a flogging. I saw Periphanes buying straps,
      and there together with him was Apoecides. I believe
      they're looking for me now. They've realized it, they
      know that they've been fooled.

STRA (*approaching Epidicus*) How are you, my Opportunity?

EPI   Just like a wretch.

STRA What's wrong with you? 615

EPI   Why don't you prepare me provisions to escape before I
      get killed? The two old men I fleeced are looking for me
      throughout the city and they're carrying ropes with them
      in their hands.

STRA Cheer up.

EPI   (*sarcastically*) Yes, because freedom is awaiting me.

STRA I'll watch over you.

EPI   They'll do so better if they get hold of me.[30] But who is 620
      that girl and that gray-haired man who's coming along?

*Enter the MONEYLENDER with a purse and TELESTIS from
the left.*

STRA This is the moneylender and this is that girl I bought from
      the spoils.

EPI   Is that her?

STRA That's her. Isn't she just as I told you? Look at her and ob-
      serve, Epidicus: from the tip of her toe to the top of her
      head she's absolutely delightful. Isn't she just as if you'd
      spotted a beautifully painted picture?

625 EPI   e tuis uerbis meum futurum corium pulchrum praedicas,
          quem Apelles ac Zeuxis duo pingent pigmentis ulmeis.

STRA di immortales! sicin iussi ad me ires? pedibus plumbeis
          qui perhibetur prius uenisset quam tu aduenisti mihi.

DAN   haec edepol remorata med est.

STRA   siquidem istius gratia
630   id remoratu's quod ista uoluit, nimium aduenisti cito.

DAN   age age, apsolue ‹me› atque argentum numera, ne comi-
          tes morer.

STRA pernumeratum est.

DAN   tene cruminam: huc inde.

STRA   sapienter uenis.
          opperire dum effero ad te argentum.

DAN   matura.

STRA   domi est.

EPI   satin ego oculis utilitatem optineo sincere an parum?
635   uideone ego Telestidem te, Periphanei filiam,
          ex Philippa matre natam Thebis, Epidauri satam?

TEL   quis tu homo es qui meum parentum nomen memoras et
          meum?

EPI   non me nouisti?

TEL   quod quidem nunc ueniat in mentem mihi.

EPI   non meministi me auream ad te afferre natali die
640   lunulam atque anellum aureolum in digitum?

TEL   memini, mi homo.
          tune is es?

627 socio iussi admirer *P*, sicin iussi ad me ires *Leo* pulmunes *BE*,
pulmones *J*, plumbeis *Brix*   631 me *add. Camerarius*

---

[31] The two most famous Greek painters, living in the fourth and
fifth centuries, respectively.   [32] Unclear reference.

EPI   According to your words, you're predicting that *my* skin   625
will be beautiful; that pair Apelles and Zeuxis[31] will paint
it with elm pigments.

STRA   (*to the moneylender*) Immortal gods! Did I tell you to
come to me like this? The proverbial man with feet of
lead[32] would have come earlier than you did.

MON   This girl delayed me.

STRA   Well, if you delayed for her sake, because she wanted it,   630
you've come far too quickly.

MON   Come on, come on, pay me off and count out the money
so that I don't delay my companions.

STRA   It's counted.

MON   Take my purse: put it in here. (*hands over his wallet*)

STRA   You've come discreetly provided. Wait while I bring the
money out to you.

MON   Hurry up.

STRA   It's in the house.

Exit STRATIPPOCLES into the house of Chaeribulus.

EPI   Do I have unimpaired eyesight or not? Is it you I see,   635
Telestis, the daughter of Periphanes, born of her mother
Philippa in Thebes, but conceived in Epidaurus?

TEL   Who are you? You're stating the names of my parents and
of myself.

EPI   Don't you know me?

TEL   No, not as far as comes to my mind now.

EPI   Don't you remember me bringing you a little golden
moon on your birthday and a little golden ring for your   640
finger?

TEL   I do remember it, my dear man. Is that you?

EPI   ego sum, et istic frater qui te mercatust tuos.
      *** alia matre, uno patre.

TEL   quid pater meus? uiuost?

EPI   animo liquido et tranquillo es, tace.

TEL   di me ex perdita seruatam cupiunt si uera autumas.

645 EPI   non habeo ullam occasionem ut apud te falsa fabuler.

STRA   accipe argentum hoc, danista. hic sunt quadraginta
        minae.
        siquid erit dubium immutabo.

DAN   bene fecisti, bene uale.

STRA   nunc enim tu mea es.

TEL   soror quidem edepol, ut tu aeque scias.
        salue, frater.

STRA   sanan haec est?

EPI   sana, si appellat suom.

650 STRA   quid? ego ⟨quo⟩ modo huic ⟨sum⟩ frater factus, dum in-
        tro eo atque exeo?

EPI   quod boni est id tacitus taceas tute tecum et gaudeas.

STRA   perdidisti et repperisti me, soror.

EPI   stultu's, tace.
        tibi quidem quod ames domi praesto est, fidicina, opera
        mea;
        et sororem in libertatem idem opera concilio mea.

655 STRA   Epidice, fateor—

EPI   abi intro ac iube huic aquam calefieri;
        cetera haec posterius faxo scibis ubi erit otium.

---

    642 nullam lacunam indicant *BEJ*, *uestigia in A* (*ex quibus* ⟨he⟩m
m⟨eus frater ille⟩ ut f⟨iat?⟩ *Leo uersum uirgini tribuens*)
    650 quo *et* sum *add. Redslob*

EPIDICUS

EPI	Yes, and that's your brother who bought you. *** from a different mother, but one father.
TEL	What about my father? Is he alive?
EPI	Be calm and relaxed, be quiet.
TEL	The gods want to turn me from lost into saved if you're telling the truth.
EPI	I have no occasion to lie to you. 645

Enter STRATIPPOCLES with a full purse.

STRA	Take this money, moneylender. There are forty minas here. If anything is doubtful, I'll exchange it.
MON	Thank you. Goodbye.

Exit MONEYLENDER to the right.

STRA	*(to Telestis)* Now you belong to me.
TEL	Yes, as your sister, so that you know it as well as I do. Hello, my brother.
STRA	*(to Epidicus)* Is she in her right mind?
EPI	She is, if she addresses the one who is hers.
STRA	What? How did I become her brother while I went in and 650 out?
EPI	Be quietly quiet about the good you have and be happy.
STRA	*(with a sigh)* You've lost and found me, my sister.
EPI	You're being silly, be quiet. You have something to love, that is the lyre girl, ready for you at home, thanks to my efforts. And I'm bringing your sister back to freedom through my efforts.
STRA	Epidicus, I admit— 655
EPI	*(interrupting)* Go inside and have water warmed up for her. I'll let you know about the rest later when we have leisure.

STRA   sequere hac me, soror.

EPI   ego ad uos Thesprionem iussero

huc transire. sed memento, si quid saeuibunt senes,

suppetias mihi cum sorore ferre.

STRA   facile istuc erit.

660 EPI   Thesprio, exi istac per hortum, affer domum auxilium mihi,

magna est res. minoris multo facio quam dudum senes.

remeabo intro, ut accurentur aduenientes hospites.

eadem haec intus edocebo quae ego scio Stratippoclem.

non fugio, domi adesse certum est; neque ille haud obi-
ciet mihi

665   pedibus sese prouocatum. abeo intro, nimis longum lo-
quor.

V. ii: PERIPHANES. APOECIDES. EPIDICVS

PER   satine illic homo ludibrio nos uetulos decrepitos duos habet?

AP   immo edepol tuquidem miserum med habes mi-
seris modis.

PER   tace sis, modo sine me hominem apisci.

AP   dico ego tibi iam, ut scias:

alium tibi te comitem meliust quaerere; ita, dum te se-
quor,

670   lassitudine inuaserunt misero in genua flemina.

PER   quot illic homo hodie me exemplis ludificatust atque te,

ut illic autem exenterauit mihi opes argentarias!

657 hac me soror *BEJ*, me soror hac *A*

658 saeuiuit senex *A*, saeuiunt senes *B*, seuiunt senes *JE*³ (sic uiuit senes *E*), saeuibunt senes *Dousa*

STRA (*going toward his house*) Follow me this way, my sister.
EPI (*accompanying the two*) I'll tell Thesprio to come over to
you. (*to Stratippocles*) But remember to come to my as-
sistance with your sister if the old men are furious.
STRA That'll be easy.

Exeunt STRATIPPOCLES and TELESTIS into his house.

EPI (*calling toward the door of Chaeribulus*) Thesprio, come   660
out that way through the garden, bring me home some
help. It's a big business. (*to the audience*) I care much less
about the old men than before. I'll go back inside so that
the guests are taken care of on their arrival. At the same
time I'll teach Stratippocles inside what I know. I'm not
running away, I'm resolved to stay at home. And he shan't
throw at me that he was challenged to a footrace. I'm go-   665
ing inside, I've been talking for far too long.

Exit EPIDICUS into his master's house.
*Enter PERIPHANES and APOECIDES from the right, carry-
ing straps.*

PER Is that chap really turning us two decrepit old men into
laughingstocks?
AP No, *you* are turning me into a wretch in wretched fash-
ion.
PER Be quiet, will you, just let me get hold of him.
AP I'm telling you now so that you know: you'd better find
yourself another companion. While I was following you,
a swelling crept into my knees from exhaustion, poor me.   670
PER In how many ways he tricked you and me today, and how
he disemboweled my monetary resources!

407

AP   apage illum a me! nam ille quidem Volcani irati est filius:
      quaqua tangit, omne amburit, si astes, aestu calefacit.

675 EPI duodecim dis plus quam in caelo deorum est immorta-
      lium
      mihi nunc auxilio adiutores sunt et mecum militant.
      quicquid ego male feci, auxilia mi et suppetiae sunt domi,
      apolactizo inimicos omnis.

PER   ubi illum quaeram gentium?

AP   dum sine me quaeras, quaeras mea causa uel medio in
      mari.

680 EPI quid me quaeris? quid laboras? quid hunc sollicitas? ecce
      me.
      num te fugi, num ab domo apsum, num oculis concessi
      tuis?

682   ***
      nec tibi supplico. uincire uis? em, ostendo manus;
      tu habes lora, ego te emere uidi: quid nunc cessas? col-
      liga.

685 PER ilicet! uadimonium ultro mi hic facit.

EPI   quin colligas?

AP   edepol mancupium scelestum!

EPI   te profecto, Apoecides . . .
      nil moror mihi deprecari.

AP   facile exoras, Epidice.

EPI   ecquid agis?

PER   tuon arbitratu?

EPI   meo hercle uero atque hau tuo
      colligandae haec sunt tibi hodie.

PER   at non lubet, non colligo.

682 *uestigia in A, uersus deest in P*

33 The god of fire.

408

AP   Away with him from me! He's the son of Vulcan[33] in an-
ger: he burns everything, wherever he touches, and if
you stand close by, he boils you with his heat.

Enter EPIDICUS from the house of Periphanes, unseen.

EPI   Twelve gods more than there are immortal gods in   675
heaven are now helping me with their support and fight-
ing on my side. Whatever I did wrong, I have help and
support at home. I spurn all my enemies.

PER   Where on earth should I look for him?

AP   So long as you look for him without me, you can even look
for him in the middle of the sea for all I care.

EPI   (*to Periphanes, as he approaches him*) Why are you look-   680
ing for me? Why are you working so hard? What are you
keeping this chap busy for? Here I am. Did I run away
from you? Am I away from home? Did I avoid your eyes?
*** and I don't seek your goodwill. You want to bind me?
Here, I'm showing you my hands. (*holds out his hands*)
You have straps, I saw you buy them. What are you hesi-
tating now? Bind me.

PER   (*to Apoecides*) It's no use! He even volunteers to offer me   685
bail.

EPI   Why won't you tie me up?

AP   (*to Periphanes*) He's a nasty piece of a slave!

EPI   No, Apoecides, you are ... not to beg for pardon for me.

AP   (*with sarcasm*) You persuade me with ease, Epidicus.

EPI   (*to Periphanes*) Are you doing something or not?

PER   At your wish?

EPI   Yes, at my wish and not at yours you have to bind these
hands of mine today.

PER   But I don't feel like it, I'm not binding them.

690   AP   tragulam in te inicere adornat, nescioquam fabricam
                facit.

      EPI   tibi moram facis quom ego solutus asto. age, inquam, col-
                liga.

      PER   at mi magis lubet solutum te rogitare.

      EPI   at nil scies.

      PER   quid ago?

      AP   quid agas? mos geratur.

      EPI   frugi es tu homo, Apoecides.

      PER   cedo manus igitur.

      EPI   morantur nihil. atque arte colliga,
695   nihil uero ⟨hoc⟩ obnoxiose.

      PER   facto opere arbitramino.

      EPI   bene hoc habet. age nunciam ex me exquire, rogita quod
                lubet.

      PER   qua fiducia ausu's primum quae empta est nudiustertius
                filiam meam dicere esse?

      EPI   lubuit: ea fiducia.

      PER   ain tu? lubuit?

      EPI   aio. uel da pignus, ni ea sit filia.

700   PER   quam negat nouisse mater?

      EPI   ni ergo matris filia est,
                in meum nummum, in tuom talentum pignus da.

      PER   enim istaec captio est.
                sed quis ea est mulier?

      EPI   tui gnati amica, ut omnem ⟨rem⟩ scias.

      PER   dedin tibi minas triginta ob filiam?

      EPI   fateor datas
                et eo argento illam me emisse amicam fili fidicinam
705   pro tua filia: istam ob rem te tetigi triginta minis.

        695 hoc *add. Goetz*   702 rem *add. Pylades*
        705 istaa- *A*, iste abore tetigi *BEJ*, istam ob rem te tetigi *Pareus*

410

| AP | He's preparing to throw a spear at you, he's devising some trick. | 690 |

| EPI | *(to Periphanes)* You're wasting your own time when I'm standing here free. Go on, I insist, tie me up. |

| PER | But I prefer to question you while you're free. |

| EPI | But you won't learn anything like that. |

| PER | *(to Apoecides)* What am I to do? |

| AP | What are you to do? Humor him. |

| EPI | You're a decent chap, Apoecides. |

| PER | Give me your hands then. |

| EPI | *(holds them out)* They aren't delaying. And tie them up tightly, without any compunction. | 695 |

| PER | *(as he ties him up brutally)* Judge when the work is done. |

| EPI | That does it. Go on now, question me, ask what you like. |

| PER | First, on what assurance did you dare to say that the lyre girl bought two days ago is my daughter? |

| EPI | I felt like it: on that assurance. |

| PER | Do you say so? You felt like it? |

| EPI | I do say so. If you like, make a bet if she isn't the daughter. |

| PER | The daughter whom the mother says she doesn't know? | 700 |

| EPI | Well then, make a bet for a small coin on my side and a talent on your side that she isn't her mother's daughter.[34] |

| PER | That's a trick. But who is this woman? |

| EPI | So that you know everything, your son's girlfriend. |

| PER | Didn't I give you thirty minas for my daughter? |

| EPI | I admit that you did and that with this money I bought that girlfriend of your son, the lyre girl, instead of your daughter: because of this business I tricked you out of thirty minas. | 705 |

[34] If Epidicus' coin is one sesterce piece, Periphanes' stake is 24,000 times as high; if it is a drachma, 6,000 times as high; and if it is a didrachma, 3,000 times as high.

411

PER	quo modo me ludos fecisti de illa conducticia
	fidicina!
EPI	factum hercle uero et recte factum iudico.
PER	quid postremo argento factum est quod dedi?
EPI	dicam tibi:
	nec malo homini nec benigno tuo dedi Stratippocli.
710 PER	quor dare ausu's?
EPI	quia mi lubitum est.
PER	quae haec, malum, impudentia est?
EPI	etiam inclamitor quasi seruos?
PER	quom tu es liber gaudeo.
EPI	merui ut fierem.
PER	tu meruisti?
EPI	uise intro: ego faxo scies
	hoc ita esse.
PER	quid est negoti?
EPI	iam ipsa res dicet tibi.
	abi modo intro.
AP	i, illuc non temere est.
PER	asserua istum, Apoecides.
715 AP	quid illuc, Epidice, est negoti?
EPI	maxuma hercle iniuria
	uinctus asto, quoius haec hodie opera inuenta est filia.
AP	ain tu te illius inuenisse filiam?
EPI	inueni et domi est.
	sed ut acerbum est pro bene factis quom mali messim
	metas!
AP	quamne hodie per urbem uterque sumus defessi quae-
	rere?
720 EPI	ego sum defessus reperire, uos defessi quaerere.

714 non illuc *P, transp. Leo dubitanter*

PER	How you fooled me about that hired lyre girl!	
EPI	Yes, that was done indeed and I judge that it was done rightly so.	
PER	What happened to the money I gave you in the end?	
EPI	I'll tell you: I gave it to a man who is neither bad nor well-disposed toward you: Stratippocles.	
PER	Why did you dare to give it to him?	710
EPI	Because I felt like it.	
PER	Damn it, what impudence is this?	
EPI	Am I still being shouted at as if I were a slave?	
PER	(*with irony*) I'm happy that you're free.	
EPI	I've deserved to become so.	
PER	You've deserved it?	
EPI	Look inside: I'll make sure you know that's how it is.	
PER	What business is this?	
EPI	The facts will speak for themselves in a moment. Just go inside.	
AP	(*to Periphanes*) Go, there must be something in it.	
PER	Watch over him, Apoecides.	

Exit PERIPHANES into his house.

AP	What business is that, Epidicus?	715
EPI	It's a great injustice that I'm standing here tied up: through my efforts this daughter of his has been found today.	
AP	Are you saying that you've found his daughter?	
EPI	Yes, I have found her and she's at home. But how bitter it is to reap a harvest of evil in return for your good deeds!	
AP	The daughter that we're both exhausted from looking for throughout the city today?	
EPI	I am exhausted from finding her, *you* are exhausted from looking for her.	720

413

PER	quid isti oratis opere tanto? ‹me› meruisse intellego
	ut liceat merito huius facere. cedo tu ut exsoluam manus.
EPI	ne attigas.
PER	ostende uero.
EPI	nolo.
PER	non aequom facis.
EPI	numquam hercle hodie, nisi supplicium mihi das, me sol-
	ui sinam.

725 PER optumum atque aequissumum oras. soccos, tunicam,
      pallium
     tibi dabo.

EPI   quid deinde porro?

PER   libertatem.

EPI   at postea?
     nouo liberto opus est quod pappet.

PER   dabitur, praebebo cibum.

EPI numquam hercle hodie, nisi me orassis, solues.

PER   oro te, Epidice,
     mihi ut ignoscas siquid imprudens culpa peccaui mea.

730   at ob eam rem liber esto.

EPI   inuitus do hanc ueniam tibi,
     nisi necessitate cogar. solue sane si lubet.

V. iii: GREX

hic is homo est qui libertatem malitia inuenit sua.
plaudite et ualete. lumbos porgite atque exsurgite.

721 me *add. Geppert*

Enter PERIPHANES from his house, followed by STRATIP-POCLES and TELESTIS.

PER   Why are you two entreating me so much for him? I real-
ize that I've earned the right to do what he deserves. (*to
Epidicus*) Give me your hands so I can untie them.

EPI   Don't touch me.

PER   Show them, come on.

EPI   I don't want to.

PER   You aren't behaving fairly.

EPI   I'll never allow myself to be untied today unless you
make amends to me.

PER   What you say is very good and fair. I'll give you shoes, a   725
tunic, and a cloak.

EPI   What else?

PER   Your freedom.

EPI   But after that? A new freedman needs something to
munch.

PER   You'll be given something, I'll provide you with food.

EPI   You'll never untie me today unless you beg me.

PER   I beg you, Epidicus, to forgive me if I made a mistake un-
knowingly through my own fault. But because of that you   730
shall be free.

EPI   I give you this indulgence unwillingly, but I'm forced by
necessity. Untie me then if you like. (*holds out his hands
and is untied by Periphanes*)

Exeunt ALL who are still on stage.
Enter the whole TROUPE.

TROUPE   This is the man who found his freedom through his
slyness. Applaud and farewell. Stretch your loins and
rise.

MENAECHMI

INTRODUCTORY NOTE

The *Menaechmi*, being the basis of Shakespeare's *Comedy of Errors*, occupies an important position in English studies. But while the basis of Shakespeare's play is thus well known, it is unclear who wrote Plautus' Greek original. It has been said that it might be Posidippus, because like him the two main characters are originally from Sicily; but that is no more than speculation. It is completely unclear what the Greek original was called or when it was first staged.

We do, however, have some indications concerning the first performance of the *Menaechmi*. Of these, the most relevant is the connection between *Most.* 858–61 and *Men.* 983ᵃ–83ᵇ. It seems that the passage in the *Menaechmi* is a nonliteral quotation of the well-known passage in the *Mostellaria*, which gives us the relative chronology of the two plays. The reference to Pellio in *Men.* 404 is probably irrelevant for the date of the play. In *Bacch.* 214–15 it is said that the play *Epidicus* is wonderful, except when Pellio stages it. This has sometimes been taken to indicate that Plautus had fallen out with his producer Pellio. The absence of a negative tone in the passage in our play could point to a still positive relationship. However, not too much should be made of the passage in the *Bacchides*, which may be no more than a good-humored joke. In l. 412

418

it is said that the present ruler in Sicily is Hiero. Hiero died in 215. But we should not conclude for this reason that the *Menaechmi* is one of the earliest plays. The reference to Hiero merely indicates that he was still remembered by most spectators. It is well known that Plautus increased his *mutatis modis cantica* in the later plays, and since the *Menaechmi* has an intermediate amount of *cantica* it may well belong to Plautus' middle period.

The story is about identical twins, both of whom have the name Menaechmus. Originally one was called Sosicles, the other Menaechmus; but Menaechmus was taken from his home in Syracuse to Tarentum by his father and got lost there, so that the boys' grandfather changed Sosicles' name to Menaechmus, partly in order to honor the memory of the lost brother. The lost brother was kidnapped in Tarentum and taken to Epidamnus, where he grew up. In order to avoid confusion, I shall continue to refer to the brothers as Sosicles and Menaechmus in what follows, not as Menaechmus I and Menaechmus II, which is the practice in some editions. The name Menaechmus is cleverly chosen: in the fourth century there was a Syracusan mathematician of the same name, who solved the problem of the duplication of the cube; and "duplication problems" are at the heart of this comedy.

Menaechmus is rich because the Epidamnian who adopted him married him to a lady of means and in addition left him a large inheritance when he died. But Menaechmus does not get on with his wife and has a mistress, the prostitute Erotium. The play begins when Menaechmus robs his wife of an expensive *palla*, a special kind of female garment with no precise English equivalent, but

419

perhaps closest to what we call a mantle. He wants to give it to Erotium in exchange for sexual services and a meal, the latter to be shared with his hanger-on Peniculus. When Erotium receives the mantle, she sends her cook Cylindrus to buy food. While preparations for the meal are under way, Menaechmus and Peniculus go to the forum, where the former has to assist a client in a lawsuit.

At this moment Sosicles arrives in Epidamnus with his slave Messenio. Sosicles has spent much time looking for his twin in various countries, but so far in vain. He meets Cylindrus and Erotium and is addressed as Menaechmus, the name he normally uses. He is surprised, but accepts the invitation to the meal; Messenio tries to warn him about Epidamnian prostitutes, but is sent away by his master, who quickly realizes that there is some confusion and that he can take advantage of the situation and enjoy himself. Sosicles has a pleasant meal, sleeps with the prostitute, and takes the mantle with him when Erotium asks him to repair it; his plan is to sell it and keep the money for himself.

Now Peniculus is on his way back from the forum, where he lost sight of Menaechmus. He meets Sosicles, believes that he is his patron Menaechmus, and comes to the conclusion that his patron has deliberately finished the meal without him. When Sosicles in addition denies knowing Peniculus, the hanger-on has enough and goes to the wife of Menaechmus to tell her what her husband is up to.

The wife of Menaechmus and Peniculus then meet not Sosicles but the original Menaechmus, who promptly gets a hard time from the two. Completely unnerved, he agrees to bring back the mantle. But when he asks Erotium for it, he naturally hears from her that he has already taken it. Again he gets a hard time.

Now Sosicles appears again, still with the mantle, and meets his brother's wife. When she scolds him for his behavior, he claims that he does not know her and that he never stole any mantle. As she sees him holding the mantle in his hands, she is particularly incensed and summons her father. Again Sosicles states that he does not know him, and the wife and her father declare him mad. Sosicles plays along and pretends to be insane in order to get rid of the two. The wife rushes home and her father fetches a doctor.

When the old man and the doctor come onstage, they meet not Sosicles but the original Menaechmus. The doctor tries to diagnose the illness and annoys Menaechmus, who knows that he is perfectly healthy. The conclusion the doctor draws is that Menaechmus is mad, and the old man brings four slaves to drag Menaechmus to the doctor. The slaves begin to grapple with Menaechmus.

Now Messenio appears again and saves Menaechmus, whom he wrongly believes to be his master. He asks Menaechmus to free him, and Menaechmus does so when he realizes that it is futile to claim not to know Messenio. Messenio promises to bring him back his wallet and Menaechmus happily agrees, hoping to make some profit.

On his way, Messenio meets his master Sosicles, who denies having freed him. They see Menaechmus. With Messenio's help they realize that they are twins. The brothers decide to return to Sicily together and Messenio gets his freedom.

The *Menaechmi* is universally regarded as one of Plautus' masterpieces, despite the fact that the leading figures

421

have flawed characters: Menaechmus has a mistress and
is happy to cheat Messenio out of his money, even though
this slave saved his life not much earlier; and Sosicles has
no qualms about deceiving Erotium in order to get food,
drink, sex, and a valuable mantle. By contrast, flaws of
composition are absent. It has been claimed that the
scenes with the doctor (ll. 889–956) are a Plautine addition
because they disrupt the flow and symmetry of the play
and contribute nothing to the plot; but on these criteria
much of Plautine—and indeed Greek—comedy could be
considered pointless padding, and it has to be said that
these scenes are among the most humorous in the entire
play. While the scenes with the doctor were probably al-
ready in the original, Plautus seems to have created or
at least expanded the scene in which Sosicles pretends
to be mad (ll. 831–71). In Greek tragedy and comedy,
real (as distinct from presumed) madness and its conse-
quences are not staged at all, though they can be reported
in messenger speeches. But madness is depicted in En-
nius' *Alcumeo*, so that we could be dealing with a parody of
Roman tragedy.

SELECT BIBLIOGRAPHY

Editions and Commentaries

Brix, J., Niemeyer, M., and Conrad, F. (1929), *Plautus:
    Ausgewählte Komödien*, vol. 3: *Menaechmi*, 6th ed.
    (Leipzig).
Gratwick, A. S. (1993), *Plautus: Menaechmi* (Cambridge).
Thoresby Jones, P. (1918), *T. Macci Plauti Menaechmi:
    Edited, with Introduction and Notes* (Oxford).

MENAECHMI

Criticism

Fantham, E. (1968), "Act IV of the *Menaechmi*: Plautus and His Original," in *Classical Philology* 63: 175–83.

Leach, E. W. (1969), "*Meam quom formam noscito*: Language and Characterization in the *Menaechmi*," in *Arethusa* 2: 30–45.

Raffaelli, R., and Tontini, A. (eds.) (2007), *Lecturae Plautinae Sarsinates X: Menaechmi (Sarsina, 30 settembre 2006)* (Urbino).

Woytek, E. (1982), "Zur Herkunft der Arztszene in den Menaechmi des Plautus," in *Wiener Studien* NS 16: 165–82.

MENAECHMI

ARGVMENTVM

Mercator Siculus, quoi erant gemini filii,
Ei surrupto altero mors optigit.
Nomen surrepticii indit illi qui domi est
Auos paternus, facit Menaechmum e Sosicle.
5 Et is germanum, postquam adoleuit, quaeritat
Circum omnis oras. post Epidamnum deuenit;
Hic fuerat alitus ille surrepticius.
Menaechmum omnes ciuem credunt aduenam
Eumque appellant meretrix, uxor, et socer.
10 I se cognoscunt fratres postremo in uicem.

PERSONAE

PENICVLVS parasitus
MENAECHMVS I adulescens
EROTIVM meretrix
CYLINDRVS coquos
SOSICLES/MENAECHMVS II adulescens
MESSENIO seruos
ANCILLA

arg. 3 illi indit *P, transp. Gratwick*

424

THE TWO MENAECHMUSES

PLOT SUMMARY

A Sicilian merchant who had twin sons died after one was kid-
napped. The paternal grandfather gave the name of the stolen
son to the one who was at home. He made a Menaechmus out of
a Sosicles. And after he grew up, he kept looking for his twin   5
around all shores. Later he ends up in Epidamnus. Here that
kidnapped boy had been raised. All people think that the new-
comer is the citizen Menaechmus, and the latter's prostitute,
wife, and father-in-law address him as such. Finally the two   10
brothers recognize each other.

CHARACTERS

PENICULUS a hanger-on; sponges on Menaechmus I
MENAECHMUS I a young man; unhappily married in Epi-
damnus and in love with Erotium
EROTIUM a prostitute; charming, but greedy
CYLINDRUS a cook; works for Erotium
SOSICLES/MENAECHMUS II a young man; from Syracuse,
twin of Menaechmus I
MESSENIO a slave; loyal to his master Sosicles/Menaechmus
II
SERVANT GIRL works for Erotium

MATRONA
SENEX
MEDICVS
LORARII

SCAENA

Epidamni

MENAECHMI

A MARRIED WOMAN wife of Menaechmus I
AN OLD MAN father-in-law of Menaechmus I
A DOCTOR very convinced of his own skills
SLAVES WITH STRAPS work for the old man

STAGING

The stage represents a street in Epidamnus. The left-hand side
of the street leads to the harbor, the right-hand side to the city
center. On the street there are two houses; the left one belongs
to Menaechmus I, the other belongs to Erotium.

PROLOGVS

PRO Salutem primum iam a principio propitiam
      mihi atque uobis, spectatores, nuntio.
      apporto uobis Plautum . . . lingua, non manu:
      quaeso ut benignis accipiatis auribus.
5   nunc argumentum accipite atque animum aduortite;
      quam potero in uerba conferam paucissuma.
      atque hoc poetae faciunt in comoediis:
      omnis res gestas esse Athenis autumant,
      quo illud uobis graecum uideatur magis;
10   ego nusquam dicam nisi ubi factum dicitur.
72   haec urbs Epidamnus est dum haec agitur fabula:
73   quando alia agetur aliud fiet oppidum;
74   sicut familiae quoque solent mutarier:
75   modo hic habitat leno, modo adulescens, modo senex,
76   pauper, mendicus, rex, parasitus, hariolus.
11   atque adeo hoc argumentum graecissat, tamen
      non atticissat, uerum sicilicissitat.
      †huic argumento antelogium hoc fuit.†
      nunc argumentum uobis demensum dabo,
15   non modio nec trimodio, uerum ipso horreo:
      tantum ad narrandum argumentum adest benignitas.

72–76 *post 10 posuit Gratwick*
13 ante elo(n)gium *P*, antelogium *Muretus*

PROLOGUE

Enter the SPEAKER OF THE PROLOGUE.

SPEA First and foremost I announce that Salus is well-disposed
toward myself and you, spectators.[1] I'm bringing you
Plautus . . . with my tongue, not my hand. I ask you to re-
ceive him with benevolent ears. Now receive the plot   5
summary and pay attention. I'll put it in as few words as I
can. This is what writers do in comedies: they claim that
everything took place in Athens, intending that it should
seem more Greek to you. I shall say what happened   10
nowhere except where it is said to have happened. This   72
city is Epidamnus as long as this play is being staged.
When another is staged it'll become another town, just as
households too always change. At one time a pimp lives   75
here, at another a young man, at yet another an old one, a   76
pauper, a beggar, a king, a hanger-on, a soothsayer. And   11
besides, this plot summary has a Greek air; nevertheless,
it doesn't have an Attic air, but a Sicilian one. †This was
the preamble to this plot summary.† Now I'll give you
your ration of the plot, not by the peck or the triple peck,   15
but by the granary itself;[2] so benevolent am I when it

---

[1] Salus is the goddess of well-being. The speaker of the prologue is
playing a magistrate announcing the result of an augury.

[2] A *modius* "peck" was nine litres; after the triple-peck with twenty-
seven litres we expect the Attic *medimnus* with fifty-four litres rather
than the whole granary.

mercator quidam fuit Syracusis senex,
ei sunt nati filii gemini duo,
ita forma simili pueri ut mater sua
20 non internosse posset quae mammam dabat,
neque adeo mater ipsa quae illos pepererat—
ut quidem ille dixit mihi qui pueros uiderat:
ego illos non uidi, ne quis uostrum censeat.
postquam iam pueri septuennes sunt, pater
25 onerauit nauim magnam multis mercibus;
imponit geminum alterum in nauim pater,
Tarentum auexit secum ad mercatum simul,
illum reliquit alterum apud matrem domi.
Tarenti ludi forte erant quom illuc uenit.
30 mortales multi, ut ad ludos, conuenerant:
puer aberrauit inter homines a patre.
Epidamniensis quidam ibi mercator fuit,
is puerum tollit auehitque Epidamnum eum.
pater eius autem postquam puerum perdidit,
35 animum despondit eaque is aegritudine
paucis diebus post Tarenti emortuost.
postquam Syracusas de ea re rediit nuntius
ad auom puerorum, puerum surruptum alterum
patremque pueri ess' Tarenti emortuom,
40 immutat nomen auos huic gemino alteri;
ita illum dilexit qui surruptust alterum:
illius nomen indit illi qui domi est,
Menaechmo, idem quod alteri nomen fuit;
et ipsus eodem est auos uocatus nomine;
45 propterea illius nomen memini facilius,

19 *uel* uti
31 puer inter homines aberrauit *P, transp. Acidalius*

comes to telling you the summary. There was a certain
old merchant in Syracuse. Two twin sons were born to
him, boys of such similar looks that their wet nurse who   20
gave them the breast could not tell them apart, nor for
that matter the mother herself who'd given birth to
them—at least someone who'd seen the boys told me so.
I haven't see them, in case any of you supposes that I did.
When the boys were now seven years old, their father
loaded a large ship with much freight. The father put one   25
twin onto the ship and took him with him to Tarentum
to the market. He left the other one at home with his
mother. In Tarentum there was by chance a festival when
he arrived. Many people had gathered, as they do at festi-   30
vals. The boy strayed from his father among the crowd.
There was a certain merchant from Epidamnus there.
He picked the boy up and carried him off to Epidamnus.
But after his father lost the boy, he despaired and be-   35
cause of his grief for him died a few days later in Taren-
tum. After the news about this came back to Syracuse
to the grandfather of the boys, that the one boy had
been kidnapped and that the boy's father had died in
Tarentum, the grandfather changed the name of this   40
other twin; so much did he love that other one who was
snatched. He gave his name to the one who was at home,
Menaechmus, the same name the other one had. And the
grandfather himself was called by the same name. I re-   45
member his name more easily for the simple reason that

---

33 Epidamnium *P*, Epidamnum eum *Seyffert*
39 Tarenti esse *P*, *transposui*

quia illum clamore uidi flagitarier.
ne mox erretis, iam nunc praedico prius:
idem est ambobus nomen geminis fratribus.
nunc in Epidamnum pedibus redeundum est mihi,
50   ut hanc rem uobis examussim disputem.
si quis quid uestrum Epidamnum curari sibi
uelit, audacter imperato et dicito,
sed ita ut det unde curari id possit sibi.
nam nisi qui argentum dederit, nugas egerit;
55   qui dederit . . . magis maiores nugas egerit.
uerum illuc redeo unde abii atque uno asto in loco.
Epidamniensis ill' quem dudum dixeram,
geminum illum puerum qui surrupuit alterum,
ei liberorum nisi diuitiae nil erat:
60   adoptat illum puerum surrupticium
sibi filium eique uxorem dotatam dedit,
eumque heredem fecit quom ipse obiit diem.
nam rus ut ibat forte, ut multum pluerat,
ingressus fluuium rapidum ab urbe hau longule,
65   rapidus raptori pueri subduxit pedes
apstraxitque hominem in maxumam malam crucem.
illi diuitiae euenerunt maxumae.
is illic habitat geminus surrupticius.
nunc ille geminus, qui Syracusis habet,
70   hodie in Epidamnum uenit cum seruo suo
71   hunc quaeritatum geminum germanum suom.
***

71–77 *prologus in A longior fuisse uidetur*

I saw him being dunned loudly. So that you aren't soon
mistaken, I'm already telling you now in advance: both
twin brothers have the same name. Now I have to re-
turn to Epidamnus on foot in order to set you right on   50
this other account: if anyone of you wants any business
sorted out in Epidamnus, let him command me boldly
and speak out, but in such a way that he gives the money
from which this business can be sorted out; if anyone
doesn't give me the money, he's behaving like a fool. But 55
if he does give me the money . . . he's behaving even more
like a fool. Well, I'm returning to the location I left and
yet I'm standing in one and the same place. That man
from Epidamnus I was talking about a moment ago, the
man who kidnapped that other twin, he had no children
except for his wealth.[3] He adopted that kidnapped boy as 60
his son and gave him a wife with a big dowry, and he made
him his heir when he himself died: when he happened to
go to the country, after much rain had fallen, he stepped
into a racing river not far from the city; the racer pulled 65
away the feet of the child-displacer and dragged him
off to a very sticky end. That young man got very great
riches. This kidnapped twin lives there. Now that twin
who lives in Syracuse has come to Epidamnus today with 70
his slave in order to look for this twin brother of his. *** 71

Exit the SPEAKER OF THE PROLOGUE.

[3] Which he loved like children.

433

PLAUTUS

ACTVS I

I. i: PENICVLVS

77 PEN iuuentus nomen fecit Peniculo mihi,
   ideo quia . . . mensam quando edo detergeo.
   homines captiuos qui catenis uinciunt
80 et qui fugitiuis seruis indunt compedis,
   nimis stulte faciunt mea quidem sententia.
   nam homini misero si ad malum accedit malum,
   maior lubido est fugere et facere nequiter.
   nam se ex catenis eximunt aliquo modo.
85 tum compediti anum lima praeterunt
   aut lapide excutiunt clauom. nugae sunt eae.
   quem tu asseruare recte ne aufugiat uoles
   esca atque potione uinciri decet.
   apud mensam plenam homini rostrum deliges;
90 dum tu illi quod edit et quod potet praebeas,
   suo arbitratu, ad fatim, cottidie,
   numquam edepol fugiet, tam etsi capital fecerit,
   facile asseruabis, dum eo uinclo uincies.
   ita istaec nimis lenta uincla sunt escaria:
95 quam magis extendas tanto astringunt artius.
   nam ego ad Menaechmum hunc eo, quo iam diu
   sum iudicatus; ultro eo ut me uinciat.
   nam illic homo homines non alit, uerum educat
   recreatque: nullus melius medicinam facit.
100 ita est adulescens ipsus; escae maxumae,

85 compediti i *P ut uidetur, sed sine pronomine B et Non.*

434

ACT ONE

Enter PENICULUS from the right.

PEN The youngsters have given me the name "Peniculus, the 77
Brush" because . . . when I eat I wipe the table clean.[4]
People who bind prisoners with chains and who put 80
shackles on runaway slaves behave very stupidly, at least
in my opinion: if an unlucky fellow finds one bad thing
added to another, he's all the more eager to run away and
behave badly. Yes, they get themselves out of the chains
in some way or other. Then those in shackles rub through 85
the link with a file or knock the rivet off with a stone.
That's just nonsense. Someone you want to watch over
well so he doesn't run away ought to be bound with food
and drink. At a full table you can tie down a man's snout.
So long as you provide him with food and drink, at his 90
own discretion, to repletion, every day, he'll never run
away, even if he's committed a capital crime. You'll guard
him easily so long as you bind him with this bond. Those
food chains are terribly tough indeed: the more you 95
stretch them, the more tightly they tie; I'm going to
Menaechmus here, the bond servant of whose household
I've been for a long time already. I'm going of my own ac-
cord so that he can bind me. Yes, he doesn't simply feed
men, but nurtures and restores them. No one practices
the medical profession better. That's what the young man 100

---

[4] The pun is hard to reproduce. Hangers-on often have obscene
nicknames. *Peniculus* can mean "little dick." We expect an obscene ex-
planation, but in fact get an innocuous one because the other meaning
is "brush."

Cerealis cenas dat, ita mensas exstruit,
tantas struices concinnat patinarias:
standum est in lecto si quid de summo petas.
sed mi interuallum iam hos dies multos fuit:
105   domi domitus sum usque cum caris meis.
nam neque edo neque emo nisi quod est carissumum.
id quoque iam, cari qui instruontur deserunt.
nunc ad eum inuiso. sed aperitur ostium.
Menaechmum eccum ipsum uideo, progreditur foras.

I. ii: MENAECHMVS. PENICVLVS

110   MEN   ni mala, ni stulta sies,
110ᵃ   ni indomita imposque animi,
111   quod uiro esse odio uideas,
111ᵃ   tute tibi odio habeas.
112   praeterhac si mihi tale post hunc diem
              faxis, faxo foris uidua uisas patrem.
114   nam quotiens foras ire uolo,
114ᵃ   me retines, reuocas, rogitas,
115   quo ego eam, quam rem agam, quid negoti geram,
              quid petam, quid feram, quid foris egerim.
              portitorem domum duxi, ita omnem mihi
              rem necesse eloqui est, quicquid egi atque ago.
              nimium ego te habui delicatam; nunc adeo ut facturus
                 dicam.
120   quando ego tibi ancillas, penum,
121   lanam, aurum, uestem, purpuram
121ᵃ   bene praebeo nec quicquam eges,
122   malo cauebis si sapis,
122ᵃ   uirum opseruare desines.

---

5 Goddess of growth and crops; her feast is the harvest festival.

himself is like. The portions are enormous, he gives dinners fit for the feast of Ceres,[5] to judge from the way he creates heaps on the tables and from the height of the piles of pans he puts together. You have to stand on your couch if you want to take something from the top. But now I've had a gap of many days past. I'm constantly   105
housebound in my house with my dear ones: I neither eat nor buy except what is dearest. And now these dear ones who are being marshaled are deserting me. Now I'll visit him. (*stops in front of Menaechmus' house*) But the door is opening. Look, I can see Menaechmus himself, he's coming out. (*steps aside to the left*)

Enter MENAECHMUS from his house, wearing a mantle under his regular cloak; he does not notice Peniculus.

MEN   (*into his house*) If you weren't bad, if you weren't stupid,   110
if you weren't unrestrained and unable to control your mind, you yourself would hate what you can see your husband hates. If after this day you do something further of this sort to me, I'll pack you off to your father as a divorced woman. Whenever I want to go out you hold me back, call me back, and ask me where I'm going, what I'm   115
doing, what business I'm carrying out, what I'm seeking, what I'm up to, what I've done outside. I've married a customs officer: I have to state everything, whatever I've done and am doing. I've spoiled you far too much. Now I'll tell you what I'm going to do. Since I'm providing you   120
well with slave girls, food, wool, gold, clothes, and purple, and you don't lack anything, you'll watch out for a hard time if you're wise and you'll stop spying on your husband. (*aside, as he walks to Erotium's house*) And so

123		atque adeo, ne me nequiquam serues, ob eam industriam
		hodie ducam scortum ad cenam atque aliquo condicam
		foras.
125	PEN	illic homo se uxori simulat male loqui, loquitur mihi;
		nam si foris cenat, profecto me, haud uxorem, ulciscitur.
	MEN	euax! iurgio hercle tandem uxorem abegi ab ianua.
		ubi sunt amatores mariti? dona quid cessant mihi
		conferre omnes congratulantes quia pugnaui fortiter?
130		hanc modo uxori intus pallam surrupui, ad scortum fero.
		sic hoc decet, dari facete uerba custodi catae.
		hoc facinus pulchrum est, hoc probum est, hoc lepidum
		est, hoc factum est fabre:
		meo malo a mala apstuli hoc, ad damnum deferetur.
		auorti praedam ab hostibus nostrum salute socium.
135	PEN	heus adulescens! ecqua in istac pars inest praeda mihi?
	MEN	perii! in insidias deueni.
	PEN	immo in praesidium, ne time.
	MEN	quis homo est?
	PEN	ego sum.
	MEN	o mea Commoditas, o mea Opportunitas,
		salue.
	PEN	salue.
	MEN	quid agis?
	PEN	teneo dextera genium meum.
	MEN	non potuisti magis per tempus mi aduenire quam adue-
		nis.
140	PEN	ita ego soleo: Commoditatis omnis articulos scio.

as to give you a good reason to guard me, in return for that officiousness I'll take a prostitute to dinner today and engage myself somewhere outside.

PEN   (*aside*) He's pretending to tell off his wife, but he's telling   125
me off: if he dines outside, he's in fact punishing me, not his wife.

MEN   Hurray! At last I've driven my wife away from the door with my invective. Where are the married lovers? Why don't they bring me presents, all of them, and congratulate me for fighting bravely? I've just stolen this mantle   130
(*points to it*) from my wife inside and I'm bringing it to a prostitute. That's how it should be: the clever guard must be tricked smartly. This deed is noble, moral, stylish, and professional: I've nicked this piece (*holds on to the mantle*) from the nasty piece, with a nasty outcome for myself, and it will be led to its ruin. I took the booty away from the enemy with our allies safe and sound.

PEN   (*loudly*) Hey there, young man! Do I get any share in this   135
booty?

MEN   I'm dead! I've been detected.

PEN   No, you've been protected, stop being afraid.

MEN   Who is it?

PEN   It's me.

MEN   (*spotting him*) O my Timeliness, o my Opportunity, my greetings to you.

PEN   And mine to you. (*grabs his hand*)

MEN   What are you up to?

PEN   I'm holding my good spirit with my right hand.

MEN   You couldn't have come at a better time than the one you're coming at.

PEN   That's my custom; I know all the critical moments of   140
Timeliness.

MEN uin tu facinus luculentum inspicere?

PEN quis id coxit coquos?
iam sciam, si quid titubatum est, ubi reliquias uidero.

MEN dic mi, enumquam tu uidisti tabulam pictam in pariete
ubi aquila Catamitum raperet aut ubi Venus Adoneum?

145 PEN saepe. sed quid istae picturae ad me attinent?

MEN age me aspice.
ecquid assimulo similiter?

PEN qui istic ornatust tuos?

MEN dic hominem lepidissumum esse me.

PEN ubi esuri sumus?

MEN dic modo hoc quod ego te iubeo.

PEN dico: homo lepidissume.

MEN ecquid audes de tuo istuc addere?

PEN atque hilarissume.

150 MEN perge, ⟨perge⟩.

PEN non pergo hercle nisi scio qua gratia.
litigium tibi est cum uxore, eo mi aps te caueo cautius.

MEN clam uxorem est ubi pulcre habeamus, [atque] hunc
comburamus diem.

PEN age sane igitur, quando aequom oras, quam mox incendo
rogum?

154–
55 dies quidem iam ad umbilicum est dimidiatus mortuos.

MEN te morare mihi quom obloquere.

PEN oculum effodito per solum
mihi, Menaechme, si ullum uerbum faxo nisi quod ius-
seris.

143 numquam *P*, enumquam *Brix*   146 est ornatus *P*, orna-
tust *Lindsay in apparatu*   150 perge[2] *add. Schwabe*
152 est *Charisius, om. P*   sepulchrum *P*, pulchre *Ussing* atque
del. Brix

MEN Do you want to see something splendid?

PEN What cook cooked it? I'll know at once if some mistake
     has been made when I see the leftovers.

MEN Tell me, have you ever seen a mural painting where an
     eagle carries off Ganymede or Venus carries off Adonis?[6]

PEN Often. But what do those pictures have to do with me? 145

MEN Go on, look at me. Do I resemble them in a similar way?

PEN (*noticing the mantle*) What are you dressed up for like
     that?

MEN Say that I'm a jolly good fellow.

PEN Where are we going to eat?

MEN Just say what I'm telling you.

PEN All right: jolly good fellow.

MEN Do you want to add something of your own to it?

PEN And jolly charming fellow.

MEN Go on, go on! 150

PEN I'm not going on unless I know what for. You're having a
     quarrel with your wife, that's why I'm taking extra-careful
     care for myself against trouble from you.

MEN There's a place where we can have a good time behind my
     wife's back and where we can burn this day to cinders.

PEN Go on then, since what you ask is fair, how soon shall I set
     fire to the pyre? Half the day is already dead, right up to 155
     its navel.

MEN You're delaying yourself by interrupting me.

PEN Gouge out my eye by the roots, Menaechmus, if I utter a
     single word except for what you tell me.

---

[6] Zeus found Ganymede irresistible, turned himself into an eagle,
and carried him off. Similarly, Venus fell in love with Adonis.

MEN	concede huc a foribus.
PEN	fiat.
MEN	etiam concede huc.
PEN	licet.
MEN	etiam nunc concede audacter ab leonino cauo.

160 PEN   eu edepol! ne tu, ut ego opinor, esses agitator probus.

    MEN   quidum?

    PEN   ne te uxor sequatur respectas identidem.

    MEN   sed quid ais?

    PEN   egone? id enim quod tu uis, id aio atque id nego.

    MEN   ecquid tu de odore possis, si quid forte olfeceris,
            facere coniecturam cu- ***?

165 ⟨PEN⟩ *** captum sit collegium.

    MEN   agedum odorare hanc quam ego habeo pallam. quid
            olet? apstines?

    PEN   summum oportet olfactare uestimentum muliebre,
            nam ex istoc loco spurcatur nasum odore illutili.

    MEN   olfacta igitur hinc, Penicule. lepide ut fastidis!

    PEN   decet.

170 MEN   quid igitur? quid olet? responde.

    PEN   furtum, scortum, prandium.
            tibi fuant ***

    MEN   elocutu's, nam *** ⟨prandium⟩.
            nunc ad amicam deferetur hanc meretricem Erotium.
            mihi, tibi atque illi iubebo iam apparari prandium.

    PEN   eu!

175 MEN   inde usque ad diurnam stellam crastinam potabimus.

    164–65 *sic A, unus uersus P*   167 oportet summum olfactare
P, transp. Guyet, summum olefactare oportet *F. Skutsch*
    168 inlutibili *Nonius,* inlutili *Ritschl,* inlucido *P*
    171–72 *desunt in P, uestigia in A*   prandium *add. Lindsay*
    175 eu *om. P*

MEN   Come over here from the door.

PEN   Yes. (*does so*)

MEN   Come over here, a bit more.

PEN   All right. (*obeys*)

MEN   Now boldly come over even further from the lioness's den.

PEN   (*doing so*) Goodness! You'd really be a good charioteer, I 160 think.

MEN   How so?

PEN   You keep looking behind you to check that your wife isn't catching up with you.

MEN   But what do you say?

PEN   I? I say yes and no to whatever you wish.

MEN   If you happened to smell something, could you make a conjecture from the smell ***?

PEN   *** the college of sniffers were stuck.   165

MEN   Go on, smell this mantle I have. (*shows it, lifting up the lower part*) What does it smell of? You're staying away?

PEN   One ought to smell the top of a female dress, because from that spot one's nose is contaminated with a smell that can't be washed off.

MEN   Then smell here, Peniculus. (*points to the top*) How charmingly you give yourself airs!

PEN   That's appropriate. (*sniffs*)

MEN   What now? What does it smell of? Answer me.   170

PEN   Theft, a prostitute, a lunch. You might have ***

MEN   You've said it, because *** lunch. Now this (*points to mantle*) will be brought to my girlfriend, the prostitute Erotium here. I'll now have a lunch prepared for myself, you, and her.

PEN   Brilliant!

MEN   Then we shall drink till tomorrow's morning star.   175

PEN   [eu!]
          expedite fabulatu's. iam fores ferio?

MEN   feri.
          uel mane etiam.

PEN   mille passum commoratu's cantharum.

MEN placide pulta.

PEN   metuis, credo, ne fores Samiae sient.

179   f- ***

180 MEN mane, mane opsecro hercle: eapse eccam exit. oh! solem uides
          satin ut occaecatust prae huius corporis candoribus?

I. iii: EROTIVM. PENICVLVS. MENAECHMVS

ERO anime mi, Menaechme, salue.

PEN   quid ego?

ERO   extra numerum es mihi.

PEN idem istuc aliis ascriptiuis fieri ad legionem solet.

184–85 MEN ego istic mihi hodie apparari iussi apud te proelium.

ERO hodie id fiet.

MEN   in eo uterque proelio potabimus.

PEN uter ibi melior bellator erit inuentus cantharo
     tu seligito ac iudicato cum utro . . . hanc noctem sies.

MEN ut ego uxorem, mea uoluptas, ubi te aspicio, odi male!

190 PEN interim nequis quin eius aliquid indutus sies.

ERO quid hoc est?

MEN   induuiae tuae atque uxoris exuuiae, rosa.

179 *lacuna in A, deest in P*
188 tuestlegio adiudicato *P*, tu selegito ac iudicato *Ussing*

444

PEN You've spoken clearly. Shall I knock on the door?

MEN Yes, do. (*pauses*) Or wait still.

PEN You've delayed the goblet a mile.

MEN Knock gently.

PEN You're afraid, I believe, that the door is Samian earthenware.[7] ***

MEN Wait, wait please. Look, she's coming out herself. Oh! 180
Can you see how the sun has been blotted out in the light
of her body's radiance?

*Enter EROTIUM from her house, followed by two slave girls,
who stand at a slight distance.*

ERO My sweetheart, Menaechmus, hello.

PEN What about me?

ERO You don't count to me.

PEN That same thing is always said to happen to supernumeraries like me in the army too.

MEN (*to Erotium*) I ordered that a battle should prepared for 185
myself here at your place today.

ERO It shall take place today.

MEN In this battle we shall both drink.

PEN (*aside*) You choose which of us is found to be the better
warrior there with the jug and decide with which of us . . .
you spend this night.

MEN My darling, how badly I hate my wife when I look at you!

PEN (*aside*) In the meantime you can't help wearing some- 190
thing of hers.

ERO What is this? (*points to the mantle*)

MEN You are robed and my wife is robbed, my rose.

---

[7] Of low quality and fragile.

ERO   superas facile ut superior sis mihi quam quisquam qui imperant.

PEN   meretrix tantisper blanditur, dum illud quod rapiat uidet;

194–95   nam si amabas, iam oportebat nasum abreptum mordicus.

MEN   sustine hoc, Penicule: exuuias facere quas uoui uolo.

PEN   cedo; sed opsecro hercle, salta sic cum palla postea.

MEN   ego saltabo? sanus hercle non es.

PEN   egone an tu magis? si non saltas, exue igitur.

MEN   nimio ego hanc periculo

200   surrupui hodie. meo quidem animo ab Hippolyta succingulum
    Hercules haud aeque magno umquam apstulit periculo.
    cape tibi hanc, quando me uiuis meis morigera moribus.

ERO   hoc animo decet animatos esse amatores probos.

PEN   qui quidem ad mendicitatem properent se detrudere.

205 MEN   quattuor minis ego emi istanc anno uxori meae.

PEN   quattuor minae perierunt plane, ut ratio redditur.

MEN   scin quid uolo ego te accurare?

ERO   scio, curabo quae uoles.

MEN   iube igitur tribus nobis apud te prandium accurarier
    atque aliquid scitamentorum de foro opsonarier,

210   glandionidam suillam, laridum pernonidam,
    aut sincipitamenta porcina aut aliquid ad eum modum,

192 impetrant *P*, imperant *Ussing*
201 haud Hercules Ω, *transp. Lambinus*
204 properent se *A*, se proderent *P*

---

8 Through passionate kissing.   9 Taking the girdle away from Hippolyta, queen of the Amazons, was one of the labors of Hercules; but speaking of an undergirdle turns this into something ridiculous.

ERO You easily gain the upper hand so that for me you are
   above any of those who command me.

PEN A prostitute only flatters as long as she can see something
   she can snatch: if you loved him, you ought to have bitten   195
   off his nose by now.[8]

MEN Lift up my cloak, Peniculus; I want to dedicate the spoils
   I vowed.

PEN Give it to me. (*takes the cloak*) But please, dance with the
   mantle like this afterward.

MEN I shall dance? You're insane.

PEN Who is more so, I or you? Well, if you aren't dancing, take
   it off.

MEN (*taking off the mantle*) I stole this in enormous danger. In   200
   my opinion Hercules didn't steal Hippolyta's undergirdle
   in such great danger.[9] Take it for yourself, since you alone
   follow my ways. (*hands it over*)

ERO Decent lovers ought to have this attitude.

PEN (*aside*) Yes, those who're rushing to hurl themselves into
   poverty.

MEN I bought that mantle for my wife for four minas a year   205
   ago.[10]

PEN (*aside*) The four minas are quite lost according to ac-
   count rendered.

MEN (*to Erotium*) Do you know what I want you to take care
   of?

ERO I know, I'll take care of what you want.

MEN Then have a lunch prepared at your place for the three of
   us, and have some delicacies bought from the market,
   sweetbreads the pig's daughters, bacon the son of ham, or   210
   pigs' heads or something of that sort which, when put on

---

[10] An exceptionally high price.

madida quae mi apposita in mensam miluinam sugge-
rant;
atque actutum.

ERO   licet ecastor.

MEN   nos prodimus ad forum.
iam hic nos erimus: dum coquetur, interim potabimus.

215 ERO quando uis ueni, parata res erit.

MEN   propera modo.
sequere tu.

PEN   ego hercle uero te et seruabo et te sequar,
neque hodie ut te perdam meream deorum diuitias mihi.

ERO euocate intus Cylindrum mihi coquom actutum foras.

I. iv: EROTIVM. CYLINDRVS

ERO sportulam cape atque argentum. ecquos tris nummos
habes?

220 CYL habeo.

ERO   abi atque opsonium affer; tribus uide quod sit satis:
nec defiat nec supersit.

CYL   quoius modi hisce homines erunt?

ERO ego et Menaechmus et parasitus eius.

CYL   iam isti sunt decem;
nam parasitus octo hominum munus facile fungitur.

ERO elocuta sum conuiuas, ceterum cura.

CYL   licet.

225   cocta sunt, iube ire accubitum.

ERO   redi cito.

CYL   iam ego hic ero.

215 propera modo *dant Menaechmo Leo et Lindsay*

219 eccos *P*, ecquos *Gratwick*   221 h(ic) (*uel* his) homines *A*,
hiomines *P* (hi homines *B²*), hisce homines *scripsi*

223 octo⟨num⟩ *Gratwick*

the table in front of me cooked, gives me an appetite as keen as a kite's; and at once.

ERO   Yes, of course.

MEN   We're off to the forum. We'll be back soon. While it's being cooked, we'll drink.

ERO   Come when you wish, it will be ready.   215

MEN   Just hurry. (*to Peniculus*) You, follow me.

PEN   Yes, I will watch you and follow you, and I wouldn't earn the wealth of the gods today if it meant losing you.

Exeunt MENAECHMUS and PENICULUS to the right.

ERO   (*to the slave girls*) Call out the cook Cylindrus at once.

Exeunt slave girls into Erotium's house.
Enter CYLINDRUS from Erotium's house.

ERO   Take a basket and money. Do you have three sesterces?

CYL   Yes, I do.   220

ERO   Go and bring food. Make sure it's enough for three. It should be neither too little nor too much.

CYL   What sort of people will they be?

ERO   Myself and Menaechmus and his hanger-on.

CYL   That's already ten: the hanger-on easily does the job of eight people.

ERO   I've told you about the guests, take care of the rest.

CYL   Okay. It's as good as cooked, tell them to go and recline at 225
table.

ERO   Return quickly.

CYL   I'll be back soon.

Exit CYLINDRUS to the right, exit EROTIUM into her house.

PLAUTUS

ACTVS II

II. i: SOSICLES. MESSENIO

SOS   uoluptas nulla est nauitis, Messenio,
        maior meo animo quam quom ex alto procul
        terram conspiciunt.

MES   maior, non dicam dolo,
        [quam] si adueniens terram uideas quae fuerit tua.

230   sed quaeso, quam ob rem nunc Epidamnum uenimus?
        an quasi mare omnis circumimus insulas?

SOS   fratrem quaesitum geminum germanum meum.

MES   nam quid modi futurum est illum quaerere?
        hic annus sextus est postquam ei rei operam damus.

235   Histros, Hispanos, Massiliensis, Hilurios,
        mare superum omne, Graeciamque exoticam,
        orasque Italicas omnis, qua aggreditur mare,
        sumus circumuecti. si acum, credo, quaereres,
        acum inuenisses, si appareret, iam diu.

240   hominem inter uiuos quaeritamus mortuom;
        nam inuenissemus iam diu, si uiueret.

SOS   ergo istuc quaero certum qui faciat mihi,
        qui sese dicat scire eum esse emortuom:
        operam praeterea numquam sumam quaerere.

245   uerum aliter uiuos numquam desistam exsequi.
        ego illum scio quam carus sit cordi meo.

MES   in scirpo nodum quaeris. quin nos hinc domum
        redimus nisi si historiam scripturi sumus?

229 quam *del. Acidalius*
234 est *om. A*
246 carus sit cordi *A*, cordi sit carus *P*

MENAECHMI

ACT TWO

Enter SOSICLES and MESSENIO from the left, each with a traveling bag, followed by slaves carrying the heavy luggage.

SOS   Seamen feel no greater pleasure in my opinion, Messenio, than when they see land in the distance from the sea.

MES   You feel an even greater pleasure, I'll tell you frankly, if on your arrival you see the land that was yours. But 230 please, why have we come to Epidamnus now? Are we going round all islands like the sea?

SOS   To look for my twin brother.

MES   Well, what limit is there to looking for him? This is already the sixth year that we've been busy with it. We've 235 sailed round the people near the Danube, the Spaniards, the people of Marseille, the Illyrians, the entire Adriatic, Sicily, and all Italian shores, wherever the sea reaches. I believe if you were looking for a needle, you'd have found the needle long ago if it were ever to appear. We're 240 searching for a dead man among the living: if he were alive, we'd have found him long ago.

SOS   Well then, I'm looking for someone who can report this to me, who can say he knows that he's dead; I'll never make an effort to find him beyond that. But on no other 245 condition will I give up looking for him while I live. I know how dear he is to my heart.

MES   You're looking for a knot in the bulrush.[11] Why don't we go back home unless we're going to write a travel book?

---

[11] I.e. something that does not exist.

451

	SOS	dictum facessas, datum edis, caueas malo.
250		molestus ne sis, non tuo hoc fiet modo.
	MES	em!

illoc enim uerbo esse me seruom scio.
non potuit paucis plura plane proloqui.
uerum tamen nequeo contineri quin loquar.
audin, Menaechme? quom inspicio marsuppium,

255 uiaticati hercle admodum aestiue sumus.
ne tu hercle, opinor, nisi domum reuorteris,
ubi nil habebis, geminum dum quaeres, gemes.
nam ita est haec hominum natio: in Epidamniis
uoluptarii atque potatores maxumi;

260 tum sycophantae et palpatores plurumi
in urbe hac habitant; tum meretrices mulieres
nusquam perhibentur blandiores gentium.
propterea huic urbi nomen Epidamno inditum est,
quia nemo ferme huc sine damno deuortitur.

265	SOS	ego istuc cauebo. cedodum huc mihi marsuppium.
	MES	quid eo uis?
	SOS	iam aps te metuo de uerbis tuis.
	MES	quid metuis?
	SOS	ne mi damnum in Epidamno duis.

tu amator magnus mulierum es, Messenio,
ego autem homo iracundus, animi perciti,

270 id utrumque, argentum quando habebo, cauero,
ne tu delinquas neue ego irascar tibi.

	MES	cape atque serua. me lubente feceris.

257 quaeres A, queris P
258 natioinepidamnieis A, gemes natio epidamnia/nam ita est hec
hominum P
264 huc sine damno P, sine damno huc A

SOS Do what you're told, eat what you're given, watch out for a beating. Don't be a nuisance, this won't be done your 250 way.

MES (*aside*) There you go! Through this word I know I'm a slave. He couldn't have said more things so plainly in such few words. But still, I can't help speaking out. (*to his master*) Can you hear me, Menaechmus? When I look into the wallet, our supply for travel is very summery. 255 Unless you return home, I believe you'll be sorry when you're left with nothing while trying to catch sight of your twin; this nation of people is like this: among the Epidamnians there are the greatest hedonists and drinkers. Then lots of impostors and cajolers live in this city. And 260 then the prostitutes are said to be the most coaxing anywhere. This city is called Epidamnus because practically nobody puts up here without being damnified.

SOS I'll be on my guard against it. Give me the wallet. 265

MES What do you want with it?

SOS Because of your words I'm afraid of you now.

MES What are you afraid of?

SOS That you may cause me some damnification in Epidamnus. You are a great lover of the ladies, Messenio, but I am an irascible man, with a quick temper. When I have 270 the money I'll prevent both these things: you committing an offense and me being angry with you.

MES (*handing it over*) Take it and watch over it. I'll be delighted.

---

268 magnus amator *P*, magis amator *A*, amator magnus *Fleckeisen*
269 perditi *P*, perciti *Lipsius*

II. ii: CYLINDRVS. SOSICLES. MESSENIO

	CYL	bene opsonaui atque ex mea sententia,
		bonum anteponam prandium pransoribus.
275		sed eccum Menaechmum uideo. uae tergo meo!
		prius iam conuiuae ambulant ante ostium
		quam ego opsonatu redeo. adibo atque alloquar.
		Menaechme, salue.
	SOS	di te amabunt quisquis ⟨es⟩.
	CYL	quisquis d- *** ⟨quis⟩ ego sim?
280	SOS	non hercle uero.
	CYL	ubi conuiuae ceteri?
	SOS	quos tu conuiuas quaeris?
	CYL	parasitum tuom.
	SOS	meum parasitum? certe hic insanust homo.
	MES	dixin tibi esse hic sycophantas plurumos?
284	⟨CYL⟩	*** -rincu- * -sm- * -n- *** -tu- ***
285	SOS	quem tu parasitum quaeris, adulescens, meum?
	CYL	Peniculum.
	MES	eccum in uidulo saluom fero.
	CYL	Menaechme, numero huc aduenis ad prandium.
		nunc opsonatu redeo.
	SOS	responde mihi,
		adulescens: quibus hic pretiis porci ueneunt
290		sacres sinceri?
	CYL	nummis.
	SOS	nummum a me accipe:
		iube te piari de mea pecunia.
		nam equidem insanum esse te certo scio,
		qui mihi molestu's homini ignoto quisquis es.

278 es *add. Bentley*   279 quis *add. Bentley*
282 certe . . . homo *dat Cylindro Lindsay*

Enter CYLINDRUS from the right with shopping.

CYL   I've shopped cheaply and according to my wishes. I'll put
a good lunch before the lunchers. But look, I can see   275
Menaechmus. Bad luck to my back! The guests are al-
ready walking in front of the door before I've returned
from shopping. I'll approach and accost them. Hello,
Menaechmus.

SOS   May the gods love you, whoever you are.

CYL   Whoever *** who I am?

SOS   No, honestly not.   280

CYL   *(laughs at the answer he got)* Where are the other guests?

SOS   What guests are you looking for?

CYL   Your hanger-on.

SOS   My hanger-on? *(to Messenio)* This man is certainly mad.

MES   Didn't I tell you there are lots of impostors here?

CYL   ***

SOS   What hanger-on of mine are you looking for, young man?   285

CYL   The Brush.

MES   *(producing a brush)* Look, I have it safe and sound in my
traveling bag.

CYL   Menaechmus, you've come back to lunch too early. I've
returned from the shopping only now.

SOS   Answer me, young man: for what price are sacred, un-
blemished pigs sold here?   290

CYL   For a sesterce each.

SOS   *(taking out his wallet)* Take a sesterce from me; have
yourself purified at my expense. I know for sure that
you're mad: you're annoying me, a man you don't know,
whoever you are.

---

284 *om. P, uestigia A*

	CYL	Cylindrus ego sum: non nosti nomen meum?
295	SOS	si tu Cylindrus seu Coriendru's, perieris.
		ego te non noui nec nouisse adeo uolo.
	CYL	est tibi Menaechmo nomen.
	SOS	tantum, quod sciam,
		pro sano loqueris quom me appellas nomine.
		sed ubi nouisti me?
	CYL	ubi ego te nouerim,
300		qui amicam habes eram meam hanc Erotium?
	SOS	neque hercle ego habeo nec te quis homo sis scio.
	CYL	non scis quis ego sim, qui tibi saepissume
		cyathisso apud nos, quando potas?
	SOS	ei mihi,
		quom nihil est qui illi homini dimminuam caput!
305		tun cyathissare mihi soles, qui ante hunc diem
		Epidamnum numquam uidi nec ueni?
	CYL	negas?
	SOS	nego hercle uero.
	CYL	non tu in illisce aedibus
		habes?
	SOS	di illos homines qui illic habitant perduint!
	CYL	insanit hicquidem, qui ipse male dicit sibi.
310		audin, Menaechme?
	SOS	quid uis?
	CYL	si me consulas,
311		nummum illum quem mi dudum pollicitu's dare
314–		iubeas, si sapias, porculum afferri tibi;
15		
312		nam tu quidem hercle certo non sanu's satis,
313		Menaechme, qui nunc ipsus male dicas tibi.

299 ⟨tu⟩ me *Pylades (fortasse recte, nam spatium apparet in A)*
308 habitas *P*, habes *Seyffert*   *uel* habitas . . . illi[c]
314–15 *hic posuit Camerarius*

CYL   (*refusing the money*) I'm Cylindrus. Don't you know my name?

SOS   Whether you're Cylindrus or Coriendrus,[12] go to hell. I 295 don't know you and I don't want to know you.

CYL   Your name is Menaechmus.

SOS   This much, as far as I know, you're speaking like a sane man, when you're addressing me by my name. But where did you get to know me?

CYL   Where did I get to know you? You have Erotium here, my 300 mistress, as your girlfriend. (*points to her house*)

SOS   No, I don't, and I don't know who you are.

CYL   Don't you know who I am? I very often ladle out wine for you at our place when you drink.

SOS   (*aside*) Dear me! Not to have anything I can smash this person's head with! (*to Cylindrus*) Are you regularly la- 305 dling out wine for me? I've never seen or set foot in Epidamnus before this day.

CYL   You deny it?

SOS   I do indeed deny it.

CYL   Don't you live in that house there? (*points to the house of Menaechmus*)

SOS   May the gods ruin the people who live there!

CYL   (*aside*) He's mad: he's cursing himself. (*loudly*) Can you 310 hear me, Menaechmus?

SOS   What do you want?

CYL   If you ask me, for that sesterce you promised to give me 311 a while ago you'd have a piglet brought for yourself if 314–15 you're smart: you're certainly not in your right mind, 312–13 Menaechmus, since you're cursing yourself now.

[12] Made-up name punning on *coriandrum* "coriander."

316	MES	eu hercle hominem multum et odiosum mihi!
	CYL	solet iocari saepe mecum illoc modo.
		quam uis ridiculus est, ubi uxor non adest.
		quid ais tu? quid ais, inquam. satin hoc quod uides
320		tribus uobis opsonatum est, an opsono amplius,
		tibi et parasito et mulieri?
	SOS	quas [tu] mulieres,
		quos tu parasitos loquere?
	MES	quod te urget scelus
		qui huic sis molestus?
	CYL	quid tibi mecum est rei?
		ego te non noui: cum hoc quem noui fabulor.
325	MES	non edepol tu homo sanus es, certo scio.
	CYL	iam ergo haec madebunt faxo, nil morabitur.
		proin tu ne quo abeas longius ab aedibus.
		numquid uis?
	SOS	ut eas maxumam malam crucem.
	CYL	ire hercle meliust te . . . interim atque accumbere,
330		dum ego haec appono ad Volcani uiolentiam.
		ibo intro et dicam te hic astare Erotio,
		ut te hinc abducat potius quam hic astes foris.
	SOS	iamne abiit? ⟨abiit.⟩ edepol hau mendacia
		tua uerba experior esse.
	MES	opseruato modo:
335		nam istic meretricem credo habitare mulierem,
		ut quidem ille insanus dixit qui hinc abiit modo.
	SOS	sed miror qui ille nouerit nomen meum.

321 tu *del. Pylades*
333 abiit[2] *add. Gruterus*

---

[13] The god of fire.

MES   Honestly, I'm sick and tired of this chap!   316

CYL   (*aside*) He often jokes with me in that way. He's as funny as you could wish for when his wife isn't around. (*to Menaechmus*) What do you say? What do you say, I ask. Is what you can see enough shopping for the three of you,   320 or should I buy more for you, the hanger-on, and the lady?

SOS   What ladies, what hangers-on are you talking about?

MES   (*to Cylindrus*) What the hell has got into you to annoy this man?

CYL   What business have you with me? I don't know you. (*pointing to Menaechmus*) I'm talking to this man, whom I do know.

MES   You aren't in your right mind, I know that for sure.   325

CYL   (*to Menaechmus*) I'll take care then that this is cooked in a minute, there won't be any delay. So don't go anywhere too far from the house. Do you want anything?

SOS   Yes, go and be hanged.

CYL   It's better if *you* go . . . in the meantime and recline at table, while I'm subjecting this to the violence of Vulcan.[13]   330 I'll go inside and tell Erotium that you're standing here, so that she may lead you off inside rather than leave you standing here outside.

Exit CYLINDRUS into Erotium's house.

SOS   Has he left? He has left. I realize that your words aren't lies.

MES   Just watch: I believe a prostitute lives there, according to   335 what that madman said who just left.

SOS   But I wonder how he knew my name.

MES   minime hercle mirum. morem hunc meretrices habent:
       ad portum mittunt seruolos, ancillulas;
340   si qua peregrina nauis in portum aduenit,
       rogitant quoiatis sit, quid ei nomen siet,
       postilla extemplo se applicant, agglutinant:
       si pellexerunt, perditum amittunt domum.
       nunc in istoc portu est nauis praedatoria,
345   aps qua cauendum nobis sane censeo.
SOS   mones quidem hercle recte.
MES   tum demum sciam
       recte monuisse, si tu recte caueris.
SOS   tacedum parumper, nam concrepuit ostium:
       uideamus qui hinc egreditur.
MES   hoc ponam interim.
350   asseruatote haec sultis, nauales pedes.

         II. iii: EROTIVM. SOSICLES. MESSENIO

ERO   sine fores sic, abi, nolo operiri.
       intus para, cura, uide, quod opust fiat:
       sternite lectos, incendite odores; munditia
354–55   illecebra animo est amantium.
       amanti amoenitas malo est, nobis lucro est.
       sed ubi ille est quem coquos ante aedis esse ait? atque ec-
          cum uideo,
       qui mi est usui et plurumum prodest.
359   item hinc ultro fit, ut meret, potissumus
359ᵃ   nostrae domi ut sit;

344 portu stat Ω, portust *Bentley*
354–55 amantium *B*, amantum *CD*

MES That's no surprise at all. Prostitutes have this habit: they
send slaves and slave girls to the harbor. If any foreign 340
ship arrives in the harbor, they ask the owner where he's
from and what his name is. After that they immediately
attach and glue themselves to him. If they seduce him,
they send him off home when he's ruined. Now in that
harbor (*points to Erotium's house*) there's a pirate ship
which I think we need to be on our guard against. 345

SOS You're giving me proper advice.

MES I will only know that I've given you proper advice if you
take proper precautions.

SOS (*listening attentively*) Be quiet for a moment: the door
has creaked. Let's see who is coming out from here.

MES I'll put this down in the meantime. (*putting down his bag* 350
and turning to the slaves) Watch over this, will you, feet
of the ship.[14]

Enter EROTIUM from her house; a slave girl stands in the door.

ERO (*to slave girl*) Leave the door like this, go away, I don't
want it to be closed. Get ready inside, take care, and
make sure that what's needed is done. (*to those inside, as*
the slave girl goes back in) Lay out the couches, burn the
incense. (*to the audience*) Elegance is an enticement 355
for lovers' hearts. For a lover loveliness leads to loss, for
us, to profit. But where's the man who the cook says
is standing in front of the house? Look, I can see him,
the man who is of the greatest use and benefit to me. I re-
ciprocate of my own accord, as he deserves, so that he's
the most important person in our house. Now I'll ap- 360

[14] The rowers.

360	nunc eum adibo, alloquar ultro.
	animule mi, mi mira uidentur
	te hic stare foris, fores quoi pateant,
	magis quam domus tua domus quom haec tua sit.
	omne paratum est, ut iussisti
365	atque ut uoluisti, nec tibi est
	ulla mora intus.
	prandium, ut iussisti, hic curatum est:
	ubi lubet, ire licet accubitum.

SOS   quicum haec mulier loquitur?

ERO   equidem tecum.

SOS   quid mecum tibi

370   fuit umquam aut nunc est negoti?

ERO   quia pol te unum ex omnibus

         Venus me uoluit magnuficare neque id haud immerito
                 tuo.

         nam ecastor solus benefactis tuis me florentem facis.

SOS   certo haec mulier aut insana aut ebria est, Messenio,
         quae hominem ignotum compellet me tam familiariter.

375 MES   dixin ego istaec hic solere fieri? folia nunc cadunt,
         praeut si triduom hoc hic erimus: tum arbores in te ca-
                 dent.

         nam ita sunt hic meretrices: omnes elecebrae argen-
                 tariae.

         sed sine me dum hanc compellare. heus mulier, tibi dico.

ERO   quid est?

MES   ubi tu hunc hominem nouisti?

ERO   ibidem ubi hic me iam diu,

380   in Epidamno.

---

364 para tutius sisti *B¹*, paratus iussisti *B⁴*, parasitus tutius sisti *CD*,
paratum est ut iussisti *Camerarius*

proach him and take the initiative in addressing him. (*approaches Sosicles*) My sweetheart, it seems strange to me that you're standing outside here: the door stands open for you, since this house is more yours than your own house is. Everything is prepared, as you ordered and as you wanted. There's no delay for you inside. The lunch has been seen to, as you told me. We can go and recline at table as soon as you wish.

SOS (*to Messenio*) Who is this woman talking to?

ERO To you of course.

SOS What business have I ever had with you or have I now?

ERO Because out of all men Venus wanted me to hold you alone in esteem, and not undeservedly so: you alone let me flourish through your generosity.

SOS (*again to Messenio*) This woman is definitely either mad or drunk, Messenio: she addresses me, a total stranger, so intimately.

MES Didn't I tell you that it always happens like this here? Now only leaves are falling compared with what'll happen if we're here for two days: then entire trees will fall onto you. Yes, the prostitutes here are like this: they're all magnets for silver. But let me address her. (*turning to Erotium*) Hey there, woman, I'm speaking to you.

ERO What is it?

MES Where did you get to know this man?

ERO In the same place where he got to know me, long ago already, in Epidamnus.

365-66 tibi est . . . mora *P*, tibi . . . mora est *Leo et Lindsay*

MES   in Epidamno? qui huc in hanc urbem pedem
nisi hodie numquam intro tetulit?

ERO   heia! delicias facis.
mi Menaechme, quin, amabo, is intro? hic tibi erit rec-
tius.

SOS   haec quidem edepol recte appellat meo me mulier no-
mine.
nimis miror quid hoc sit negoti.

MES   oboluit marsuppium
385   huic istuc quod habes.

SOS   atque edepol tu me monuisti probe.
accipedum hoc. iam scibo utrum haec me mage amet an
marsuppium.

ERO   eamus intro, ut prandeamus.

SOS   bene uocas: tam gratia est.

ERO   quor igitur me tibi iussisti coquere dudum prandium?

SOS   egon te iussi coquere?

ERO   certo, tibi et parasito tuo.

390 SOS   quoi, malum, parasito? certo haec mulier non sana est
satis.

ERO   Peniculo.

SOS   quis iste est peniculus? qui extergentur baxeae?

ERO   scilicet qui dudum tecum uenit, quom pallam mihi
detulisti quam ab uxore tua surrupuisti.

SOS   quid est?
tibi pallam dedi quam uxori meae surrupui? sanan es?
395   certe haec mulier cantherino ritu astans somniat.

ERO   qui lubet ludibrio habere me atque ire infitias mihi
facta quae sunt ?

SOS   dic quid est id quod negem quod fecerim?

ERO   pallam te hodie mihi dedisse uxoris.

MES   In Epidamnus? He never set foot in this city except today.

ERO   Goodness! You're pulling my leg. (*turning to Menaechmus*) My dear Menaechmus, please, why don't you go inside? Here you'll have a better time.

SOS   (*to Messenio*) This woman is addressing me correctly by my name. I'm very curious what business this is.

MES   She's smelled that wallet you have.   385

SOS   Yes, you've given me good advice. (*handing over the wallet*) Take this. I'll find out in a minute whether she loves me or my wallet more.

ERO   Let's go inside to have lunch.

SOS   Thanks for inviting me, but no thanks.

ERO   Then why did you tell me a while ago to have a lunch cooked for you?

SOS   I told you to have one cooked?

ERO   Yes, certainly, for you and your hanger-on.

SOS   Damn it, for what hanger-on? (*aside*) This woman is certainly not in her right mind.   390

ERO   For the Brush.

SOS   What brush is that? The one sandals are cleaned with?

ERO   Of course the one who came with you a while ago when you brought me the mantle you stole from your wife.

SOS   What's that? I gave you a mantle I stole from my wife? Are you in your right mind? (*aside*) This woman is certainly dreaming the way horses do, while standing.   395

ERO   Why do you wish to poke fun at me and to deny what's happened?

SOS   Tell me what I've done that I'm now denying.

ERO   That you've given me your wife's mantle today.

SOS   etiam nunc nego.
ego quidem neque umquam uxorem habui neque habeo neque huc
400   umquam, postquam natus sum, intra portam penetraui pedem.
prandi in naui, inde huc sum egressus, te conueni.

ERO   eccere,
perii misera! quam tu mihi nunc nauem narras?

SOS   ligneam,
saepe tritam, saepe fixam, saepe excussam malleo;
quasi supellex Pellionis, palus palo proxumust.

405 ERO iam, amabo, desiste ludos facere atque i hac mecum simul.

SOS nescioquem ⟨tu⟩, mulier, alium hominem, non me quaeritas.

ERO non ego te noui Menaechmum, Moscho prognatum patre,
qui Syracusis perhibere natus esse in Sicilia,
409–10   ubi rex Agathocles regnator fuit et iterum Phintia,
tertium Liparo, qui in morte regnum Hieroni tradidit,
nunc Hiero est?

SOS   hau falsa, mulier, praedicas.

MES   pro Iuppiter!
num istaec mulier illinc uenit quae te nouit tam cate?

414–15 SOS hercle opinor, pernegari non potest.

MES   ne feceris.
periisti, si intrassis intra limen.

SOS   quin tu tace modo.
bene res geritur. assentabor quicquid dicet mulieri,
si possum hospitium nancisci. iam dudum, mulier, tibi

---

405 desine *P*, desiste *Fleckeisen*   406 tu *add. Fleckeisen*

SOS I'm denying it even now. I for one have never had a wife, nor do I have one now, and I never put my foot here in- 400 side the city gate since I was born. I had lunch on my ship, then I came out here and met you.

ERO Look! Dear me, I'm ruined! What ship are you telling me about now?

SOS A wooden one, often battered, often pierced, often shaken by the mallet;[15] just like the stage material of Pellio, stake next to stake.

ERO Please, stop playing the clown now and come with me 405 this way.

SOS My good woman, you're looking for some other man, not me.

ERO Don't I know you, Menaechmus, scion of your father Moschus, you who are said to have been born in Syracuse in Sicily, where King Agathocles was ruler and then 410 Phintias, thirdly Liparo, who passed the kingdom on to Hiero when he died, and now it's Hiero?[16]

SOS You aren't telling lies, my good woman.

MES Oh Jupiter! Has that woman come from there since she knows you so well?

SOS (taking Messenio aside) I think it can't be denied. 415

MES Don't do it. You're dead if you cross the threshold.

SOS Just be quiet. Things are going well. I'll agree with what-ever she says to see if I can get hospitality. (returning to

[15] Sosicles refers to different types of damage, so the mallet is prob-ably a weapon or projectile.
[16] Agathocles: ruler of Syracuse 317–289; Phintias: ruler of Agri-gentum ca. 280; Liparo: bogus name; Hiero: ruler of Syracuse 269–15.

419–
20 non imprudens aduorsabar: hunc metuebam ne meae
uxori renuntiaret de palla et de prandio.
nunc, quando uis, eamus intro.

ERO   etiam parasitum manes?
SOS neque ego illum maneo nec flocci facio nec, si uenerit,
eum uolo intro mitti.
ERO   ecastor haud inuita fecero.
425 sed scin quid te amabo ut facias?
SOS   impera quid uis modo.
ERO pallam illam quam dudum dederas, ad phrygionem ut
deferas,
ut reconcinnetur atque una opera addantur quae uolo.
SOS hercle qui tu recte dicis: eadem ⟨ea⟩ ignorabitur,
ne uxor cognoscat te habere, si in uia conspexerit.
430 ERO ergo mox auferto tecum, quando abibis.
SOS   maxume.
ERO eamus intro.
SOS   iam sequar te. hunc uolo etiam colloqui.
432–
33 eho Messenio, accede huc.
MES   quid negoti est?
⟨SOS⟩   sciscito.
MES quid eo opust?
SOS   opus est.
MES   scio ut mendices: tanto nequior.

427 ut opera *P*, una opera *Leo*
428 ea *add. Ritschl*
432–33 sussciri *P* (*sine nota personae*) (*B*[2] *addit* lege: scisscitari),
sciscito *Leo in apparatu* (*propter Festum, qui scribit*: nam *scisscito*
significat "sententiam dicito ac suffragium ferto")
434 *partes sic distribuit Gratwick*   me dicas *B*[1]*CD*, me dices *B*[2],
mendices *Gratwick*

Erotium) My dear woman, a while ago I contradicted you   420
deliberately. I was afraid that this chap might tell my wife
about the mantle and the lunch. Now when you wish, let's
go inside.

ERO Won't you wait for your hanger-on?

SOS No, I'm not waiting for him and I don't care for him at all,
and if he comes, I don't want him to be let in.

ERO Honestly, I'll do so happily. But do you know what I'd   425
love you to do?

SOS Just command me whatever you want.

ERO Take that mantle you gave me earlier to the embroiderer
so that it can be repaired and so that at the same time the
additions that I want can be made.

SOS How right you are! That way it'll also become unrecog-
nizable, so that my wife won't realize that you have it if
she spots you in the street.

ERO Then take it away with you soon, when you go.   430

SOS Certainly.

ERO Let's go inside.

SOS I'll follow you in a moment. I still want to speak to this
chap.

Exit EROTIUM into her house.

SOS Hey there, Messenio, come here.

MES What's the matter?

SOS Find out.

MES What's that necessary for?

SOS It is necessary.

MES I know, it is necessary for you to become a beggar: all the
worse of you.

435	SOS	habeo praedam: tantum incepi operis. i quantum potes,
		abduc istos in tabernam actutum deuorsoriam.
		tum facito ante solem occasum ut uenias aduorsum mihi.
	MES	non tu istas meretrices nouisti, ere.
	SOS	tace, inquam, ‹atque hinc abi.›
		mihi dolebit, non tibi, si quid ego stulte fecero.
440		mulier haec stulta atque inscita est; quantum perspexi modo,
		est hic praeda nobis.
	MES	perii! iamne abis? periit probe:
		ducit lembum dierectum nauis praedatoria.
		sed ego inscitus qui domino me postulem moderarier:
		dicto me emit audientem, haud imperatorem sibi.
445		sequimini, ut, quod imperatum est, ueniam aduorsum temperi.

ACTVS III

III. i: PENICVLVS

PEN	plus triginta annis natus sum, quom interea loci
	numquam quicquam facinus feci peius nec scelestius
	quam hodie, quom in contionem mediam me immersi miser.
	ubi ego dum hieto, Menaechmus se supterduxit mihi
450	atque abit ad amicam, credo, nec me uoluit ducere.

438 atque hinc abi *add. Ritschl*
443 quid (quod *B*) rome *P*, qui domino me *Bothe*
448 in *om. A*

470

SOS   I have booty, I've begun such a great deed. Go as quickly 435
as you can and take those people to the inn at once
(*points to the slaves*). Then make sure you come to meet
me before sunset.

MES   You don't know those prostitutes, master.

SOS   Be quiet, I tell you, and go away. *I* will feel the pain, not
you, if I do something stupid. This woman is stupid and 440
naive; as far as I could see just now, there's booty in here
for us.

Exit MENAECHMUS into Erotium's house.

MES   (*calling after him*) I'm done for! Are you going away
already? (*to the audience*) He's perished properly. The
pirate ship is leading our sailing boat to its ruin. But it's
stupid of me to expect to restrain my master. He bought
me as his servant, not as his commander. (*to the slaves*) 445
Follow me, so that I can go to him in good time, as com-
manded.

*Exit MESSENIO to the left, followed by the slaves with the lug-
gage.*

ACT THREE

Enter PENICULUS from the right.

PEN   I'm more than thirty years old, and up till now I've never
committed a worse or more wicked crime than today
when I plunged myself into the middle of the assem-
bly, poor wretch that I am. While I was gaping there,
Menaechmus stole himself away from me and went off to 450
his girlfriend, I believe, and he didn't want to take me

qui illum di omnes perduint qui primus commentust
⟨male⟩
contionem habere, qui homines occupatos occupat!
non ad eam rem otiosos homines decuit deligi,
qui nisi assint quom citentur, Consus capiat ilico?
455 qu**quam senatus deu**contionem**
456 ***
affatim est hominum in dies qui singulas escas edint,
quibus negoti nihil est, qui esum nec uocantur nec uo-
cant:
eos oportet contioni dare operam atque comitiis.
460 si id ita esset, non ego hodie perdidissem prandium,
quoi tam credo datum uoluisse quam me uideo uiuere.
ibo: etiamnum reliquiarum spes animum oblectat
meum.
sed quid ego uideo? Menaechmus cum corona exit foras.
sublatum est conuiuium, edepol uenio aduorsum tem-
peri.
465 opseruabo quid agat. hominem post adibo atque allo-
quar.

III. ii: SOSICLES. PENICVLVS

SOS potin ut quiescas? ego tibi hanc hodie probe
lepideque concinnatam referam temperi.
non faxo eam esse dices: ita ignorabitur.
PEN pallam ad phrygionem fert confecto prandio
470 uinoque expoto, parasito excluso foras.

451 commentu est *P*, commentust ⟨male⟩ *Ritschl*, ⟨hoc⟩ commen-
tus est *Vahlen*
454 census *P*, Consus *Gratwick*
455–56 *uestigia in A, uersus non inueniuntur in P*
461 *uersus nonnullis edd. corruptus esse uidetur*

along. May all the gods ruin the man who first had the
bad idea to hold an assembly, who keeps busy people
busy! Shouldn't one have chosen men of leisure for this,
whom Consus[17] would snatch at once if they weren't
present when called upon? *** than the senate *** an as-   455
sembly ***. There are plenty of people who eat just once
a day, who have nothing to do, and who neither receive
invitations to meals nor issue any. *They* ought to get busy
with the assembly and meetings. If it were like that, I   460
wouldn't have lost my lunch today, I, to whom I believe
he wanted it to be given as much as I can see that I'm
alive. I'll go. Even now the hope of leftovers gives joy to
my heart.

Enter SOSICLES from Erotium's house, wearing a flower gar-
land and carrying the mantle.

PEN   But what do I see? Menaechmus is coming out with a
garland. The meal is finished; (*sarcastically*) I'm really
coming toward him in good time. I'll observe what he's   465
doing. I'll approach and address him afterward.

SOS   (*into the house*) Can't you be quiet? I'll return it to you in
good time today, refashioned properly and charmingly.
I'll make sure you'll say it's not the same, so unrecogniz-
able will it be.

PEN   (*still standing at a distance*) He's taking the mantle to
the embroiderer after the lunch is finished off, the wine   470
drunk out, and the hanger-on locked out. I'm not the

---

[17] A god of agriculture, commonly associated with assemblies be-
cause of the formal similarity with *consilium*.

473

non hercle ⟨ego⟩ is sum qui sum, ni hanc iniuriam
meque ultus pulchre fuero. opserua quid dabo.

473– SOS pro di immortales! quoi homini umquam uno die
74
475   boni dedistis plus qui minus sperauerit?
prandi, potaui, scortum accubui, apstuli
hanc, quoius heres numquam erit post hunc diem.

PEN nequeo quae loquitur exaudire clanculum;
satur nunc loquitur de me et de parti mea?

480 SOS ait hanc dedisse me sibi atque eam meae
uxori surrupuisse. quoniam sentio
errare, extemplo, quasi res cum ea esset mihi,
coepi assentari: mulier quicquid dixerat,
idem ego dicebam. quid multis uerbis ⟨opust⟩?

485   minore nusquam bene fui dispendio.

PEN adibo ad hominem, nam turbare gestio.

SOS quis hic est qui aduorsus it mihi?

PEN   quid ais, homo
leuior quam pluma, pessume et nequissume,
flagitium hominis, subdole ac minimi preti?

490   quid de te merui qua me causa perderes?
ut surrupuisti te mihi dudum de foro!
fecisti funus med apsente prandio.
quor ausu's facere, quoi ego aeque heres eram?

SOS adulescens, quaeso, quid tibi mecum est rei
495   qui mi male dicas homini hic ignoto insciens?
an tibi malam rem uis pro male dictis dari?

PEN post eam quam edepol te dedisse intellego.

471 ego *add. Ritschl*
476–77 apstuli/hanc *P*, apstuli hanc/⟨pallam⟩ *Wagner*
484 opust *add. Pylades*
485 nusquam *P*, numquam *Gratwick*

474

man I am if I don't take revenge for this injustice and my-
self beautifully. Watch what I'll give you.

SOS   Immortal gods! What man expecting it less have you ever   475
given more good to in a single day? I had lunch, I had
drinks, I lay with a prostitute, and I took away this here
(*holds up the mantle*), whose heir she shall never be after
this day.

PEN   I can't hear what he's talking about secretly; is he full now
and talking about me and my share?

SOS   She said that I'd given it to her and that I'd stolen it from   480
my wife. When I realized that she was mistaken, I imme-
diately began to agree with her, as if I had dealings with
her. Whatever she said, I'd say the same. What need is
there for many words? I've never had a good time at   485
lower cost.

PEN   I'll approach him: I'm keen to cause trouble.

SOS   Who is this who is coming toward me?

PEN   (*to Menaechmus*) What do you say, you man lighter than
a feather, you most evil and disgraceful creature, you
crime of a man, you worthless trickster? What did I do to   490
deserve that you should ruin me? How you gave me the
slip in the forum a while ago! You buried the lunch in my
absence. How did you dare to do it? I was equally much
its heir.

SOS   Young man, please, what business have you with me?
You're giving me hard words, without knowing me, a man   495
unknown here. Or do you want to get a hard time for the
hard words?

PEN   After the one which I see you've already given me.

---

495 homini hic noto B^1, homini hic ignoto B^2, hic noto *CD*
497 post *P*, pol *A*   quidem Ω, quam *Goldbacher*

	SOS	responde, adulescens, quaeso, quid nomen tibi est?
	PEN	etiam derides quasi nomen non noueris?
500	SOS	non edepol ego te quod sciam umquam ante hunc diem
		uidi nec noui; uerum certo, quisquis es,
		si aequom facias, mihi odiosus ne sies.
	PEN	Menaechme, uigila.
	SOS	uigilo hercle equidem quod sciam.
	PEN	non me nouisti?
	SOS	non negem si nouerim.
505	PEN	tuom parasitum non nouisti?
	SOS	non tibi
		sanum est, adulescens, sinciput, intellego.
	PEN	responde, surrupuistin uxori tuae
		pallam istanc hodie ac dedisti Erotio?
	SOS	neque hercle ego uxorem habeo neque ego Erotio
510		dedi nec pallam surrupui.
	PEN	satin sanus es?
		occisa est haec res. non ego te indutum foras
		exire uidi pallam?
	SOS	uae capiti tuo!
		omnis cinaedos esse censes quia tu es?
514–15		tun med indutum fuisse pallam praedicas?
	PEN	ego hercle uero.
	SOS	non tu abis quo dignus es?
		aut te piari iube, homo insanissume.
	PEN	numquam edepol quisquam me exorabit quin tuae
		uxori rem omnem iam, uti sit gesta, eloquar;
520		omnes in te istaec recident contumeliae:
		faxo haud inultus prandium comederis.
	SOS	quid hoc est negoti? satine, uti quemque conspicor,
		ita me ludificant? sed concrepuit ostium.

508 atque ‹eam› *Bentley*   522 quemque *CD*, quemquem *B*

476

SOS   Please answer me, young man, what's your name?

PEN   Are you even poking fun at me as if you didn't know my name?

SOS   As far as I know, I've never seen you or got to know you 500 before this day. But certainly, whoever you are, if you're prepared to act reasonably, don't annoy me.

PEN   Menaechmus, be awake.

SOS   I am awake, as far as I know.

PEN   Don't you know me?

SOS   I wouldn't deny it if I did.

PEN   You don't know your hanger-on? 505

SOS   Young man, you don't have a sane pighead, I can see that.

PEN   Answer me, didn't you steal that mantle from your wife today and give it to Erotium?

SOS   I don't have a wife and I didn't give the mantle to Ero- 510 tium, nor did I steal it.

PEN   Are you in your right mind? This is the end. Didn't I see you come out wearing a mantle?

SOS   Curse you! Do you think everyone's a catamite just be- cause you are one? Are you telling me that I was wearing 515 a mantle?

PEN   Yes, I am indeed.

SOS   Won't you go off to where you deserve to be? Or have yourself exorcised, you complete madman.

PEN   No one will ever prevail on me not to tell your wife how the entire thing happened. All those insults will fall back 520 onto you. I'll make sure that you haven't eaten the lunch without punishment. (*walks to the house of Menaech- mus, knocks and enters*)

SOS   What does this mean? Is everyone I set eyes on making fun of me? But the door has creaked.

III. iii: ANCILLA. SOSICLES

	ANC	Menaechme, amare ait te multum Erotium,
525		ut hoc una opera ⟨sibi⟩ ad auruficem deferas,
		atque huc ut addas auri pondo unciam
		iubeasque spinter nouom reconcinnarier.
	SOS	et istuc et aliud si quid curari uolet
		me curaturum dicito, quicquid uolet.
530	ANC	scin quid hoc sit spinter?
	SOS	nescio nisi aureum.
	ANC	hoc est quod olim clanculum ex armario
		te surrupuisse aiebas uxori tuae.
	SOS	numquam hercle factum est.
	ANC	non meministi, opsecro?
		redde igitur spinter, si non meministi.
	SOS	mane.
535		immo equidem memini. nempe hoc est quod illi dedi.
		istuc: ubi illae armillae sunt quas una dedi?
	ANC	numquam dedisti.
	SOS	nam pol hoc unum dedi.
	ANC	dicam curare?
	SOS	dicito: "curabitur."
539–40		et palla et spinter faxo referantur simul.
	ANC	amabo, mi Menaechme, inauris da mihi
		faciendas pondo duom nummum, stalagmia,
		ut te lubenter uideam, quom ad nos ueneris.
	SOS	fiat. cedo aurum; ego manupretium dabo.
545	ANC	da sodes aps te: post ⟨ego⟩ reddidero tibi.

525 sibi *add. Ussing*
545 ego *add. Pylades*

Enter SERVANT GIRL from Erotium's house, carrying a golden bracelet.

SER   Menaechmus, Erotium says she's asking you very kindly to bring this bracelet here to the goldsmith for her at the 525 same time and to add an ounce of gold and have it repaired as new.

SOS   Tell her I'll take care of this and anything else, if she wants anything to be taken care of, whatever she wants.

SER   Do you know what bracelet this is? 530

SOS   I don't know, except that it's made of gold.

SER   This is the one you said you once furtively stole from your wife's cabinet.

SOS   That never happened.

SER   Please, you don't remember? Then give me back the bracelet if you don't remember.

SOS   Wait. Yes, I do remember. (*takes the bracelet*) This is the 535 one I gave her. By the by, tell me: where are those armlets I gave her together with it?

SER   You never gave her any.

SOS   Yes, I only gave her this here.

SER   Shall I say you're taking care of it?

SOS   Tell her: "It'll be taken care of." I'll make sure the mantle 540 and bracelet will be brought back together.

SER   Please, my dear Menaechmus, have earrings made for me, two denarii[18] in weight, in the shape of drops, so that I'm happy to see you when you come to us.

SOS   Yes. Give me the gold; I'll pay for the labor.

SER   Please give it from your pocket. I'll return it to you later. 545

---

[18] This is the most likely coin here; the weight is thus 9 grams.

	SOS	immo cedo aps te: ego post tibi reddam duplex.
	ANC	non habeo.
	SOS	at tu, quando habebis, tum dato.
	ANC	numquid [me] uis?
	SOS	haec me curaturum dicito . . .
		ut quantum possint quique liceant ueneant.
550		iamne abiit intro? abiit, operuit fores.
550ᵃ		***i***a***am
551		di me quidem omnes adiuuant, augent, amant.
		sed quid ego cesso, dum datur mi occasio
		tempusque, abire ab his locis lenoniis?
		propera, Menaechme, fer pedem, confer gradum.
555		demam hanc coronam atque abiciam ad laeuam manum,
		ut, si sequentur me, hac abiisse censeant.
		ibo et conueniam seruom si potero meum,
		ut haec, quae bona dant di mihi, ex me sciat.

ACTVS IV

IV. i: MATRONA. PENICVLVS

	MAT	egone hic me patiar frustra in matrimonio,
560		ubi uir compilet clanculum quicquid domi est
		atque ea ad amicam deferat?
	PEN	quin tu taces?
		manufesto faxo iam opprimes: sequere hac modo.
		pallam ad phrygionem cum corona ebrius

548 me *del. Acidalius*   550 intro habiit *B¹CD*, abiit intro *B²*
550ᵃ *uestigia apparent in A, uersus deest in P*
555 hanc *Nonius, om. P*   556 si qui sequatur hac me *P*, si
sequentur me hac *Nonius*, si sequantur me hac *Lindsay*
559 frustrat *A, om. P*, frustra *plerique edd.*

SOS No, give it from *yours*. I'll return it to you later, twice over.

SER I don't have any.

SOS Well, then give it to me when you do have some.

SER Do you want anything else?

SOS Say that I'll take care of this . . . (*aside*) that it'll be sold as quickly and expensively as possible.

Exit the SERVANT GIRL into Erotium's house.

SOS Has she gone inside now? She's gone, she's closed the 550
door. *** All the gods help, support, and love me. But
what am I hesitating to leave these pimp places while I'm
given the opportunity and the time? Hurry, Menaech-
mus, move your foot, carry on your step. I'll take off this 555
garland and throw it away to the left (*throws it to his left,
our right*) so that they think I went this way if they follow
me. I'll go and meet my slave if I can so that he knows
from me about the good things the gods are giving me.

Exit SOSICLES to the left.

ACT FOUR

*Enter WIFE OF MENAECHMUS from her house, followed by
PENICULUS.*

WIFE Should I tolerate being treated like an idiot here in my
marriage, where my husband's furtively stealing every- 560
thing that's at home and taking it to his mistress?

PEN Why won't you be quiet? I'll make sure you catch him in
the act in a minute. Just follow me this way. With a gar-
land on and drunk he was carrying the mantle to the

481

		ferebat hodie tibi quam surrupuit domo.
565		sed eccam coronam quam habuit. num mentior?
		em hac abiit, si uis persequi uestigiis.
		atque edepol eccum optume reuortitur;
		sed pallam non fert.
	MAT	quid ego nunc cum illoc agam?
	PEN	idem quod semper: male habeas; sic censeo.
570		huc concedamus: ex insidiis aucupa.

IV. ii: MENAECHMVS. PENICVLVS. MATRONA

	MEN	ut hoc utimur maxume more moro,
		molesto atque multo! atque uti quique sunt op-
		tumi maxume morem habent hunc! clientes
		sibi omnes uolunt esse multos: bonine an
575		mali sint, id hau quaeritant; res magis quae-
576		ritur quam clientum fides quoius modi clue-
577–78 579		at. si est pauper atque hau malus nequam habetur,
		sin diues malust, is cliens frugi habetur.
580		qui nec leges neque aequom bonum usquam colunt,
		sollicitos patronos habent.
		datum denegant quod datum est, litium
		pleni, rapaces uiri, fraudulenti,
584		qui aut faenore aut periuriis
584ᵃ		habent rem paratam; mens est in quo ***
585		eis uiris ubi dicitur dies,
585ᵃ		simul patronis dicitur,
586		quipp' qui pro illis loquimur quae male fecerunt.
		[aut ad populum aut in iure aut apud aedilem res est.]

572 molesto atque multo *A*, molestoque multum *P*

584ᵃ mens est *W*, mensae *uel* mense *ceteri Palatini*   -n quo la *A*, in quo re *B¹*, in quoi rem *B⁴*, in quo ire *CD*, in querellis *W*

embroiderer, the one he took from your house today. But   565
look, the garland he had. Am I lying? (*pointing to the exit
on the right*) There, he went away this way, if you want to
follow him by his tracks. And look, perfect, he's coming
back. But he isn't carrying the mantle.

WIFE What should I do with him now?

PEN The same as always: give him a hard time. That's what I
think. Let's go over here: catch him from an ambush.   570

*Enter MENAECHMUS from the right, not seeing his wife or
Peniculus.*

MEN What incredibly stupid, tedious, and bothersome custom
we have! And the more respected people are, the more
they have this custom! Everybody wants to have many
clients: whether they're good or bad they don't ask; they   575
ask about the money rather than the reputation of the cli-
ents' reliability. If someone's poor and not bad, he's con-
sidered useless, but if a rich one's bad, he's considered a
useful client. People who don't honor the laws or what's   580
fair and good anywhere keep their patrons busy. They
deny that what's been given has been given, are full of
lawsuits, and are greedy and dishonest men, who have
gained their money either on interest or through perju-
ries. Their mind is in which ***. When these men are   585
called to court, their patrons are called to court at the
same time since we speak for those who've committed of-
fenses. [The case comes before the people or the court or

---

585 eis u- *A*, lis uiris *BC*, lis iuris *D*, his uiris *Bergk*, uiris *dell. Leo et
Lindsay*   586 loquimur . . . fecerunt *A*, loquantur . . . fecerint *P*
587 apud aedilem *A*, ad iudicem *P*   *uersum secl. Ussing*

sicut me hodie nimis sollicitum cliens quidam habuit nec
    quod uolui
agere aut quicum licitum est, ita med attinuit, ita deti-
    nuit.

590   apud aedilis pro eius factis plurumisque pessumisque
dixi causam, condiciones tetuli tortas, confragosas:
haud plus, haud minus quam opus fuerat dicto dixeram,
    controrsim
ut sponsio fieret. quid ille †qui praedem dedit?
nec magis manufestum ego hominem umquam ullum te-
    neri uidi:

595   omnibus male factis testes tres aderant acerrumi.
596   di illum omnes perdant, ita mihi
596a   hunc hodie corrupit diem,
597   meque adeo, qui hodie forum
597a   umquam oculis inspexi meis.
598   diem corrupi optumum:
598a   iussi apparari prandium,
599   amica exspectat me, scio.
599a   ubi primum est licitum, ilico
600   properaui abire de foro.
600a   irata est, credo, nunc mihi;
600b   placabit palla quam dedi,
601   quam hodie uxori apstuli atque huic detuli Erotio.

PEN   quid ais?
MAT   uiro me malo male nuptam.
PEN   satin audis quae illic loquitur?
MAT   satis.
MEN   si sapiam, hinc intro abeam, ubi mi bene sit.

589 quicum *P*, ait qu(o)quam *A*, aut quicum *Ritschl*

the aedile.[19] This is how a certain client kept me very
busy today and how I couldn't do what I wanted or who I
wanted to do it with, to such an extent did he delay and
detain me. Before the aediles I spoke in defense of his   590
countless misdeeds and proposed complicated and ob-
scure provisos. I spoke no more and no less than was re-
quired, so that a settlement came about on both sides.
What did the man do †who gave a surety?† I've never
seen anyone caught more red-handed. For all his mis-   595
deeds three most stern witnesses stood present. May all
the gods destroy him: he ruined this day for me today,
and me to, whoever set my eyes on the forum today. I've
wasted a perfect day. I had a lunch prepared for me. My
girlfriend's expecting me, I know that. As soon as I could,
I rushed off from the forum. She's angry with me now, I   600
believe; the mantle I gave her will mollify her, the one I
took away from my wife today and took to Erotium here.

PEN (*to the wife, quietly*) What do you say?

WIFE That I'm badly married to a bad husband.

PEN Can you hear well enough what he's saying?

WIFE Yes.

MEN If I were smart, I'd go off inside, where I'd have a good
time.

---

[19] A Roman magistrate mainly in charge of buildings and public
events, but also responsible for legal matters.

---

592 aut . . . aut Ω, haut . . . haut *Teuffel*   fuerat *A*, erat *P*
controuersiam Ω, controrsim *Havet*
   593 *aliquid deesse uidetur*
   596ª corrupit *B*[2], corrumpit *ceteri Palatini*
   601 huic detuli *P, transp. Ritschl*

PEN	mane; male erit potius.
MAT	ne illam ecastor faenerato apstulisti.
PEN	sic datur.
605 MAT	clanculum te istaec flagitia facere censebas pote?
MEN	quid illuc est, uxor, negoti?
MAT	men rogas?
MEN	uin hunc rogem?
MAT	aufer hinc palpationes.
PEN	perge tu.
MEN	quid tu mihi
	tristis es?
MAT	te scire oportet.
PEN	scit sed dissimulat malus.
MEN	quid negoti est?
MAT	pallam—
MEN	pallam?
MAT	quidam pallam—
PEN	quid paues?
610 MEN	nil equidem paueo.
PEN	nisi unum; palla pallorem incutit.
	at tu ne clam me comesses prandium. perge in uirum.
MEN	non taces?
PEN	non hercle uero taceo. nutat ne loquar.
613 MEN	non hercle ego quidem usquam quicquam nuto nec nicto
	tibi.
615 PEN	nihil hoc confidentius; quin quae uides ea pernegat.
MEN	per Iouem deosque omnis adiuro, uxor—satin hoc est
	tibi?—
	me isti non nutasse.

617 mei si non *B*, meisi inon *CD*, me isti non *Pylades*   istis *P*, isto
Bothe

PEN (*going toward Menaechmus*) Wait. You'll rather have a
     bad time.
WIFE (*also going toward him*) Yes, you took that away on inter-
     est.
PEN That's the stuff to give him.
WIFE (*to Menaechmus*) Did you think you could commit those 605
     offenses in secret?
MEN What do you mean, my wife?
WIFE Are you asking me?
MEN Do you want me to ask him? (*tries to pat her*)
WIFE Stop your caresses.
PEN Continue, you.
MEN (*to his wife*) Why are you upset with me?
WIFE You ought to know.
PEN He does, but he's pretending not to, the criminal.
MEN What's the matter?
WIFE The mantle—
MEN The mantle?
WIFE The mantle, someone—
PEN (*to Menaechmus*) What are you afraid of?
MEN I'm not afraid of anything.   610
PEN Except for one thing; the mantle is dismantling your con-
     fidence. Well, you shouldn't have eaten up the lunch
     behind my back. (*to the wife*) Continue against your hus-
     band.
MEN Won't you be quiet?
PEN No, I definitely will not be quiet. (*to the wife*) He's nod-
     ding at me that I shouldn't speak.
MEN I am certainly not nodding or winking at you about any- 613
     thing anywhere.
PEN Nothing is bolder than him: he denies what you can see. 615
MEN I swear by Jupiter and all the gods, my wife—is this
     enough for you?—that I didn't nod to him.

	PEN	credit iam tibi de isto: illuc redi.
	MEN	quo ego redeam?
	PEN	equidem ad phrygionem censeo; i, pallam refer.
619	MEN	quae istaec palla est?
	PEN	taceo iam, quando haec rem non meminit suam.
614	MAT	ne ego ecastor mulier misera.
	MEN	qui tu misera es? mi expedi.
620		numquis seruorum deliquit? num ancillae aut serui tibi
		responsant? eloquere. impune non erit.
	MAT	nugas agis.
	MEN	tristis admodum es. non mi istuc satis placet.
	MAT	nugas agis.
	MEN	certe familiarium aliquoi irata es.
	MAT	nugas agis.
	MEN	num mihi es irata saltem?
	MAT	nunc tu non nugas agis.
625	MEN	non edepol deliqui quicquam.
	MAT	em rursum nunc nugas agis.
	MEN	dic, mea uxor, quid tibi aegre est?
	PEN	bellus blanditur tibi.
	MEN	potin ut mihi molestus ne sis? num te appello?
	MAT	aufer manum.
	PEN	sic datur. properato apsente me comesse prandium,
		post ante aedis cum corona me derideto ebrius.
630	MEN	neque edepol ego prandi neque hodie huc intro tetuli
		pedem.
	PEN	tun negas?
	MEN	nego hercle uero.

618 et *P*, ei *Gruterus*
614 *uersum hic posuit Kiessling*
622 est *B¹CD*, es *B²*

488

PEN	She believes you about "him" now. Return there.	
MEN	Where should I return?	
PEN	To the embroiderer, I think. Go, bring back the mantle.	
MEN	What mantle is that?	619
PEN	(*aside*) I'm quiet now since she doesn't remember her own business.	
WIFE	(*to Menaechmus*) I really am a wretched woman.	614
MEN	How come you're wretched? Explain it to me. Did any of the servants commit an offense? Do the slave girls or the slaves talk back to you? Tell me. It won't go unpunished.	620
WIFE	You're talking rubbish.	
MEN	You're in quite a bad mood. I'm not happy about it.	
WIFE	You're talking rubbish.	
MEN	You're definitely angry with one of the slaves.	
WIFE	You're talking rubbish.	
MEN	Surely at any rate you can't be angry with me?	
WIFE	Now you're not talking rubbish.	
MEN	I haven't done anything wrong.	625
WIFE	There, now you're talking rubbish again.	
MEN	Tell me, my dear wife, what are you upset about?	
PEN	(*to the wife*) Your beau is buttering you up.	
MEN	Can't you stop being a nuisance? I'm not addressing you, am I? (*tries to pat his wife again*)	
WIFE	Take off your hand.	
PEN	That's the stuff to give him. (*to Menaechmus*) Hurry to eat up the lunch in my absence, then mock me in front of the house with your garland on and drunk.	
MEN	I haven't had any lunch and I haven't set foot in here today.	630
PEN	Do you deny it?	
MEN	Yes, I do indeed deny it.	

	PEN	nihil hoc homine audacius.

PEN   nihil hoc homine audacius.

         non ego te modo hic ante aedis cum corona florea
         uidi astare? quom negabas mi esse sanum sinciput
         et negabas me nouisse, peregrinum aibas esse te?

635 MEN   quin ut dudum diuorti aps te, redeo nunc demum do-
           mum.

     PEN   noui ego te. non mihi censebas esse qui te ulciscerer.
         omnia hercle uxori dixi.

     MEN   quid dixisti?

     PEN   nescie!

         eam ipsus [i] roga.

     MEN   quid hoc est, uxor? quidnam hic narrauit tibi?

639   quid id est? quid taces? quin dicis quid sit?

     MAT   quasi tu nescias.

[639a   palla mi est domo surrupta.

     MEN   palla surrupta est tibi?]

640 MAT me rogas?

     MEN   pol hau rogem te si sciam.

     PEN   o hominem malum,
         ut dissimulat! non potes celare rem: noui⟨t⟩ probe.
         omnia hercle ego edictaui.

     MEN   quid id est?

     MAT   quando nil pudet
         nec uis tua uoluntate ipse profiteri, audi atque ades.
         et quid tristis ⟨sim⟩ et quid hic mi dixerit faxo scias.

645   palla mi est domo surrupta.

     MEN   palla surrupta est mihi?

---

637 nescio *P*, nescie *Gratwick*
638 eam plus *B¹*, eam ipsus *B²*, eampsus ei *CD*
639ᵃ *uersum secl. Acidalius*   641 noui⟨t⟩ *Acidalius*
644 sim *add. Pylades*

PEN Nothing is bolder than him. Didn't I see you standing here in front of the house with a flower garland just now? When you claimed that I didn't have a sane pighead and that you didn't know me, and when you said you were a foreigner?

MEN No, after leaving you a while ago I'm only returning 635
home now.

PEN I know you. You didn't think I have any means of revenge. I told your wife everything.

MEN What did you tell her?

PEN You innocent! Ask her yourself.

MEN What's this, my wife? What on earth did he tell you? What is it? What are you silent for? Why don't you tell me what it is?

WIFE As if you didn't know. [My mantle has been stolen from home.

MEN Your mantle has been stolen?]

WIFE You're asking me? 640

MEN I wouldn't ask you if I knew.

PEN What a bad man, how he's pretending. (to Menaechmus) You can't conceal it: she knows it properly. I've spilled the beans.

MEN What's that?

WIFE Since you aren't ashamed and don't want to admit it yourself voluntarily, listen and pay attention. I'll let you know what I'm in a bad mood for and what this chap here has told me. My mantle has been stolen from home. 645

MEN My mantle has been stolen?

PEN   uiden ut ⟨te⟩ scelestus captat? huic surrupta est, non
         tibi.

         nam profecto tibi surrupta si esset . . . salua non foret.

MEN   nil mihi tecum est. sed tu quid ais?

MAT   palla, inquam, periit domo.

MEN   quis eam surrupuit?

MAT   pol istuc ille scit qui illam apstulit.

650 MEN   quis is homo est?

MAT   Menaechmus quidam.

MEN   edepol factum nequiter.

         quis is Menaechmust?

MAT   tu istic, inquam.

MEN   egone?

MAT   tu.

MEN   quis arguit?

MAT   egomet.

PEN   et ego. atque huic amicae detulisti Erotio.

MEN   egon dedi?

MAT   tu, tu istic, inquam.

PEN   uin afferri noctuam,

         quae "tu tu" usque dicat tibi? nam nos iam defessi sumus.

655 MEN   per Iouem deosque omnis adiuro, uxor—satin hoc est
         tibi?—

         non dedisse.

PEN   immo hercle uero, nos non falsum dicere.

MEN   sed ego illam non condonaui, sed sic utendam dedi.

MAT   equidem ecastor tuam nec chlamydem do foras nec pal-
         lium

646 te *add. Lambinus*
654 nos iam nos *P*, nos iam *F*, nos nos *Gratwick*

492

PEN (*to the wife*) Can you see how the criminal's trying to trick you? (*to Menaechmus*) *Her* mantle has been stolen, not *yours*. If yours had been stolen . . . it wouldn't be safe.[20]

MEN (*to Peniculus*) I have nothing to do with you. (*to his wife*) But what do *you* say?

WIFE I'm telling you, a mantle has disappeared from home.

MEN Who stole it?

WIFE Well, the man who took it away knows that.

MEN Who is it? 650

WIFE A certain Menaechmus.

MEN Honestly, an appalling act. Who is that Menaechmus?

WIFE You there, I'm telling you.

MEN I?

WIFE You.

MEN Who is accusing me?

WIFE I am.

PEN And so am I. And you brought it to your mistress Erotium here.

MEN I gave it to her?

WIFE You, you there, I'm telling it to you.

PEN (*to Menaechmus*) Do you want an owl to be brought along which constantly says "to wit to you" to you? We are already exhausted.

MEN I swear by Jupiter and all the gods, my dear wife—is that 655 enough for you?—that I haven't given it to her.

PEN No, rather that we aren't lying.

MEN But I didn't give it to her as a present, but just like this, on loan.

WIFE I certainly don't give your cloak or your tunic on loan to

---

[20] Rather than being at the embroiderer's.

	quoiquam utendum. mulierem aequom est uestimentum muliebre
660	dare foras, uirum uirile. quin refers pallam domum?
MEN	ego faxo referetur.
MAT	ex re tua, ut opinor, feceris;
	nam domum numquam introibis nisi feres pallam simul.
	eo domum.
PEN	quid mihi futurum est qui tibi hanc operam dedi?
MAT	opera reddetur, quando quid tibi erit surruptum domo.
665 PEN	id quidem edepol numquam erit, nam nihil est quod perdam domi.
	cum uiro cum uxore, di uos perdant! properabo ad forum,
	nam ex hac familia me plane excidisse intellego.
MEN	male mi uxor sese fecisse censet, quom exclusit foras;
	quasi non habeam quo intro mittar alium meliorem locum.
670	si tibi displiceo, patiundum: at placuero huic Erotio,
	quae me non excludet ab se, sed apud se occludet domi.
	nunc ibo, orabo ut mihi pallam reddat quam dudum dedi;
	aliam illi redimam meliorem. heus! ecquis hic est ianitor?
	aperite atque Erotium aliquis euocate ante ostium.

IV. iii: EROTIVM. MENAECHMVS
675 ERO quis hic me quaerit?

anyone. It's proper for a woman to give a woman's gar-
ment on loan and for a man, a man's. Why don't you bring   660
the mantle back home?

MEN   I'll make sure it's brought back.

WIFE You'll do this to your own advantage, I think: you'll never
enter the house unless you bring the mantle with you.
I'm going home.

PEN   What reward am I going to get, who did you this service?

WIFE I'll return the favor when something's been stolen from
your house.

Exit the WIFE OF MENAECHMUS into her house.

PEN   That'll be never: I don't have anything at home that I   665
could lose. Both husband and wife, may the gods ruin
you! (*to the audience*) I'll rush to the forum. I can see that
I've plainly fallen out from this household.

Exit PENICULUS to the right.

MEN   My wife thinks she's done me a bad turn by locking me
out; as if I didn't have a better place where I'll be let in. If   670
you dislike me, I'll have to put up with it. But Erotium
here will like me, who will not lock me out from her
place, but will lock me in at her home. Now I'll go and ask
her to give me back the mantle I gave her a while ago. I'll
buy her another, better one instead. (*knocks at her door*)
Hey there! Is there any porter here? Let someone open
and call Erotium out here in front of the door.

Enter EROTIUM from her house.

ERO   Who is looking for me here?   675

MEN	sibi inimicus magis quam aetati tuae.
ERO	mi Menaechme, quor ante aedis astas? sequere intro.
MEN	mane.

scin quid est quod ego ad te uenio?

ERO	scio, ut tibi ex me sit uolup.
MEN	immo edepol pallam illam, amabo te, quam tibi dudum dedi,

mihi eam redde. uxor resciuit rem omnem, ut factum est, ordine.

680 ego tibi redimam bis tanta pluris pallam quam uoles.

ERO   tibi dedi equidem illam, ad phrygionem ut ferres, paullo prius,

et illud spinter, ut ad auruficem ferres, ut fieret nouom.

MEN   mihi tu ut dederis pallam et spinter? numquam factum reperies.

nam ego quidem postquam illam dudum tibi dedi atque abii ad forum,

685 nunc redeo, nunc te postillac uideo.

ERO   uideo quam rem agis.

quia commisi, ut me defrudes, ad eam rem affectas uiam.

MEN   neque edepol te defrudandi causa posco—quin tibi dico uxorem resciuisse—

ERO   nec te ultro oraui ut dares:

tute ultro ad me detulisti, dedisti eam dono mihi;

690 eandem nunc reposcis: patiar. tibi habe, aufer, utere

uel tu uel tua uxor, uel etiam in loculos compingite.

tu huc post hunc diem pedem intro non feres, ne frustra sis;

quando tu me bene merentem tibi habes despicatui,

mihi feres argentum frustra, me ductare non potes.

695 aliam posthac inuenito quam habeas frustratui.

691 oculos *P*, loculos *Balbach*   694 nisi *P*, mihi *Gratwick*

496

MEN An enemy to himself rather than to your life.

ERO My dear Menaechmus, why are you standing in front of the house? Follow me in.

MEN Wait. Do you know what the reason is why I'm coming to you?

ERO Yes, so that you can get some pleasure from me.

MEN No, please return that mantle I gave you a while ago. My wife's found out how the whole thing happened, from first to last. I'll buy you another mantle instead, twice as 680 expensive, of your own choice.

ERO I gave it to you a little earlier to take to the embroiderer, and that bracelet to take to the goldsmith to have a makeover.

MEN You gave me the mantle and the bracelet? You'll never find that this happened; after I gave it to you a while ago and went off to the forum, I'm returning now, I'm seeing 685 you now for the first time after that.

ERO I see what you're up to. Because I gave you the opportunity to cheat me, you're taking that path.

MEN No, I'm not asking for it in order to cheat you—rather, I told you that my wife's found out—

ERO (interrupting) Well, I didn't ask you to give it to me in the first place. You yourself brought it to me of your own accord and gave it to me as a present. Now you demand 690 back that same mantle. I'll put up with it. Have it for yourself, take it away, use it, you or your wife, or even shut it away in your money box. After this day you won't set a foot in here, don't fool yourself. Since you despise me even though I deserve well of you, you'll bring me your money for nothing, you can't trick me. From now on 695 find another woman to deceive.

Exit EROTIUM into her house.

MEN   nimis iracunde hercle tandem. heus tu, tibi dico, mane,
        redi. etiamne astas? etiam audes mea reuorti gratia?
        abiit intro, occlusit aedis. nunc ego sum exclusissumus:
        nec domi neque apud amicam mihi iam quicquam credi-
        tur.

700   ibo et consulam hanc rem amicos quid faciendum cen-
        seant.

ACTVS V

V. i: SOSICLES. MATRONA

SOS   nimis stulte dudum feci quom marsuppium
        Messenioni cum argento concredidi.
        immersit aliquo sese, credo, in ganeum.
MAT   prouisam quam mox uir meus redeat domum.
705   sed eccum uideo. salua sum, pallam refert.
SOS   demiror ubi nunc ambulet Messenio.
MAT   adibo atque hominem accipiam quibus dictis meret.
        non te pudet prodire in conspectum meum,
        flagitium hominis, cum istoc ornatu?
SOS   quid est?
710   quae te res agitat, mulier?
MAT   etiamne, impudens,
        muttire uerbum unum audes aut mecum loqui?

MEN (*calling after her*) You really are acting too angrily. Hey there, I'm speaking to you, wait, come back. Will you stand still? Will you return for my sake? (*to the audience*) She's gone inside and locked the house. Now I'm completely locked out. Neither at home nor at my girlfriend's am I still believed in anything. I'll go and consult my 700 friends what they think I should do about this matter.

Exit MENAECHMUS to the right.

ACT FIVE

Enter SOSICLES from the left, still carrying the mantle and bracelet.

SOS I behaved really stupidly some time ago when I entrusted my wallet with the money to Messenio. He's plunged himself somewhere into a pub, I believe.

Enter the WIFE OF MENAECHMUS from her house with a servant girl.

WIFE I'll check how soon my husband's returning home. But 705 look, I can see him. I'm safe, he's bringing the mantle back.

SOS (*to himself*) I wonder where Messenio is walking around now.

WIFE I'll approach him and welcome him with the words he deserves. (*loudly*) Aren't you ashamed to come under my eyes with that gear, you disgrace of a man?

SOS What is it? What's troubling you, woman? 710

WIFE You shameless individual, do you even dare to utter a single word or speak with me?

499

	SOS	quid tandem ammisi in me ut loqui non audeam?
	MAT	rogas me? ‹o› hominis impudentem audaciam!
	SOS	non tu scis, mulier, Hecubam quapropter canem
715		Graii esse praedicabant?
	MAT	non equidem scio.
	SOS	quia idem faciebat Hecuba quod tu nunc facis:
		omnia mala ingerebat quemquem aspexerat.
		itaque adeo iure coepta appellari est Canes.
	MAT	non ego istaec ‹tua› flagitia possum perpeti.
720		nam med aetatem uiduam esse mauelim
		quam istaec flagitia tua pati quae tu facis.
	SOS	quid id ad me, tu te nuptam possis perpeti
		an sis abitura a tuo uiro? an mos hic ita est
		peregrino ut aduenienti narrent fabulas?
725	MAT	quas fabulas? non, inquam, patiar praeterhac,
		quin uidua uiuam quam tuos mores perferam.
	SOS	mea quidem hercle causa uidua uiuito
		uel usque dum regnum optinebit Iuppiter.
	MAT	at mihi negabas dudum surrupuisse te,
730		nunc eandem ante oculos attines: non te pudet?
	SOS	eu hercle! mulier, multum et audax et mala es.
		tun tibi hanc surruptam dicere audes quam mihi
		dedit alia mulier ut concinnandam darem?
	MAT	ne istoc mecastor iam patrem accersam meum
735		atque ei narrabo tua flagitia quae facis.
		i, Deceo, quaere meum patrem, tecum simul

713 o *add. Pylades*
719 tua *add. Ritschl*
734 istuc *P,* istoc *Brix*

SOS Really now, what offense did I commit that I shouldn't
     dare to speak?

WIFE You're asking me? Oh, the petulant boldness of the man!

SOS Don't you know, woman, why the Greeks said that Hec- 715
     uba[21] was a bitch?

WIFE No, I don't.

SOS Because Hecuba was doing the same thing you are doing
     now: she heaped all sorts of insults on anyone she saw.
     For that reason she rightly came to be called "the bitch."

WIFE I can't tolerate those shocking acts of yours: I'd rather 720
     live the rest of my life as a divorcee than tolerate those
     shocking acts of yours which you commit.

SOS What do I care whether you can tolerate being married
     or will leave your husband? Or is it custom here to tell
     gossip to new arrivals from abroad?

WIFE What gossip? I'm telling you, I won't put up with it from 725
     now on, I'll live as a divorcee rather than tolerate your
     habits.

SOS Live in divorce, for all I care, as long as Jupiter keeps his
     kingship if you wish.

WIFE But a moment ago you denied that you'd stolen it from
     me (*points to the mantle*), and now you're holding the 730
     very same in front of my eyes. Aren't you ashamed?

SOS Goodness! Woman, you're very bold and bad. Do you
     dare to say that this one was stolen from you? Another
     woman gave it to me to have it repaired.

WIFE Right! That does it! Right now I'll bring my father to
     you and tell him about the shameful acts you commit. 735
     (*to the servant girl*) Go, Deceo, look for my father, so that

---

[21] Wife of king Priam in the Iliad, embittered after the loss of her
husband and children.

    ut ueniat ad me: ⟨sub⟩ita⟨m⟩ rem esse dicito.
    iam ego aperiam istaec tua flagitia.
SOS   sanan es?
    quae mea flagitia?
MAT   pallas atque aurum meum
740   domo suppilas ⟨tua⟩ tuae uxori et tuae
    degeris amicae. satin haec recte fabulor?
SOS   quaeso hercle, mulier, si scis, monstra quod bibam
    tuam qui possim perpeti petulantiam.
    quem tu hominem ⟨me esse⟩ arbitrere nescio;
745   ego te simitu noui cum Porthaone.
MAT   si me derides, at pol illum non potes,
    patrem meum qui huc aduenit. quin respicis?
    nouistin tu illum?
SOS   noui cum Calcha simul:
    eodem die illum uidi quo te ante hunc diem.
750 MAT negas nouisse me? negas patrem meum?
SOS   idem hercle dicam si auom uis adducere.
MAT ecastor pariter hoc atque alias res soles.

     V. ii: SENEX. MATRONA. SOSICLES
SEN ut aetas mea est atque ut hoc usus facto est
    gradum proferam, progredi properabo.
755   sed id quam mihi facile sit hau sum falsus.

737 ita *P*, subitam *Gratwick*
739 pallam *P*, pallas *Vahlen*
740 tua *add. Gratwick*
744 me esse *add. Pylades*
754 progredi⟨ri⟩ *Bothe ut integer tetrameter fiat*

he comes to me with you. Tell him it's an emergency.
Right now I'll reveal those shameful acts of yours. (*Deceo
leaves the stage on the right*)

SOS   Are you in your right mind? Which shameful acts of
mine?

WIFE You steal mantles and my gold, from your wife, from your   740
home, and carry them to your mistress. Aren't I speaking
the truth?

SOS   Please, woman, if you know, prescribe me something to
drink in order to be able to put up with your rudeness. I
don't know who you think I am. I got to know you at the   745
same time as Porthaon.[22]

WIFE (*spotting Deceo and her father*) Even if you're laughing
at me, you can't laugh at that man, my father, who is com-
ing here. Why don't you look back? Do you know him?

SOS   I got to know him together with Calchas;[23] I saw him on
the same day on which I saw you before this day.

WIFE You deny knowing me? You deny knowing my father?   750

SOS   Yes, and I'll say the same if you wish to bring here your
grandfather.

WIFE Honestly, that's just in keeping with the other things you
always do.

*Enter the OLD MAN with a walking stick, accompanied by
Deceo.*

OM   As fast as my age allows and the situation demands I'll
move my step, I'll hurry to walk along. But I'm not mis-   755
taken about how easy that is for me. My swiftness is de-

22 Son of Meriones; an obscure person.
23 Greek seer in the Iliad.

nam pernicitas deserit: consitus sum
senectute, onustum gero corpus, uires
reliquere: ut aetas mala est! merx mala aegro est.
nam res plurumas pessumas, quom aduenit, fert,
760   quas si autumem omnis, nimis longus sermo est.
sed haec res mihi in pectore et corde curae est,
quidnam hoc sit negoti quod filia sic
763   repente expetit me, ut ad sese irem.
763^a nec quid id sit mihi certius facit, quid
763^b uelit, quid me accersat.
764   uerum propemodum iam scio quid siet rei.
765   credo cum uiro litigium natum esse aliquod.
ita istaec solent, quae uiros supseruire
sibi postulant, dote fretae, feroces.
et illi quoque haud apstinent saepe culpa.
uerum est modus tamen, quoad pati uxorem oportet;
770   nec pol filia umquam patrem accersit ad se
nisi aut quid commissi aut iurgi est causa.
sed id quicquid est iam sciam. atque eccam eampse
ante aedis et eius uirum uideo tristem.
id est quod suspicabar.
775   appellabo hanc.

MAT   ibo aduorsum. salue multum, mi pater.
SEN   salua sis. saluen aduenio? saluen accersi iubes?
quid tu tristis es? quid ille autem aps te iratus distitit?
nescioquid uos uelitati estis inter uos duos.
loquere, uter meruistis culpam, paucis, non longos logos.

758 ergo *P*, aegro *Gratwick*
759 fert *B¹*, affert *uel* adfert *B⁴CD*
763^b accersit *P*, accersat *Lambinus*

serting me, I'm overgrown with old age, I'm moving a
burdened body, my strength has left me. How bad old
age is! It's a bad lot for an ill man: it brings countless trou-
bles when it comes. If I were to speak about all of them, 760
my talk would be far too long. But this matter is a worry
in my breast and in my heart, what this business is that
my daughter has asked me suddenly like this to come to
her. And she doesn't inform me what it is, what she wants,
what she's summoning me for. But I practically know al-
ready what's the matter. I believe some argument has 765
arisen with her husband. They're always like that, those
women who expect their husbands to act as their slaves,
relying on their dowries and generally savage. And the
husbands are often not blameless either. But there's a
limit to what a wife ought to put up with. And a daughter 770
never summons her father unless the reason is some
offense or argument. But whatever it is, I'll know in a
moment. And look, I can see her in person in front of the
house, and her husband with an unhappy expression. It's
what I suspected. I'll address her. 775

WIFE I'll go toward him. (*loudly*) Many greetings, my dear
father.

OM And to you. Am I finding everything well? Is all well, that
you have me summoned? What are you upset about? And
why does he stand at a distance from you? You've had
some fight between you two. Tell me which of you is
guilty, but briefly, no long stories.

---

773 tristem uirum uideo *P*, uirum uideo tristem *Brix*, uirum tristem
uideo *Bothe*

775 *partes sic distribuit Gulielmus*

777 destitit *P*, distitit *Lambinus*

780   MAT   nusquam equidem quicquam deliqui: hoc primum te ap-
                    soluo, pater.
              uerum uiuere hic non possum nec durare ullo modo.
              proin tu me hinc abducas.

      SEN   quid istuc autem est?

      MAT   ludibrio, pater,
              habeor.

      SEN   unde?

      MAT   ab illo quoi me mandauisti, meo uiro.

      SEN   ecce autem litigium! quotiens tandem edixi tibi
785   ut caueres neuter ad me iretis cum querimonia?

      MAT   qui ego istuc, mi pater, cauere possum?

      SEN   men interrogas?

787– MAT   nisi non uis.
88
      SEN   quotiens monstraui tibi uiro ut morem geras,
              quid ille faciat ne id opserues, quo eat, quid rerum gerat.

790   MAT   at enim ille hinc amat meretricem ex proxumo.

      SEN   sane sapit
              atque ob istanc industriam etiam faxo amabit amplius.

      MAT   atque ibi potat.

      SEN   tua quidem ille causa potabit minus,
              si illic siue alibi lubebit? quae haec, malum, impudentia
                est?
              una opera prohibere ad cenam ne promittat postules
795   neu quemquam accipiat alienum apud se. seruirin tibi
              postulas uiros? dare una opera pensum postules,
              inter ancillas sedere iubeas, lanam carere.

      MAT   non equidem mihi te aduocatum, pater, adduxi, sed uiro.
              hinc stas, illim causam dicis.

787–88 non uis *P*, neuis *Bothe*

WIFE I didn't do anything wrong anywhere. I'll free you from   780
that worry first, my father. But I can't live here and I can't
endure it in any way. So you must take me away from
here.

OM What's that?

WIFE I'm being ridiculed, my father.

OM By whom?

WIFE By the man you gave me to, my husband.

OM Look at that, an argument! How often did I tell you to be   785
on your guard against either of you coming to me with a
complaint?

WIFE How can I be on my guard against that, my dear father?

OM You ask me?

WIFE Unless you object.

OM How often did I teach you to obey your husband, not to
observe what he's doing, where he's going, and what he's
up to!

WIFE But he makes love to a prostitute from here next door.   790

OM He's just doing the smart thing and because of your of-
ficiousness I bet he'll make love to her even more.

WIFE And he drinks there.

OM Will he drink less for your sake if he wants to drink there
or anywhere else? What impudence is this, damn it? By
the same token you could demand to forbid him to accept
a dinner invitation or to receive anyone else at his place.   795
Do you demand that men should be your slaves? By the
same token you could demand to give him something to
spin, to tell him to sit among the slave girls, and to card
the wool.

WIFE I brought you here not as *my* advocate, my father, but as
my *husband's*. You stand here but you plead his case from
there.

507

	SEN	si ille quid deliquerit,
800		multo tanta illum accusabo quam te accusaui amplius.

        quando te auratam et uestitam bene habet, ancillas, pe-
            num

        recte praehibet, melius sanam est, mulier, mentem su-
            mere.

MAT   at ille suppilat mihi aurum et pallas ex arcis domo,

        me despoliat, mea ornamenta clam ad meretrices de-
            gerit.

805 SEN male facit, si istuc facit; si non facit, tu male facis

        quae insontem insimules.

MAT   quin etiam nunc habet pallam, pater,

        ⟨et⟩ spinter, quod ad hanc detulerat, nunc, quia resciui,
            refert.

SEN   iam ego ex hoc, ut factum est, scibo. ⟨ibo⟩ ad hominem

        atque ⟨al⟩loquar.

        dic mi istuc, Menaechme, quod uos dissertatis, ut sciam.

810   quid tu tristis es? quid illa autem irata aps te distitit?

SOS   quisquis es, quicquid tibi nomen est, senex, summum
            Iouem

        deosque do testis—

SEN   qua de re aut quoius rei rerum omnium?

SOS   —me neque isti male fecisse mulieri quae me arguit

        hanc domo ab se surrupuisse atque apstulisse.

⟨MAT⟩   peierat.

815– SOS si ego intra aedis huius umquam ubi habitat penetraui
16   ⟨pedem⟩,

        omnium hominum exopto ut fiam miserorum miser-
            rumus.

807 et ꞩ   808 ibo *add. Camerarius*   adquemloquar *P* (atque
loquar *B²*), atque adloquar *Saracenus*

    810 destituis *B*, dedistitus *CD*, distitit *Lambinus*

OM If *he* commits any offense, I'll accuse him many times as 800
severely as I accused you. Since he keeps you well sup-
plied with jewelry and clothes and provides you with
slave girls and food as he ought, it would be better to
adopt a healthy attitude, woman.

WIFE But he's stealing my gold and mantles from my chests
from home, he's robbing me, he's secretly carrying off my
jewelry to prostitutes.

OM He behaves badly if he behaves like this. If he doesn't 805
behave like this, *you* are behaving badly by accusing an
innocent man.

WIFE But even now he has the mantle, my father, and the
bracelet he'd taken to her; now that I've found out about
it he's returning them.

OM In a moment I'll know from him how it happened. (*ap-
proaching him*) I'll go to him and address him. Tell me
this, Menaechmus, what you're arguing about, so that I
know. What are you upset about? And why does she stand 810
at a distance from you, angry?

SOS Whoever you are, whatever your name is, old man, I give
you Jupiter above and all the gods as my witnesses—

OM (*interrupting*) For what or on account of what on this
earth?

SOS —that I haven't wronged that woman, who is accusing
me of having stolen this (*shows the mantle*) from her
house and of having carried it off.

WIFE He's perjuring himself.

SOS If I ever set foot into the house where this woman lives, I 815
wish to become the most wretched of all wretches.

---

814 delurat *P* (deiurat *B*²), peierat *matronae interrumpenti dedit
Schoell*

815–16 pedem *add. Pylades*

	SEN	sanun es qui istuc exoptes aut neges te umquam pedem
		in eas aedis intulisse ubi habitas, insanissume?
820	SOS	tun, senex, ais habitare med in illisce aedibus?
	SEN	tu⟨n⟩ negas?
	SOS	nego hercle uero.
	SEN	immo hercle inuero negas;
		nisi quo nocte hac ⟨e⟩migrasti. ⟨tu⟩ concede huc, filia.
		quid tu ais? num hinc emigrasti⟨s⟩?
	MAT	quem in locum aut ⟨quam⟩ ob rem, opsecro?
	SEN	non edepol scio.
	MAT	profecto ludit te hic. non tu[te] tenes?
825	SEN	iam uero, Menaechme, satis iocatu's. nunc hanc rem
		gere.
	SOS	quaeso, quid mihi tecum est? unde aut quis tu homo es?
		⟨quid debeo⟩
		tibi aut adeo isti, quae mihi molest⟨i⟩ae est quoquo
		modo?
	MAT	uiden tu illi⟨c⟩ oculos uirere? ut uiridis exoritur colos
829–30		ex temporibus atque fronte, ut oculi scintillant, uide!
843	SOS	ei mihi! insanire me aiunt, ultra quom ipsi insaniunt.
831		quid mi meliust quam, quando illi me insanire praedi-
		cant,
		ego med assimulem insanire, ut illos a me apsterream?
	MAT	ut pandiculans oscitatur! quid nunc faciam, mi pater?
	SEN	concede huc, mea nata, ab istoc quam potest longissume.

821 tu⟨n⟩ *Bothe*   ludere *P*, inuere *Lindsay*, inuero *Gratwick*, ludis si *Kayser*   822 ⟨ex⟩migrasti, ⟨tu⟩ *Schoell*
823 emigrasti⟨s⟩ *Acidalius*   quam *add. Beroaldus*
824 tute *P*, tu *Mueller*   826 quid debeo *add. Leo*
827 molest⟨i⟩ae *Schoell*
828 illi⟨c⟩ *Ritschl*   iurere *CD*, uire- *B¹*, uirere *B²*
829–30 atque ⟨ex⟩ *Gratwick*

OM   Are you in your right mind, wishing for this or denying that you ever set foot into the house where you live, you complete madman?

SOS   Do you, old man, claim that I live in that house?   820

OM   Do you deny it?

SOS   I do deny it, in all truth.

OM   No, you deny it in all untruth; unless you moved out somewhere last night. (*turning to his daughter*) You come over here, my daughter. What do *you* say? Did you two move out from here?

WIFE   Where to or why, please?

OM   I don't know.

WIFE   He's plainly making fun of you. Don't you get it?

OM   You've really joked enough now, Menaechmus. Now pay   825
attention.

SOS   Please, what business have I with you? Where are you from, or who are you? What do I owe you, or for that matter this woman, who is a nuisance to me in every conceivable way?

WIFE   (*to her father*) Can you see how green his eyes are? How a pale color is arising from his temples and his forehead,   830
how his eyes are flaming, look!

SOS   (*aside*) Dear me! They say *I* am mad, when on the con-   843
trary they themselves are. Since they say that I'm mad,   831
what's better for me than to pretend to be mad in order to drive them away from me? (*moves and acts strangely*)

WIFE   How he's gaping with a grimace! What should I do now, my dear father?

OM   Come over here, my daughter, as far away from him as possible.

---

843 *uersum hic posuit Acidalius*   832 ego me *P*, egomet *Gratwick*

835	SOS	euhoe Bacche, Bromie, quo me in siluam uenatum uocas?

835 SOS euhoe Bacche, Bromie, quo me in siluam uenatum
uocas?
audio, sed non abire possum ab his regionibus,
ita illa me ab laeua rabiosa femina asseruat canes,
poste autem ille Cercops alius, qui saepe aetate in sua
perdidit ciuem innocentem falso testimonio.
840 SEN uae capiti tuo!
SOS   ecce, Apollo mihi ex oraclo imperat
ut ego illic oculos exuram lampadibus ardentibus.
842 MAT perii! mi pater, minatur mihi oculos exurere.
844 SEN filia, heus!
MAT   quid est? quid agimus?
SEN   quid si ego huc seruos cito?
845 ibo, adducam qui hunc hinc tollant et domi deuinciant
prius quam turbarum quid faciat amplius.
SOS   enim haereo;
ni occupo aliquid mihi consilium, hi domum me ad se au-
ferent.
pugnis me uotas in huius ore quicquam . . . parcere,
ni a meis oculis apscedat in malam magnam crucem.
850 faciam quod iubes, Apollo.
SEN   fuge domum quantum potest,
ne hic te optundat.
MAT   fugio. amabo, asserua istunc, mi pater,
ne quo hinc abeat. sumne ego mulier misera quae illaec
audio?

835 eubi (eum *B¹*, heu *B²*) atque heu Bromie *P, corr. Ritschl*
838 illi circo salus *P*, ille Cercops alius *Gratwick*, illic hircus alius
Beroaldus, alii alia
841 illi *P*, illic *nonnulli edd.*   lampadi[bu]s *Geppert*
844 *partes sic distribuit Acidalius*

SOS (*loudly*) Woohoo, Bacchus, Bromius,[24] where are you 835
      calling me to hunt in the woods? I can hear you, but I
      can't leave these regions: that rabid bitch on my left is
      keeping watch, and behind me that other Cercops,[25] who
      often ruined an innocent citizen through false evidence
      in his day.

OM   Curse you!   840

SOS Look, Apollo[26] tells me through a divine utterance to
      burn out that woman's eyes with flaming torches.

WIFE I'm dead! My dear father, he's threatening to burn out my 842
      eyes.

OM   Hey there, my daughter!   844

WIFE What is it? What are we doing?

OM   What if I summon slaves here? I'll go and fetch people to 845
      lift him up from here and tie him up at home before he
      makes any more trouble.

SOS (*aside*) I'm stuck. Unless I get hold of some trick, they'll
      carry me off to their house. (*loudly*) You tell me to spare
      her face with my fists . . . in no way, unless she leaves my
      sight and goes to be hanged. I'll do what you tell me,   850
      Apollo.

OM   Run off home as fast as possible so that he doesn't beat
      you.

WIFE Yes. Please, watch over him, my dear father, so that he
      doesn't go away anywhere. Aren't I a wretched woman to
      hear those things?

Exit the WIFE OF MENAECHMUS into her house with Deceo.

[24] Bromius is a cultic name of Bacchus, the god of wine and intoxication.

[25] The Cercopes were dwarfs, turned into monkeys by Jupiter.

[26] The god of music, poetic inspiration, and oracles.

SOS   hau male illanc amoui; ⟨amoueam⟩ nunc hunc impuris-
        sumum,
    barbatum, tremulum Titanum, qui cluet Cynos pater.

855   ita mihi imperas ut ego huius membra atque ossa atque
        artua
    comminuam illo scipione quem ipse habet.

SEN   dabitur malum,
    me quidem si attigeris aut si propius ad me accesseris.

SOS   faciam quod iubes; securim capiam ancipitem atque
        hunc senem
    osse fini dedolabo assulatim uiscera.

860 SEN   enim uero illud praecauendum est atque accurandum est
        mihi;
    sane ego illum metuo, ut minatur, ne quid male faxit
        mihi.

SOS   multa mi imperas, Apollo: nunc equos iunctos iubes
    capere me indomitos, ferocis, atque in currum inscen-
        dere,
    ut ego hunc proteram leonem uetulum, olentem, eden-
        tulum.

865   iam astiti in currum, iam lora teneo, iam stimulum: in
        manu est.
    agite equi, facitote sonitus ungularum appareat
    cursu celeri; facite in flexu sit pedum pernicitas.

SEN   mihin equis iunctis minare?

SOS   ecce, Apollo, denuo
    me iubes facere impetum in eum qui ⟨hic⟩ stat atque oc-
        cidere.

853 amoueam *add.* Persson, *alii alia*   854 Titanum *P et Prisci-
anus*, Tithonum *Meursius*   Cygno prognatum patre *P*, qui lucet
(cluet *Scaliger*) Cygno patre *Priscianus*, qui cluet Cynospater *Gratwick*

SOS I didn't get rid of her badly; now I'll get rid of that
     most filthy, bearded, trembling Titan,[27] who is called the
     Bitch-Father. This is your command, that I should smash   855
     his limbs, bones, and joints to pieces with his own walk-
     ing stick.

OM   You'll get a beating if you touch me or come any closer
     to me.

SOS I'll do what you tell me: I'll take a double-edged ax and
     hew away this old man's flesh, bit by bit, down to the
     bone.

OM   (*aside*) I really have to be on my guard against that and   860
     be careful. I'm horribly afraid, given the nature of his
     threats, that he could do me some harm.

SOS You give me many commands, Apollo: now you're telling
     me to take a span of horses, untamed and wild, and to get
     onto a chariot in order to trample this old, smelly, tooth-
     less lion underfoot.[28] (*pretends to mount a chariot*) Now   865
     I'm standing on my chariot, now I'm holding the reins,
     now the goad: it's in my hand. Go on, my horses, let the
     ring of your hooves be audible in your swift gallop; let
     there be speed in the bending of your legs.

OM   Are you threatening me with a span of horses?

SOS Look, Apollo, again you tell me to assault the man stand-

[27] Earlier he referred to the old man as a Cercops; he uses the con-
trast between the dwarf and the giant to show how mad he is.
[28] He is called a lion because of his beard.

867 inflexu *P*, in flexu *Lambinus*, inflexa *Dousa senior*
869 hic *add. Bothe*

870		sed quis hic est qui me capillo hinc de curru deripit?
		imperium tuom demutat atque edictum Apollinis.
872	SEN	eu hercle morbum acrem ac durum! ***
872ᵃ		*** di, uostram fidem!
873		uel hic qui insanit quam ualuit paullo prius!
		ei derepente tantus morbus incidit.
875		ibo atque accersam medicum iam quantum potest.

V. iii: SOSICLES. SENEX

	SOS	iamne isti abierunt, quaeso, ex conspectu meo,
		qui me ui cogunt ut ualidus insaniam?
		quid cesso abire ad nauem dum saluo licet?
879–80		uosque omnis quaeso, si senex reuenerit,
		ne me indicetis qua platea hinc aufugerim.
	SEN	lumbi sedendo, oculi spectando dolent,
		manendo medicum dum se ex opere recipiat.
		odiosus tandem uix ab aegrotis uenit,
885		ait se obligasse crus fractum Aesculapio,
		Apollini autem bracchium. nunc cogito
		utrum me dicam ducere medicum an fabrum.
		atque eccum incedit. moue formicinum gradum.

V. iv: MEDICVS. SENEX

	MED	quid esse illi morbi dixeras? narra, senex.
890		num laruatust aut cerritus? fac sciam.
		num eum ueternus aut aqua intercus tenet?

872–72ᵃ *lacunam indicauit Schoell*
889 esset illi *P* (esse illi *F*), illi esse *Fleckeisen*

---

[29] Divine healer.
[30] Ceres was a goddess of growth, but also connected with death, hence the link to madness.

ing here and to kill him. But who is that dragging me off 870
the chariot by my hair? The power over you and Apollo's
behest is failing. (*falls to the ground*)

OM   Goodness! A bitter and harsh illness! *** gods, your pro-
tection! For instance this madman, how healthy he was a
little earlier! Suddenly such a severe illness has befallen
him. I'll go and fetch the doctor as quickly as possible.   875

Exit the OLD MAN to the right.

SOS   (*getting up*) Have they left my sight now, please? They
force me to act crazy even though I'm healthy. What do I
hesitate to go off to the ship while I can still do so safely?
(*to the audience*) I entreat you all: if the old man comes   880
back, don't tell him what street I ran away on.

Exit SOSICLES to the left, enter the OLD MAN from the right.

OM   My loins hurt from sitting, my eyes from watching, from
waiting for the doctor to return from work. With dif-
ficulty and after much time the pest came from the sick.
He said he'd bandaged the broken shin of Aesculapius[29]   885
and the arm of Apollo. Now I'm wondering whether I
should say I'm hiring a doctor or a sculptor. Look, here he
comes. Move your antlike step.

Enter the DOCTOR from the right.

DOC   What illness did you say he has? Tell me, old man. Is he   890
possessed by evil spirits or by Ceres?[30] Inform me. Does
lethargy or dropsy hold him in its grip?

SEN   quin ea te causa duco ut id dicas mihi
        atque illum ut sanum facias.

MED   perfacile id quidem est;
        sanum futurum, mea ego id promitto fide.

895 SEN   magna cum cura ego illum curari uolo.

MED   quin suspirabo plus sescenta in die:
        ita ego eum cum cura magna curabo tibi.

SEN   atque eccum ipsum hominem. opseruemus quam rem
        agat.

V. V: MENAECHMVS. SENEX. MEDICVS

MEN   edepol ne hic dies peruorsus atque aduorsus mi optigit.

900   quae me clam ratus sum facere, ea omnia fecit palam
        parasitus qui me compleuit flagiti et formidinis,
        meus Vlixes, suo qui regi tantum conciuit mali.
        quem ego hominem, siquidem uiuo, uita euoluam sua.

905   sed ego stultus sum, qui illius esse dico quae mea est:
        meo cibo et sumptu educatust. anima priuabo uirum.
        condigne autem haec meretrix fecit, ut mos est meretri-
        cius:
        quia rogo palla ut referatur rursum ad uxorem meam,
        mihi se ait dedisse. eu edepol! ne ego homo uiuo miser.

SEN   audin quae loquitur?

MED   se miserum praedicat.

SEN   adeas uelim.

910 MED   saluos sis, Menaechme. quaeso, quor apertas brac-
        chium?
        non tu scis quantum isti morbo nunc tuo facias mali?

---

896 in dies *P*, in die *Lambinus*   *uersus propter hiatum et sensum parum clarum nonnullis edd. suspectus est*
    897 illum *P*, eum *Kämpf*
    900 ea omnia *P, transp. Bothe*
    903 ⟨iam⟩ uita *Ritschl*

OM   Well, I'm hiring you to tell me that and to heal him.

DOC   That's very easy. He shall be well, I promise you that on my honor.

OM   I want him to be taken care of with great care.   895

DOC   Yes, I'll sigh more than six hundred sighs per day, which goes to show with what great care I'll take care of him for you.

OM   Look, the man himself. Let's observe what he's up to.

Enter MENAECHMUS from the right, without noticing anyone.

MEN   This day has really come upon me as an evil and bad one. My hanger-on revealed everything which I thought I was   900 doing in secret. He filled me with shame and fear, this Ulysses of mine, who stirred up so much trouble for his king.[31] As truly as I live, I'll send him spinning out of his life. But it's stupid of me to call his what's mine: he was   905 raised on my food and at my expense. I'll deprive him of life. And this prostitute behaved in accordance with the habit of prostitutes: because I ask her that the mantle be brought back to my wife, she says she's given it to me. Wonderful! Yes, I am a poor wretch.

OM   *(to the doctor)* Can you hear what he's talking about?

DOC   He says he's a wretch.

OM   I'd like you to go to him.

DOC   Hello, Menaechmus. Please, why are you exposing your   910 arm? Don't you know how much worse you're making your illness now?

---

[31] Allusion taking its point of departure from the double meaning of *rex*: "king" and "patron of a hanger-on." Ulysses was known for his trickery. Here there could be a reference to Ulysses persuading king Agamemnon to sacrifice his daughter.

MEN   quin tu te suspendis?

MED   ecquid sentis?

MEN   quidni sentiam?

MED   non potest haec res ellebori iungere optinerier.
        sed quid ais, Menaechme?

MEN   quid uis?

MED   dic mihi hoc quod te rogo:

915   album an atrum uinum potas?

MEN   quin tu is in malam crucem?

MED   iam hercle occeptat insanire primulum.

MEN   quin tu [me inter]rogas
        purpureum panem an puniceum soleam ego esse an lu-
            teum?
        soleamne esse auis squamosas, piscis pennatos?

SEN   papae!

919–20   audin tu ut deliramenta loquitur? quid cessas dare
        potionis aliquid prius quam percipit insania?

MED   mane modo, etiam percontabor alia.

SEN   occidis fabulans.

MED   dic mihi hoc: solent tibi umquam oculi duri fieri?

MEN   quid? tu me locustam censes esse, homo ignauissume?

925 MED dic mihi: enumquam intestina tibi crepant, quod sentias?

MEN   ubi satur sum, nulla crepitant; quando esurio, tum cre-
        pant.

MED   hoc quidem edepol hau pro insano uerbum respondit
        mihi.
        perdormiscin usque ad lucem? facilin tu dormis cubans?

916 tu me interrogas *P*, tu rogas *Bothe*, me interrogas *Lindsay*

MEN   Why don't you hang yourself?

DOC   (*pinching him*) Do you feel anything?

MEN   Why shouldn't I?

DOC   (*to the old man*) Even with a wagonload of hellebore this can't be achieved. (*proceeding with the diagnosis*) But what do you say, Menaechmus?

MEN   What do you want?

DOC   Tell me what I ask you: do you drink white wine or red?[32]   915

MEN   Why don't you go to the devil?

DOC   (*to the old man*) Now he's beginning to go crazy for the first time.

MEN   Why don't you ask if I normally eat purple bread or crimson or yellow? If I normally eat birds with scales and fish with feathers?

OM   (*to the doctor*) Amazing! Can you hear how he's talking   920
nonsense? What are you hesitating to give him some potion before he has a fit?

DOC   Just wait, I will still ask about other things.

OM   You're killing me with your talking.

DOC   (*to Menaechmus*) Tell me this: are your eyes ever apt to become hard?

MEN   What? Do you think I'm a lobster, you disgraceful creature?

DOC   Tell me, do your intestines ever rumble, as far as you   925
know?

MEN   When I'm full, they don't rumble at all; when I'm hungry, they do.

DOC   (*to the old man*) On this issue he didn't answer me like a madman. (*to Menaechmus*) Do you sleep through till dawn? Do you sleep easily when you go to bed?

---

[32] Lit. "black"; dark wine was said to have laxative qualities (Cato *agr.* 157. 9), white wine to be astringent.

929–
30   MEN   perdormisco, si resolui argentum quoi debeo.
931–
33   qui te Iuppiter dique omnes, percontator, perduint!
      MED   nunc homo insanire occeptat: de illis uerbis caue tibi.
935   SEN   immo Nestor nunc quidem est de uerbis, praeut dudum
                 fuit;
            nam dudum uxorem suam esse aiebat rabiosam canem.
      MEN   quid ego dixi?
      SEN   insanu's, inquam.
      MEN   egone?
      SEN   tu istic, qui mihi
            etiam me iunctis quadrigis minitatu's prosternere.
939–
40   egomet haec te uidi facere, egomet haec ted arguo.
      MEN   at ego te sacram coronam surrupuisse Iouis ‹scio›,
            et ob eam rem in carcerem ted esse compactum scio,
            et postquam es emissus, caesum uirgis sub furca scio;
            tum patrem occidisse et matrem uendidisse etiam scio.
945   satin haec pro sano male dicta male dictis respondeo?
      SEN   opsecro hercle, medice, propere quicquid facturu's face.
            non uides hominem insanire?
      MED   scin quid facias optumum est?
            ad me face uti deferatur.
      SEN   itane censes?
      MED   quippini?
            ibi meo arbitratu potero curare hominem.
      SEN   age ut lubet.

___

937 quid ego dixi insanus *P*, MEN quid ego dixi SEN insanis ς, MEN q.
e. dixi SEN insanu's *Gratwick*, MEN quid ego SEN dix‹t›i insanus *Leo*
941 iouis *B*, lo iouis *CD*, Iouis scio *Pylades*, aio Iouis *Pareus*

___

33 King of Pylos, a wise statesman in the Iliad.

MEN I sleep through if I've paid everyone I owe money to. 930
May Jupiter and all the gods ruin you, questioner!

DOC (to the old man) Now he's beginning to have a fit. Be careful on account of those words.

OM No, now he's a Nestor[33] with regard to his words, com- 935
pared with how he was a moment ago: a moment ago he
said his wife was a rabid bitch.

MEN What did I say?

OM You're mad, I'm telling you.

MEN I?

OM Yes, you there: you even threatened to lay me low with
yoked chariot horses. I myself saw you do this, I myself 940
am accusing you of it.

MEN But I know that you stole the sacred crown of Jupiter,[34]
and I know that you were thrown into prison because of
that, and I know that you were beaten with rods under
the fork[35] after you were released; then I also know that
you murdered your father and sold your mother. Am I re- 945
plying well enough for a sane man with my insults to your
insults?

OM Please, doctor, do quickly whatever you're going to do.
Can't you see that he's crazy?

DOC Do you know what you'd better do? Have him taken to
my place.

OM Do you advise that?

DOC Naturally. There I'll be able to take care of him as I see fit.

OM Do as you please.

---

[34] An impious crime, but also an impossible one: the statue on the
Capitol stood on a high column (Trin. 85–7).

[35] A punishment for slaves; the slave's neck is put into the fork, the
arms are fastened to the projecting ends.

950	MED	elleborum potabis faxo aliquos uiginti dies.
	MEN	at ego te pendentem fodiam stimulis triginta dies.
	MED	i, arcesse homines qui illunc ad me deferant.
	SEN	quot sunt satis?
	MED	proinde ut insanire uideo, quattuor, nihilo minus.
	SEN	iam hic erunt. asserua tu istunc, medice.
	MED	immo ibo domum,
955		ut parentur quibus paratis opus est. tu seruos iube
		hunc ad me ferant.
	SEN	iam ego illic faxo erit.
	MED	abeo.
	SEN	uale.
	MEN	abiit socerus, abiit medicus: [nunc] solus sum. pro Iup-
		piter!
		quid illuc est quod med hisce homines insanire praedi-
		cant?
		nam equidem, postquam natus sum, numquam aegrotaui
		unum diem
960		neque ego insanio nec pugnas neque ego litis coepio.
		saluos saluos alios uideo, noui ‹ego› homines, alloquor.
		an illi perperam insanire me aiunt, ipsi insaniunt?
		quid ego nunc faciam? domum ire cupio: uxor non sinit;
		huc autem nemo intro mittit. nimis prouentum est ne-
		quiter.
965		hic ero usque; ad noctem saltem, credo, intro mittar do-
		mum.

957 nunc *del. Guyet*
958 me hic *P*, ‹nunc› me hisce *Mueller*
961 ego *add. Ritschl*
963 cupio *P*, coepio *Schoell*

524

DOC   (*to Menaechmus*) I'll make you drink hellebore for some   950
      twenty days.
MEN   But *I* shall hang you up and jab you with cattle prods for
      thirty days.
DOC   (*to the old man*) Go, fetch men to take him to me.
OM   How many does it take?
DOC   Considering how crazy I can see him acting, four, no less.
OM   They'll be here in a moment. You watch over him, doctor.
DOC   No, I'll go home so that what needs to be prepared is pre-   955
      pared. You tell your slaves to bring him here to me.
OM   I'll make sure he'll be there in a moment.
DOC   I'm off.
OM   Goodbye.

*Exit the DOCTOR to the right, followed shortly by the OLD
MAN.*

MEN   Gone is my father-in-law, gone is the doctor. I'm alone.
      Oh Jupiter! Why is it that they say I'm mad? I've never
      been ill for a single day since birth; I'm not mad and I   960
      don't start fights or arguments. As a healthy man I see
      others being healthy, I know people and address them.
      Or are they wrong to say that I am crazy and are crazy
      themselves? What should I do now? I wish to go home;
      my wife doesn't let me. And no one allows me in here
      (*points to Erotium's house*). This went awfully badly. I'll   965
      be here throughout; at nightfall at least I'll be let into the
      house, I believe.

V. vi: MESSENIO

MES spectamen bono seruo id est, qui rem erilem
    procurat, uidet, collocat cogitatque,
    ut apsente ero ⟨tam⟩ rem eri diligenter
    tutetur quam si ipse assit aut rectius.

970   tergum quam gulam, crura quam uentrem oportet
    potiora esse quoi cor modeste situm est.

972   recordetur id,

972ᵃ   qui nihili sunt, quid eis preti

973   detur ab suis eris, ignauis, improbis uiris:
    uerbera, compedes,

975   molae, [magna] lassitudo, fames, frigus durum,
    haec pretia sunt ignauiae.
    id ego male malum metuo: propterea bonum esse cer-
      tum est potius quam malum;
    nam magis multo patior facilius uerba: uerbera ego odi,
    nimioque edo lubentius molitum quam molitum prae-
      hibeo.

980   propterea eri imperium exsequor, bene et sedate seruo
      id;
    atque mihi id prodest.
    alii [esse] ita ut in rem esse ducunt, sint: ego ita ero ut me
      esse oportet;

983   metum [id] mihi adhibeam, culpam apstineam, ero ut
      omnibus in locis sim praesto:

983ᵃ   serui qui quom culpa carent metuont, i solent esse eris
      utibiles.

983ᵇ   nam illi qui nil metuont, postquam malum promeriti,
      tunc ei metuont.

984   metuam hau multum. prope est quando †ceruso faciam†
      pretium exsoluet.

985   ⟨eo⟩ ego exemplo seruio,

Enter MESSENIO from the left.

MES This is the touchstone for a good servant: that one is good
who secures, watches, arranges, and has in mind his mas-
ter's business, so that when his master is away he guards
his master's business as diligently as if he were present in
person or even better. A slave who has his heart in its   970
proper place has to put his back above his gullet, his shins
above his belly. Let him remember what reward those
who are worthless are given by their masters, the lazy and
shameless ones: beatings, shackles, the mill, exhaustion,   975
hunger, harsh cold, these are the rewards of laziness. I'm
terribly afraid of this terrible suffering. That's why I'm
resolved to be good rather than bad. I can bear a chiding
much more easily: I hate a hiding, and I much prefer to
eat what has been milled to doing the milling. For this   980
reason I'm following my master's command and carry it
out well and calmly. And that's to my own good. Let oth-
ers be as they think it's advantageous. I shall be as I ought
to be. I should retain a sense of fear and steer clear of   983
guilt, so that I'm there for my master in all places. Those
slaves who are afraid when they're free from guilt are
usually useful to their masters. Those who are not afraid
of anything are afraid after deserving a trashing. I shan't
be greatly afraid. The time is close when my master will
reward me. I serve him on that principle, as I think it ad-   985

---

968 tam *add. Ritschl*   975 magna *del. Ritschl*
980 id *B⁴CD, om. B¹*   981 mihi id *B*, id mihi *CD*
982 aliis *B¹CD*, alii *Bᶜ*   esse *del. Pylades*
983 id *del. Camerarius*   983ᵇ promeritum que *P*, promeriti
(sunt) tunc *Pylades*   984 *uersus sanari non potest*
985 eo *add. Spengel*

985ª   tergo ut in rem esse arbitror.

986   postquam in tabernam uasa et seruos collocaui, ut ius-
            serat,

        ita uenio aduorsum. nunc fores pultabo, adesse ut me
            sciat,

        nequamque erum ex hoc saltu damni saluom ut educam
            foras.

        sed metuo ne sero ueniam depugnato proelio.

V. vii: SENEX. MENAECHMVS. MESSENIO

990 SEN   per ego uobis deos atque homines dico ut imperium
            meum

        sapienter habeatis curae, quae imperaui atque impero:

        facite illic homo iam in medicinam ablatus sublimis siet,

        nisi quidem uos uostra crura aut latera nihili penditis.

        caue quisquam quod illic minitetur uostrum flocci
            fecerit.

995   quid statis? quid dubitatis? iam sublimem raptum opor-
            tuit.

        ego ibo ad medicum: praesto ero illi, quom uenietis.

MEN   occidi!

        quid hoc est negoti? quid illisce homines ad me currunt,
            opsecro?

        quid uoltis uos? quid quaeritatis? quid me circumsistitis?

        quo rapitis me? quo fertis me? perii, opsecro uostram
            fidem,

1000   Epidamnienses, subuenite, ciues! quin me mittitis?

MES   pro di immortales! opsecro, quid ego oculis aspicio meis?

        erum meum indignissume nescioqui sublimem ferunt.

985ª tergo *B*, terge *CD*, tergi *Merula*
988 neque utrum *P*, nequamque erum *Gratwick*

vantageous for my back. After putting up the luggage and
slaves in the inn, as he'd told me to, I'm coming to meet
him. Now I'll knock on the door so that he knows I'm
here and so that I can take my worthless master out of
this den of damage safe and sound. But I'm afraid that
I'm coming too late, after the battle's been fought.

Enter the OLD MAN with four slaves with straps from the right.

OM   I'm ordering you by the gods and men to follow my   990
command wisely, what I have commanded and what I
am commanding. Make sure that he's carried off in the
air to the doctor's at once, unless you don't care about
your shins and sides. Let no one take any account of his
threats. Why are you standing around? Why are you hesi-   995
tating? By now he ought to have been carried off. I'll go
to the doctor. I'll be there when you come.

Exit the OLD MAN to the right. The four slaves are beginning to carry Menaechmus off.

MEN   I'm dead! What business is this? Why are those men run-
ning toward me, please? What do you want? What are
you looking for? Why are you surrounding me? Where
are you dragging me? Where are you carrying me? I'm
done for! I implore your protection, citizens of Epidam-   1000
nus, come to my help! Why won't you let me go?
MES   (*spotting the scene*) Immortal gods! Please, what must I
see with my eyes? Some people are carrying off my mas-
ter in a most shameful way!

---

997 illic *P,* illisce *Brix*

	MEN	ecquis suppetias mi audet ferre?
	MES	ego, ere, audacissume.
1004		o facinus indignum et malum,
1004ᵃ 1005		Epidamnii ciues, erum
		meum hic in pacato oppido
1005ᵃ 1006		luci deripier in uia,
		qui liber ad uos uenerit!
		mittite istunc.
	MEN	opsecro te, quisquis es, operam mihi ut des
		neu sinas in me insignite fieri tantam iniuriam.
	MES	immo et operam dabo et defendam et subuenibo sedulo.
1010		numquam te patiar perire, me perire est aequius.
		eripe oculum istic, ab umero qui tenet, ere, te opsecro.
		hisce ego iam sementem in ore faciam: pugnos[que] op-
		seram.
		maxumo hercle hodie malo uostro istunc fertis. mittite.
	MEN	teneo ego huic oculum.
	MES	face ut oculi locus in capite appareat.
1015		uos scelesti, uos rapaces, uos praedones!
	LOR	periimus!
		opsecro hercle!
	MES	mittite ergo.
	MEN	quid me uobis tactio est?
		pecte pugnis.
	MES	agite abite, fugite hinc in malam crucem.
		em tibi etiam! quia postremus cedis, hoc praemi feres.
		nimis [aut] bene ora commetaui atque ex mea sententia.
1020		edepol, ere, ne tibi suppetias temperi adueni modo.

1012 que *del. Fraenkel*
1013 hodie malo hercle P, *transp. Bothe*
1015 perimus P, periimus *Camerarius*

MEN   Won't anyone bring me help?

MES   Yes, master, I will do so very boldly. (*loudly*) An unworthy
and evil crime, citizens of Epidamnus: my master's being   1005
dragged off in the street in broad daylight, here in a city
that is at peace. He came to you as a free man! (*to the
slaves*) Let go of him.

MEN   (*to Messenio*) I beg you, whoever you are, help me and
don't let such a strikingly great injustice happen to me.

MES   Yes, I'll help you, defend you, and come to your assis-
tance eagerly. I'll never let you die, I'd rather die myself.   1010
Master, I beg you, tear out the eye of the man who is
holding you at the shoulder. Now I'll do some sowing in
their faces: I'll plant my fists there. (*to the slaves*) You'll
pay dearly for trying to carry him off today. Let go of him.

MEN   I'm holding this one by the eye.

MES   Make sure that the eye's socket shows in his head. (*to the*   1015
slaves) You criminals, you robbers, you thugs!

SLAVES   We're dead! Please!

MES   Let go of him then.

MEN   (*also to the slaves*) What did you touch me for? (*to Mes-
senio*) Comb them with your fists.

MES   (*to the slaves*) Go on, run off, flee from here and be
hanged! (*as they run off, hitting the last one*) There's one
for you! Since you're leaving last, you'll carry off this
prize. (*to Menaechmus*) I've surveyed their faces really
well and to my liking. Yes, master, I've brought you help   1020
just in the nick of time.

1019 aut *del. Bothe*   hora *P*, ora *F*

MEN   at tibi di semper, adulescens, quisquis es, faciant bene.
nam apsque te esset, hodie numquam ad solem occasum
    uiuerem.
MES   ergo edepol, si recte facias, ere, med emittas manu.
MEN   liberem ego te?
MES   uerum, quandoquidem, ere, te seruaui.
MEN   quid est?
1025   adulescens, erras.
MES   quid, erro?
MEN   per Iouem adiuro patrem,
med erum tuom non esse.
MES   non taces?
MEN   non mentior;
nec meus seruos umquam tale fecit quale tu mihi.
MES   sic sine igitur, si negas tuom me esse, abire liberum.
MEN   mea quidem hercle causa liber esto atque ito quo uoles.
1030 MES   nemp' iubes?
MEN   iubeo hercle, si quid imperi est in te mihi.
MES   salue, mi patrone. "quom tu liber es, Messenio,
gaudeo." credo hercle uobis. sed, patrone, te opsecro,
ne minus imperes mihi quam quom tuos seruos fui.
apud ted habitabo et quando ibis, una tecum ibo domum.
1035 MEN   minime.
MES   nunc ibo in tabernam, uasa atque argentum tibi
referam. recte est opsignatum in uidulo marsuppium
cum uiatico: id tibi iam huc afferam.
MEN   afler strenue.
MES   saluom tibi ita ut mihi dedisti reddibo. hic me mane.

1027 umquam *CD*, numquam *B*
1028 tuom negas *P*, *transp. Bothe*

MEN	May the gods always bless you, young man, whoever you are: if it hadn't been for you, I'd never have lived till sunset today.
MES	Then if you were to do the right thing, master, you'd set me free.
MEN	I should free you?
MES	Yes, since I've saved you, master.
MEN	What's that? Young man, you're mistaken.
MES	What, I'm mistaken?
MEN	I swear by Father Jupiter that I'm not your master.
MES	Won't you be quiet?
MEN	I'm not lying. My slave has never done anything of the sort you did for me.
MES	Then let me go off like this, as a free man, if you say I don't belong to you.
MEN	As far as I'm concerned you can be free and go where you wish.
MES	Are you telling me to do so?
MEN	Yes, I am, if I have any authority over you.
MES	Greetings, my patron. (*shaking his own hand*) "Messenio, I'm happy that you're free." "I'm sure you mean it." But, my patron, I ask you not to command me any less than when I was your slave. I'll live with you and when you go home, I'll go together with you.
MEN	Certainly not.
MES	Now I'll go to the inn and return the luggage and money to you. The wallet with the traveling money is correctly sealed in the traveling bag. I'll bring it here to you now.
MEN	Yes, bring it quickly.
MES	I'll return it to you safe and sound, just as you gave it to me. Wait for me here.

Line numbers in right margin: 1025, 1030, 1035

	MEN	nimia mira mihi quidem hodie exorta sunt miris modis:
1040		alii me negant eum esse qui sum atque excludunt foras;
1040ª		***
1041		etiam hic seruom se meum esse aiebat quem ego emisi manu,
1042		[uel ille qui se petere argentum modo, qui seruom se meum
1042ª		esse aiebat, ‹med erum suom,› quem ego modo emisi manu]
1043		is ait se mihi allaturum cum argento marsuppium:
		id si attulerit, dicam ut a me abeat liber quo uolet,
1045		ne tum, quando sanus factus sit, a me argentum petat.
		socer et medicus me insanire aiebant. quid sit mira sunt.
		haec nihilo esse mihi uidentur setius quam somnia.
		nunc ibo intro ad hanc meretricem, quamquam suscenset mihi,
		si possum exorare ut pallam reddat quam referam domum.

V. viii: SOSICLES. MESSENIO

1050	SOS	men hodie usquam conuenisse te, audax, audes dicere,
		postquam aduorsum mi imperaui ut huc uenires?
	MES	quin modo
		erupui, homines qui ferebant te sublimem quattuor,
		apud hasce aedis. tu clamabas deum fidem atque hominum omnium,
		quom ego accurro teque eripio ui, pugnando, ingratiis.
1055		ob eam rem, quia te seruaui, me amisisti liberum.
		quom argentum dixi me petere et uasa, tu quantum potest
		praecucurristi obuiam, ut quae fecisti infitias eas.

1040ª *lacunam indicauit Ritschl*   1042–42ª *desunt in A*

534

Exit MESSENIO to the left.

MEN Very strange things have happened to me today in
strange ways. Some people deny that I am the one I am   1040
and lock me out; ***. This chap, whom I freed, even said
he was my slave. [For example that chap who just said he
was getting the money, who claimed that he was my slave
and that I was his master, and whom I just freed.] He said
he was going to bring me the wallet with the money. If he
brings it, I'll tell him to go away from me as a free man
wherever he likes, so he doesn't claim back the money   1045
from me when he's become sane again. My father-in-law
and the doctor said I was mad. I wonder what this is all
about. It seems to be nothing short of dreams. Now I'll go
inside to that prostitute, however angry she is with me, if
I can persuade her to return the mantle to me so I can
carry it back home. (*walks toward Erotium's house*)

Enter SOSICLES and MESSENIO from the left.

SOS You dare say, you brazen creature, that I met you any-   1050
where today since the time I told you to come here and
meet me?

MES But just now, at this house, I rescued you from four
men who had lifted you up and were carrying you off.
You were imploring the protection of gods and all men
when I ran to you and rescued you with might and main,
against their will. For that reason, because I rescued you,   1055
you sent me off as a free man. When I said I was getting
the money and the luggage, you ran ahead as fast as you
could to meet me so that you could deny what you did.

1042ᵃ med erum suom *add. Lindsay*

SOS   liberum ego te iussi abire?

MES   certo.

SOS   quin certissumum est
     mepte potius fieri seruom quam te umquam emittam
     manu.

V. ix: MENAECHMVS. MESSENIO. SOSICLES

1060   MEN   si uoltis per oculos iurare, nihilo hercle ea causa magis
     facietis ut ego ‹hinc› hodie apstulerim pallam et spinter,
     pessumae.

MES   pro di immortales! quid ego uideo?

SOS   quid uides?

MES   speculum tuom.

SOS   quid negoti est?

MES   tua est imago. tam consimilest quam potest.

SOS   pol profecto haud est dissimilis, meam quom formam
     noscito.

1065   MEN   o adulescens, salue, qui me seruauisti, quisquis es.

MES   adulescens, quaeso hercle ‹e›loquere tuom mi nomen,
     nisi piget.

MEN   non edepol ita promeruisti de me ut pigeat quae uelis
     ‹opsequi›. mihi est Menaechmo nomen.

SOS   immo edepol mihi.

MEN   Siculus sum, Syracusanus.

SOS   ea domus et patria est mihi.

1070   MEN   quid ego ex te audio?

SOS   hoc quod res est.

MES   noui equidem hunc: erus est meus.
     ego quidem huius seruos sum, sed med esse huius cre-
     didi.

1061 hinc *add. Ritschl*   1066 ‹e›loquere *Fleckeisen*

SOS I told you to go away as a free man?

MES Certainly.

SOS No, it's absolutely certain that I'd rather become a slave myself than ever free you.

MEN (*shouting outside the door of Erotium's house*) Even if 1060 you want to swear by your eyes, you won't make it any more true for that reason that I took away the mantle and bracelet from here today, you witches.

MES Immortal gods! What do I see?

SOS What do you see?

MES Your mirror image.

SOS What's the matter?

MES It's your spitting image. He's as similar as he can be.

SOS He's indeed not dissimilar when I look at myself.

MEN (*to Messenio*) Greetings, young man who saved me, who- 1065 ever you are.

MES Young man, please tell me your name, unless you object.

MEN You certainly didn't treat me in such a way that I could object to obeying your wishes. My name is Menaechmus.

SOS No, *my* name is.

MEN I'm a Sicilian from Syracuse.

SOS That's *my* home and country.

MEN What do I hear from you? 1070

SOS The facts.

MES (*pointing to Menaechmus*) I know this chap: he's my master. I am this man's slave, but I thought I am his (*points to*

1068 opsequi *add.* Vahlen
1069 et patria *P*, ea patria *Gratwick*

537

       ego hunc censebam ted esse, huic etiam exhibui nego-
         tium.

       quaeso ignoscas si quid stulte dixi atque imprudens tibi.

SOS   delirare mihi uidere: non commeministi simul

1075   te hodie mecum exire ex naui?

MES   enim uero aequom postulas.

       tu erus es: tu seruom quaere. tu salueto: tu uale.

       hunc ego esse aio Menaechmum.

MEN   at ego me.

SOS   quae haec fabula est?

       tu es Menaechmus?

MEN   me esse dico, Moscho prognatum patre.

SOS   tun meo patre es prognatus?

MEN   immo equidem, adulescens, meo;

1080   tuom tibi neque occupare nec praeripere postulo.

MES   di immortales, spem insperatam date mihi quam suspico!

       nam, nisi me animus fallit, hi sunt gemini germani duo.

       nam et patriam et patrem commemorant pariter quae
         fuerint sibi.

       seuocabo erum. Menaechme.

MEN + SOS   quid uis?

MES   non ambos uolo,

1085   sed uter uostrorum est aduectus mecum naui.

MEN   non ego.

SOS   at ego.

MES   te uolo igitur. huc concede.

SOS   concessi. quid est?

MES   illic homo aut sycophanta aut geminus est frater tuos.

       nam ego hominem hominis similiorem numquam uidi al-
         terum.

    1081 suspicor *B*[2]
    1083 et patrem et matrem *P*, et patriam et patrem *Lipsius*

      Sosicles). (*to Sosicles*) I thought that you are this one (*points to Menaechmus*), and I was a nuisance to him. (*to Menaechmus*) Please forgive me if I said anything stupid to you without being aware of it.

SOS   You seem to be crazy; don't you remember that you left 1075
      the ship together with me today?

MES   Yes, you're right. (*to Sosicles*) You are my master; (*to Menaechmus*) you must look for a slave. (*to Sosicles*) Hello to you; (*to Menaechmus*) goodbye to you. I say that this one (*points to Sosicles*) is Menaechmus.

MEN   But I say it's me.

SOS   What does this mean? You are Menaechmus?

MEN   I say that I am, a scion of my father Moschus.

SOS   Are you a scion of *my* father?

MEN   No, young man, of mine. I have no intention to appropri- 1080
      ate yours or steal him from you.

MES   Immortal gods, fulfill this unhoped-for hope which I sus-
      pect I have! Indeed, unless I'm mistaken, they are twin
      brothers: they mention both the country and the father
      that they had in the same way. I'll call aside my master.
      Menaechmus.

MEN + SOS What do you want?

MES   I don't want both, but the one of you that came here with 1085
      me by ship.

MEN   I didn't.

SOS   But I did.

MES   Then I want you. Come over here.

SOS   (*obeying*) All right. What is it?

MES   That man is either an impostor or your twin brother: I've
      never seen one man more similar to another. Believe me,

---

1088 homini *P*, hominis *Wesenberg*

<table>
<tr><td></td><td></td><td>neque aqua aquae nec lacte est lactis, crede mi, usquam similius</td></tr>
</table>

neque aqua aquae nec lacte est lactis, crede mi, usquam
    similius
1090   quam hic tui est, tuque huius autem; poste eandem pa-
    triam ac patrem
    memorat. meliust nos adire atque hunc percontarier.
SOS   hercle qui tu me ammonuisti recte et habeo gratiam.
    perge operam dare, opsecro hercle; liber esto, si inuenis
    hunc meum fratrem esse.
MES   spero.
SOS   et ego item spero fore.
1095 MES quid ais tu? Menaechmum, opinor, te uocari dixeras.
MEN ita uero.
MES   huic item Menaechmo nomen est. in Sicilia
    te Syracusis natum esse dixisti: hic natust ibi.
    Moschum tibi patrem fuisse dixti: huic itidem fuit.
    nunc operam potestis ambo mihi dare et uobis simul.
1100 MEN promeruisti ut ne quid ores quod uelis quin impetres.
    tam quasi me emeris argento, liber seruibo tibi.
MES   spes mihi est uos inuenturum fratres germanos duos
    geminos, una matre natos et patre uno uno die.
MEN mira memoras. utinam efficere quod pollicitu's possies.
1105 MES possum. sed nunc agite uterque id quod rogabo dicite.
MEN ubi lubet, roga: respondebo. nil reticebo quod sciam.
MES est tibi nomen Menaechmo?
MEN   fateor.
MES   est itidem tibi?
SOS   est.
MES   patrem fuisse Moschum tibi ais?

1089 lacti *P*, lactis *Ritschl*
1090 postea *P*, post eandem *Bothe*
1094 idem *P*, item *Seyffert*

540

water isn't more similar to water anywhere or milk to
milk than he is to you and you in turn to him. Then he 1090
mentions the same country and father. It's better if we
approach and question him.

SOS Indeed, you've given me good advice and I'm grateful.
Continue to make this effort, please. You shall be free if
you find out that he's my brother.

MES I hope it'll turn out to be like that.

SOS And I hope so too.

MES (*to Menaechmus*) What do you say? I think you said 1095
you're called Menaechmus.

MEN Yes, indeed.

MES This one's name is also Menaechmus. You said you were
born in Sicily, in Syracuse: *he* was born there. You said
your father was Moschus: he was also this man's father.
Now you can both help me and yourselves at the same
time.

MEN You've deserved that you shouldn't ask for anything with- 1100
out achieving your wish. Just as if you'd bought me for
money, I'll serve you, even though I'm free.

MES I have the hope of finding that you're two twin brothers,
born from one mother and one father on one day.

MEN You're telling a strange tale. I hope you can succeed with
what you've promised.

MES I can. But now come on, each of you tell me what I ask. 1105

MEN Ask when you like: I'll answer. I won't keep anything I
know quiet.

MES Is your name Menaechmus?

MEN I admit it.

MES (*to Sosicles*) Is it also yours?

SOS Yes.

MES (*to Menaechmus*) Do you say that your father was
Moschus?

| MEN | ita uero. |

MEN   ita uero.

SOS   et mihi.

MES esne tu Syracusanus?

MEN   certo.

MES   quid tu?

SOS   quippini?

1110 MES optume usque adhuc conueniunt signa. porro operam date.
quid longissume meministi, dic mihi, in patria tua?

MEN cum patre ut abii Tarentum ad mercatum, postea
inter homines me deerrare a patre atque inde auehi.

SOS Iuppiter supreme, serua me!

MES   quid clamas? quin taces?

1115 quot eras annos natus quom te pater a patria auehit?

MEN septuennis: nam tunc dentes mihi cadebant primulum.
nec patrem umquam postilla uidi.

MES   quid? uos tum patri
filii quot eratis?

MEN   ut nunc maxume memini, duo.

MES uter eratis, tun an ille, maior?

MEN   aeque ambo pares.

1120 MES qui id potest?

MEN   gemini ambo eramus.

SOS   di me seruatum uolunt.

MES si interpellas, ego tacebo.

SOS   ⟨ego⟩ potius taceo.

MES   dic mihi:
uno nomine ambo eratis?

MEN   minime. nam mihi hoc erat,
quod nunc est, Menaechmo: illum tum uocabant Sosiclem.

542

MEN Yes, precisely.

SOS Mine too.

MES (*to Menaechmus*) Are you from Syracuse?

MEN Certainly.

MES (*to Sosicles*) What about you?

SOS Naturally.

MES The signs have been in perfect agreement so far. Con- 1110
tinue to pay attention. (*to Menaechmus*) Tell me, what's
the earliest thing you remember in your country?

MEN It's that when I went with my father to Tarentum to the
market, I then wandered off from my father into the
crowd and was taken away from there.

SOS Jupiter above, save me!

MES (*to Sosicles*) What are you shouting for? Why won't you
be quiet? (*to Menaechmus*) How many years old were 1115
you when your father took you away from your country?

MEN Seven: at that time my teeth were falling out for the first
time. I never saw my father after that.

MES Well then? How many sons did your father have at that
time?

MEN As I remember it now, two.

MES Which of you was older, you or he?

MEN We were both exactly the same age.

MES How can that be? 1120

MEN We were both twins.

SOS The gods want me saved!

MES (*to Sosicles*) If you interrupt, I'll be quiet.

SOS No, *I* am quiet rather.

MES (*to Menaechmus*) Tell me, did you have the same name?

MEN Certainly not: I had the name I have now, Menaechmus;
people called that other one Sosicles at the time.

1121 ego *add. anon. apud Schoell*

	SOS	signa adgnoui, contineri quin complectar non queo.
1125		mi germane, gemine frater, salue. ego sum Sosicles.
	MEN	quo modo igitur post Menaechmo nomen est factum tibi?
1127	SOS	postquam ad nos renuntiatum est te ***
1127ᵃ		*** et patrem esse mortuom,

auos noster mutauit: quod tibi nomen est, fecit mihi.

1129
–30   MEN   credo ita esse factum ut dicis. sed mi hoc responde.

    SOS   roga.

    MEN quid erat nomen nostrae matri?

    SOS   Teuximarchae.

    MEN   conuenit.

o salue, insperate, multis annis post quem conspicor.

    SOS frater, et tu, quem ego multis miseriis, laboribus

usque adhuc quaesiui quemque ego esse inuentum gaudeo.

1135 MES hoc erat quod haec te meretrix huius uocabat nomine:

hunc censebat te esse, credo, quom uocat te ad prandium.

    MEN namque edepol hic mi hodie iussi prandium apparier,

clam meam uxorem, quoi pallam surrupui dudum domo.
eam dedi huic.

    SOS   hanc, dicis, frater, pallam quam ego habeo?

    MEN   ⟨haec ea est.⟩

1140   quo modo haec ad te peruenit?

    SOS   meretrix ⟨quae⟩ huc ad prandium

me abduxit me sibi dedisse aiebat. prandi perbene,
potaui atque accubui scortum, pallam et aurum hoc
  ⟨apstuli⟩.

1127–27ᵃ *unus uersus in codicibus, sed lacunam indicauit Ritschl*
1132 multis annis *CD*, annis multis *AB*

SOS	I've recognized the signs, I can't refrain from embracing you. My true twin brother, my greetings. I am Sosicles.	1125
MEN	Then how did you get the name Menaechmus later on?	
SOS	After we received the message that you *** and that our father had died, our grandfather changed it. He gave me the name you have.	
MEN	I believe it happened the way you say. But answer me this.	1130
SOS	Ask.	
MEN	What was our mother's name?	
SOS	Teuximarcha.	
MEN	Correct. My greetings, unhoped-for brother, whom I see after so many years.	
SOS	And mine to you, my brother, whom I've been looking for with much hardship and toil until now and whom I'm happy to have found.	
MES	(to Sosicles) That was why this prostitute addressed you by this man's name. She thought you are him, I believe, when she invited you to lunch.	1135
MEN	Yes, indeed; I had a lunch prepared for me here today, behind my wife's back; I stole a mantle from her from home a while ago. I gave it to her.	
SOS	My brother, do you mean this mantle I have? (produces it)	
MEN	This is the one. How did it come into your hands?	1140
SOS	The prostitute who took me to lunch here said I'd given it to her. I had a very good lunch, I drank, and lay with the prostitute, and I took away this cloak and gold.	

1133 partes sic distribuunt *CD*, frater *Menaechmo I dat B*
1139 haec ea est *add. Vahlen*, papae *add. Gratwick*
1140 quae *add. Ritschl*   1142 apstuli *add. Onions*

MEN   gaudeo edepol si quid propter me tibi euenit boni.

1144   nam illa quom te ad se uocabat, me‹met› esse credidit.
–45

MES   numquid me morare quin ego liber, ut iusti, siem?

MEN   optumum atque aequissumum orat, frater: fac causa
           mea.

SOS   liber esto.

MEN   quom tu es liber, gaudeo, Messenio.

1149 MES   sed meliore est opus auspicio, ut liber perpetuo siem.
–50

SOS   quoniam haec euenere, frater, nobis ex sententia,
        in patriam redeamus ambo.

MEN   frater, faciam, ut tu uoles.
        auctionem hic faciam et uendam quicquid est. nunc in-
           terim
        eamus intro, frater.

SOS   fiat.

MES   scitin quid ego uos rogo?

1155 MEN quid?

MES   praeconium mi ut detis.

SOS   dabitur.

MES   ergo nunciam
        uis conclamari auctionem?

MEN   fore quidem die septumi.

MES   auctio fiet Menaechmi mane sane septumi.
        uenibunt serui, supellex, fundi, aedes, omnia.
        uenibunt quiqui licebunt, praesenti pecunia.

1160   uenibit . . . uxor quoque etiam, si quis emptor uenerit.
        uix credo tota auctione capiet quinquagesies.
        nunc, spectatores, ualete et nobis clare plaudite.

1144–45 me‹met› *Ritschl*   1151 frater nostra Ω, frater nobis
Camerarius, nostra frater *Gratwick*
   1154 frater *dederunt Sosicli Schoell et Seyffert*

MEN I'm really happy if something good came your way be-
cause of me: when she invited you, she thought that you 1145
are me.

MES (*to Sosicles*) Do you have any objections against me being
free, as you said I should be?

MEN What he asks is absolutely good and fair, my brother. Do
it for my sake.

SOS (*to Messenio*) Be free.

MEN I'm happy that you're free, Messenio.

MES But I need a better omen in order to be free for good. 1150

SOS My brother, since this went according to our wishes, let's
both return to our country.

MEN My brother, I'll do as you wish. I'll hold an auction here
and sell whatever there is to sell. Now in the meantime
let's go inside, my brother.

SOS Yes.

MES Do you two know what I'm asking you for?

MEN No; what is it? 1155

MES Let me be the auctioneer.

SOS Yes.

MES So do you want the auction to be announced now?

MEN Yes, it's to be in six days.

MES (*loudly, to the audience*) The auction of Menaechmus
will take place very early in six days. Slaves will be on sale,
furniture, country estates, the house, everything. This
will be on sale for whatever price it fetches in cash. There 1160
will also be on sale . . . a wife, if any buyer comes. I hardly
believe he'll get five million sesterces in the entire auc-
tion. Now, spectators, farewell and give us your loud
applause.

METRICAL APPENDIX

CASINA

arg., 1–143 ia^6
144–146 ba^4
147 cr^2 + ith
148 extra metrum
149–150 cr^2 + ith
151 cr^4
152–154 cr^3
155 tr^7
156–157 ba^4
158 cr^4
159 tr$^{4\wedge}$
160 cr^1 + tr^2
161 c^r
162–163 ba^4
164 c^r + c^r
165–166 an^8
167 an^4
168–169 cr^4
170–171 ia^4 + adon
172–173 an^4 + adon
174–175 c^r + c^r
176–177 ia^6

178 c^r + c^r
179 an^4
180–181 c^r + c^r
182 an^8
183–183^a cr^c
184 ba^4
185–194 cr^4
195–198 tr$^{4\wedge}$
199–202 cr^4
203 cho^2 + cr^c
204–205 an^7
206–207 an^8
208–209 an^7
210–212 an^8
213 an^4
214 an^4 + an^2
215–216 cr^2 + cr^c
217 an^8
218 an^7
219 an^8
220 an^7
221–227 an^8

228 an^7

229–231^a ia^4

232–235 cr^4

236–236^a ia^4

237 cr^2 + tr$^{4\wedge}$

238 tr^8

239 an^8

240 an^7

241 an^8

242 an^7

243–246 tr^8

247 cr^4

248 cr^c + cr^c

249–250 an$^{4\wedge}$ + an$^{4\wedge}$

251 ia^8

252–308 tr^7

309–352 ia^6

353–423 tr^7

424–514 ia^6

515–562 tr^7

563–618 ia^6

619 extra metrum

620 ia^6

621–627 cr^4

628 cr^2 + tr$^{4\wedge}$

629 cho^2

629^a–630 wil

630^a cho^2

631–633 tr^8

634 wil

634^a cho^2

635–636 ia^4 + cr^c

637–640 ia^4

641–643 cr^4

644 diph

645 cho^2 + adon

646–647 an^4

648–649 ba^4

650 ba^2 + ba^c

651–653 ba^4

654 ba^3

654^a ba^c

655 ba^4

656 ba^2 + ba^c

657 ba^4

658 ba^2 + ba^c

659 ba^3

659^a ba^2

660–661 an^4

662 ba^2 + ba^c

663 ba^c + ba^c

664 ba^4

665 ba^2 + ba^c

666 ba^c + ba^2

667–672 ba^4

673 ba^2 + ba^c

674 ba^c + ba^1

675 ba^2 + ba^c

676 ba^4

677–680 tr sy^{10}

681 tr$^{4\wedge}$

682–683 tr^7

684 ba^4
685 ba^2 + ba^c
686–690 ba^4
691 ba^c + ba^c
692–693 ba^4
694–695 ba^2 + ba^c
696 ba^c + ba^2
697–701 ba^4
702 ba^2 + ba^c
703 ba^c + ba^c
704–705 ba^4
706–707 tr^8
708–718 ia sy$^{11\text{metr}}$
719 an^8
720–723^a an^4
723^b an^2
724 an^4
725 an$^{4\wedge}$
726 ?
727–728 an^8
729–729^a cr^1
730 tr^2 + ith
731 ion$^{2\wedge}$ a minore
732–733 ion^1 a minore
734 ia^4
735 an^4 + c^r
736 c^r
737–739 ba^4
740–741 ion^1 a minore
742–744 an$^{4\wedge}$
745 an^7

746 an^4 + an^2
747–747^a wil
748 an$^{4\wedge}$
748^a cr^2 + cr^c
749 v^r
750–754 c^r
755 v^r
756–757 c^r
758 v^r
759–797 ia^6
798–799 tr^7
800 c^r + extra metrum
801–807 tr^7
808 c^r + extra metrum
809–814 tr^7
815–816 ion^4 a maiore
817 cr^2 + cr^c
818 ith
819–822 an^8
823 an^4
824 ith
825 ia^7
826 v^r
827–828 ba^4
829 an^4
830 ith
831 ba^2 + ia$^{4\wedge}$
832 ba^4
833 ia$^{4\wedge}$
834 ba^c + ba^c
835 ba^4

836 $\text{ia}^{4\wedge}$
837 ba^4
838 $\text{ia}^{4\wedge}$
839 $\text{ba}^3 + \text{ia}^2$
840 $\text{ba}^2 + \text{ba}^\text{c}$
841 an^4
842 ba^4
843–845 c^r
846 $\text{ia}^{4\wedge}$
847–854 ia^6
855–858 ba^4
859 tr^8
860–863 ba^4
864 ba^c
865–866 $\text{cr}^2 + \text{cr}^\text{c}$
867 $\text{ba}^2 + \text{ba}^\text{c}$
868 c^r
869 $\text{ba}^1 + \text{ia}^2$
870–872 ?
873 $\text{cr}^2 + \text{cr}^\text{c}$
874 c^r
875–878 an^7
879–882 an^8
883–885 cr^4
886 ?
887 wil + c^r
888 $\text{cr}^2 + \text{cr}^\text{c}$
888[a] ith
889–891 an^8
892 $\text{tr}^{4\wedge} + \text{c}^\text{r}$
893–895 $\text{ia}^4 + \text{an}^2$

896 $\text{c}^\text{r} + \text{ia}^{4\wedge}$
897–908[a] ?
909 wil + c^r
910 tr^7
911 tr^8
912–913 ia^7
914 $\text{tr}^{4\wedge}$
915–916 tr^8
917–918 ia^7
919 $\text{ia}^{4\wedge}$
920 ba^4
921 tr^7
922 tr^8
923–928 ?
929 v^r
930–933[a] ia^4
934 $\text{tr}^{4\wedge} + \text{c}^\text{r}$
935 $\text{ia}^{4\wedge} + \text{c}^\text{r}$
936 $\text{tr}^{4\wedge} + \text{ith}$
937–940 wil
941 $\text{tr}^{4\wedge}$
942 $\text{cr}^\text{c} + \text{cr}^\text{c}$
943–949 ?
950 cr^4
951 wil + cr^c
952–953 ia^4
954–956 wil + cr^c
957 ?
958 c^r
959–962 wil + adon
963–1018 tr^7

CISTELLARIA

arg. ia^6	37 ba^2 + ia$^{4\wedge}$
1 ia$^{4\wedge}$ + ba^2	38–58 ia^7
2–3 ba^4	59–119 tr^7
4 ba^2 + ba^c	120–202 ia^6
5–7^a tr sy$^{12\mathrm{metr}}$	203–205 an^7
8 ba^2 + an$^{4\wedge}$	206–210 an sy$^{8\mathrm{metr}}$
9 ia$^{4\wedge}$	211–212 an^7
10 an^4	213–220 an sy$^{13\mathrm{metr}}$
11–13 ba^4	221–222 an^7
14 tr^4 + sp^2	223–229 an sy$^{12\mathrm{metr}}$
14^a cr^2	230 ?
15 tr^4 + tr^2	231–266 tr^7
15^a cr^2	267–304 ia^6
16 cr^c	305–373^a ia^7
17–18 tr^8	374–408 ia^6
19–21 ba^4	409–446 ia^6 ?
22 tr^7	449 ?
23 ba^4	450–454 ia^8
24 tr$^{4\wedge}$	455 ?
25 an^8	456–457 tr^7
26 an^7	458 ?
27 ia^8	459 ith
28 ia^7	460 tr^7
29–31 ba^4	461–462 ?
32 tr$^{4\wedge}$	463 ia^8
33 tr^7	464 thy
34 ba^4	465–535 tr^7
35 ba^2 + ba^c	536–630 ia^6
36 ba^4	631–670 tr^7

671–672 an^7

673–676 ba^4

677 ba$^{3\wedge}$

678–679 an^8

680–687 ba^4

688–689 an^4

690–691 cr^4

692–694 ba^2 + ba^c

695–696 ia^7

697–701^a an sy$^{16\text{metr}}$

702–703 an^7

704–746 ia^7

747–773 ia^6

774–787 tr^7

fr. xiv–xvi ?

fr. xvii ia^6

fr. xviii ?

CVRCVLIO

arg., 1–95 ia^6

96–97 diph

97^a an^4

98 ia^2 + cr^c

98^a ia^4

99–100 cr^4

101–102 c^r + ia^2

103–104 ia^4 + ith

105–109 cr^4

110–110^b ia^7

111 tr$^{4\wedge}$

112 cr^1 + cr^c

113 ba^4

113^a cr^2

114 tr^4

115 ba^4

116 ba^2 + ba^c

117 cr^2 + cr^c

118–119 cr^4

119^a ith

120 c^r + c^r

121–122 an^4 + c^r

123–125 ia^7

126–131^a an^8

132 an^7

133 cr^4

134 tr^4

135 cr^4

136 wil

137 tr^4

138 an^7

139–141^a an sy$^{10\text{metr}}$

142–146 an^7

147–154 cr^4

155–157 wil + cr^c

158–215 tr^7

216–279 ia^6

280–370 tr^7

371–461 ia^6

462–486 tr^7

487–532 ia^7

533–634 tr^7

635–678 ia^6

679–729 tr^7

EPIDICVS

arg. ia^6

1–2 tr^7

3–6 tr$^{4\wedge}$

7–8 ia^8

9 cr^2

9^a ia^4

9^b extra metrum

10 tr^7

11–11^a tr$^{4\wedge}$

12–17 tr^7

18–22 ia^8

23 tr^7

24 ia^6

25–26 ia^8

27–28^a ia^4

29 cr^2

29^a ia^4

30 tr^7

30^a–31 tr$^{4\wedge}$

32–36 tr^7

37–43 ia^8

44–45 tr^7

46–47 ia^6

48–49 ia^8

50–51 tr^7

52 cr^2

52^a tr$^{4\wedge}$

53–56 tr^7

57 cr^2

57^a ia^4

58 ia^8

59–60^a ia^4

61 ia^8

62–63 ia^8

64 tr^7

65 cr^2

65^a tr$^{4\wedge}$

66 tr^7

67–67^a cr^c

68 ia^8

69–71^a tr sy^{12metr}

72 tr^7

73–74 tr$^{4\wedge}$

75–76 cr^2

77–79^a tr sy^{12metr}

80–84 tr^7

85–85^a cr^1

86 tr^7

87–87^a cr^1

88 tr^7

89–89^a cr^1

90 tr^7

90^a–90^b cr^1

91 tr^7

92–92^a cr^1

93 tr^7

94–94^a cr^1

95 tr^7

96–96^a cr^1

97 tr^7

98–98^a cr^1

99–163 tr^7

164–165 ia^8

166–166^a cr^2 + cr^c

167 c^r

168 cr^4

169 cr^2 + cr^c

170 c^r

171–172 an^8

173 cr^4

174 tr$^{4\wedge}$ + cr^2

175–176 cr^4

177 cr^c + tr$^{4\wedge}$

178 cr^4

179–180 ia^7

181 extra metrum

182 ia^4

183–184 an$^{4\wedge}$ + c^r

185–186 ia^8

187 ia^4

188 ia^8

189 ia^4

190–193 tr^7

194–195 ia^8

196–305 tr^7

306–319 ia^6

320–323 cr^4

324 ia^8

325 ia^6

326 tr^7

327 cr^3

328 ith

329 tr^8

330 cr^3

330^a tr$^{4\wedge}$

331 ia^8

332 ia^7

333 tr^7

334 ia^8

335 cr^4

336–338 ia^7

339 wil

339^a ith

340 wil

340^a ith

341–381 ia^7

382–525 ia^6

526 tr^8

527–528 ba sy^7

529–530 ba^2 + ba^c

531–532 ia^8

533–536 wil

536^a ia^4

537 cho^3

537^a c^r

538–539 cr^4

540–540^a ?
540^b an^4
541 an^2
541^a an^4
541^b c^r

542–544 tr sy^{10metr}
544^a–545 tr sy^{4metr}
545^a ith
546 ith + ith
547–733 tr^7

MENAECHMI

arg., 1–109 ia^6
110–110^a cho^2
111 wil
111^a ith
112–113 cr^4
114–114^a wil
115–118 cr^4
119 tr^8
120–122^a ia^4
123–127 tr^7
128–129 ia^8
130 tr^7
131–132 ia^8
133–134 ia^7
135–225 tr^7
226–350 ia^6
351 an^4
352 ia^4 + an^2
353 an^2 + an^4
354–355 ia^4
356 ia^6
357 an^7
358 an^4
359 ia^6

359^a c^r
360 an$^{4\wedge}$
361–364 an^4
365 ia^4
366 an^2
367–368 an^4
369–465 tr^7
466–570 ia^6
571–579 ba sy^{32}
580 cr^4
581 ba$^{3\wedge}$
582 ba^2 + ba^c
583 ba^c + ba^2
584 ia^4
584^a ba^2 + ?
585–585^a ia^4
586 ia^6
587 ?
588 an^8
589 an^7
590–592 tr^8
593 ?
594 tr^8
595 tr^7

596–600^b ia^4

601 tr^7

602–603 an^7

604–700 tr^7

701–752 ia^6

753 ba^4

754 ba^2 + ba^c

755–759 ba^4

760 ba^c + ba^2

761 ba^4

762 ba^2 + an^2

763–763^a ba^2 + ba^c

763^b ba^2

764–770 ba^4

771 ba^2 + ba^c

772–773 ba^4

774 ia$^{4\wedge}$

775–871 tr^7

872–898 ia^6

899–965 tr^7

966–968 ba^4

969 ba^2 + ba^c

970 ba^4

971 ba^2 + ba^c

972 ba^c

972^a ia^4

973 tr^7

974 ba^c

975 ba^4

976 ia^4

977–978 ?

979 ia^8

980 ia^7

981 c^r

982 tr^8

983–983^b an^8

984 ?

985–985^a tr$^{4\wedge}$

986–987 ia^8

988–994 tr^7

995–1003 ia^8

1004–1006 ia^4

1007 tr^8

1008–1059 tr^7

1060–1062 ia^8

1063–1162 tr^7

INDEX OF PROPER NAMES

The index is limited to names of characters in the plays and of characters, persons, towns, countries, regions, peoples, and deities mentioned in the plays. Names for which established English forms or translations exist are listed under the English forms, for instance, *Jupiter* or *Underworld*.

INDEX